INTERCULTURAL ACTING AND PERFORMER TRAINING

Intercultural Acting and Performer Training is the first collection of essays from a diverse, international group of authors and practitioners focusing on intercultural acting and voice practices worldwide. This unique book invites performers and teachers of acting and performance to explore, describe, and interrogate the complexities of intercultural acting and actor/performer training taking place in our twenty-first century, globalized world.

As global contexts become multi-, inter- and intra-cultural, assumptions about what acting "is" and what actor/performer training should be continue to be shaped by conventional modes, models, techniques and structures. This book examines how our understanding of interculturalism changes when we shift our focus from the obvious and highly visible aspects of production to the micro-level of training grounds, studios, and rehearsal rooms, where new forms of hybrid performance are emerging.

Ideal for students, scholars and practitioners, *Intercultural Acting and Performer Training* offers a series of accessible and highly readable essays which reflect on acting and training processes through the lens offered by "new" forms of intercultural thought and practice.

Phillip B. Zarrilli is Artistic Director of The Llanarth Group and Emeritus Professor of Performance Practice at Exeter University, UK. Zarrilli is widely known for his publications on acting, including: *Psychophysical Acting: an intercultural approach after Stanislavski* (2009, 2010 Outstanding Book of the Year, ATHE); *Acting (Re)Considered: Theories and Practices;* and *Acting: interdisciplinary and intercultural perspectives* (co-author).

T. Sasitharan is Co-Founder and Director of the Intercultural Theatre Institute (ITI). He has worked as an actor, performer, director and producer and writes and lectures on art, theatre training, performance practice and Singapore culture. He received the Cultural Medallion, Singapore's highest award for artists in 2012.

Anuradha Kapur is a theatre maker and presently Visiting Professor at Ambedkar University, Delhi. She is the author of *Actors, Pilgrims, Kings and Gods: the Ramlila at Ramnagar*, and her writings on performance have been widely anthologized. She completed her term as Director National School of Drama, New Delhi in 2013.

INTERCULTURAL ACTING AND PERFORMER TRAINING

*Edited by Phillip B. Zarrilli, T. Sasitharan
and Anuradha Kapur*

Routledge
Taylor & Francis Group

LONDON AND NEW YORK

First published 2019
by Routledge
2 Park Square, Milton Park, Abingdon, Oxon OX14 4RN

and by Routledge
52 Vanderbilt Avenue, New York, NY 10017

Routledge is an imprint of the Taylor & Francis Group, an informa business

British Library Cataloguing-in-Publication Data
A catalogue record for this book is available from the British Library

Library of Congress Cataloging-in-Publication Data
A catalog record for this book has been requested

ISBN: 978-1-138-35213-1 (hbk)
ISBN: 978-1-138-35214-8 (pbk)
ISBN: 978-0-429-43487-7 (ebk)

Typeset in Bembo
by Apex CoVantage, LLC

MIX
Paper from
responsible sources
FSC
www.fsc.org   FSC™ C013985

Printed in the United Kingdom
by Henry Ling Limited

CONTENTS

FIGURES

INTRODUCTION IN THREE PARTS

Phillip B. Zarrilli,[1] T. Sasitharan and Anuradha Kapur

Intercultural Acting and Actor-Performer Training originated as a specific edition of *Theatre Dance and Performance Training* (7 March, 2016). This expanded book version is intended to make this important and timely collection of essays more widely available to actors, performers, teachers and students of acting and performance throughout the world. For this collection, contributors were invited to explore, describe and interrogate the complex issues, structures, practices, techniques, paradigms, histories, and/or discourses of intercultural acting and actor/performer training taking place in the spaces "between" in our twenty-first century, globalized world.

The three co-editors have each been deeply engaged in reshaping and reframing contemporary actor training from an intercultural perspective throughout our professional and pedagogical careers. Professionally, politically and personally we are all invested in ongoing processes that reconsider how we think about, talk about, as well as create performance and training in the interstices "between" in an increasingly globalized world. As a prelude and introduction to the chapters that follow, we each reflect in our own ways on intercultural acting and actor-training today.

Part 1: Reframing intercultural acting and actor training in the twenty-first century

Phillip Zarrilli

In the twenty-first century, contemporary theatre practices and modes of actor/performer training are being reshaped and reframed within the crucible of a global, (largely) urban, cosmopolitan context, which is inherently multi-, inter- and or intra-cultural. To take one example, Kay Li explains that "Hong Kong is a globalized city" with a "long history of cosmopolitanism and capitalism"; therefore, "theatre in

Hong Kong captures the city's response to the challenges of globalization" and as "a meeting place between Eastern and Western cultures" (2007, pp. 440–2). A similar process of mixing and meeting could be said of con-urbanized metropolises such as Singapore, Johannesburg, Shanghai, Seoul, Melbourne, New York, Tehran, Cairo, Mumbai, Berlin, London, or Jakarta. The internet provides immediate access to the multiple "worlds" of performance and actor/performer trainings available today. For good and/or ill, global higher education means that most young people today aspiring to become actors/performers/dancers/performance makers have received an education shaped at least in part by Western pedagogies, institutional models and modes of reflection.

Any consideration of acting and performance processes and practices, concepts and paradigms of acting, as well as of actor/performer training today must address our global, urban, multi-, inter-, intra-cultural paradigms, perspectives and realities as *the norm* rather than the exception. Consider the following examples, arranged in no particular order:

- In 1994 Veenapani Chawla moved to Pondicherry in south India to found Adishakti in order to pursue a "hybrid" theatre between traditional and contemporary practices (Gokhale 2014).
- In 1963 A.C. Scott (1909–1985) founded the Asian Experimental Theater Program at the University of Wisconsin-Madison US where he established a studio with *taiqiquan* as the primary preparation for the American actors training in his studio, and during this same period internationally known director Herbert Blau was using *taiqi* as a daily training with actors in his company, KRAKEN.
- In Singapore Kuo Pao Kun and T. Sasitharan established the Intercultural Theatre Institute in 2000 – a programme in which students are immersed equally in Asian and Western modes of training (see Part 3 and Chapter 1).
- In Chicago, new modes of "polycultural" theatre are being created in the work of relatively new theatres such as Silk Road Rising.
- In Berlin one of the major "state" theatres, The Maxim Gorki, recently programmed its repertory season around what is called "post-migrant theatre" – a decision which has meant the employment of a multi-ethnic group of professional German actors.

As dance dramaturg Guy Cools recently asked in his discussion of the work and lives of two of the most important European choreographers today – Belgian-Moroccan Sidi Larbi Cherkaoui and British-Bengali Akram Khan –, "Aren't we all migrating bodies?" living "on the frontiers" of identities located in between through either forced or (for the fortunate) voluntary migration. (2015, pp. 13, 43).[2] And wherever people move and meet, encountering difference(s), hasn't there always been a "migration" of acting/training techniques, concepts and practices?

The chapters in this book are concerned with the inter-, intra-, multi-cultural spaces "between" – locations where differences are encountered within an individual, between people in the studio, as well as in the spaces between at local, regional, national and international levels. These thresholds or spaces "between" are literal, metaphorical and imaginary locations where techniques, processes, practices and differences are constantly (re)negotiated individually, socially, aesthetically and politically. But these locations between, and the processes of negotiation are not neutral. The spaces between are always fraught with actual and/or potential imbalances of power, and these imbalances must be recognized and addressed.

Contrary to the plurality and between-ness of our global and national realities, the vast majority of professional/conservatory-based training programmes in Europe, the UK, US and Australia with a few exceptions have not yet fully embraced these multi-, inter-, intra-cultural realities in their structure or pedagogical practices. The name "conservatory" reflects the often inherently "conservative" nature of conservatories that train actors and performers. Assumptions about what acting "is" and how acting is taught, continue to be shaped by often conventional modes, models, techniques and structures that resist critical, creative and institutional self-examination. This book is an intentional provocation to professional and university actor/performer training programmes, teachers and students throughout the world to address and reframe some of the key questions addressed by the contributors to this volume:

- What modes of actor training are needed to create new modes/forms of hybrid, "polycultural"/national and global modes of mixing "between"?
- What alternative models or paradigms of interculturalism might better illuminate issues of intercultural and/or intracultural exchange?
- What is the "view" from "elsewhere" on issues of intercultural actor training? Is the "default" training of contemporary actors in non-Western countries still Stanislavskian-based approaches and, if so, how do these fall short in terms of the needs of intercultural training programmes?
- When considering acting as a phenomenon and process, what happens if we set aside or bracket "psychology" and reconsider acting using alternative paradigms and concepts of experience from other cultures?
- What new techniques, models and programmes for training today's (intercultural) actors in a globalized world have emerged, and how are they different from the iconic Western drama/acting school model?
- How is contemporary training being negotiated institutionally, programmatically, practically, and/or theoretically outside of Europe/North America in Africa, Asian, Latin America?
- What happens if, and when we shift the focus from the obvious and highly visible aspects of production to a micro-level of the training grounds, studio, and/or rehearsal room where face-to-face/body-to-body/consciousness-to-consciousness transactions "between" are taking place?

Most theories and analyses of interculturalism in theatre have focused on and around production and reception of iconic Western performances directed by

Brook, Mnouchkine, Barba, et cetera or more recent productions such as those of Singaporean TheatreWorks director, Ong Ken Sen. Insufficient attention has been given to numerous but much less visible "small" intercultural performances staged throughout the world that negotiate difference(s) in new and compelling ways. Charlotte McIvor's *Migration and Performance in Contemporary Ireland: Towards a New Interculturalism* (2016) and McIvor and King's edited collection of essays, *Interculturalism and Performance Now: New Directions?* (2019) significantly expand the scope and range of scholarship focused on what are being described as "new" interculturalisms.

Perhaps most importantly for this book, far too little attention has been given to processes of intercultural exchange, interaction and modes of "interweaving" that take place both within individual actors/performers when they received a diverse set of intercultural trainings, as well as between individuals and/or theatre groups when they share techniques, embodied practices, concepts and discourses at a micro-level of exchange *in the studio* and *on the stage in performances by individual actors*.

The term "interweaving" has been suggested by Erika Fischer-Lichte in lieu of "intercultural" as the latter problematically presupposes "the feasibility of clearly recognizing the cultural origins of each element and distinguishing between what is 'ours' and what is 'theirs'. This implies the notion that a culture is essentially monadic and self-contained" (2010, pp. 14–5). Crucially, Fischer-Lichte's use of "interweaving" captures the processual "nature and generation of new differences" and can occur in the spaces between (2010, p. 15) which have clearly been part of modernity and through which potentially positive changes and transitions have often taken place.

In a lengthy discussion with Fischer-Lichte, Rustom Bharucha has argued that "all the problems associated with 'interculturalism'" do not necessarily "disappear with the introduction of 'interweaving'", especially "problems relating to the distribution of power, stereotyping, etc." (2011, p. 6). For Bharucha using the term "Interculturalism" continues to be both useful and important in that it "encompasses a spectrum of exchanges that . . . go beyond the cultural domain" (2011, p. 9). Whether we label the body-to-body, technique-to-technique, concept-to-concept processes that characterize studio-based exchanges as modes of interweaving or intercultural interaction, it is imperative to be attentive to the dynamics of power operative in each specific context.[3]

We also need to realize that issues and practices of intra-, multi- and interculturalism(s) are part of the larger dynamics of political struggle that are part of our increasingly fraught world today across the local, regional, national and international domains we inhabit. The movement of peoples – especially those who are fleeing distress, danger and violence, or those who are forcefully moved or removed – are ubiquitous in human history. In this historical sense, we *have* all migrated or been moved "from" somewhere at some point in the past. However problematic, processes of interweaving and of intercultural theatre practice might be, the practices of intercultural interaction in the studio are one way of attempting to address the essential question(s) of difference in the face of the currents of reactionary male authoritarianism at work throughout the world. Jason Stanley's recent book, *How Fascism Works: The Politics of US and THEM* (2018) provides a highly accessible analysis of the dilemma we face as emboldened authoritarian "leaders" are manipulating national and global discursive spaces with polarizing narratives where there will always be an "US" set against a "THEM". In the body-to-body, person-to-person collaborative exchanges of the intercultural studio there is no place for an US against a THEM mentality.

Reconsidering how we think and talk about acting

In a number of my own previous publications about acting – *Acting (Re)considered* (2002), *Psychophysical Acting: an intercultural approach after Stanislavsky* (2009), and the Introduction to *Acting: Psychophysical Phenomenon and Process, an Intercultural and Interdisciplinary View* (2013),[4] I have attempted to help reshape how we think and talk about contemporary acting by displacing exclusively Euro-American paradigms and introducing alternative paradigms from other cultures. Ever since the seminal work of Stanislavsky (1863–1938), the dominant commonplace paradigm informing how Westerners usually think and talk about acting is psychology – a discipline and field invented in the nineteenth century at the same time theatrical realism and naturalism focused attention on the individual self as understood in the West. Kevin Page's recent book, *Psychology for Actors: Theories and Practices for the Acting Process* (2019) provides actors with a sensible and readable overview of psychology *in the plural*, i.e., of the *varied* ways in which each strand of psychology from Freud to Jung to Adler to Horney, Erickson, Maslow, and/or Wilber might illuminate specific aspects of the actor's work on character.

But *beyond* the various strands of psychology through which acting might be approached, there are alternative paradigms that can guide us and help us better understand and re-frame acting/performance as a phenomenon and process, and that can help us better understand and articulate our experience(s) of acting and/or voicing. Exemplified in Chapter 6 (Kim and Yoo) and Chapter 7 (McAllister-Viel) in this book, as well as Jeungsook Yoo's *A Korean Approach to Actor Training* (2018) and Tara McAllister Viel's *Training Actors' Voices: Towards an Intercultural/Interdisciplinary Approach* (2019), an intercultural perspective on acting and voice invite us to reframe discussions of contemporary acting by displacing normative paradigms informing acting (psychology) or voice (the natural voice) from their primary explanatory positions by either replacing them, or placing them alongside alternative ways of understanding acting as a phenomenon and process.

Non-Western and especially Asian philosophies, paradigms of embodiment, and understanding of the body-mind relationship such as yoga and yoga philosophy have long had a tremendous and lasting influence on shaping many of the major Western theorist/practitioners including Stanislavsky, Michael Chekhov, Brecht, Grotowski, Barba, as well as the development of my own approach to training actors.[5] This is also the case with most of the major alternative approaches to movement and body work, from Alexander Technique to Feldenkrais work as well as Pilates. Among the numerous relatively early publications exploring this territory is Richard Heckler's *The Anatomy of Change: East/West Approaches to Body/Mind Therapy* (1985) which uses the disciplines of Japanese Aikido and Lomi bodywork as practices that might assist individuals towards developing an embodied awareness. The most recent manifestation of non-Western and especially Asian influences on actor training are the use of meditation and/or "mindfulness" practices for actors.[6] But in all such intercultural interventions, the questions and problems presented by intercultural "borrowing" are *always* present, especially if/when "borrowing" is shallow and takes place at a superficial level. These issues continue to need both professional scrutiny as well as scholarly attention, along with a considered human sensitivity about issues of potential cultural appropriation in any interaction "between".

In addition to reframing discussions of contemporary acting and voice and the paradigms through which we consider acting, there are also the next-to-invisible histories of how contemporary non-Western actors and directors have negotiated *their* encounters with realist drama, Stanislavskian-based techniques, or the techniques/legacies of Grotowski, Michael Chekhov, and other approaches to contemporary acting/performance making. Only recently have publications begun to address the complex intercultural negotiations, displacements and replacements that began to take place in the twentieth century between Stanislavsky and Chinese acting (Tian 2008, pp. 159–74) and Stanislavsky and Indonesia (Winet 2010, pp. 134–40). As noted in more detail below, Chapter 11 by Kathy Foley and Chapter 12 by Marco Adda make significant additional contributions to our historical understanding of West to East influences on acting in modern Southeast Asian acting practices.

In Parts 2 and 3 of this Introduction, Anuradha Kapur and T. Sasitharan provide further provocations toward a reconsideration of intercultural acting and actor training today. Immediately following these provocations, I provide a brief overview of the fourteen chapters.

Part 2: Recalibrating intercultural acting/training today

Anuradha Kapur

Modes of access/conditions of transmission

This collection of chapters is prompted by the recognition that the principles and methods of instruction for the actor in the twenty-first century are different from those that shaped the actor in the twentieth century. Modes of access to theatre knowledge, among other knowledges, and the way these are transmitted to and borne by an actor's body, have been radically changed by the processes of globalization and new information technologies.

Globalization has brought about circulations of various kinds: on the one hand the unprecedented movement of goods, information and knowledges; and on the other, a stringent control on that circulation via authorizations, sanctions and permits. Likewise, digitization and new information technologies have made the storage and retrieval of vast amounts of data exceptionally easy and blindingly fast. Online databases present multiple options to the trainee to learn music, dance and acting skills across languages and geographical locations. Yet, this instant access to texts and forms from across the world in the digital format puts forth the question of classification. By what architecture, by what mandate and by what authorizing procedures (via universities, private enterprises, dot.coms) is such hyper availability made possible? Many conflicting principles and interests are thrown up, and their success or failure is determined not least by the commercial well-being of the structuring/sponsoring agency.

In the process of this kind of travel of knowledges and lexicons, the interculturalist project needs once again to be recalibrated. In seeking to set up a dialogue between cultures, and in attempting to reaffirm a common humanity, the project was seen to have a utopic potential in the 1970s; it was also seen to be, simultaneously, a contemporary form of imperialism that raids the resources of another culture; but then as Erika Fischer-Lichte points out there have been different and varying historical conjunctions when dialogue between practices and an exchange of performance grammars has been germane to the act of theatre making.[7]

As traffic between nations and cultures increases at an unprecedented and urgent scale, what is subject to interrogation once again is an interrelated set of ideas; in the largest frame, the idea of cultural exchange, following that, the formats of transmission, the practice of memory and the implication of embodied knowledge. The material nature of the performer's body, as well as the assumption that transmission too is material, requires to be tested and annotated anew.

I wish to enter these frames via the motif of translation and translatability because translations are an ongoing project; a constant process of negotiation, and conceptualization; of transplanting ideas, and resituating concerns.[8] Walter Benjamin provides the following articulation of this process:

> Just as a tangent touches a circle lightly and at but one point-establishing, with this touch rather than with the point, the law according to which it is to continue on its straight path to infinity-a translation touches the original lightly and only at the infinitely small point of the sense, thereupon pursuing its own course according to the laws of fidelity in the freedom of linguistic flux.[9]

Retranslation/hybridization

Although hybrids have a long history of generating new knowledges *hybridization*, as Homi Bhabha points out, it is not a "happy, consensual mix of diverse cultures; it is the strategic, translational transfer of tone, value, signification, and position – a transfer of power".[10] Here, for me, translational transfers are key. They pull and push and articulate, with difficulty, new and sometimes oppositional experiences.

They can cause, variously, disputation, dissonance and hybrid vigour, in the course of relocation. Being interpretations of interpretations, they do not necessarily call up a single prior text; and mutation is inbuilt in translational energy. Bhabha compares translation to slow-release tablets "where elements of the anterior object will emerge in different places at different times and constitute different things".[11]

What might translation be when we think of it in the context of performance training? I wish to put before you two examples – very different from each other, but taken from my experience as a teacher in classrooms over many years, especially at the National School of Drama.[12] When an actor in a modern theatre institution in India – modern as in a rupturing of traditional learning systems, such as the *guru–shishya parampara* and the *gharana* (family-line), privileges that occur because of a democratized admission policy – is immersed in a three-month schedule of training in an eleventh-century form such as Kutiyattam, what is to be gained by such training?

I take the example of Kutiyattam because it has recently become a teaching module across many institutions in India (as also in Singapore, among other countries). Traditional training in Kutiyattam takes years; a three-month module cannot, therefore, afford a transference of skills. Instead, like Bhabha's slow-release tablet it makes a student aware of shifting substances in her own body. In the strict economy of the form, breath instigates emotion, which is then inscribed on the topography of the face; precisely delineated *mudras* form a physical language for the hands. Through the twitch of muscle and dilation of eyes, the face records the experience of being part of a universe of flowers, trees, animals and humans that are unitedly affected by atmosphere and event. In a performance of Kalidasa's early Sanskrit drama, *Sakuntala*, when she finds that her husband has forgotten her – at this precise moment of rejection – flowers wilt and the deer stands stock still. A densely populated world *rematerializes* via acute observation, *in* the eyes and *on* the face. Experientially the student learns to register an entire world on the face: equally, she also learns that her particular physiognomy defines the landscape she manifests. The nose and the eyes, the muscle and bone of the performer determine the height, weight and scale of mountains – the rapidity of the flow of a river, the flight of a swarm of bees. The intricate connection between habitat and body refigures the way interiors and exteriors are conceptualized in performance vocabularies today. But more of that later.

Several students have given the name "inner monologue" to the intense focus they achieve during Kutiyattam training, channelling actorly vocabularies drawn from realism for that purpose. I would like to suggest that there is an intriguing disalignment between the spatial understanding of the inner monologue situated within realist conventions and the exercises of Kutiyattam in this formulation. The governing convention of the psychologized monologue is that it arises in the chiaroscuro interior of the character and is materialized by summoning personal memories of the actor. The Kutiyattam "monologue", on the other hand, is not self-directed. It is perfectly poised along a thin permeable line separating the inner world of the character and an ever-widening, ever-wondrous outer world. The character inhabits the universe, and the intricate delineation of the universe produces the character.

During a Kutiyattam workshop, students remember being instructed to experience their bodies as a *universe* and attend to its sensations with the greatest of care, the inner world and the abundant outer world being aligned.[13] In searching for a linguistic approximation – by employing words such as inner monologue, *swagat*, soliloquy, to name this translocation, the performer is engaging with perplexing, dissonant, even disorientating concepts. This process of alignment which is also a disalignment, produces a pedagogical disagreement that for me is of particular importance. Because of the disagreement, the student attempts a rearticulation. She brings two forms of experience together and sutures them. Into the vocabulary of psychological realism is inserted another kind of spatiality and into the lexicon of Kutiyattam is brought the force of the concrete present (in which the student lives and breathes). By interjecting contemporary corporeality into the experience of an ancient performance protocol, notions of cultural continuity as also notions of an easy negotiability between forms is put to question.

Horizontality/synchronicity

The second example is that of an audition of a young aspirant to a drama school (here National School of Drama) who performs a Michael Jackson number before the jury. The moves have obviously been learned via YouTube. Yet the performer owns them; he sees them as accurately describing his self-conception – his own understanding of his assumed and assigned social roles.[14] Cultural memory, cultural intersection, citation, embodied knowledge – words that are very much a part of studio-based acting pedagogy – are turned into a complex mix. In countries like India which see themselves as having long (supposedly uninterrupted) histories of training and performance protocols, this mix can be both exhilarating (for the performer) and confounding (for the teacher). Manoeuvring a sliding scale between tradition, translation and practice, between contemporaneity and its components, between hybridity and its opposite, authenticity, is to be risked again and again.

In India today, an actor needs to work with a variety of protocols synchronically – pedagogies shaped by global institutional models such as the Stanislavsky toolkit *and* the several traditional vocabularies in practice today. She needs to be alert to the fertile energies that *adjacency* of forms and genres produce; uneven and jolting energies that cause defamilarization and dissonance in the experience of training.[15]

I expand the argument by suggesting another metaphor, that of interweaving/entanglement from Erika Fischer-Lichte, and modify it for my purposes.[16] Entanglement can be uncomfortable and vexing. Slubs, knots and holes – from the vocabulary of weaving – need always to be attended to. The difficulties of putting two different strands together produces in the very weave of the fabric an unevenness which in turn produces an appreciation, however vexing it may be, of the separation between them. Separation is an uncomfortable place to start from because work is required to critically examine the nature of the separation, examining for instance the threads "dyed, plied and interwoven" for their particular material character. Fischer-Lichte is eloquent about the "backbreaking" labour that such weaving entails. She describes the action of entangling and disentangling as being prone to failure and even disaster, because, as cultural forms are processual, they continuously produce new differences and ever newer disputes.[17]

The journey between forms is not teleological, in that the end is not predetermined. There is nothing like an already composed or built up conclusion to be found.[18] In that case, the meaning of *destination*, in terms of training, and in terms of practice, needs to be spun around and reorientated.

As I have tried to show, actors today are caught up in hybrid spaces and entangled histories: their bodies are in the process of being recomposed by these very histories and entanglements. Intercultural performance grammars, as they get fitted into curricula and institutional frames, need to annotate the specific contexts of the forms and genres that they practise. Furthermore, they need to be ever alert to being absorbed or assimilated within dominant teaching methodologies. Such methodologies *draw in* a student to their orbit (who is being trained for what purpose) and obscure issues of self-composition (how students align their assigned and assumed social roles via training) which is an action that is actually a *drawing* away from a fixed orbit.

Training modules that are clear about the direction that they set down for their travellers shape their expectations and prepare them for placement, especially in the industry.[19] But training that is adaptive and elastic leads the actor not towards a finale but onwards on a jagged line, even a landscape of jagged lines, into an expanded field and makes certain that a "sensitivity and commitment to the otherness of technique assures that it is not a fixed or determined end in itself but rather is alive and adaptable according to the development of the performer. If technique is considered like language, it is then like enabling speakers to change language itself and not simply improve their proficiency".[20]

Translatability

In terms of institutional imagination, placing contradictory teaching modules contiguous to each other in academic planning (a classical, codified form followed by a marginalized form such as circus) as was done at the National School of Drama in an intensive rethink some years ago, produces a pattern of slots and segments. This sought to develop not an escalation of skills but contradiction, resistance, traction and chaos. Cognitive dissonance impels a student to cover the distance between forms through their own body and in their own exceptional way. There is no model journey nor is there a predestined endpoint. The binaries between knowledge and ignorance, emptiness and fullness, lack and plenitude, may not, in such an imagination, describe the relation of *guru* and *shishya*. Perhaps their relationship can be better imagined as something more cooperative in that the journey may not be a means to an end. Training and transmission then may be envisaged as being about "wayfaring" as Tim Ingold would have it,[21] an urging out of disciplinary boundaries, into an expanded field, where they *affect*, (defined as bearing upon, or having a bearing on) life; and *effect*, (understood as having consequences on) life choices.

Translation makes mobile performance grammars and repurposes them for different needs and contexts. The body bears these changing grammars. The historical value of these grammars is reassessed through the course of training. Practise – rehearsal, drill, improvization, massage – evaluates their particular effects. In making and remaking the body through practise, the body itself is understood to be processual and dynamic; specific to the point that even an individual's bone structure is modified so as to attune it to a particular form. It is from this degree of precision and particularity that we have to calibrate the global issue of intercultural translation of forms.

Part 3: The "hot crucible" of intercultural actor training: the Singaporean context

T. Sasitharan

As a Singaporean, like so many of my people, I am a whole and a fragment, connected and disjointed, in situ and displaced. I am part of one of the oldest living civilizations on earth and yet nothing more than a washed-up immigrant on a sliver of an island at the tip of the Malaysian peninsular, the southernmost point of Asia; flotsam and jetsam of a diasporic dispersion long before the Second World War (1939–1945). If I can be certain of anything at all it is that my children will be far, far more plural and diverse than I can even begin to imagine. This is what it is to be alive today. We are many, many things and many things are within us.

> I think we are seeing signs that the privilege given to natural languages and, as it were, natural cultures is dissolving. These objects and epistemological grounds are now appearing as constructs, achieved fictions, containing and domesticating heteroglossia. In a world with too many voices speaking all at once, a world where syncretism and parodic invention are becoming the rule, not the exception, an urban, multinational world of institutional transience – where American clothes made in Korea are worn by young people in Russia, where everyone's "roots" are in some degree cut – in such a world it becomes increasingly difficult to attach human identity and meaning to a coherent "culture" or "language".[22]

The "post-cultural" crisis that James Clifford identifies above is nowhere more truly, more palpably and more extremely experienced than in Singapore. The rootlessness, syncretism and dissonances of "constructed" culture and language are the norms of life in this ethnically diverse, mostly immigrant, postcolonial society. Singapore willingly embraced globalization long before it became the de rigueur mode of development for emerging economies. In 1972, less than a decade after its independence, Singapore's then Minister for Foreign Affairs S. Rajaratnam declared:

> But times are changing and there will be less and less demand for the traditional type of entrepot services Singapore has rendered for well over a century. Its role as the trading city of South-East Asia, the market place of the region, will become less and less important. This is because it is transforming itself into a new kind of city – the Global City. It is a new form of human organisation and settlement that has, as the historian Arnold Toynbee says, no precedent in man-kind's past history. People have become aware of this new type of city only very recently. They have found a name for this distinctive type of city. They call it Ecumenopolis – the world embracing city.
>
> [...] the Global City, now in its infancy, is the child of modern technology. It is the city that electronic communications, supersonic planes, giant tankers and modem economic and industrial organisation have made inevitable. Whether the Global City would be a happier place than the megalopolis out of whose crumbling ruins it is emerging will depend on how wisely and boldly we shape its direction and growth.[23]

This then is the crucial context; the social, historical and cultural milieu of the Intercultural Theatre Institute (ITI) in Singapore.

Since its inception in 2000 ITI has been dedicated to forging a new vision of contemporary theatre training; a vision based on practices of theatre making founded on a deep understanding of the cultural diversity and differences inherent in Singapore and in virtually all other societies today. The primary aim of ITI is to study, develop and run a comprehensive, systematic contemporary actor training programme that combines classical Asian theatre traditions with contemporary Western theatre practice and which emphasizes the active, practical modalities of studio work and training without neglecting the relevant theoretical concerns of theatre as art. The ITI curriculum is intertwined with the history and development of the actual practice of contemporary theatre in Singapore. Specifically, it emerges out of the work of the Singaporean playwright and dramatist Kuo Pao Kun (1939–2002).

From the 1960s to the time of his death at the age of 63, Kuo was one of the most important dramatists, playwrights and cultural activists in Singapore. Effectively bilingual in Chinese and English, his significant legacy includes a substantial number of critically acclaimed plays, theatre productions and considerable cultural criticism, unrivalled in its intellectual engagement and insight. His plays have been translated to Malay, Tamil, Hindi, German, French and Japanese, and notable works include *The Coffin Is Too Big For The Hole* (1986), *Mama Looking For Her Cat* (1988) and *Descendants of the Eunuch Admiral* (1995). Kuo was arrested and imprisoned without trial as a political detainee from 1976 to 1980.

Since the 1950s Singapore contemporary theatre has been a world of shifting sands and melting shadows; the lay of the land has often been transformed by new ideas, a maturing political scene and constantly changing social realities all of which were fostered by the most rapid pace of economic development known to man. Holding up a mirror to *this* reality was and continues to be a real struggle. Theatre artists here have always been scrambling to capture, frame and represent on stage "Singaporean life and consciousness", for ever-younger, better-educated publics, with shorter attention spans and even shorter memories.

Theatre, more than any other art form, is inextricably linked with the living forms of life. It feeds off life, and life, in turn, feeds theatre. Like the great river systems of the world which channel mountain waters down to the ground, transforming the land and sustaining life, theatre carries the ideas, ideals, values, customs and wisdom of a society and scatters these like so many seeds on the life-soil of people. Conversely, the reception of theatre by people, by audiences and the various publics, loops lived-reality back into the art.

Historically it is an endless and mostly, virtuous cycle. There is a natural ebb and flow, constant and continuous, as old as the seas. If the cycle is broken, then the quality of life and theatre suffer and start to wither. Both are diminished and reduced. But only until the next inevitable rejuvenation and renewal. In the context of Singapore's contemporary theatre practice, ITI is an attempt at just such a rejuvenation and renewal.

A fundamental premise of ITI is that any serious attempt at training contemporary actors in Singapore should draw from the rich resources of the various heritages and cultures that influence the people of Singapore. The aim is to research all Singaporean cultures and heritages, to experiment with styles and themes that are coherent with a multiracial and multicultural society, and to allow for the natural growth of a truly Singaporean theatre that reflects a contemporary, multicultural, globalized society.

ITI is a highly specialized and selective programme intended for small groups of serious, highly motivated professional actors interested in expanding their skills and expertise. At the heart of the vision that informs ITI is an article of faith. It is the belief that the established and inherited systems of performance making which continue to serve as standards of excellence in world theatre, like Noh, *Xiqu* (Beijing or Kun Opera), Kutiyattam (or *Bharatha Natyam*) and *Wayangwong*, are relevant and invaluable resources in the training and the making of the contemporary actor.

To put it another way, the underlying belief that informs and animates ITI is that the programmatic disciplines and the intricate aesthetics of these traditional forms can still speak volumes to actors today; and that by way of their rigour and precision, system and spirituality, technique and commitment, humility and grace hold out the promise of raising the art of contemporary theatre to new and hitherto unattained heights.

What is unique about ITI is that it immerses the actor-student in these four traditional theatre forms even as they are trained in a range of contemporary acting methods. To try and do more, take on more techniques or methods, would be impossible in a three-year programme. ITI is compact, comprehensive and uncompromising. And it is so to cultivate, engender and (sometimes) provoke the awakening of a "historical sense"; T.S. Eliot's idea that the artist must possess a sense of the deep timelessness that permeates all changing realities in any historical context.[24]

> Yet if the only form of tradition, of handing down, consisted in following the ways of the immediate generation before us in a blind or timid adherence to its successes, 'tradition' should positively be discouraged. We have seen many such simple currents soon lost in the sand; and novelty is better than repetition. Tradition is a matter of much wider significance. It cannot be inherited, and if you want it you must obtain it by great labour. It involves, in the first place, the historical sense, which we may call nearly indispensable to anyone who would continue to be a poet beyond his twenty-fifth year; and the historical sense involves a perception, not only of the pastness of the past, but of its presence; . . . This historical sense, which is a sense of the timeless as well as of the temporal and of the timeless and of the temporal together, is what makes a writer traditional. And it is at the same time what makes a writer most acutely conscious of his place in time, of his contemporaneity.[25]

The "historical sense" is the sense of "timelessness within temporality", an imagination of eternity palpable in the present. It is a sense that is instantly apprehensible in all great works of art – poetry, painting, sculpture, music or theatre. The fundamental premise of the ITI curriculum is that training in contemporary theatre is no different. To produce great works of contemporary theatre, the actor too must be imbued with the "historical sense".

This entails that the student learns and is trained in multiple, sometimes conflicting, pedagogical processes concurrently. It involves a practical, immersive and intensive core of studio work and practicums, traditional theatre training juxtaposed with training in contemporary acting methods, coupled with disciplined, rigorous, systematic training in pure craft and technical skills: Voice and Speech, Movement, Mask Work, Corporeal Mime and paratheatrical body disciplines like Taiji, Yoga and *kalarippayattu*.[26]

The ITI student will never at the end of their course be a Noh performer, a Beijing Opera artist, a *Kutiyattam* performer or a *Wayangwong* actor. This is not the objective of the programme. What they will able to do is recombine, for themselves and themselves alone, the deep-learning experience they have had of these traditional systems with the methodology and techniques of contemporary acting, as they have been developed within the Western canon of theatre, primarily that of Constantin Stanislavsky (1863–1938).

The acting techniques of Stanislavsky broadly assume that an actor's stage actions are determined, defined and ultimately shaped by the character's "internal need" – motivation, desire, psychology, biography, context, situation and given circumstances as set out in a script – in a word, it is concerned with the actor understanding, uncovering and finally identifying with the "truth" of the character, and then sustaining, nurturing and keeping vital the "through line" of this discovered truth throughout the play's duration.

Even as they are trained in the Stanislavski system, ITI students are taught to go beyond its bounds and break free of the cognitive and discursive limits privileged within the method. ITI students are concurrently taught "alternative approaches to acting" – ones that unlock the truth of a character by working from the "external" towards the "internal" and which draw as much upon the actor's kinaesthetic and physical impulses as their intellectual or rational capacities. In this "alternative approach" – and to be sure it is just an approach; nothing quite like a system – the actor is constantly enjoined to be "holistic" on stage; to be a whole being, a complete psychophysical entity; rather than be alive only from the shoulders up.

This co-mingling of the Stanislavski system and more recent alternative approaches to actor training is excellent not only in preparing the actor to work in improvizational situations and in devising dramatic contexts for performance, but also in unlocking new possibilities to make meaning particularly during the early stages of the rehearsal process when a script is first encountered or unavailable.

All the core ITI training modules, both the traditional and contemporary, the technical and creative, share the following key characteristics:

1   Established pedagogies for training, presentation and representation
2   Significant and recognized repertoire of content
3   Vivid, dramatic characterizations
4   Well-formed, stable dramaturgies
5   Recognizable aesthetics of performance

The learning and the training in ITI are grounded squarely in the practical and the performative. In that it is situated (happens) in both the doing and the being, in both action (deed/task) and thought. It is thoroughly experiential and existential; about being in and bounded by specific, definable empirical realities of life. In other words, all ITI training processes emphasize a radical corporeality (in the Kantian sense). Recalling the novelist Toni Morrison: "In a sea of distress you have the body in motion and you have the *obligation* (my emphasis) of seeing the body as the real and final home".[27]

Bear in mind also that actor training in ITI happens in a learning context that is very specific and unusual. Where the "Intercultural" is foregrounded, highlighted, interrogated and explored. This is the "hot crucible" which forges in the student-actor's mind-body (the "bastard-body" as one student called it), a unity of all the contested, disputed and displaced processes of becoming an actor.

So, what exactly is the "intercultural learning context"? It is one in which the student must confront and comport with differences every single day; by recombining diversities of craft and culture, by re-examining histories and traditions, by rediscovering the possibility of speaking with conviction and belief about new values of life in our sprawling, globalized, post-industrial societies. Theatre itself must be made anew, for a world consisting of unstable truths, dissipated aspirations of common humanity, a depleted, devastated planet and the terrifying prospect of life without hope and faith.

Implicit in "the Intercultural" is the tension between identifying difference on the one hand and seeking commonality on the other. Difference must be acknowledged in order to name the Other as a "culture", but some transcendence of that difference must be found to allow for "inter"action to happen.[28] This search for commonality (for transcendence) while identifying and acknowledging difference, is the very heart and kernel of the ITI process of actor training. The process also includes devising exercises, training routines and regimens that enable the transfer and transmission of specific skills and techniques from traditional theatre forms to the student. This entails containing, shaping and directing the teaching of the "master teachers" and the outcomes of the training in the various traditional forms.

What all ITI teachers emphasize, the goal they all work towards, is to prepare and enable the student, at the end of three years of programmatic training, to be "autonomous". To be able to determine and direct their own learning and practice. This is achieved by clearly stating the objectives and outcomes of all work, encouraging open, continual, off-floor critique of training methods and providing continuous feedback on how students are performing, outlining errors and suggesting corrections. To borrow a coinage of the philosopher Richard Rorty we were attempting to create technology that "helped break down the traditional distinction between the 'high' wisdom of the priests and theorists and the 'low' cleverness of the artisan . . . ."[29]

The Post-modular Labs (PML) and the work of the Final Year Individual Project (FYiP), all of which are initiated and driven by the students themselves, offer possibilities for recombining the classical with the contemporary, the past with the present and of transcending differences in culture, form, language and technique. It offers, in short, the possibility of making new art.

Each of the four theatre traditions being taught brings with it a paradigm of expression and representation that is anchored in the body of the actor in a precise and specific manner. These paradigms are still relevant – by way of their rigour and precision, system and spirituality (a co-mingling of rationality and emotion), technique and commitment and humility and grace – to actors today. The trick is to find the key for each student; a way to unlock and unpack these monolithic paradigms to plumb, select and draw on their elements – of gesture, voice, movement, rhythm, breath control, presentational modes and form – which may be recombined and situated within the specific realities of their own communities, locales and situations.

After 18 years of training very different cohorts of students from all over the world, we are just beginning to get a glimpse of what the key might be to unlock those monolithic systems of theatre technology which contain within them the "secret knowledge" – of stage action and representation, of self-awareness and availability and of owned speech and voice – so that the actor "be not too tame but let his/her own discretion be their tutor: suit the action to the word, the word to the action; with this special observance, that they o'erstep not the modesty of nature; . . . ".[30]

The key we seek is not to be found in the person of a single teacher or director (some guru figure), nor in some supreme, overriding method, technique, precept, formula, skill or ability, that the actor can learn, repeat and master in good time. It is a kind of nous; a rigorous, disciplined, practical intelligence derived from a way of being, a way of practising and seeing, something of a sensibility. Perhaps it is a capacity, a cast of mind, an aspect of spirit, a way of thinking and feeling with both body and mind. In short, it is a personality; an actor's personality capable of manifesting specific, well-defined cultural truths intended for a moment, drawing its impulse from the deep well-springs of peoples' lives and politics.

We are many, many things and many things are within us.[31] This sensibility is in fact far more complex than is implied here. For it is not merely artists and audiences who are so interpellated. This thing we call "culture" is similarly complicated.

> A culture is not a self-enclosed world. It is not an identity but a system of differences held together by history. Not being self-complete, it opens out to other possibilities. Then one finds the other within oneself. I do not understand all my motives, choices, and desires. The stranger and the foreigner are right in my neighbourhood. My culture and the other culture are not separated as the known, the familiar and the unknown and the unfamiliar, but rather by degrees of familiarity, foreignness, strangeness. Sometimes, I understand myself only through the other, at other times the reverse happens. The boundaries are shifting.[32]

To everything there must be balance, and the spontaneity and spark that the "alternative" approach to actor training engenders in the rehearsal process has to be tempered by the rigorous, empirical grounding that the Stanislavski system brings to bear. There is the constant ebb and flow of movement, sensitivity and consciousness between these modalities that the ITI student is expected to master and deploy in both rehearsal and performance. This process of selection, excavation and combination and recombination would have to be played out again and again many times in the mind and body of the student-actor until a new aesthetic equilibrium is achieved, a new *discordia concors*; some unheard, unseen harmony, gained by the combination of disparate or even conflicting elements. The result, of course, would be a renewal of contemporary theatre practice.

It is worth noting that the traditional theatre systems are not taught in isolation at ITI, as they normally would be in their places/cultures of origin – in isolation and to the exclusion of all other traditional or contemporary systems. In ITI the traditional theatre systems are contextualized, elaborated and juxtaposed with other systems. Nothing can live and grow in isolation; life is possible only because of the connections we make, and are willing to make, as human beings; to each other, to things, to ideas and to life itself. Art is possible because, ideologically, we believe in the connectedness, or at the very least in the connectivity, of all ideas, of all things and of all beings through the human imagination. This sensibility is epitomized in Kuo Pao Kun's notion of the "open culture":

> [Open Culture] contemplates a transcendence of the individual from race and tradition-bound communities to embrace a diverse global community. [It] provides resources for and provokes dynamic interaction. Open Culture begets open futures.[33]

Open culture is possible only as the outcome of an act of imagination. The urgency to re-imagine tradition to this end has never been greater. As far as theatre and the performing arts are concerned, this revolution or "ferment" had emerged in many parts of Asia (India, Indonesia, Taiwan, Japan and Singapore) over the last decade. As one critic put it:

> At the core of the ferment is the deep-seated desire of the community of artists and thinkers in this part of the globe to re-negotiate their artistic identities from within their own rich resource of a plural form-language, and yet remain free of the constraints and limitations that such conventions imply. Tradition is what enables a set of defining ideas and concepts to renew themselves and stay relevant over time – not something meant to be pickled and bottled with built-in artificial shelf-life. As Chandralekha, the Indian dancer and choreographer has repeated on many occasions: "Preserving tradition is fine. But we need to pause periodically to pull it off the shelf, dust it vigorously, and hold it against the sun to see if it still reflects light".[34]

This is the critical question: Are the traditional theatre systems of Asia, particularly the ones that are studied and deployed in ITI, capable at all of standing in the sunlight of ordinary life and are they able to reflect some of this light? If they are capable of doing so, if they are still relevant, significant and vital, they will able to connect with and revitalize the contemporary theatre practice of actors. Not only for the Asian actor, but for all actors.

What is the actor's role in today's changing world? More specifically what is the impact of ITI's approach to intercultural theatre on contemporary performance works and acting pedagogies? What emerges is an approach which has specific, defining values:

- a predisposition for "working *with* and working *out* difference"
- a respect for the creative collaborator's agency
- a sensibility which leans towards attending to the decentred, the marginalized, the fringe in oneself and others
- the search for an independence from ideological structures and homogenizing forces (be it constrictive market demands or government agendas)
- a respect for the body-mind as a complex multilayered site of interconnectedness
- a curiosity (respectful and not superficial or exploitative) towards traditions, cultures and new practices, one's own and others'
- an enquiring "mind" seeking to understand the socio-historic context, philosophy and functioning of embodied practices
- an enquiring "body", ready to immerse itself in unfamiliar modes of being to search new forms through them
- a courage to challenge oneself to stay in that uncomfortable and fragile space "in between" that is the "inter"-cultural[35]

This is the mode of intercultural actor training which emerges from ITI in Singapore.

An overview of the chapters

Phillip B. Zarrilli

The ubiquity of serious interest in and practice of multi-, inter-, intra-cultural approaches to acting/actor training today is reflected in the fact that for the original TDPT special issue, we received over fifty proposals from scholars and practitioners throughout the world. The breadth and depth of the contributions have been gratifying. We are pleased to provide the reader with this expanded collection of chapters curated to create a journey through the various descriptions, discussions, and analyses of processes and/or problems of "interweaving" between.

Extending the discussion offered by T. Sasitharan in the third part to this Introduction about the Intercultural Theatre Institute, in Chapter 1 Giorgia Ciampi provides a first-person account from her perspective as a former student of the ITI's intensive three-year professional training programme in Singapore. In multicultural/multilingual Singapore, the ITI programme exemplifies a bold attempt to create not "an actor" but an actor whose body-mind has experienced multiple interweavings – shaped and reshaped by one's own socio-cultural background and creative impulses and interests. Ciampi's account provides insight into the process of interculturalism at work within individual actors.

The contributions by Odem and Calamoneri in Chapters 2 and 3 focus on two of the best-known twentieth contemporary Japanese "trainings" that have become interwoven into Western contemporary actor/performer/dance training programmes – Suzuki's specific mode of training actors, and *butoh*. While Suzuki Tadashi's work has been the subject of numerous publications, Odem's careful interrogation of multiple notions of subjectivity in his theatre practice offers a model of how to methodologically and analytically illuminate practice/technique by focusing on a specific issue – in this case the entailments of "subjectivity" in the Japanese post-war period. Calamoneri provides a description and analysis of the use of *butoh* in the work of the actor – a case study focused on how RSC actor, Greg Hicks makes use of *butoh*'s transformative imagination in creating an embodied sub-score. Read alongside Frances Barbe's Chapter 10, Calamoneri helps us understand how *butoh* can lead to a dynamically alive inner world manifest in the individual performer's embodiment of a specific role – Hamlet.

Parallel to Calamoneri's primary focus on a single actor whose process makes integral use of *butoh*, Chen's Chapter 4 focuses on the seminal process of transformation of a Taiwanese *jingju* actor, Wu Hsing-Kuo when he encountered the work of renowned Cloud Gate dance company, and came to perform *Macbeth*. The essays by Calamoneri and Chen allow us to see interweaving processes at work East to West, and then West to East – both of which have been transformative for these noted actors.

In Chapter 5, David Peimer's account of the shifting landscape of actor training in post-apartheid Johannesburg takes us into an alternative socio-cultural and geopolitical landscape where stereotypical assumptions about "training" and acting/performance "theories" are thrown into question by life as it is – lived. It is to be hoped that Peimer's contribution may inspire other future publications in/around issues of intercultural actor training in Africa.

Editorially, we were in the unique position of having essays submitted by two Korean actors/authors, each of whom was reflecting from "inside" their work as actors on a new intercultural theatre production, *playing "the maids"*. In Chapter 6, Yoo and Kim draw upon key Korean and/or Buddhist concepts to discuss their acting processes, shedding an alternative light on how we can think and talk about acting and performance beyond the ubiquitous use of "psychology".

Another dynamic pair of contributions follow in Chapters 7 and 8 on issues of intercultural voice training by Tara McAllister-Viel and Electa Behrens. Both authors question in their own way "normative" notions of what contemporary voice training in professional actor-training programmes should/might be like, and offer up alternative pedagogical and conceptual strategies for reconsidering voice trainings today.

In Chapter 9, Christel Weiler provides a thoughtful reflection on the "inspirations and starting points" of integrating *taiqiquan* into contemporary actor training. Weiler's careful questioning of the purpose of movement training for the contemporary actor invites reflection on the tremendous value that *taiqiquan* might offer actor training programmes today. Weiler offers a tantalizing glimpse of the long-term value and benefits offered by this type of training. Immediately following in Chapter 10, Frances Barbe provides a detailed account and specific examples of her use of selected *butoh*-based techniques in training and expanding the contemporary performer's embodied imagination. Barbe's account of her selective use of *butoh*-based training exercises exemplifies how (selective) interculturalism is "at work" in the studio today. Barbe's chapter should be read alongside Tanya Calamoneri's Chapter 3 account of one specific actor's use of *butoh*-based work in creating the specific role of Hamlet.

Chapters 11 and 12 provide important contributions that illuminate contemporary approaches to acting in Southeast Asia. Kathy Foley's chapter contextualizes the wonderfully urgent and always almost chaotic "mixed salad" (*gado-gado*) in-between that characterizes modern Indonesian "new theatre" as exemplified in the work and experience of two key formative figures – Arafin C. Noer and Putu Wijaya. Foley traces each director's often chaotic journey and experience "between" the West and Indonesia, and provides insights into how each has (s)mashed together – interwoven is too polite a term for their processes – their own unique contributions to contemporary Indonesian theatre. In Chapter 12 Marco Adda provides a complementary account to Foleys, but about the tremendously important work of W.S. Rendra and his approach to acting that developed in and through his experiences of actor training in the United States.

In Chapter 13 concepts and perceptions of "otherness" are explored by Carmencita Palermo. Palermo examines issues of otherness through her experience of introducing Balinese techniques when working with actors in Brazil. Palermo's chapter invites us to (re)consider how all intercultural processes and modes of interaction and/or interweaving necessarily must address issues of the other and otherness.

In the final chapter, Josh Stenberg and Tsai Hsin-hsin provide an important and detailed account of institutional changes in a traditional form of Taiwanese "opera" (*xiqu*). Stenberg and Hsin-hsin's account begins to shed light on the seldom examined but often radical changes wrought by modernization as pedagogies have been reshaped by new, Western-influenced modes of institutional organization and notions of teaching.[36]

Notes

1 I want to acknowledge with thanks the support of the International Research Centre (IRC), "Interweaving Performance Cultures", at Freie Universität that provided time and support for the development of this collection of essays for TDPT, and for this expanded book version. Without the support of Prof. Dr. Erika Fischer-Lichte and Dr. Christel Weiler, and the staff and colleagues at IRC, this collection of essays would never have materialized. I also want to thank Rustom Bharucha for his thoughtful response to this type of collection of essays.

2 For an important study of migration and the type of "new" interculturalism in theatre that responds to migration in Ireland, see McIvor (2019).

3 For further extensive discussions see the numerous reflections in the "Textures" section of the International Research Centre, "Interweaving Performance Cultures" website, Freie Universität, Berlin (www.textures-platform.com).

4 In addition, see Zarrilli (2015, 2012, 2011).

5 On yoga and Stanislavsky see Tcherkasski (2016), Carnicke (2009), as well as Kapsali (2013).

6 For example, see Kevin Page's *ACT: Advanced Consciousness Training for Actors, Meditation Techniques for the Performing Artist* (2018). Based on interviews with teachers of acting at major US actor-training programmes, Page provides an overview and practical guide to the use of meditation/mindfulness training in acting schools, as well as providing an account of his specific approach to deepening the actor's ability to concentrate, focus and be attentive.

7 See Erika Fischer-Lichte, Torsten Jost and Saskya Iris Jain. (eds.). (2014). *The Politics of Interweaving Performance Cultures Beyond Postcolonialism.* New York and Abingdon: Routledge, p. 2.

8 Maria M. Delgado. (2014). Translation, Cultural Ownership. In Bryan Reynolds, ed., *Performance Studies: Key Words, Concepts and Theories.* London and New York: Palgrave Macmillan, p. 103.

9 Walter Benjamin. (1996). The Task of The Translator. In Marcus Bullock and Michael W. Jennings, eds., *Selected Writings, Volume 1, 1913–1926.* Cambridge and London: The Belknap Press of Harvard University Press, pp. 253–63, p. 261.

10 Homi Bhabha cited in Rajeev S. Patke. (2006). Postcolonial Cultures. *Theory Culture & Society, Problematizing Global Knowledge,* Special Issue, 23(2–3), pp.369–71, p. 369, March–May.

11 Homi Bhabha. (2017). Cultural Appropriation: A Roundtable. *Artforum,* Summer. Available at: www.artforum.com/inprint/issue=201706&id=68677.

12 In India, the 1950s saw the formation of several arts institutions like the Sahitya Akademi (the Academy of Literature), the Sangeet Natak Akademi (the Academy of Music Theatre and Dance), the Lalit Kala Akademi, (The Akademi of Visual Arts), the National Gallery of Modern Art, and the Film and Television Institute of India. These initiatives were part of a larger Nehruvian vision to create an infrastructure for the practice and public manifestation of the arts in the newly independent nation. The Asian Theatre Institute

(ATI), which later came to be called the National School of Drama, was initiated by Bhartiya Natya Sangh with UNESCO support in 1958. It was a year-long theatre education programme with two courses – Rural Theatre and Children's Theatre. Both courses were conceived as ways of pulling together ideas of education and social development through cultural practice. This programme was taken over by Sangeet Natak Akademi in 1959 and named National school of Drama and Asian Theatre Institute – a two-year consolidated course in Theatre Arts. In 1975 NSD became autonomous from the SNA; ATI was dropped from its name but its conceptual interest in the theatre practices of the "East" remained.

13 Personal conversation with Priyanka Pathak who recounted the instructions given by G. Venu, Kudiattam guru and practitioner to the National School of Drama students in 2010–2011.
14 Raymond Williams. (1982). *The Sociology of Culture*. New York: Schoken Books, p. 145.
15 See B. Ananthakrishnan and Jane Collins. (2018). Against a Hierarchy of Expressive Means: Arguments for New Pedagogies in Performer Education in India and the UK. *Studies in Theatre and Performance*, 6. doi:10.1080/14682761.2018.1429758 for a discussion of the fertile ground between forms.
16 See Erika Fischer-Lichte, Torsten Jost and Saskya Iris Jain. (eds.). (2014). *The Politics of Interweaving Performance Cultures Beyond Postcolonialism*. New York and Abingdon: Routledge.
17 Ibid., p. 11.
18 See Tim Ingold. (2015). *The Life of Lines*. Abingdon and New York: Routledge.
19 See Frank Camilleri. (2009). Of Pounds of Flesh and Trojan Horses: Performer Training in the Twenty-First Century. *Performance Research*, 14(2), pp. 26–34. doi:10.1080/13528160903319232.
20 Ibid., p. 3.
21 Tim Ingold. (2015). *The Life of Lines*. Abingdon and New York: Routledge.
22 James Clifford. (1988). *The Predicament of Culture*. Cambridge, MA and London: Harvard University Press, p. 95.
23 S. Rajaratnam. Singapore: Global City. Text of address to Singapore Press Club, 6 Feb 1972. www.nas.gov.sg/archivesonline/data/pdfdoc/PressR19720206a.pdf
24 T.S. Eliot. (1921). Tradition and the Individual Talent. In *The Sacred Wood: Essays on Poetry and Criticism*. New York: Alfred A. Knopf, p. 43.
25 Ibid.
26 *Kalarippayattu* is the traditional martial art of Kerala, South India. It dates from approximately the tenth century ACE.
27 Ihab Hassan. (2008). Literary Theory in an Age of Globalization. *Philosophy and Literature*, 32 (1), pp. 1–10.
28 Jennifer Lindsay. (2007). Intercultural Expectations I La Galigo in Singapore. *TDR: The Drama Review*, 51(2, T194), Summer.
29 Richard Rorty. (1992). A Pragmatist View of Rationality and Cultural Difference. *Philosophy East and West*, 42(4), pp. 581–96.
30 William Shakespeare, *Hamlet*, Act 3 Scene 2.
31 T. Sasitharan. (2009). *Freedom of Expression and Cultural Sensitivity or Fucking the Powerless*, 4th World Summit on Arts and Culture of the International Federation of Arts Councils and Culture Agencies, Johannesburg, South Africa, 24 September.
32 Jitendra Nath Mohanty. (2000). *The Self and Its Other: Philosophical Essays*. New Delhi and Oxford: Oxford University Press, p. 19.
33 Pao Kun Kuo. (1998). *Contemplating an Open Culture: Transcending Multiracialism*. Edited by Mahizhnan Arun and Tsao Yuan Lee. Singapore: Re-Engineering Success.
34 Menon, Sadanand. (2002). *"Tradition" as a Limiting Notion Within Indian Performing Arts*. Singapore: Talk at the Asian Civilisations Museum, 21 September.
35 Giorgia Ciampi. (2017). *Asian Intercultural Conference, Theatre Wars: The Return of the Artist*, convened by I.T.I., Singapore, 27–30 November.

36 As another example, see the earlier extended analysis of the history of institutional and pedagogical changes in Kerala, India's *kathakali* dance-drama training, see Phillip Zarrilli's. (1984). *The Kathakali Complex: Actor, Performance, Structure*. New Delhi: Abhinav, pp. 261–356.

References

Carnicke, S. (2009). Stanislavsky in Focus. London: Routledge Press.

Cools, G. (2015). *In-Between Dance Cultures: On the Migratory Artistic Identity of Sidi Larbi Cherkaoui and Akram Khan*. Amsterdam: Antennae.

Fischer-Lichte, E. (2010). Interweaving Cultures in Performance: Different States of Being In-Between. *Textures*, 11 August. Available at: www.textures-platform.com.

Fischer-Lichte, E. and Bharucha, R. (2011). Dialogue: Erika Fischer-Lichte, Erika and Rustom Bharucha. *Textures*, posted 6 August. Available at: www.textures-platform.com.

Gokhale, S. (ed.). (2014). *The Theater of Veenapani Chowla: Theory, Practice, and Performance*. New Delhi: Oxford University Press.

Heckler, R. S. (1985). *The Anatomy of Change: East/West Approaches to Body/Mind Therapy*. Boston and London: Shambala.

Kapsali, M. (2013). The Presence of Yoga in Stanislavski's Work. *Stanislavski Studies*, 3, 139–150.

Li, K. (2007). Performing the Globalized City: Contemporary Hong Kong Theatre and Globalized Connectivity. *Asian Theatre Journal*, 24(2), 440–469.

McAllister-Viel, T. (2019). *Training Actors' Voices: Towards an Intercultural/Interdisciplinary Approach*. London: Routledge Press.

McIvor, C. (2016). *Migration and Performance in Contemporary Ireland: Towards a New Interculturalism*. Basingstoke: Palgrave Macmillan.

McIvor, C. and King, J. (eds.). (2019). *Interculturalism and Performance Now: New Directions?* Switzerland: Springer Nature.

Page, K. (2018). *ACT: Advanced Consciousness Training for Actors, Meditation Techniques for the Performing Artist*. New York and London: Routledge.

Page, K. (2019). *Psychology for Actors: Theories and Practices for the Acting Process*. New York and London: Routledge.

Stanley, J. (2018). *How Fascism Works: The Politics of US and THEM*. New York: Random House.

Tcherkasski, S. (2016). *Stanislavsky and Yoga*. Holstebro and London: ICARUS and Routledge.

Tian, M. (2008). *The Poetics of Difference and Displacement: Twentieth Century Chinese-Western Intercultural Theatre*. Hong Kong: Hong Kong University Press.

Winet, E. D. (2010). *Indonesian Postcolonial Theatre: Spectral Geneologies and Absent Faces*. New York: Palgrave Macmillan.

Yoo, J. (2018). *A Korean Approach to Actor Training*. London: Routledge Press.

Zarrilli, P. B. (1984). *The Kathakali Complex: Actor, Performance, and Structure*. New Delhi: Abhinav Publishers.

Zarrilli, P. B. (2009). *Psychophysical Acting: An Intercultural Approach After Stanislavski*. London: Routledge Press.

Zarrilli, P. B. (2011). Altered Consciousness in Performance: West and East. In Etzel Cardena and Michael Winkelman, eds., *Altering Consciousness: Multidisciplinary Perspectives, Vol. I: History, Culture and the Humanities*. Santa Barbara: Praeger, pp. 301–326.

Zarrilli, P. B. (2012). ' . . . presence . . . ' as a Question and Emergent Possibility: A Case-Study from the Performer's Perspective. In Gabriella Giannachi and Nick Kaye, eds., *Archeologies of Presence*. London: Routledge, pp. 119–152.

Zarrilli, P. B. (2013). 'Introduction', 'Chapter 1: Psychophysical Acting in India', 'Chapter 2: Psychophysical Acting in Japan'. In *Acting: Psychophysical Phenomenon and Process (Intercultural and Interdisciplinary Perspectives)*. [Book Co-authored with Jerri Daboo and Rebecca Loukes]. Basingstoke: Palgrave Macmillan.

Zarrilli, P. B. (2015). ' . . . beneath the surface' of *Told by the Wind:* An Intercultural Experiment in Performance Dramaturgy and Aesthetics. *Asian Theatre Journal*, 32(1), 47–78.

1

ACTOR TRAINING AT THE INTERCULTURAL THEATRE INSTITUTE OF SINGAPORE

Giorgia Ciampi Tsolaki

Introduction

The Theatre Training and Research Program (TTRP) (now Intercultural Theatre Institute, ITI)[1] was founded in Singapore in 2000 by playwright Kuo Pao Kun and theatre practitioner Thirunalan Sasitharan. The school is based on Kuo Pao Kun's:

> vision of intercultural actor training using a matrix of traditional theatre systems and conceptions of theatre making from different cultures with a view to producing original contemporary theatre and socially engaged artists
>
> *(ITI website http://iti.edu.sg/ 2011)*

This kind of training enables the actor to become aware, through regular and in-depth forms of practice, of the broader cultural context in which different theatre traditions were born and developed. The objective of practising the traditional forms is hardly to perfectly reproduce them, but rather to open the actor's sensibility to different modes of perception and possibilities of practice. It is the actor's work that goes into embodying these forms – into making them present through the body-mind – that allows the actor to be traversed by different kinds of energy, rhythms, images, feelings from different places and times. A deep practical understanding of these theatre traditions allows the actor to make mindful choices in relation to their practice and develop new contemporary work.

The traditional teachers at the school are deeply aware of this: the Noh theatre practitioner Hideo Kanze (descendant of the Zeami lineage) once told a student who asked if he could change a Noh gesture: "Change it! But know why you're doing it!"

In this chapter, I will concentrate on how the different theatre training systems meet, intersect or contradict each other within the body-mind of the student-actor at ITI. I will reflect on ITI's intercultural programme, through a series of interviews with the ITI/TTRP alumni themselves.

The context

ITI/TTRP: a brief history

I will start by contextualizing ITI/TTRP within the Singapore cultural landscape.

Why does the need for this intercultural school arise at the heart of multicultural Singapore?

There are many aspects about ITI's project that are contextually specific to the socio-historical and economic context of Singapore. I will try to capture some of them. The 2015 ethnic composition of Singapore is: 74.3% Chinese, 13.3% Malays, 9.1% Indians, 3.3% Others. This terminology and subdivision is the specific result of the CMIO - for consistency's sake with later examples model (Chinese Malay Indian Other), which represents the "racial governmentality of late twentieth-century Singapore, which endows each of its citizens with a racialised identity and speaks to them through race" (Holden 2006)[2]. It is the British, whose colonization of Singapore lasted from 1819 to 1965, who were responsible for bringing to Malaya immigrant workers from their other Chinese and Indian colonies (PuruShotam 1998, p. 56). After Singapore achieved independence in 1965, its "nationalist discourse, to an even greater extent than in most postcolonial nationalisms, borrowed many of the elements of self-fashioning from the colonial state". With the initial aim "to contain ethnic conflict", the CMIO model ended up reproducing, as "a glove inside out" (Holden 2006, n.p.), the separation of different racial communities and cultures, which had previously been endorsed by the British colonialists.

It is within this context of separated cultural coexistence, that Kuo Pao Kun's vision of an "open culture" can be understood. He believes that seeds of this open culture are to be cultivated in the field of education. In fact he comments:

> There are no in-depth education programmes in school or society to make the communities understand each other's customs and practices, culture and religion, their deeper emotions and higher aspirations.
>
> *(Kuo 1998, p. 52)*

Kuo Pao Kun here highlights the urgent need for a space where the different cultures can begin to communicate with each other. ITI's function within this context is thus coming into focus.

After Singapore's independence, the government's emphasis on economic growth, together with policies of multiracialism, has caused the cultural and social development to be dictated by global economic laws. As a consequence:

> Singapore's cultural and social landscape are saturated with signs of other modernities held up as objects of desire: Japanese popular music and fashion,

Korean soap operas dubbed into Mandarin, Dutch banks, American seminars on entrepreneurship and self-help books.

(Holden 2006, n. p.)

It is against this fast-growing and barren saturation, that Kuo Pao Kun's project proposes to recognize "what is currently ours, within us and around us" (Kuo 1998, p. 56) within the richness and fertility of the existing cultures of Singapore. Within a historically forced multicultural *coexistence*, there can be born a willingness to understand and be part of each other's *existences*. For this willingness to understand each other's cultures and traditions to flourish, the mere presence of different cultures is not sufficient. Culture and tradition are not automatically inherited; they must be gradually discovered and acquired through study and effort.

The structure of the ITI/TTRP programme and the issue of the "intercultural"

I will now give a brief overview of the organization of the ITI/TTRP three-year programme and of its subjects. During the first two years, the students undergo an intense training regime from 8am to 6pm every day. In the third year they work with Singaporean or international directors to create three contemporary theatre productions.

During the two-year training period, the mornings (from 8am to 1pm) are dedicated to the core modules: Movement, Voice, Tai Chi and Humanities. The afternoons (from 2.15pm to 6pm) are dedicated to the particular theatre training (traditional or contemporary) that the students are practising in that period. Each year they experience two "training immersions" in traditional Asian forms (each immersion lasting from two to three months) and two contemporary theatre techniques. The uniqueness of the school consists in offering practitioners from all cultures and backgrounds a "training immersion" in four traditional Asian theatre techniques (Kutiyattam Theatre from India,[3] Beijing Opera from China,[4] Noh Theatre from Japan[5] and Wayang Wong Opera from Indonesia),[6] alongside various contemporary techniques from all over the world.

I attended ITI from 2012 to 2014 and I reflect here on the modules that I experienced during this time: the "Movement" module was based on techniques of corporeal mime and theatre anthropology, taught by Leela Alaniz. Within the "Voice" module, teacher Robin Payne, (trained in Cicely Berry and Linklater techniques), challenged us to turn back to the popular voices of our ancestors, to rediscover *our* voice. "Tai Chi for actors" was conceived by Taijigong Shifu from Wu Tu Nan lineage, Sim Pern Yiau. During the weekly "Humanities" class, the director T. Sasitharan had the students discuss several theoretical readings, often contextualizing the particular form they were practising in that period. Some examples of the contemporary theatre approaches I was exposed to are: Phillip Zarrilli's "psychophysical training", Iben Nagel Rasmussen's "wind dance technique" employed in the research of "organic" action and clown, taught by actor/director Guillermo

Angelelli, Stanislavskian technique and Shakespearean text with director Aarne Neeme, *Butoh* training with teacher/practitioner Frances Barbe.

This created a unique combination of training systems and vocabularies, which pulled our body-minds in all directions, stirred all sorts of conflicts and contradictions within us, and lit up our sensibilities to an incredibly different range of theatres/performances/cultures. Every time we would think we were beginning to grasp the inner workings of a particular form, the rug was pulled out from under our feet, the rules changed and all was to be discovered anew. Andy from the very first batch of TTRP, explains:

> I don't see any other programme or school that addresses so emphatically the conflicts of culture. The programme itself is a conflict; teachers taught contrasting things. For example, one teacher asked me to learn how to relax, and another teacher may require me to hold tension in some body parts. I needed to find my own way and this is the true training of it.
>
> *(Q&A with Andy Ng, ITI blog,*
> *https://itiblog.org/2015/01/08qa-with-andy-ng/)*

However, the "interculturality" of the school's teaching space doesn't come from the variety of techniques but from developing the capacity for accepting, negotiating and containing all the contradictory aspects, from not trying to smooth them out or make them agree with each other. This attitude towards the contradictions inherent in the training emerges both from the daily practice and from the space for reflection on the practice, initiated in the "Humanities" class. Through this space, the issue of the "intercultural" is brought to the centre of the students' enquiry from the very beginning of the programme. I believe this inspires the way the students welcome the different teachers and receive their teachings: as a gift. Sasitharan finds this idea of the "gift" to be at the heart of the intercultural exchange.

> Intercultural exchange happens at its purest when the two parties decide to make a gift of their art. The person who offers doesn't expect anything else but the receiver to receive the gift. This is the only kind that preserves the artistic integrity. That's the way we work with all the teachers. They don't come to teach a formula but just to give you a gift.
>
> *(Sasitharan 2012)*

In fact, all the teachers carefully selected a limited part of the taught repertoire in order to be able to concentrate on the quality and the depth of the work: even if it was just a walk in Noh theatre that we were learning or a way of stretching our eyes open, or learning how to perform only one sentence through the *mudras*[7] in Kutiyattam Theatre. This created a breathing space between the different cultural forms. It seems to me that it resisted the sense of Singapore's cultural saturation and instead opened up a space *in between* cultures, a space where cultures could breathe, interact, enter into dialogue, debate, exchange, "imagine and re-imagine themselves", (Sasitharan 2009, p. 5).

But what was the students' experience of this training? What was the process of encountering the different theatre systems like? How did the different types of energy, rhythms, images, which underpin each theatrical culture, affect the student-actors at ITI? How did they cope with the different philosophical and practical approaches to the body-mind? And how do the practitioners, who have completed training at ITI, organize these experiences to nourish their own practice and contemporary theatre?

I posed these questions to the alumni themselves who generously shared their experiences. It is through their testimonies that I will reflect on the intercultural training at ITI and its relevance to contemporary theatre practice.

Conversations between practitioners

The ITI programme provides no formula or "guidelines" for how all the different theatre trainings might come together or emerge in the work of each practitioner. From the testimonies of the alumni, it becomes apparent that each one of them has operated a unique synthesis of the different techniques. I have organized their reflections according to certain emergent themes:

1 The training: a synthesis of techniques
2 The concept of the actor
3 The transformation of the performance space and time
4 A shifting centre
5 The actor creator/thinker/theatre maker

A natural conversation between practitioners emerges by gathering the alumni's thoughts around these core ideas. Their reflections highlight, question, contradict and challenge one another, while perhaps unwittingly containing the seed for multifaceted and transient answers. All their testimonies are dotted with examples of their experiences as actors, teachers and directors of contemporary work.

Three of the practitioners I interviewed were my colleagues in ITI between 2012 and 2014:

> Shakeel Ahmmad – actor, teacher and director, founder of the "Spinning Tree"Theatre Company, Karnataka, India
>> *(personal communication, 8 May 2015)*

> Pedro Simoni – freelance actor currently performing in Singapore, former professional violinist, originally from Bolivia
>> *(video recording, 1 August 2015)*

> Adèle Frantz – actress and co-founder of the "Compagnie Canopée", Paris, France
>> *(personal communication, 10 August 2015)*

Two alumni of the previous edition of the school (TTRP) also contributed by sharing their views:

> Noushad Mohamed Kunju (graduated in 2005) – actor/director currently associate professor at the Central University of Hyderabad (India)
> *(personal communication, 14 July 2015)*

> Sim Pern Yiau (graduated in 2003) – Taijigong Shifu from Wu Tu Nan lineage, former full-time theatre maker (Singapore).
> *(personal communication, 2 September 2015)*[8]

Since during the various interviews the alumni use certain terms or mention certain exercises as part of a TTRP/ITI-shared vocabulary, I will intervene to fill in the gaps, clarify or explain (the alumni's words will be in italics).

1. The training: a synthesis of techniques

Within this section, I collect the practitioners' accounts of how they work on activating or shaping their energy to support their practice. We can observe how each one found their own synthesis, blending different techniques and experiences of the training.

Noushad

I consider Noh Theatre and Kutiyattam Theatre as the core of my body. They give me inner immobility, intensity and will. They create an energy channel through the body.
 Noushad refers to Noh and Kutiyattam as the core of his practice because of the fundamental role they have in awakening the sense of the vertical axis that sustains the actor's life/energy. This comes from a yogic concept of the body where the seven energy centres (*chakra-s*) are placed on the fundamental three channels (*nadi-s*), which occupy the central vertical line of the body. In Kutiyattam, the actor's posture favours circulation of the energy along these channels to activate the energy centres, one by one, from the lowest, situated at the base of the spinal column, to the highest, situated on top of the head.[9] In fact in the traditional *aramandala* stance,

> the feet are placed a hand span apart and turned outwards to form a straight line, the knees are bent in a deep squatting position and turned outwards. The spine forms a straight line from the occipital bone to the coccyx [. . .].
> *(Pfaff 1997, p. 147)*

Kutiyattam teacher Venu G explains how this position allows the performer to gather a "storehouse of energy at the base of the spine", which is extraneous to the individual's everyday experience (Venu 2012, Kutiyattam training). From this "storehouse", the energy can be deployed, shaped and channelled – it departs from the coccyx, travels up the spine and is distributed to the extremities of the body. By means of a combination of power and precision developed through training, the actors become endowed with an extra-daily energetic connection to their perception, which greatly differs from the quality of the individual's daily interactions and responses.

As for the Noh training, this central energetic channel of the body is developed through the basic walk of the Noh actor: the most important aspect of this walk is to keep the pelvis stable and always at the same distance from the floor. In order to do this, the knees must be slightly bent, the tailbone must be perpendicular to the floor and the heels must never leave the floor. The chin must be tucked in towards the chest in order not to break the verticality of the spine at the level of the neck's vertebrae. This gives a particular rhythm to the Noh movement phrases, which is captured in the "jo, ha, kiu" principle. This principle was never actually mentioned by the Noh teachers, and it cannot really be explained, but only gradually felt through countless repetitions of the form. However, we can approximately describe it as follows: beginning each movement phrase slowly, gradually increasing intensity and speed and then punctuating the end through a brief suspension which brings us again to the beginning of the cycle. This allows the attainment of a distilled and concentrated energy, which Noushad describes as "inner immobility, intensity and will".

It is fascinating that, within Noushad's account, this sensation of inner stillness is not the legacy of only one technique, but it appears as the result of a blending process, within the actor's body-mind, of Kutiyattam and Noh training. It's as if the stratification of these two experiences had intensified the feeling of the vertical channel of energy within the actor's self-awareness.

The importance of the activation of the spine appears in Pedro's and Adèle's accounts of their practice as well. In Pedro's case, through Phillip Zarrilli's psychophysical training and the work on the breath:

Pedro

Through exercises of tension and release, relaxing the hips and backbone (spine), connecting to the breath and the sky. The connection to the breath is essential to my psychophysical practice.

Zarrilli's psychophysical training, which is one of the modules in ITI, consists of a combination of exercises from Asian martial arts: Taiji, Yoga and Kalarippayattu (Indian martial art). Through regular practice, the students access a deeper connection to their breath, which allows the subtle harnessing, cultivation and growth of the actor's "inner-breath" (in yogic terms *prana vayu* is the life/breath or energy) (Zarrilli 2008, p. 4). It is the emphasis on never breaking the line of the spine which allows the development of this deep connection to the breath, and therefore to one's concentrated energy (Figure 1.1).

Adèle takes an in interest in the work on relaxing the spine as the starting point of her practice:

FIGURE 1.1 Psychophysical Training with Phillip Zarrilli at ITI, October 2012

Photo by the Intercultural Theatre Institute

Adèle

Now, in order to warm up, I always start with the "back exercise", which stretches out my spine and allows the muscles around the spine to relax. During performance, it happens that I suddenly become aware of my hands and my feet (energy points in Taiji) and I feel the wave of energy which circulates.

The sense of relaxation of the spine comes for Adèle from both the Jigong practice and from Thomas Leabhart's "back exercise".

In the Jigong, the students are invited to imagine drawing a wave of energy from the ground like warm air or water, which gradually fills up their bodies from toes, feet, ankles, knees, pelvis, waist, chest, shoulders, elbows, wrists, palms and fingers. They need to meticulously follow this journey until it becomes a cycle, which naturally sustains and underscores every movement (Figure 1.2). The imagined

FIGURE 1.2   Taiji for Actors with Pern Yiau at ITI, January 2012

Photo by the Intercultural Theatre Institute

sensation of water or air filling up the body allows a certain relaxation within the verticality of the spine, as if the body was a balloon being blown into shape. No unnecessary muscular tension goes into standing upright, since the actor's spine is imaged as the structural connection between earth and sky.

The flexible quality of the spine is further developed through Thomas Leabhart's "back exercise" or "back exploration", taught by movement teacher Leela Alaniz. It consists of lying on the back, knees bent, soles of the feet in contact with the ground and in line with knees and hips. The students begin to feel how subtly shifting the contact of the pelvis with the ground has a repercussion on the serpentine movement of the spine. While exploring this sensation, they initiate a small pulsation at the level of the pelvis, which then travels vertically up and down the spine. This creates some micro-movements within and around the spine that allow the students to feel the space between their vertebrae expanding. As a result of the regular practice of this training, it is possible to feel a constant inner dance of the spine, like a spiral, which grows within the central vertical channel of the body.

This description of Leabhart's work on the spine invites a parallel with the work on the core energetic channel of the body discussed above in relation to Noh and Kutiyattam practice. It appears that, while Noushad is left with a strong impression of how the central channel creates the conditions for inner stillness within the moving body, Adèle is sensitive to the constant inner movement of the spine within the apparently still body. Pedro, for his part, finds himself responsive to the work on the breath, in order to sense the central channel of energy. The practitioners' accounts offer us a glimpse into the complex and subtle sensibilities awakened in the students through the intersection of different, often contradictory techniques.

So, throughout the various modes of training and performance experienced, how did the students find their own identity as actors? What concept of the actor did they form for themselves and how?

2. The concept of the actor

Different theatre traditions develop different concepts of the actor. In each tradition the actor must train to embody certain fundamental qualities, which belong to that specific form. For example, the traditional forms taught in ITI privilege different aspects within the actor's work. While in Noh training, the actor is supposed to contain and distil expression, Kutiyattam practice is based on the full expression of emotion. While Wayang Wong privileges fluid slow movement weaved with the *gamelan*[10] through improvization, in Beijing Opera the quick staccato movements are sharply coordinated with specific parts of the music. Despite the different ideas of the actor encountered, the alumni emphasize the need to develop a basic state of openness and readiness. As we will observe in their reflections, the journey through different performance traditions required them to analyse themselves closely and develop a better understanding of the inner workings of their "self", in order to access this state of concentrated awareness.

Pedro

I need to know myself as a person in order to go onstage because that's my raw material. It takes daily practice "to achieve an actor inside oneself". When I go onstage, I go myself, but it's an extended self, a multiplied, an all-embracing self that goes onstage.

Pedro's concept of the actor is influenced by Kutiyattam practice where Venu G utilizes the expression: "To achieve an actor inside oneself". In fact, traditional Indian theatre training is based on the concept of the distinction between "individual, actor and character": "the individual 'creates' a performer inside herself through training; that performer becomes the character".[11] Whilst powerful emotions, in the individual's life, tend to override her capability to exercise self-control, in Kutiyattam, the attainment of a heightened perceptual awareness allows the performer to embody the overwhelming sensations that accompany these emotions, while maintaining a "crystal clear mind" (Venu 2012) and maximum precision in the form.

Adèle joins Pedro in emphasizing the importance of the work on the self in order to train as an actor. The individual must work on the awareness of their body, their energy and their emotions:

Adèle

The awareness of one's body (thanks to the work on the "centre"):[12] Knowing how to relax or tense one's body at will. Tasting neutrality. Not being afraid of going beyond one's habits, not being content with what we already know, but rather continue to search ceaselessly. Living the failures, due to the limits of our bodies, and at the same time being amazed by our bodies' memory, accuracy and faithfulness.

The awareness of one's energy: The actor as a "ferryman" [of energy], an energy which goes through every part of our bodies (like in Taiji), through our breathing (like in Wayang Wong). A "ferryman without a face" as described by Georges Banu about the Noh actor.[13] *An actor made of holes, like the Gruyère cheese, who lets the light shine through.*

The awareness of one's emotions: According to Arnaud Desjardins,[14] *[. . .] in ordinary life, we're constantly preys of our emotions and so we're not free. So what of the actor's emotions? When the actor provokes certain emotions in herself, she becomes prey of other emotions as well (when I evoke fear, I also feel joyous excitement, or tenderness, or the sense of being reassured . . .) The actor should go deep in the search of the self, in order to stay neutral onstage while being in the grip of a very strong emotion. She is required to live it intensely, it's paradoxical. Neutral, intense, free? How is it possible? [. . .]*

While risking her freedom, the actor must stay calm, she must find tranquillity in her fury, she must have worked on herself so much that she can be aware of all her emotions and manage them.

Adèle's subdivision is helpful in identifying the different areas of awareness that the student can address during the training at ITI. She also highlights the paradoxical nature of the actor's experience in relation to these areas: the body's potential accuracy vis-à-vis its limitations; the actor's search for energetic balance, while faced with the uncontrollable nature of emotions. Therefore, while dealing with a storm of contrasting sensations and thoughts, the ITI student explores their intricate relationships and searches their way through them.

In the next section, the alumni's reflections are centred around the relationship between the actors' work on their perceptions and the transformation of the performance space and time.

3. The transformation of the performance space and time

Under this theme, we can observe how the experience of the intercultural training often challenges the student's perception, by limiting it, making it difficult and unfamiliar. While dealing with the challenges posed by the different trainings, the student undergoes a process of psychophysical transformation, which in turn allows for transformation of the performance space and time. In fact, through the alumni's considerations, we discover how transformation of space/time is not just a theatre convention or a formality but is deeply embedded in the actors' complex work on their senses, emotions and energy.

Let's look at some examples of this process of transformation:

Noushad

The body presence has to talk of the atmosphere, the five senses have to work. What is the body experiencing head to toe? For example in Beijing Opera, there is a scene where the actor will walk fast around the stage in a big round shape in order to show the passing of one day from dawn to dusk and then he looks into the sunset. The time transition can also be shown through the body.

Noushad demonstrates how to show looking into the horizon: his eyes start widening and his body retreating and his breath deepening, his body is simultaneously the man who looks at the sunset, the space and the air between him and the sunset, he is the sunset itself. He evokes the type of detailed embodied work which can be seen in a Kutiyattam performance without necessarily showing the codified form.

He goes on to make a connection about his teaching experience.

In modern times the participants or students don't have "sense", because they are not bringing their awareness to that.[15] They are drinking coffee, they are drinking tea, but they are not tasting it, they are not smelling it, they are doing something else at the same time, and not allowing their body to experience. So, like in the traditional forms, I do exercises with them to select which sense they are working with. I limit their vision and give them something to smell or taste (coffee, tea, sugar, salt, honey), to touch (mango dry leaves, rose petals, paper, drops of water). (Figure 1.3)

Another way is to limit their mobility by having them sitting down in a row of chairs. I developed an exercise with them from a version of Zarrilli's structured improvisation[16] and Kutiyattam work on Navarasa.[17] So while the students are in the structured improvisation mode, I ask them to put one word into their mind (i.e. I am jealous, I am burning etc . . .). I tell them that it's like a cell of cancer, which is developing and spreading all over their bodies. I ask them to follow it with their "inner eye"[18] while it gradually grows. I will guide them,

FIGURE 1.3   Reflections: student performance directed by Noushad, Hyderabad, 2012

Photo by permission of Noushad Mohammed Kunju.

as if I were a light fader, telling them: 5%, 10%, 20% etc . . . Bit by bit, they convert this feeling into whispered sound, and that sound will grow louder and louder as I increase the percentage until 100%. They can never stand up from that chair, they are confined to that particular space, so they can only concentrate on the body sensations and the sounds. Then I will gradually bring them back to 0%. When they reach the peak point: saliva will come out, tears, panting, body muscles will be warmed up. This kind of work can't be done every day, it gives a very concentrated experience to the students.

These are some of the exercises Noushad derived from ITI's training in order to enhance his students' perceptual awareness in connection with their emotions. As in the intercultural training, the awakening of the senses passes through limiting and challenging their perception.

Now we'll look at an example from Noh theatre where the unfamiliarity and difficulty of perception leads the actor through the process of transformation of space and time. The Noh actor needs to move with precision and grace underneath five heavy layers of costume, with a tight headgear, which muffles their hearing and a mask, which reduces their vision to two minuscule holes. What is left of "reality"? What of perceptions? The only parts of the skin feeling the touch of the air are the hands, masterfully steering a fan. So the actor needs to learn how to perceive anew, and this new perception slowly leads them through silence and darkness to an unfamiliar way of moving the body through space. The unfamiliarity of the actor's movement reshapes the audience's sense of space, transfiguring the human body, turning time into a meditative state (Figure 1.4).

FIGURE 1.4 Noh presentation, March 2013

Photo by the Intercultural Theatre Institute

Japanese writer Tanizaki describes the experience of appreciating a particular decoration within the dark meanders of a Japanese house. While training in Noh theatre, it struck me how this can be a very suitable metaphor for revealing how the Noh movement furtively and quietly etches itself in the perception of the viewer.

> And surely you have seen, in the darkness of the innermost rooms, [...] how the gold leaf of a sliding door or screen will pick up a distant glimmer from the garden, then suddenly send forth an ethereal glow, a faint golden light cast into the enveloping darkness, like the glow upon the horizon at sunset. [...] You walk past turning to look again, and yet again; and as you move away the golden surface of the paper glows ever so deeply, changing not in a flash but glowing slowly steadily brighter [...].
>
> (Tanizaki 1997, p. 35)

So in this image, when the substance of the gold is stretched through time, its brightness gradually intensifies; it acquires a quality that is made of layers and depth. In the same way a simple action, like raising the fan, stretched through time and filtered through the pulsing of the "jo ha kiu", profoundly carves the space. The glow it releases gradually intensifies and hovers in the space beyond the end of the action itself; we're thus caught in a cyclical experience where there is no before or after, just the present awakening of our senses.

The immersion in different cultural theatre forms allows for experiencing different perceptions of time and space, which often challenge linear and monocentric notions of theatre, to open towards new perspectives. We can find an interesting example of this in Pern Yiau's description of the performance he devised with another four ITI alumni in 2012:

In *Transformations*, the actors and I created four characters each in their own worlds. And each of these settings is best described in different psychic terms. One realist, one metaphorical, one primeval-metaphysical, one between dream and waking. At the same time, they all exist in one common setting on stage. In this setting, sometimes their worlds enter each others', sometimes not. Thus, at the most multidimensional moments, a character can be existing in three space-times concurrently. To me, this is not a theatre device, nor about play structure, but about reality as I sometimes experience it (Figure 1.5).

4. A shifting centre

In the previous sections, we've observed how the intercultural practice invited the students to open towards conceptions of space, which don't necessarily revolve around one centre. However, the awareness of the "centre" of the actor's body is a very concrete necessity. Many traditional and contemporary cultures join in locating the centre of the body, the point from which all movement originates, in the lower belly, more specifically, three centimetres below the navel: from the Taijigong, where it is called the "dan t'ian", to Indian yogic concepts of the body, where it is the "nabhi

FIGURE 1.5 Transformations: a piece by TTRP graduates, 2012

Photo by permission of Peter Sau.

mula" (root of the navel), to the Japanese concept, where it is identified as the *"hara"*, until the more modern technique of corporeal mime, which also locates the centre of the body "three centimetres below the navel".[19] However, throughout the different trainings, the way the practitioners perceive the various possible centres of their bodies is more complex and causes subtle shifts in the quality of their perception.

From one centre . . .

Adèle

The idea of centre became concrete for me and understood by my body through Leela's train-ing [. . .] My experience with Leela made me feel that everything started from the centre (in Leabhart's training the zone of the navel), but my centre was always tense and would never relax. I was confusing abdominal muscles and centring, I was tense. [. . .] It was the Taiji that allowed me to become aware that my centre never managed to relax, and I've never felt more fluidity and energy in my pelvis than during my period in ITI.

Adèle speaks of the complexity of the different qualities of the centre. Once we've located it, what do we do with it? It needs to sustain every movement of our body so there must be some kind of contraction involved, but at the same time it is the point to which and from which the breath travels which implies an expansion. These two apparently contrasting states are emphasized in the two trainings Adèle refers to. In Decroux's corporeal mime there is indeed an emphasis on contraction, while in the Taijigong, the emphasis is on expansion (even if of course the two disciplines don't fully exclude one or the other). However, what is important is that the body of the actor, caught in the intersection of two contrasting sensations, can be fed by both and benefit from their complementary nature. Therefore, through intensive practice of both disciplines, the body finds a more rich, complex and dynamic way of utilizing its centre.

To no centre . . .

So far we've looked at the centre of the body in relation to the body itself but what of the centre of the actor's body in relation to the performance space? Pern Yiau here widens the field to the shifting relationships between different focus points in the body and the performance space.

Pern Yiau

The idea of a centre comes from a centric view of performance, and is made too much of. Some kinds of traditions are built on dispersion, off-centredness and even centrelessness. Everywhere-ness. This is what I learned from experiencing different ways of being in theatre. [. . .] If the space is yourself then your physical centre is the space within your lower abdomen below your navel, into your guts. But when we perform, that is often not the space that the audience sees. That's why it's important to think beyond just being a performer. The audience sees the whole stage or the performance area. In this moment then it is more useful for the actor to find his centre in terms of the feet on the ground, the tailbone and through the spine. That is a verti-cal centre. And then to relate to the space in a horizontal way too, that is, how and where to focus his energies in that performance space. And where to physically place oneself in any given moment.

To many centres . . .

Finally, the practitioners' perception of where their movements originate is ever shifting and changes according to several factors. For example Shakeel here explains how his perception of his centre changes according to the different forms he embodies:

Shakeel

Take a simple stance of the Noh theatre, just a walk:
slightly bent knees,
spine straight
look far,
arms and hands at a particular angle,
very slow
At that time, how do your feet feel?
What do you feel under your feet?
In Noh I feel my feet. (Figure 1.6)

FIGURE 1.6   Noh presentation at ITI, March 2013

Photo by the Intercultural Theatre Institute

In Kutiyattam, I feel the centre of my body [three fingers below the navel]. The Kutiyat-tam stance with outward bent knees, means that the whole weight of the body goes to the thighs and knees. Since this is painful we try to pull up the weight to the centre, and that's how our centre gains strength. I think that, if we draw a circle around the Kutiyattam actor's body, it touches head, elbows, knees and feet. And the centre of this circle is the navel (or three fingers below the navel). (Figure 1.7)

In Beijing Opera I feel the chest. You put a step, and the next thing you're aware of is the chest. Any movement starts by shifting the chest, every circle drawn by the arms is generated from it. Of course the centre below the navel is still there, underlying and sustaining every movement, but the focus of my experience shifts towards the chest. (Figure 1.8)

In Wayang Wong I feel it is here (points above his head then takes a strand of hair from the top of the head and pulls it up towards the sky) it goes up up up up. The awareness is somewhere outside, which means that it is also inside everywhere! We didn't do a specific form but a free form training where the movement goes on and on until you feel every part of your body moving. Your mind becomes "flow" and it goes out of the body. You have a kind of big ball around you, which is expanding bit by bit. In that time and space, there often is a little connection which is a sort of leading point of your awareness: sometimes it is in the tip of my finger, in my stomach, in my shoulder, in my back, neck, nose, and sometimes it is a point outside in the space. That's why it's outside of the body and at the same time inside everywhere. (Figure 1.9)

FIGURE 1.7 Kutiyattam presentation at ITI, March 2012

Photo by the Intercultural Theatre Institute

From Shakeel's description, it emerges that each form makes the actor more aware of a particular part of the body. That becomes a new kind of centre, or as Pern Yiau puts it, a point of focus, which confers a different quality, rhythm and texture to the movements.

When Shakeel finished describing his different points of focus for each form, he had unconsciously traced a vertical line from the feet to the head of the actor. The order he chose was not deliberate/spontaneous but we later realized that it created a progression from the feet and below (Noh Theatre) to the belly (Kutiyattam Theatre) to the chest (Beijing Opera) through the top of the head and above (Wayang Wong). Now this is not to propose a theoretical map of how the four traditional forms might work because that experience is and must be different for each individual. However it is interesting to observe one particular actor's repeated elaboration of the traditional forms' points of focus. For Shakeel these points of focus become a way of finding different doorways through which to infuse the traditional form in contemporary practice, *"without slavishly reproducing it"*.

5. The actor creator/thinker/theatre maker

In ITI there is a particular space which is dedicated to the work of re-elaboration of each traditional theatre form, the post-modular lab. That's where the students can play with the different forms they're experiencing, improvize with them, make them their own. Shakeel comments on his point of view on the process of re-elaboration:

FIGURE 1.8   Beijing Opera presentation at ITI, October 2012

Photo by the Intercultural Theatre Institute

Shakeel

You don't need to show the technique during practical research and improvisation. That is only for training. We have to let these techniques come organically through our bodies. It was mainly through Leela's work on practical research that we could take all these different types of awareness born from the various trainings, and transform them into something else.

He goes on to give an example of how he put this into practice for his final year project at ITI, specifically of the opening scene where he was walking from the entrance to a red cloth stretched out and laid down on the floor. (Figure 1.10)

FIGURE 1.9 Wayang Wong presentation at ITI, November 2013

Photo by the Intercultural Theatre Institute

FIGURE 1.10 Final Year Individual Project at ITI, August 2014

Photo by the Intercultural Theatre Institute

It was a walk [towards the cloth] while looking at the audience. Not a Noh walk, my knees were less bent, it was not as slow, but it was slow. The angle of my body in relationship to the floor was the same as when we do Leela's "back exercise" standing against the wall. It was a blending of the sensation that I get when I detach myself from the wall [during that back exercise] mixed with the experience of the Noh walk. I could feel my feet, my eyes [...] I realised I was watching myself while I was walking: I was putting my heel on the floor, then, when I put the ball of my foot, my toes would spread open to encompass the biggest possible surface of the floor, thus adhering strongly to it and giving me rootedness. When I lifted the heel, the toes would start to close again. If one day I didn't do that, I wouldn't feel comfortable, more fragile.[20] I feel that the practice of the traditional forms (and Leela's and Phillip's trainings) compels me to watch myself from outside, I developed this capability to monitor, for example, if I'm in the right position, if it has enough strength, if my spine is straight. That consciousness and precision of watching yourself is in every form and comes unconsciously into the way I step into the creation process of my contemporary work.

Conclusion

Through the progression of the alumni's reflections, we can observe a movement from the actors' work on the inscrutable self, through their work on transformation of the performance space and time, until the appearance of an actor/practitioner now able to operate from the perceptual horizon of this ever-shifting multicentred self. We can also observe a movement from the revelation of the rich microcosm of the individual's organic inner life, through the actor's psychophysical transformation, to the awareness of the space/time macrocosm in which the practitioner is immersed. It appears to me that this movement reflects the journey of the student through ITI/TTRP: during the three years, the initial emphasis on the actor's work on the self gradually and inevitably favours the growth of the conscience of the practitioner as a whole. This practitioner is one able to reflect upon and process the trainings she underwent and the cultures she encountered. She re-elaborates them, mixing their substances to her own fibres until she's free enough to let her own form flow out of her, her own expressivity surface, her own "theatre" materialize.

One of the first things the director Sasitharan told us the day we arrived was:

"There are as many theatres as there are people". It has stayed with me since.

Notes

1 In 2008, 'TTRP suspended teaching and training activity. The organization set out to work on reviewing all aspects of the first phase of its development and to map its next phase'. It reopened as ITI in 2012.
2 "Each Singaporean citizen follows his or her father's race at birth. Race [. . .] determines the "mother tongue" language taken at school, the ethnic self-help organization to which salary deductions are credited, and even allocation of public housing' (Holden 2006, n. p.)
3 In Kutiyattam Theatre, taught by master Venu G, the actor, accompanied by the drummer, plays an epic story through a codified sequence of hand gestures/eye-movements,

while embodying all the different characters' emotional states. In the first years of TTRP the students were trained in Barathanatyam dance. Later, this discipline was replaced with Kutiyattam.

4 In Beijing Opera, taught by Mdm Li Qiu Ping, the actors combine the skills of dancing, martial arts and singing to embody one character-type throughout the play.

5 In Noh Theatre, an ancient dance-based performance taught by Yoshimasa Kanze and Kuwata Takashi, the actors' deliberate, intense, often slow movements, accompanied by singers and traditional instruments, capture the supernatural quality of the literary Noh characters.

6 In Wayang Wong, master Bambangan Besur emphasizes free-form training techniques inspired by the Indonesian islands' animalistic dances. This kind of improvization technique can last for hours and it enhances a deepening of the breath and a freeing of the physical and vocal expression.

7 Gestures expressed through the coordination of hands and eyes.

8 He taught a new module in ITI between 2012 and 2014: "Taiji for actors". In the interview he specifies that "in my experience ITI and TTRP are separate schools and thus my teaching in ITI should not be seen as a continuation of my studies or teaching in TTRP, even though my starting point was so".

9 The *chakra*-s are represented as half-open buds, which bloom through the activating power of the inner breath or life/energy.

10 Traditional music accompanying Wayang Wong performances.

11 From Venu, G.'s words during the *Kutiyattam Theatre course* at ITI.

12 This idea will be amply dealt with in section 4: A shifting centre.

13 *In his book "L'acteur qui ne revient pas".*

14 *In his book "Adhyatma Yoga, à la recherche du soi".*

15 In using the word "sense", he refers to the senses, the sensations.

16 In Zarrilli's structured improvization, the students sit on a row of chairs in front of the audience and, with every out-breath and in-breath they change focus to their hand, someone else's hand or someone else's face.

17 Kutiyattam technique passed on by Guru Ammannur Madhava Chakyar to Venu G. This technique consists of training in the actor to evoke at will different effective states of being and to communicate them to the spectators (*rasa*, only approximately translated as emotion).

18 The term comes from Zarrilli's psychophysical training.

19 "Thomas Leabhart draws on his collaboration with Arthur Lessac, [. . .] in order to help actors acquire stage presence through an awareness of the centre of their body, situated three centimetres below the navel. He defines his work as follows: 'Metaphorically, the actor draws energy from the ground, pulls it (energy, stuff, fluids, electricity, steam, water, thought) from a reservoir in the earth, through the legs, and into the place one inch below the navel'" (Alaniz 2013, p. 102).

20 There is another exercise which comes from a Grotowski technique that Leela taught us where we imagine that we are planting roots in the ground first with the ball of our feet and then with our toes.

References

Ahammad, S. (2015). *Skype Conversation*, 8 May.

Alaniz, L. (2013). The Dynamo-Rhythm of Etienne Decroux and His Successors. *Mime Journal*, 34, 25 May.

Frantz, A. (2015). *Email sent*, 10 August.

Holden, P. (2006). Histories of the Present: Reading Contemporary Singapore Novels. *Post-colonial Text*, 2(2), n. p. [online].

Kuo, P. K. (1998). Contemplating an Open Culture: Transcending Multiracialism. In *Singapore: Re-Engineering Success*. Singapore: Oxford University Press.

Mohamed Kunju, N. (2015). *Skype Conversation*, 14 July.

Pfaff, W. (1997). The Ant and the Stone: Learning Kutiyattam. *The Drama Review*, 41(4), 133–162, Winter. [online].

Purushotam, N. (1998). Disciplining Difference: Race in Singapore. In *Southeast Asian Identities*. Singapore: Institute of Southeast Asian Studies.

Sasitharan, T. (2009). *Imagining Tradition* in The 4th World Summit on Arts and Culture, Johannesburg, South Africa.

Sasitharan, T. (2012). *Interview*, 24 January.

Simoni, P. (2015). *Recorded Video Sessions* sent, 1 August.

Sim Pern Yiau. (2015). *Email* sent, 2 September.

Tanizaki, J. (1997). *In Praise of Shadows*. English Translation by Thomas J. Harper. New Haven: Columbia University, Leete's Islands Books.

Venu, G. (2012). *Kutiyattam Training*, Course Facilitated at the Intercultural Theatre Institute of Singapore, Studio 1, 21 February–30 April.

Zarrilli, P. (2008). *Psychophysical Acting: An Intercultural Approach After Stanislavski*. New York: Routledge.

2

FROM THE FLOWER TO MADNESS

The ontology of the actor in the work of Suzuki Tadashi

Glenn Odom

Several female nurses push men in wheelchairs around a sparsely decorated stage suggestive of a mental hospital. Bits of Western classics mix with fragments of other texts and paralinguistic grunts in a mad, fractured world.

These elements – fragments of texts, noticeable gender dynamics, madness, experimentation with language – are common in Suzuki Tadashi's work. Leaving aside for now the gender dynamics and disability politics, which deserve their own careful consideration, why would intercultural theatre take this mad, fragmented form? The answer to this question lies in the status of the actor as an individual, subjective presence on stage – and understanding this status requires a discussion of Japanese notions of subjectivity. To know who the actor might be is to know what constitutes a "who" in this intercultural context.

The idea of intercultural interaction is actually built into many notions of Japanese subjectivity – but this is an interculturalism built on mutually constitutive notions of uniqueness and unity rather than a contrast between the universal and the particular. Japanese ideas of unity and unique identities in relation to the world emerge in separate forms in *nō* theatre (as one of the nominal roots of many contemporary staging practices), *shutaisei* (a contested and politicized type of subjectivity), and *kokutai* (a much-debated type of nationalism focused on the body of the nation) which are discussed within Zengakuren National Students Federation (founded 1948) – an organization that served as a bellwether for the state of avant-garde theatre in Japan.

Peter Eckersall's provocative historicizing of the political "space" that shaped and was shaped by the *angura* movement (Japanese underground theatre in the 1960s and 1970s) explicitly avoids overlaying Western theoretical modes and he concludes that:

> While critiques of hybridity and appropriation in theatre offer complex political problems for scholars, it is also clear that angura's use of hybrid forms

has a radical political context [. . .] By their move to consider Japanese cultural memory from a sense of interconnectedness rather than breach, angura
artists expressed a willingness to reconsider Japanese cultural totality including factors such as the war and Japanese aggression that had been excised
from the more fragmented historical view.

(Eckersall 2006, p. 57)

He applies this totality primarily to *intra*-cultural elements within Japan, but a
broader philosophical and theatrical contextualization of post-*shingeki* theatre suggests that the same sort of unity or interconnectedness is at stake in intercultural
relations as well. While they might be related, a discourse of interconnectivity/unity
and fracture /uniqueness is not synonymous with a discourse of the universal and
particular.

What follows are four different treatments of subjectivity from an array of fields
and a consideration of how Suzuki Tadashi's theatre has reacted to these subjectivi-
ties. None of these discussions is "representative" of a field nor do they come close
to exhausting the range of discussions within Japan. I chose them precisely because
of their eclectic diversity as a means of demonstrating what concepts are the subject
of debate during the post-*shingeki* era. While this sampling only provides a limited
range of possible sides to this debate, it does credibly establish the basic parameters
of the philosophical questions with which any intercultural Japanese theatre must
grapple. In other words, while the discussions below do not speak for the entirety
of their fields, they do participate in core debates from those fields. Each of the
discourses below presents ways in which the individual can be established and ways
in which this individuality is related to a unified whole. At times this relationship is mildly antagonistic, while at others the unity and individuality are mutually
constitutive.

Zeami and the flower: non-homogenous harmony

While Suzuki Tadashi has experimented directly with *nō* techniques (even building
a *nō*-inspired theatre and directing a *nō* play), generally he created new styles that
had spiritual, aesthetic, or formal resonances with tradition rather than participating
in what would become a thriving industry of staging *nō* and Kabuki adaptations of
Western classics. That being said, the elements of *nō* in his work are often muted
and almost always secondary to other aesthetics concerns. Nonetheless, his own
theoretical writing and analysis of his method suggests a connection to the ontology of the self in *nō*.

In Zeami Motokiyo's (1363–1443) explanation of *nō*, the production is harmonious if each actor plays his own role to the best of his ability according to the tone
set by a lead actor.[1] Zeami says that actors have two duties: to "work to perfect their
individual skills and to create the impression of a truly successful and complete
performance [in which] the various skills of all the performers must be properly
harmonized together" (Zeami 1984, p. 163).

Several things are rather immediately apparent in what Zeami says. While Zeami's description of the various roles within *nō* is extremely precise, connoisseurs are attuned to the subtle variations between performers playing identical roles, even though said performers had been trained in the role by their predecessors. There is absolutely a place for skilled individuals to shine within Zeami's theatrical world. Zeami discusses individual skill with the metaphor of a flower that grows and blossoms at different stages in an actor's life. The individuality of each actor's "flower" is influenced by the actor's age, by his body, by his training, and by his temperament. Zeami is clear that all of these factors must be respected if the flower is to be the best it can be. Distinctiveness is important in *nō*.

While the individuality of the actor matters, Zeami does give overall guidance for the place of this individual within a larger framework. Firstly, all actors pass through the same developmental stages, albeit in different ways. All actors should observe the same general set of rules. All this individual skill should be working towards the creation of harmony and balance. Zeami says that performances must be "properly" harmonized, implying a limited range of ways in which they might fit together. Elsewhere he discusses finding the beauty even in coarseness – the harmony of the world is not homogeneity or lack of variety, it is, instead, like musical harmony, the creation of a more beautiful whole from a variety of distinct parts. These distinct parts retain their distinctness even as they become part of the whole.

So, from Zeami, in what (for him at least) passes as a straightforward declaration, we have distinct individuals with their own skill sets coming together to create some sort of harmony in a non-homogeneous world that has a unity dependent on the distinctiveness of each individual. Of course, Zeami is one *nō* artist and *nō* is one of many theatrical traditions in Japan. This is not the only traditional way to think of the actor and the world in Japanese theatre, but Zeami's argument about unity is one which was familiar to theatre audiences and practitioners in the post-*shingeki* era, and thus one possible piece of a discussion about subjectivity on the intercultural stage – albeit one that only establishes the idea that actors on stage are distinct from one another even as they participate in a unity.

Wartime selves: body of the nation, body of the self

This question of the place of the individual is echoed and altered in the political sphere, which provides another piece of the same discussion. Of course, the idea of *kokutai* – the body of Japan/Japan as body – embodied in the emperor, shifted over time, and other discourses on nationalism, like *nihonjinron* (the idea of Japan's fundamental uniqueness) emerged.

Official discourses on national identity like the 1937 *Cardinal Principles of National Polity* (*Kokutai No Hongi*) and the 1890 *Imperial Rescript on Education* were designed to promote a national identity – and a particular kind of nationalism. Both these works were culturally and behaviourally oriented, discussing what was appropriate and inappropriate for Japanese citizens. Kokutai originated in the Tokugawa era and was a loose set of ideas about the direct descent of the Japanese from Amaterasu (the sun goddess). In the latter half of the nineteenth century, scholars like Katō Hiroyuki and Fukuzawa Yukichi debated the relationship of *kokutai* to Japan's lack of progress relative to the West. By the Taisho Democracy in 1911 *kokutai* had become associated with the anti-socialist form it took through the war years, insisting on the right to private property.[2] Essentially Japan had the right to defend its borders, and this right extended, by proxy, to the idea that each citizen could protect the borders of their own property.

Despite this insistence on private property, *kokutai* was better at applying the idea of individuality or self to the nation than it was to individuals within the nation: Japan was unique, agentic and unified, whereas the Japanese were part of this larger body. Japan had a sovereign right to rule its own land and had specific borders – both geographically and culturally – that separated it from the rest of the world. Kokutai implied a unity – a situation where the individual body and the national body were interchangeable (and thus the private rights of the individual ought to be protected in the same way that national sovereignty must be protected). The official legal status of *kokutai* (secured by The Peace Preservation Law of 1925 and following amendments), however, ensured that discussions of the individual body must interact with the idea of a national body. The body became a marker of individual and nation simultaneously, with the relationship between these two constantly being redefined.

Like Zeami's work, ideas of *kokutai* focus simultaneously on the individual and on the individual as part of a unified group. Yoshikuni Igarashi (b 1960) notes that the body became the sight of memory and political action after the war in part because bodies had been so carefully regulated before the war (to say nothing of the damage done to bodies during the war). In this notion, the individual subject is not important except as a reflection of the all-important individuality of Japan itself. This is a model of subjection as subjectivity, where to be subject to Japan was to enact a modified form of indirect subjectivity. Yoshikuni discusses new forms of calisthenics that became popular during the war, including one in which the workout was conducted to the slogan "Bei-Ei-geki-metsu (destroy, perish America and England)" (Yoshikuni 2000, p. 49). Unlike Zeami where the unity of performance was created through the harmony of disparate elements, *kokutai* was often a system in which the route to subjectivity led through the abrogation of individuality in favour of group cohesion. In both cases unity was key – and in both cases the body played a critical role. Neither case provides us a theory of a psychologized individuality.

Pre-war Japanese philosophy: being, nothingness and the unified field

Both Zeami's work and discourses surrounding *kokutai* imply some manner of performance – the individual performing to create a whole or the individual performing to reinforce a position within the whole. Philosophical writing on the self enters from a different angle, searching for the preconditions of being, but reinforces the need to determine the relationship of one individual to a whole. Nishida Kitaro (1870–1945), credited with founding the Kyoto School of philosophy, made it his life's work to translate Western analytical philosophy into Japanese terms, to critique this philosophy, and to offer his own concise contributions to both philosophy broadly and "Japanese Philosophy" (a concept which is closely tied to the Kyoto School). Despite the government's use of many of Nishida's writings for various political purposes, his own political stance has remained the subject of debate. At a time when scholars were extremely active politically, Nishida seemed reticent to voice extensive political opinions – such were not the grounds for the analytical philosophy with which he was engaging.

In Nishida's words

> The real world is where things work on one another [. . .] Now, a thing can work on others only by self-denial [. . .] But if things working on one another make up one world in this manner, it means they lose their being things to become parts of the world [. . .] It means then they make up an unreal world because there is no more plurality in there. The real world should not be like-wise. It should always be one and plural at the same time. Each thing should never lose its individuality even if it works on others and others work on it to make up relations. The real world should not only be self-identical but also self-contradictory.
>
> *(Nishida 1949, p. 165)*

If objects are only legible when they work on each other – when their contrasts with other objects are their important feature – then, Nishida argues, they lose their independent existence. He postulates the existence of a negative void – an empty field – against which objects may be defined. His dialectic is between nothingness and being, not between two beings. As such, all being shares a similar relationship to nothingness (and is self-identical) but is markedly different from other portions of this being (self-contradictory). Difference, then, does not interrupt the unity of the field, because the field exists in contrast to nothingness.

By taking nothingness as the starting point, Nishida Kitaro's theory actually allows for radical variation between objects in the field. Individual difference is not a marker of a difference in kind, because identity is drawn from the dialectical tension with nothingness, not a contrast to other individuals in the field. This position simultaneously leaves open space for variation in identities and decreases the importance of these distinctions. The unity implied here is not the harmony of Zeami's work nor the homogeneity of *kokutai*. It is, however, different again from the self/other distinctions that hold sway in Lacanian psychoanalysis. Nishida does not pursue questions of the precise bearing of this theory on individual subjectivity, but his ideas were widely circulated during an era when identity was a primary concern.

Shutaisei: post-war active subjectivities

In the rush to figure out what had led Japan into the war, discussions of *shutaisei* (one of several words translated as subjectivity) proliferated. Japanese scholars (and the general public) wondered how responsibility for the war should be parcelled out, which, in turn, led to questions of individuality and collectivity. This discourse often combined performative, philosophical and political notions of self. Maruyama Masao (1914–1996) was one of the leading scholars in the post-war era who dedicated a large portion of his career to the exploration of concepts of *shutaisei* (subjectivity) as related to the rebuilding of Japan. He advocated active participation in political processes, although, as with many scholars, his wartime statements tainted the reception of his later work.

His arguments link individual autonomy and democratic political consciousness and he goes on to define the individual as an active force. In some of his earlier work (1946) Maruyama states that the project of "'people's rights' was from the beginning connected with theories about 'national rights' [. . .] thus in the struggle for liberalism the question of the individual's conscience never became a significant factor in determining his freedom"(Maruyama 1966, p. 5). Unlike European nationalism, which Maruyama characterizes as having ceded its moral function to individual groups within the nation after the major religious struggles following the Reformation, the Japanese nation, in its ultra-nationalist phase took on a moral component. Indeed, while "ultra" remains the preferred translated prefix, "super" in the sense of "supernatural" might be more apt, given that Maruyama is talking about a form of nationalism that assimilated most aspects of individuals' lives into itself. The conflation of nation and morality left no room for a differentiation between public and private spheres, and thus no room for "private" subjectivity. "Private life" was the subject of public scrutiny because all subjects were first and foremost subjects of Japan and of the emperor. There was no moral code outside of the nation to which it was subject. This is the negative form of subjectivity that Maruyama claims comes out of the dangerous ultra-nationalism of pre-war Japan.

So for Maruyama, early twentieth century Japanese subjectivity was subsumed entirely by the nation, to the detriment of Japan and its people, but the association with the abrogation of potential subject positions and violence was not his only issue with the formation of Japanese subjectivity. In his later work, Maruyama was particularly concerned with what he perceived as Marxists' inability to explain how the process of creation/formation (*hassei ron*) related to the idea of essence (*honshitsu ron*).[3] Maruyama saw his version of *shutaisei* as a way of bridging between essence/being and the idea of a novel genesis of new historical moments. By inserting a subjective position into history, Maruyama was able to maintain the unbroken totality of history but still account for the appearance of novel moments within it. Individual perception, the only way to analyse the historical event, might note breaks, but to understand the breaks the individual also had to perceive the totality of history. An active, value-driven individual could stand against the state and rewrite both the present and history thereby creating substantive changes in the material conditions of society. While *shukansei* (主観性) actually refers to the ontological nature of subjectivity, it is *shutaisei* (主体性) that is actually debated throughout the period. The shift of one syllable in *shutaisei* implies a subject taking action, and this new term (along with Maruyama's articulation of the subject's place in history) emphasizes the idea of an active, if not always physically active, subject who can change history. The subject has to be distinct from the state and the nation, while at the same time taking an active role in reshaping state and nation.

The same themes present in Nishida's work emerge here, albeit in a more politicized form – individuality is, in some fashion, related to totality or unity – in Murayama's case individuality interrupts and reconstructs the unity of history while fracturing and restructuring the unity of the nation-state. It is the active engagement with historical processes which promotes individual consciousness as well: the individual, history and the nation are intertwined, albeit not fully mutually constitutive. Rather than an empty field or a pre-existing ideal world, Murayama's (post-war) individual emerges from the field of historical progress.

The shift in Maruyama's analysis of the subject also indicates the freshness and contentiousness of this idea during the period. By the rise of post-*shingeki* theatre, there were a multitude of possible conceptions of the self, each of which is different from Western subjectivity (which was certainly also a familiar mode in Japan given the widespread circulation and translation of Western philosophy enacted by the Kyoto School and others).

In the above models there are five different conceptions of the self – Zeami's individual working to create a unified world, *kokutai's* individual as part of the larger body of Japan (which has its own identity), Nishida's individual emerging from a field of nothingness, and Murayama's active individual reperceiving the world. In each of these cases, unity is a key element of debate, and each model presents a dramatically different way of understanding this unity. In all but Nishida's abstract, analytical philosophy, the body of the individual becomes a proving ground for the philosophy.

Suzuki's theatre

The above constellation of notions of subjectivity provides us with a series of questions we can ask when examining the performance of subjectivity within Suzuki Tadashi's intercultural work. To what extent are these subjects active or passive? To what extent are they constituted by or constitutive of the group? What is the relationship between perception and subjectivity? To what extent does relationship to other subjects matter? To what extent is the world in which these subjects move harmonious? To what extent is it homogenous? All these questions have immediate political resonances in Japan, and each also directly impacts any notion of the intercultural. The bodies on-stage are performing/enacting/embodying/resisting the intercultural – to understand the interaction between two objects requires an understanding of the individual objects.

The post-war directors answered these questions in various ways, but the trope of madness and fracturing, the idea of energy devoted to existence, and elaborations of the mind/body relationship emerge as proving grounds for these various treatments of subjectivity on-stage – all, of course, localized in the body of the actor. For Suzuki, individuality – particularly as expressed through mad characters – is created by an examination of the dire conditions of the world, but it is also a lens through which a unique viewpoint can be established. While the intercultural elements of the post-*shingeki* directors' work are immediately obvious in the discussion below, the specific constructions of unity and the individual within this era of theatre radically shifts the possibilities of interculturalism, a point that I will address more fully in my conclusion.

While a relatively small percentage Suzuki's work since the 1966 formation of his first company was videorecorded, he has written extensively about his practice. The Toga Festival in Japan continues, often reviving older productions. Both SCOT (The Suzuki Company of Toga) and ISCOT (The International Suzuki Company) continue their training and performances. Numerous current and former members of Suzuki's various groups offer courses in variations of "The Suzuki Method", despite Suzuki's own skepticism that he has produced any consistent "method". My own analysis of and encounters with Suzuki's training have been of this degree of remove, and my encounter with his productions has been mediated through print and video.

The idea of the importance of an individual perspective in establishing the world (as seen in Maruyama's work) emerges strongly in the trope of madness, particularly in Suzuki's production featuring Kayoko Shiraishi (who was part of Suzuki's companies from 1967–1989), which focus on the odd kaleidoscopic world as seen through her eyes: "Usually an insane person is my main character; basically, the structure of my theatre is that a person with excessive illusions sits alone in a room in a real time, sometimes accompanied by an assistant. And the texts of Euripides and Shakespeare possess him or her" (Suzuki 2010, p. 196). He also remarks that he looks at humanity like Freud, in terms of individual consciousness, clarifying with a distinctive understanding of Freud, "In one body, there exist various levels of consciousness. While you are doing one thing, you can think of others, be on different levels of reality. To my mind, that's what makes humanity dramatically interesting" (Ibid.).

The individual is deeply divided internally (an idea which is not explored as deeply in Japanese philosophy as it is in Western), and divided from the rest of the world by a distinctive viewpoint. The degree of distinctiveness is defined as madness in this context, but, at the same moment, it is celebrated – there is a beauty and a harmony in the way the mad, divided individual sees the world. The divisions in the world seem to be produced by the distinct viewpoint of a divided self, which curiously makes the "foreign" material no more or less different than any other aspect of the fractured, mad perspective to which we are treated (and in this way it echoes the idea of difference found in Nishida's work). This is not a world fractured by competing global forces, but rather a world whose diverse, sometimes terrifying, beauty can best be seen from a distinctive individual vantage point.

On the other hand, the beauty of Suzuki's productions does not diminish the fact that individual subjectivity has emerged from interactions with negative aspects of the world. Suzuki claims that "nothing can ever happen beyond a human scale [. . .] the only way you can achieve anything at all is by constantly confronting yourself with a sense of poverty and wretchedness" (Bogart 1995, p. 85). This is a radical notion of individuality. Suzuki argues for individual agency that results from confronting the worst aspects of the world. Instead of a perfect nation creating individuals in its image (as with *kokutai*), a deeply flawed world creates individuals who, in turn, seek to create something else (the active individual in political processes as with Maruyama).

By the same token, the nation can have no meaning until it is perceived on the human scale – the individual creates and is created by the world. While the overarching *mise-en-scène* might be a product of the mental processes of individual characters, these processes are eventually related to "achieving" something – to taking action. Suzuki's theatre is not simply a celebration of the creation/recreation of individual subjectivity, but a question about the actions this fractured subjectivity might take in the world. This physical aspect of individuality can be seen in Suzuki's various training methods which focus intensely on each individual experiencing their own body as a means of sharpening consciousness both of the body and of the world surrounding the body. The well-documented, rigorous movements, particularly those involving the feet and legs, do not vary from person to person, but this routinization is not the reduplication of an ideal subject, but instead, a routine process that leads to an active subject.

The active individual visible in Suzuki's training and theories is also visible in the content of his productions. For example, in *Clytemnestra* (an adaptation of several variations of the house of Atreus legends which was performed in various locations from 1983–1987 and survives as a published script and a grainy video) Suzuki greatly expands the trial scene (relative to *The Eumenides*), including a memory portion where Clytemnestra and Agamemnon explain themselves. Tyndareos implores Apollo and Athena to put Electra and Orestes to death, but the final moments of the play consist of Orestes and Electra taking responsibility for their actions and allowing the ghost of Clytemnestra to kill them. Suzuki presents and then removes the possibility of divine intervention or judgement. The humans confront their own worst selves and choose to pay a heavy price for it.

Suzuki notes that this play follows his *The Trojan Women* "conceived in a traditional [Japanese] style" and *The Bacchae* "developed in a Western style" (Suzuki 1986, p. 122). He says that Clytemnestra is an "attempt – [. . .] hard to express in words – to break through those other styles and create a play that shows the relationship between them". He argues that both Greece and Japan looked for "a god who does not actually exist [who will] spurt forth nonsense as a theatrical reality that pleases an audience" and that such a desire suggests a society "rapidly approaching decadence" (Ibid.). The point Suzuki is making here is not "intercultural" in the sense that this term is deployed in Western analysis. His concern is with the nature of the similarity – not the existence of similarity. To return to Nishida's work, objects in the field draw their distinction from nothingness, not from difference between themselves. The nihilistic force against which the subjectivity of the characters in this play is formed is, in fact, the desire for a higher, external power to provide shape and form to the notion of subjectivity.

Admittedly, Electra and Orestes's declaration of their own independent subjectivity leads directly to their deaths, so this individuality is not necessarily a point of celebration – Clytemnestra's ghost stares vacantly out over the audience instead of celebrating or mourning these deaths, suggesting that no cosmic balance has been restored. This play becomes very human. Two *people*, sans national modifiers, attempt to claim personal responsibility for what they have done and die. The possibility of this being part of a perfect larger plan is suggested and then specifically foreclosed. It would be relatively easy to consider this to be Suzuki's statement about a universal human condition, which would lead to an argument of interculturalism as a force which highlights those elements of society that, like Barba's pre-expressive, exist before cultural differentiation. That move, however, ignores the fact that the philosophical context, specifically Nishida's work allows for a different notion of similarity and unity. While questions of universality may be usefully applied, another pertinent question in this context is what fills the philosophical space of "nothingness" against which a dialectical tension might form? This is not about the differences between cultures, but about those forces which are antithetical to the existence of these cultures.[4]

This idea of focusing on the construction of self independently from contrasts with other selves emerges in Suzuki's discussion of the animal energy devoted to existence. The intense physical aspects of Suzuki's training strip away the actor's preconceived notions of being and acting: the actor is left with a body and that body's connection to the earth. The actor can then attempt to reach a core of energy that is the precondition of a separation between being and nothingness. Paul Allain, a contemporary scholar who has explored actor training in multiple context, neatly summarizes Suzuki's various comments on the objectification of the self, noting that the performer is "principally in dialogue with [himself] rather than another object or character [Suzuki says that] 'The Impulse to act springs from constantly feeling the impossibility of being oneself'" (Allain 2002, p. 122). The actor is not imitating another self or some abstract notion of self-hood. Rather the actor is treating himself as the object of exploration through which the self might emerge. Subject and object reflect back in on one another with the subject's perception of the world being the only way the object can be understood even when the object in question is the self. What we see on stage is often the desperate attempt (and failure) of a person to make sense of perception through their own embodied experience.

Suzuki actually makes the madness of the world and the individual into mutually constitutive elements (not unlike being and nothingness in Nishida's work or history and the individual in Maruyama's work): the foreign scripts that possess the mad individual at once provide a distinctive voice and highlight the struggle to express individuality. Rather than individuals constructing a harmonious world, they are constructed by a non-harmonious one, which they in turn shape: the intercultural elements of Suzuki's theatre are part of the process of differentiation and unity that form the basis for Suzuki's world. It is only the simultaneous separation and connection of individual and world that allows for growth.

Conclusion

Why use intercultural elements to explore subjectivity, particularly given that Suzuki specifically discusses a Japanese body and subjectivity in his work? One of the core tensions in Western modernity surrounds its relationship to the universality of Enlightenment rationality – European modernity is at once the assumption of universal principles and the rejection of these principles (at least by post-modernity), both of which can be seen in colonial and neocolonial processes. Western criticism of Japanese intercultural theatre has tended to debate the existence of the universal. The universal presents a different model of the wholeness of the world than the Japanese discourses presented above.

The intercultural is a vital component of both identity and theatre debates. Deguchi Norio, another twentieth-century director, was the first to direct all of Shakespeare's plays in Japan. He articulates the relationship between Shakespeare and Japan in a particularly nuanced fashion.

> For me, making it "Japanese" is not the ultimate aim. The important thing is to find a place where I and the text can converge. [...] "Making it Japanese" is already about marking a border where exoticism begins. But I think exoticism is partly due to the ignorance of other nations. [...] today's Japan is only partly traditional Japan. {...} It means that "Japanese Shakespeare" production cannot be recognized unless we simplify our Japaneseness. I don't think that is universalization; Japanization is simply a particularization.
>
> *(Deguchi 2010, p. 183)*

This enigmatic passage recognizes the multiplicity of cultures in play. In doing so it specifically rejects the idea of the universal and the particular in favour of a contextualized individuality. What makes Shakespeare legible to Deguchi in the modern Japanese context is precisely its interaction with the individual voice. Finding the connection to the "I" in Shakespeare allows these performances to unify all the traditional, modern, Western and Eastern elements present in modern Japan.

The difficulty of the passage lies in the fact that it requires us to step outside of the logics of universalism (and resistances to the same) of Western interculturalism. As post-colonial critique has well established, the idea of the universal contains a built-in teleology. Certain cultures are further along the path that all cultures share. The universal is also at odds with the particular, and intercultural theatre can be a bridge between them. Either something belongs to the universal and can be understood through a process of translation or, less often, something belongs to the local and can then be maintained as a sort of artefact within a production. This leads to logics like Pavis' hourglass where source and target cultures are translated into one another through the language of theatre. At its best, Western intercultural theatre is a reminder of the things that do unite humanity in a time when dangerous fractures are emerging around the globe. This same impulse, however, can also be read as a desire to commodify and contain difference. To be clear, these are the struggles that Western heuristics have posed for Western intercultural theatre – these are the problems with which Western intercultural theatre must contend.

It is perhaps not surprising, given Western intercultural theatre's relationship with post-modernism that there is only limited space for the actor as individual within this system: The actor as universalizable body, the actor as transmitter of message – but seldom the psychological realism of modernist theatre in the West. Works like *Harlem Duets* – an adaptation of *Othello* set in Harlem in three different periods – which may or may not be considered as intercultural theatre – have posed obvious challenges to the universal impulses of the big names in Western intercultural practices by placing racially marked bodies in contrast to universal ideals. Again, the universal and the particular are at odds in the Western system, and, in the case of *Harlem Duets*, this conflict is played out in literal bodies.

If we replace the logics of universalism with the logics of unity – this whole set of debates changes. Unity from an empty field allows for infinite variation of its subjects, although it requires active agentic subjects to continually recreate and reposition this unity. Unity that comes from the top down, as seen in Zeami's work or in *kokutai* similarly must be able to account for (or remove) differentiation amongst the bodies it unifies. In either case, ideas from other cultures can, in fact, enter into this unity without disrupting it or losing their foreignness. This sort of interculturalism can maintain difference without violating unity or creating false homogeneity. Again, as Japan's fraught history with Westernization suggests, this is not an easy, straightforward, or always-accepted process, but it is a process that differs substantially from the processes of cross-cultural translation implied by Western intercultural theories. This idea of unity accounts for the reticence of Japanese directors to spell out the intercultural nature of their projects explicitly. The adoption and adaptation of Western materials is not a conflict between "own" and "foreign" or between universal and local. It is, to borrow Deguchi's word a "particularization" of material that belongs within the same, differentiated unity as any other material. It must be digested by the individual and then related back to the world.

As for the actor in this sphere, in order to see an agentic subject in relationship to the world, there must be some differentiation or division within the subject, between subjects, or between subject and the world. Fracturing is predicated on the possibility of unity: it cannot be broken if it was never whole. Curiously then, as Yukio Ninagawa (1935–2016) notes, Japan, a nation that has long rejected the selfish individualism of the West, has a long period of theatrical experimentation that accentuates (if not always positively) questions of individuality (Ninigawa 2010, p. 211).

What then, is the place of this distinctive form of interculturalism in the next project of Japanese theatre, given that many of the debates over the subject's place in philosophies of nationalism from the 1930s onwards have subsided in the twenty-first century? While Suzuki leaves his mark on contemporary Japanese theatre, it is the next generation like the vernacular plays of Oriza Hirata's Contemporary Colloquial Theatre, the Robot-Human Theatre Project, or Tadashi Kawamura's T Factory that are poised to tackle this new question. If notions of subjectivity are key to understanding the intercultural interactions of contemporary Japanese theatre, what happens to these notions when some of the subjects on stage are non-human? What other types of identities might be included in any possible unities? Are non-humans forming the new intercultural frontier? These questions, emerging as they do from an examination of the distinct concepts presented in Japanese theatre theory, diverge noticeably from the concerns of much Western scholarship and suggest new avenues of research.

Notes

1 While the story of Zeami's client-patron relationships with various Shoguns is interesting, Zeami's precise political allegiances have little bearing on the work of the post-shingeki directors. Readers interested in a richer historical contextualization should begin with Thomas Rimer's work.
2 There is, of course, a narrative about Japan's fraught relationship with both the US and, more importantly, Russia during this period with provides a different sort of justification for official proclamations on the nature of private property in Japan. It is worth drawing a distinction between an analysis of the political motivation of a given idea and its social (and later theatrical) ramifications.
3 For a detailed analysis of Maruyama's complete works in context, see Kersten (1996).
4 These questions are substantially different from those posed by scholars exploring the issue of subjectivity in relationship to Western notions of universality. For two critics wrestling with issues of Suzuki's "universalism" in interesting ways see Allain (2002) and Brandon (1990).

References

Allain, P. (2002). *The Art of Stillness*. London: Metheun.
Bogart, A. (1995). *Viewpoints*. New Hampshire: Smith and Kraus.
Brandon, J. R. (1990). Contemporary Japanese Theatre: Interculturalism and Intracultural-ism. In Erika Fischer-Lichte, ed., *The Dramatic Touch of Difference*. Tübingen: Gunther Nar Verlag.
Deguchi, N. (2010). Interview with Deguchi Norio. In Minami Ryuta et al., eds., *Performing Shakespeare in Japan*. Cambridge: Cambridge University Press.
Eckersall, P. (2006). *Theorising the Angura Space: Avant-Garde Performance and Politics in Japan, 1960–2000*. London: Brill.
Kersten, R. (1996). *Democracy in Postwar Japan: Maruyama Masao and the Search for Autonomy*. New York: Routledge.
Maruyama, M. (1966). Theory and Psychology of Ultra-Nationalism. In Ivan Morris, ed. and trans., *Thought and Behavior in Modern Japanese Politics*. London: Oxford University Press.
Ninigawa, Y. (2010). Interview with Ninagawa Yukio. In Minami Ryuta et al., eds., *Performing Shakespeare in Japan*. Cambridge: Cambridge University Press.
Nishida, K. (1949). *Zenshu IX*. Translated by Hitoshi Oshima. Tokyo: Iwanam.

Suzuki, T. (1986). *The Way of Acting: The Theatre Writings of Suzuki Tadashi*. Translated by Thomas Rimer. New York: Theatre Communications Group.

Suzuki, T. (2010). Interview with Suzuki Tadashi. In Minami Ryuta et al., eds., *Performing Shakespeare in Japan*. Cambridge: Cambridge University Press.

Yoshikuni, I. (2000). *Bodies of Memory: Narratives of War in Postwar Japanese Culture, 1945–1970*. Princeton: Princeton University Press.

Zeami, M. (1984). *On the Art of Nō Drama*. Translated by Thomas Rimer. Princeton: Princeton University Press.

3

DANCING HAMLET IN A WORLD OF FROGS

Butoh and the actor's inner landscape

Tanya Calamoneri

Dancing Hamlet in a world of frogs[1]: *butoh* and the actor's inner landscape

Butoh has joined the myriad alternative forms employed by Western theatre makers who seek out intercultural dialogue in their quest for theatrical "truth", in the resonantly human sense. I have encountered actors, directors, theatre designers, and playwrights at *butoh* workshops and performances all over the world. I have coached a few who were interested in embodying *butoh-fu*'s[2] surreal landscapes, and have witnessed an interesting cross-pollination between *butoh* and Western Theatre, both classical and experimental. This chapter investigates one such intercultural collision in Greg Hicks, a classically trained actor who has worked with the Royal Shakespeare Company for 30 years, who uses *butoh* techniques for developing the interior world of his characters (personal communication, 29 January 2016). Hicks learned *butoh* primarily from London-based *butoh* artist Marie-Gabrielle Rotie, but also researched Hijikata Tatsumi and Ohno Kazuo on his own. His experiences here are filtered through my own investigations, most extensively with Murobushi Ko, Seki Minako, Waguri Yukio, and Shinichi Koga[3], in whose company inkBoat I performed in several productions.[4] Of particular interest in my research is how an actor might use *butoh* methods to inform character, particularly at a phenomenological level.

Oftentimes *butoh* is deployed to embody the outwardly horrifying characters of a play – the three witches in Tony Tacone's 1994 *Macbeth* at Berkeley Repertory Theater, the infirm in Subjective Theater's 2003 *White Plague* in New York, or Hicks' ghost in Michael Boyd's 2004 *Hamlet* for the Royal Shakespeare Company. Los Angeles-based *butoh* artist Don McLeod has made an entire career out of playing such demons, including the lead werewolf in *The Howling*, Jack Nicholson's demonic double in *The Witches of Eastwick*, and Quasimodo in *Naked Gun 2½*. He

FIGURE 3.1   Greg Hicks in Michael Boyd's 2004 production of *Hamlet* for the Royal Shakespeare Company. Reproduced with permission from the Royal Shakespeare Company.

Photo by Manuel Harlan @ the RSC

was also the infamous angry gorilla jumping on the suitcase in the 1980s Samsonite commercials.

The grotesque is of course a logical and valid application of *butoh* in theatre, and yet I argue (and I think many *butoh* artists would agree) there is much more that *butoh* can offer to almost any character in a narrative play. Rotie says, and I concur: "*butoh* suffers from its outward aesthetic that is copied without enough exploration of the internal processes". I interviewed Rotie about her interactions with Hicks but also about her experience teaching *butoh* to actors[5] in general (personal communication, 12 January 2016). She has taught at the Royal Shakespeare Company, Royal National Theatre, and is currently on faculty at Goldsmiths College University in London. In her *butoh* work with actors she begins by dismantling that iconic aesthetic, and instead exploring energy, impulse, deteriority, stillness, doing nothing but standing and being present. She says, "for me, a good result is getting an actor to do nothing and still be captivating". She prefers to work with actors on a non-production basis because when she's working on shows she often feels there is too much pressure on the actor to produce. In the context of a class process, they can focus on a more fundamental level of theatrical expression that informs the creation of character.

As a starting point, *butoh*'s way of working with imagery is for the performer to fully transform into qualities, atmospheres, objects and creatures from a distinctly non-human perspective. Once transformed, the performer enters a new logic that is that of image and no longer concerned with intellect, psychology, or anything that one would deem to be "normal" human behaviour. The point of this is not merely strangeness; the point is to blur the expression of "normal" humanness, to question conditioned responses, and ultimately, to propose new ways of inhabiting the body. I suggest that rather than this being diametrically opposed to actor training that is invested in psychology and ego (either the actor's or the character's), that training in the human and non-human are two sides of the same coin that together can enhance a performer's presence and creative expression. Further, through a process of inhabiting atmospheres implied or described in the text, *butoh* methods can also help an actor to interpret the larger themes of the play rather than just "what does my character do?"

Hicks considers Shakespearean text/characters and *butoh* to be well-matched, alchemical theatre forms: "Macbeth says, 'full of scorpions is my mind', well you can't have a more graphically *butoh*-ish image than that, can you? Mind full of scorpions, body full of ants?" He is referencing a *butoh-fu* exercise in which dancers are instructed to sense one ant crawling on the skin. And, as Hicks says in rapid-fire succession, "then two, then three, then four, then five, then six trillion . . . and they're inside . . . that image always struck me as useful for playing anything with terrible inner [turmoil]". Having explored such an image with full physicality and outward expression, Hicks can then internalize the image and fill a simple gesture of turning the head with such a horrifying inner experience. As the skull rotates on the spine, one can sense these tiny insects scuttling about, their exoskeletons clattering on whitened bone. The sound is enough to make anyone shudder. In the RSC video trailer (2010) for Hick's *King Lear*, one can sense such an unnerving predicament in Lear's gaze.

On its face, this process sounds a bit like Psychological Gesture in the Michael Chekhov technique – filling an action or interaction with a qualitatively different (in this case) energetic body that is not expressed but nonetheless has an affect on the overall tone created by the actor's action (in this case simply turning the head). And yet there are subtle differences in the kinds of images one works with, and the interaction of ego and psychology, in each. Further, there are different pedagogical aims of *butoh* and Chekhov technique, with *butoh* aiming to break free from ossified notions of form (in performance and also human form), and Chekhov to create a character with a cohesive embodiment. I might even go as far as to say that Chekhov is generative while *butoh* is destructive, and there is a place within actor training for both.

Hicks, a classically trained actor, describes being "very bound as a young actor coming from drama school . . . 'cabined, cribbed, and confined'", he says, quoting from Macbeth. "I just was stuck. And something like *butoh* . . . has just opened that out a lot". He also credits the Brazilian martial art of capoeira, which he practises religiously before every show, with helping him break through his habits and formal training. Both forms, he says, have taught him to be comfortable upside down and off balance. "[A] fairly organised Western actor is not used to being asked to explore the world from the other way round", he quips, but for him, the process has been quite fruitful. He notes, there is the danger of developing what he calls:

> a superficial style of all your favorite ways of being, and then people say "oh god, he's doing it again, he's doing that *butoh* thing he does with his hands" . . . I can see that in itself it can become a block, that the actor would actually indulge a style that he was comfortable with . . . [but] my impulse was to look at these forms in order to try and break through my own rather stuck ego
>
> *(personal communication, 29 January 2016)*

I asked Hicks whether he felt he was drawn to these forms, at least in part, for their exoticness. He replied, "I can see that there is a danger of becoming superficially multicultural in one's approach. However, I think if you're slow and sure and you listen carefully, I think there's much to be taken from [these methods]". Beyond that, he has been steadfast in his commitment to learn. The result is, in his opinion, "I don't think I'm just talking the talk, I do think I actually use them".

Hicks found Rotie through her private classes in London before she came to teach at the RSC. According to Rotie, he already had his own particular way of working, he knew what would be valuable to acting, such as the micro-detail of the hands, face and focus, and that these would be useful to the transformation he was after. Working on *King Lear*, she said, "the play is already tied into the disorder of nature, the howling wind, air and earth, for example". Thus, Hicks had a natural bridge by which to connect the qualitative ways of working in *butoh* to this atmosphere.

More so than the grotesque, Hicks notes that the most valuable contribution of working with *butoh* methods for him is the ability to shift time. He says:

> *Butoh* just steps outside of our normal time scope, doesn't it? Time stops, or does something else, it goes in on itself . . . instead of time being linear it drops to something completely vertical . . . Actually *Macbeth* is all about that . . . seeing the future in the instant and then realising that tomorrow is an illusion and all our yesterdays, etc. etc.
>
> *(personal communication, 29 January 2016)*

Further, this shift in time signature opens up another space: referring to *Hamlet*, he says "you've got to come up with some other dimension . . . it's as bad as what happened in the States on 9/11 . . . in his head, it's that this cannot possibly be happening in front of my eyes in such a way". He invokes a sense of cognitive dissonance, a moment of being unstuck from, or more precisely, *ripped* from quotidian time, where images of a life flicker in front of one's eyes in a surreal, filmic flash.

There are several frequently cited instances of this time-space shift in *butoh*: Kurihara recounts one experience of watching Ashikawa Uzumi performing at St Mark's Church in New York City during which the space between her and performer collapsed; she remembers feeling the breeze from the dancer's hand moving slowly and delicately in space, some 20 feet away from her on-stage. She writes:

> The distance between her and me disappeared; I felt that she was simultaneously far away and directly in front of me. At that moment time stood still. Some invisible force was affecting me in a very powerful way, slipping me, for a moment, into another dimension.
>
> *(1996, pp. 44–5)*

More ominously, dance critic Miura Masahai claims that witnessing Hijikata's dance made his palms sweat and his body tremble, and that he sensed substances like oil and sand oozing from Hijikata's moving body (in Kurihara 1996, pp. 45–6). The performer's inner reality can have a profound effect on the audience, whether it is expressed outwardly or not.

When he played Lear, Hicks evoked a walking exercise he had explored with Rotie, in which one imagines that 1,000 years pass between each rise and fall of one's foot. "I don't know if anything has that kind of waiting that *butoh* has", he says. There is of course the slow-ten exercise in Suzuki training, and Shogo Ota's "aesthetics of quietude achieved through divestiture"[6] (Zarrilli 2009, p. 148), as employed in the slowed-down choreography of *The Water Station*, for example. A popular *butoh* version of the slow-motion walking exercise is *suriyashi*, referring to the sliding steps of Noh theatre, but this is combined with the following images: blades under the feet, thin sheet of paper between the knees, buckets or spears in each hand, raw eggs pinned delicately in place in the armpits, a rope around the waist pulling one forward, parachute behind, catching the wind and creating resistance to the forward motion, the eyes as mirror balls hanging in the sockets and reflecting the outer world, and either a bowl of water or a bird's nest on the head. Generally, one passage across the floor will take about ten minutes. In workshops with Su-En, Seki and Koga, I have practised this for about 30 minutes, rotating fluidly at each end of the room and repeating the journey as if it were endless. Such a walk can be internalized and used to imbue a body, even if it is not actually travelling in space, with a particularly charged tension. Waguri recounted a performance in which Hijikata stood still for 15 minutes before moving, pinned on the spot by opposing forces. In the process of Hicks imagining that each footfall takes 1,000 years, he will no doubt experience a wealth of imagery from the sheer physical effort of lifting a leg that slowly. As I imagine it, I can hear the crack of a giant redwood tree splitting and tearing up its roots as it begins to fall, or a skyscraper creaking and rumbling from its foundation. On the ground, life rushes by in its usual maddening pace, as slowly the tall structure lumbers forward in space, walking and falling, walking and falling. Each step takes 1,000 years, in which time civilizations rise and fall.

In addition to shifting time, Hicks identifies the unpredictability of *butoh* timing as an asset in helping him find authentic shifts in mood, tone and emotion. As he experiences them:

> *Butoh's* inner rhythms are a series of wonderful implosions that happen . . . it's a bit like watching those flocks of birds that suddenly "poof" fly off, or conversely, you might see a cat that is just simply sitting on a fence and you think that cat's made out of stone and then all of a sudden its ear will twitch.
> *(personal communication, 29 January 2016)*

The moment of shift is all the more arresting because of the contrasting stillness. And the timing is dictated by the progression of the image, so it is surprising to both performer and audience alike. One can see these mercurial shifts in Hicks' Leontes, as he sinks into jealous delusion. Charles Spencer of *The Telegraph* writes, "Hicks brilliantly captures the way jealousy feeds on itself and eats away at its victim from within" (2009), a further testament to Hicks' penchant for establishing a dynamic inner world.

Through imagery, Hicks creates a sub-score that he performs simultaneous to the text, almost as a polyrhythm to the timing of verse. The material substances of images have their own distinct atmosphere, time-space, and bodily consciousness. "We cannot divide time and space", says Waguri, "So my nerves reach out to 100 meter . . . and come back". As the way back is also 100 metres, he continues, "this takes time, so this time makes space". For example, in a 2009 workshop, he teaches us choreography of flower petals opening: we are seated with our legs folded to one side and sway a little side to side as our thumb and forefinger pluck and then peel a petal away from our centre. We are allowed time to improvise with the image and explore it in slow motion, and then Waguri sets the choreography to music and the entire sequence is sped up. However, even as the timing of the action is sped up, the time-space of the image is not. In the case of the flower choreography, we allow the resonance of each flower petal to linger even as we are tugging open the next one. For Hicks, perhaps his inner "flower" in this instance withered, became fetid and died, all with a unique rhythm that underscored each interaction with Hermione and also the arc of the first two acts.

What Hicks refers to as "*butoh* methods" at first glance are quite unlike the myriad well-articulated actor training systems. It is rather a collection of exercises handed down orally from Hijikata and Ohno and refined by each successive generation, yet practitioners are generally left to discern the thread between one exercise and the next. There are a few trademark *butoh* techniques, but none really offer a unique "system" as such, in my experience. As for Hijikata, the closest he came to articulating a methodology was this: "[The] [b]utoh dancer must be kidnapped, killed, reincarnated, and after that endowed with the power to talk with wind and grasses" (Mikami 1997, p. 88). While beautifully poetic, these words warrant interpretation. Dancer Nakajima Natsu, a student of both Hijikata and Ohno, phrased *butoh* methodology in somewhat more actionable terms as "becoming nothing, becoming something" (1997). And yet, how to instruct a performer to become nothing? Sankai Juku-dancer Matsuoka Dai told me, "it's more like you become something, and nothingness appears" (personal communication, 15 October 2010). In other words, as the performer disappears into the image, the doubleness and totality of being appear. There are two parts to this equation, becoming and nothingness, which I will elaborate on briefly below.

"Becoming" is an enigmatic concept, though one that is frequently applied to the actor's work. One talks of disappearing into a role, merging with the character, living and breathing as this new fictitious person. In *butoh*, becoming refers to the performer existing as an empty vessel, which is then filled with a series of images, and this causes the body to be "danced".

An apt metaphor for how performers work with images in *butoh* is "attunement". Images promote a holistic experience for body-mind, and interact with the actor on the level of the subtle body, through which *ki* circulates through one's own body and beyond. When we talk of a person "radiating" a certain quality we are talking about the tonal ambiance of their *ki*, which Japanese philosopher Nagatomo Shigenori calls the "qualitative presence of a particular personal body" (1992, p. 205). *Ki* travels much like sound waves, and gives off a vibration or a "rhythmic fluidity" (Ibid., p. 206) that can be sensed by "tuning" one's subtle body.[7] We can both project our own *ki* and sense *ki* from our ambiance, hence Nagatomo refers to relating to one's ambiance as a "bilateral coming-together" (Ibid., p. 198), or *attunement*. The process of engaging another substance through imagery involves the interaction of "touching and being touched" (to use Ichikawa's explanation of Cartesian cogito, see Nagatomo Ibid., p. 21) through which these two elements establish degrees of "inter-corporeality" (Ibid., p. 197). Through the personal body-mind, we somatically sense an "affective resonance" of engagement, which in turn shapes our "epistemological as well as actional apparatus" (Ibid., p. 213). In this circular feedback loop, we receive energy and information from our ambiance, and emit energy and information into our environment. Performer and image come together, or become *attuned*.

In his book *Handsome Blue Sky*, Hijikata describes the *butoh* body as an empty vessel that is abruptly invaded by something which "fills it to the brim" and overflows (1987 cited in Mikami 1997, p. 140). He continues, "the movement of becoming empty is the way of the vessel . . . [Through this process] his body is metamorphosed to a new one which is the present 'I'" (Ibid.). Mikami (1997, p. 140) explains that as an empty vessel, the dancer simply welcomes everything that is given to him in these choreographies, accepting any condition, "always being ready to take anything, anytime". Most importantly, the transformation process is instantaneous; Waguri says he needs to "watch, [and] already [he is] changed . . . [to] think and [then] move is too slow . . . [instead] at the same time as you watch it, you just become this thing" (personal communication, 9 September 2010).

Hicks describes attunement thus: "It's like it hits me in the gut, and it *makes* me". Speaking about his imagery work with the ghost in *Hamlet*, he refers to it as the "world under the floor" from which he emerges, literally and figuratively. The concept of nothingness also plays into Hicks' acting. In an interview with Sarah Hemming on his Lear, he says, "The Buddhist notion is that nothing is everything and you have to lose everything – most crucially your ego – before you find something. Once the ego goes, then there's a big hole and that's it: that's when you're alive" (Hemming 2010). He twists the idea around to show Lear's tragic flaw: "when Lear says, 'Nothing will come of nothing', he absolutely doesn't get it, because his ego's in the way. Maybe at the end of the play . . . " (Hemming 2010).

Nothingness, *mu*, is a concept that pervades Japanese performing arts such as *Noh* and *butoh*, as well as Zen philosophy and practice. Though it is a much larger topic that I can do justice to here, it is worthy of note as context for the discussion of performer training. Briefly, "nothing" in the context of Japanese philosophy is not the opposite of "something". It is not nihilism. Rather, "nothing" envelops both "something" and "not-something", and is the ground for both being and non-being. Opposites (something and not-something, I and not-I) are both the wave and the shore, where nothingness is the entire interrelationship, or the foundation out of which *both* identities arise. One could say it is the creative source, but this is also an illusion because of the image of a source, a font, a spring, etc. There is not such shape or substance or directionality to nothingness. In Buddhist teachings it generally appears as *mu*, as in *mu-shin* (no mind) and *musō* (no thought).[8] *Mu* has the characteristic of being prior to thought, judgement, or meaning. Says Nagatomo, *mu* can be understood as "non-conceptual awareness, non-projection, non-superimposition, mind as witnessing consciousness, or no-mind" (personal communication, 15 October 2009). The idea is to "see without being a seer", to reside in pure experience. In a practical application of this concept, *butoh* teachers often instruct students that the eyes should not see but reflect, as if they were mirror balls hanging inside the head, in order to cultivate simultaneous inner and outer awareness. There is also a desire to simply reflect sensation, and not add any personal comment on the experience. For example, Yoshito says that Hijikata directed him: "the flower has everything, so don't put yourself" (personal communication, 9 January 2010). Instead, his job was just to experience the flower, and be the flower, without adding his commentary on beauty, death or any other human assessment of the flower.

Rotie, who studied with Ohno, explains:

> In *butoh* the actor is trying to disappear . . . It's a different sense of expanding energy from within . . . *butoh* is about the impossibility of becoming nothing, it's a Zen *koan*. The effort needed to negate [oneself] is what creates the point of realisation.
>
> *(personal communication, 29 January 2016)*

Thus it is the process of trying to approach nothingness that is of interest in *butoh*.

As a training system with nothingness at the central principle, *butoh* may appear a bit vague at first. In fact, Hijikata did not actually train his dancers in any technique. Everything was created out of necessity in the rehearsal process, as Hijikata sought specific expressions from his dancers. It is through reflection (and very careful notes) that subsequent dancers and choreographers have been able to discern methodology. Nakajima Natsu is one such dancer who was around Asbestos-kan for Hijikata's late-night art lectures in the early days of *butoh*'s inception.[9]

The first step in *butoh*, says Nakajima, is to "shed" the social body and "to return to the original body" (1997, p. 8). One must interrupt habit and reinvigorate perception. The process of "shedding" is not so much a subtraction from our everyday perspective as it is a perspectival shift, and ultimately an expansion of our perceived reality. We must both widen the aperture of our senses and de-centre our normal modes of perception. Hicks' use of the 1,000 years per footfall is one such example. Just by slowing down a simple walk, he experiences each moment in significantly greater depth, filled with micro-details of sensation and imagistic associations.

Additionally, *butoh* emphasizes an off-kilter stance to disrupt the body's central axis, which is reinforced by an involuntary righting reflex. Murobushi describes Hijikata's strategy as "always unbalance", he remembers his teacher saying as Murobushi himself teeters precariously on an elbow and the knife-edge of a foot. Seki echoes this, instructing students, "stand like a pencil, not like a notebook", meaning that we should feel the sensation of always being about to fall over, as a pencil would if we were to stand it up on one end. In a 2003 workshop in Berlin, we practised balancing brooms in our hands to get the sensation of a constant falling motion and the need to continuously shift our centre of gravity in order to balance the broom.

Postmodern dance around the world – and I include *butoh* in this as a postmodern art form – made use of *ostranie* (defamiliarization), the use of radical recontextualization in order to "recover the sensation of life" amid the wartime devastation (Banes 2003, p. 5). The idea was to shock the senses awake from the numbing effects of modern life. Waguri describes Hijikata's dance as distinct from most movement forms, because "most dance asks 'what can my arm do?', whereas Hijikata asked, 'what is my arm?'" (personal communication, 10 January 2011). Hijikata worked from this place of deeply questioning all known assumptions about his own existence.

One exercise to create a sense of *ostranie* in *butoh* is to re-route movement mid-action. Waguri suggests, "if [an] artist, or dancer want[s] [to] make [the] audience surprised, you have to let yourself [be] surprised first". He suggests to "cut the movement just before". A simple pause before completing an action can build the tension of the moment, and subvert both audience and performer expectations. That tiny arrest is like a small panic; our habitual flow is interrupted and we do not know what to *do* next when we are not doing what we normally do. And that is precisely the moment in which, if we can let go of the anxiety of knowing and not *do* anything but rather just stay present for that moment, then something surprising to both performer and audience will arise. For example, in a 2005 workshop at CAVE studio in New York, Murobushi asked the students to begin with a daily action such as brushing our teeth or getting dressed and then, as if we were suddenly struck with Alzheimer's disease, to forget what we had started doing. In the pause that ensued, we were to wonder at the form our body was in – in my case, right arm at a right angle, bent at the elbow, hand in front of mouth and mouth agape – and get curious about this. Small sensations such as the warm breath on the hand or the exposure of the armpit, create the impetus for the next action. The daily action is used as a portal to find new movement.

Such an exercise as described above is a training experience to encourage the performer to notice small sensations that are typically obscured by a "known" action. Bringing this into character development, such training can aid an actor in keeping multiple realities occurring simultaneously. A similar notion might be found in the Suzuki Technique Statue Exercise in which the actor freezes their physical form in a challenging position such as balancing on one leg, and then recites a Greek or Shakespearean monologue. The idea behind this is to build energy in the body to support the speech. As one's leg begins to shake and sweat drips down the back, these added sensations help the actor stay present in the moment and encourage the sense that the text is happening *now*.

In his development of the ghost character, Hicks chose a rather intense but also well-known form as a portal: that of the so-called "Napalm girl" or Phan Thi Kim Phuc, as captured by photographer Nick Ut in 1972 as she ran from a napalm strike on her village in Vietnam (*Associated Press*, 6 August 1972). This image has the physical intensity of a Suzuki-style frozen form, and also is such an iconic image of suffering in our contemporary cultural consciousness that it could become as common as brushing one's teeth, by which I mean that it's possible to assume that form and stop there as a depiction of horror. It is what Hicks did with this form that then becomes interesting. He said "that was my *starting* point . . . And then, I would use *butoh* language, physically, which I very much used as the ghost: the broken, the unexpected, the ugly, the nothing, the beauty, the terror, the gnarled, all the things that *butoh* [language] *does*" to a body, in order to find the lived experience inside the form, and use it to build his own performance as the ghost. It's not that he transposed the character of a terrified girl into the character of the ghost, rather that her extreme, distorted posture was a filter for his "walk of 1,000 years" (as he refers to it), enabling him to "live it now" from an already off-balance place.

In comparing *butoh* methods to the Chekhov technique, I found similar approaches with different aims. The most striking similarity is the process of becoming. Lenard Petit,[10] Director of the Michael Chekhov Institute in New York, tells me, "what we mean when we say we incorporate an image . . . is that I want to feel my inner self, my energetic self, moving. It's all about concentration. Concentration is about movement and it's a movement toward the thing" (personal communication, 14 January 2016). Petit describes it as a magnetic pull, as one makes an "identification" with the object. He continues on to say "I don't have it, it has me . . . this is where the ego goes, this thing has me and then I'm free".

Hicks describes a similar experience, which echoes Waguri and Mikami's explanations of attunement as well:

In *butoh*, that ant image, it's doing you, you're not doing it, otherwise it's just demonstration, isn't it? If it's a demonstrated image, it's an outward demonstration. And I don't think *butoh* is that . . . or if it is, if it suddenly becomes extrovert, it's because the inner impulse is so strong that that's how it's translated. But you can't do that without doing the other first.

(personal communication, 29 January 2016)

I agree that one must start with the inner sense of an image. In fact, as I sidecoach my students, if I see them becoming demonstrative or moving as if on autopilot, without a felt inner sense of what they are doing, I instruct them to go back to the basic image inside the core – one fish swimming in the body searching for an exit, for example – and slowly build back up to a full-bodied engagement, say, a body full of fish.

Petit cautions that such attunement is not done in Chekhov Technique with the goal of all sense of "I" disappearing: "it's not in such a way that I can't follow directions or instructions or make choices . . . you're not in a trance . . . as an actor you need to be here and talk to this other person (a scene partner) while you are in this state because that's the only way it's useful to you".

Butoh has a similar dictum. Though one does become fully engrossed in the experience, "being danced" by images is not the same as being in a trance. The dancer must maintain a sliver of consciousness in order to be able to sense new information on a very minute level, and also sculpt the unfolding experience and movements that arise into something performance-worthy. They must observe without attachment, and without interfering too much. Waguri coaches students to find a "coolness", and Mikami calls "not drunk" (personal communication, 7 November 2010), in other words, not being in an altered state (personal communication, 9 September 2010). Hijikata admonished his students to not be seduced by their own movement. He told Waguri, "[if] *butoh* looks like [you have taken] a drug, and ahh, [I have a] good feeling, or possession . . . Such kind of dancer cannot get it". Instead, a "drunk" dancer is lost in the ego-based sensation of the personal body. They are not tuning to, or resonating with, one's environs. The dancer needs to maintain a minimal level of awareness in order to track "small things . . . [they are] very delicate and sensitive happenings" (personal communication, 9 September 2010).

And from this point, the two forms deviate. For Chekhov, Petit says that the image is never divorced from the psychology and humanness, because "we are interested in a person who has an ego and a psychology", and, further "there's a narrative arc we have to fulfill". Petit describes asking students to simply "become this stick", not as a person but just as an object. At the same time, he notes that we have all developed a psychological relationship to any image – he uses the example uncooked pasta as a particularly brittle "stick-" type person – so that is what he asks actors to draw from as they are shaping the movements of a character. More importantly, Petit is interested in interactions between people, between characters, not so much in the personal but in how the personal plays out in relationship. In this way, actors discover the psychology of the object, says Petit, "because Chekhov says there's a psychology in everything".

Butoh, on the other hand, attempts to remain in the sentient world rather than the feeling one, and engenders performance with multiple interpretations. This stems from Hijikata's (2000, p. 45) desire to create a "body shop" in the business of "human rehabilitation", which "is accomplished only in connection with young people who unceasingly experience the natural movements that kick the matrix of today's good sense". He formulates *butoh* as protest against rapidly encroaching modernity, in the context of his own political reality in 1950s Japan, however, the precepts are still applicable to contemporary capitalistic society. Invoking George Bataille ("nakedness" as a strategy for moving beyond the confines of self) and Frederic Nietzsche ("strip the costume of . . . contemporary civilization" and reinscribe it with "simple sensual passion"), Hijikata formulates a new image of humanity for young people, as naked "lethal weapons that dream" (2000, pp. 45–7). From this political statement stems a proposal for human existence that is on par with nature, rather than dominating it, hence the performer attempting to disappear into the image, to forefront something other than human existence, which can nonetheless offer comment on humanity.

To illustrate the differences in ends of *butoh* and Chekhov, consider the following image exercise devised by David Zinder, a Michael Chekhov teacher who has developed an extensive system of working with images that stem from the body moving:

> A softly cupped hand might "produce" a "gold chain," which you might then begin pouring from one hand to the other . . . or else you might put two hands out a certain distance and angle one from the other, let your imagination put something there between those two hands – say, a concertina – and then work with it for a minute or two.
>
> *(2009, p. 194)*

The state of readiness and openness needed to explore images in this way that Zinder describes is very much like the state necessary for *butoh* – soft focus, deep concentration, and a creative flow that allows images to transform into something else, not through thought but discovered through sensation. The distinction, however, is how the sensation plays out. For example, Zinder describes one possible transformation of the gold chain example:

> As you apply soft focus to the that, the gold chain goes stiff, the clasp at one end no longer tickles your palm but pricks it instead, and the other end that you are "holding" between your thumb and forefinger grows thick and bulky and – voila – the golden chain has suddenly transformed into a jewel-encrusted dagger.
>
> *(2009, p. 197)*

He cautions, "emphasise to the actors that the only way they can give us the reality of an object is by 'using' it – in other words, letting the body stoke the imagination" (2009, p. 197). Zinder says the image must remain "palpable" to the performer. Petit says the aim of imagery work is to "absorb psychological qualities" which are then applied in rehearsal.

A *butoh* approach to such an image – a gold chain that transforms into a dagger – would focus on the resulting change in the body. The cascading metal links transferred from one palm to the other would be a sensation invited into the whole body and encouraged to transform even the soles of the feet. If it were to transform into a dagger, one could imagine a variety of sensations to inhabit: being completely covered in jewels and radiating that brilliance, being surrounded by daggers and experiencing the sharp point pricking or slashing the skin, and so on.

It is certainly possible to find a psychological response to such images, but it is first important to allow the imagination full rein to transform the body itself. Rotie describes *butoh*'s sense of play thus: "It's a game we play with nothing", she says, "throwing atoms instead of balls, for example".

In his essay "From Being Jealous of a Dog's Vein",[11] Hijikata describes several experiences – real or fictitious, it is difficult to know with Hijikata – of "becoming" the landscape, such as falling in mud and not being able to get traction to stand so he starts to play with things he finds there and just accepts his mud reality and becoming a mud creature (Hijikata 2006, p. 73), or the landscape being so inundated with rain that he is no longer certain where it starts and ends. He says, "The surrounding space gets so mixed up in this time of rain with no start and no end, and there is no longer any distinction between time and space" (Ibid., p. 76). Losing his sense of self, Hijikata describes being "reborn at that place . . . as if", Hijikata writes, "my body, from its very core, returned to its starting point" (Ibid., p. 73). He reorients his body, "with my head and the soles of my feet turned upside down" (Ibid.), like babies "who treated their hands as if they were not their own . . . who make their hands eat something" (Ibid., p. 74). Similarly, he comments on a cabinet-maker's hands, which are at once weathervanes gauging the humidity and also becoming the plane that shapes the wood: "they are at once part of his body and not" (Ibid., p. 75). This disappearance marks the expression that Hijikata sought in his dance: movement that does not intend to express at all and yet expresses volumes because of its absorption in its function. It also seems that by being disassociated from "normal" function that these movements are able to discover unique meaning. In fact, he says, "my body trains itself as a matter of course . . . when you come in touch with such things [these extreme nature images and experiences] something is naturally forced out of your body" (Ibid., p. 76). Hijikata's term for investigating such internalized images and experiences is "plucking the darkness and eating it" (Ibid., p. 78), which he says these babies who eat their hands achieve because they have no concept of internal or external world, but rather, are simply wrapped up in the experience.

Says Hicks, "What fascinated me about *butoh* was that every time I did it, it forced me to confront my lack of authenticity [from working through formal training], oddly enough, and I found that dynamic really useful". Moreover, it's the surrealistic, shifting landscapes in which he finds inspiration: "'Today we dance *Hamlet* in a world of frogs'. I mean what the f – k is that? Well you could dine out on that for a year!" As Hicks embarks on his directorial debut with *Hamlet* in Brazil (and his umpteenth production of the play), he says he is certain to bring such imagery to bear in the creative process.

Notes

1 Ohno Kazuo famously said to a class of students: "Today you will dance Hamlet in a world of frogs" (cited in Viala and Masson-Sekine 1988, p. 55).
2 *Butoh-fu* are the poetic strings of imagery that Hijikata used to notate his choreography, and which performers now use to reconstruct the dances.
3 All Japanese names are listed with surname first in keeping with Japanese conventions, except Koga, who is Japanese-American.
4 Additionally, my perspective is informed by workshops with SU-EN, Nakajima Natsu, Carlotta Ikeda, Tamano Hiroko, Kasai Akira, Ohno Yoshito, Endo Tadashi, Kaseki Yuko, Masaki Iwana, Yoshimoto Daisuke, Muramatsu Takuya, and a collaboration with Endo Mariko (former Dairakudakan dancer and Kasai student) from 2011–2015.
5 Other notable *butoh* teachers who are involved in training actors include Chicago Butoh Festival-founder Nicole LeGette, who has worked frequently with classically trained actor/director and professor and University of North Carolina professor, Christopher Marino, and Frances Barbe, who has taught *butoh* to actors at the Universities of Kent and Exeter, and is currently at the Western Academy of Performing Arts in Perth, Australia. See Barbe (2011) for an illuminating discussion of "character" and "figure" in her performance training methods.
6 See also Mari Boyd's (2006) *The Aesthetics of Quietude: Ota Shogo and the Theatre of Divestiture.*
7 Matsuoka says "each dancer makes his own image for it [the movement directions] and you kind of tune to it".
8 D.T. Suzuki notes that Chinese scholars borrowed this concept from Lao-tzuan to describe the Indian Buddhist idea of *sunyata* (emptiness), which is why the *mu* is often equated with both nothingness and emptiness (1959, p. 49).
9 Nakajima did not dance with Hijikata until much later because "he only wanted to work with men". Instead, she worked with Ohno Kazuo and then later returned to Hijikata in the 1970s when he had begun working with Ashikawa Yoko. Already a developed choreographer at that point, Hijikata set several pieces on Natsu.
10 I was fortunate to work briefly with Petit on a production of *Sleeping Beauty*, produced by children's theatre storyteller David Gonzalez. I appeared in the production video as multiple roles, as the spurned fairy, the princess pricking her finger, and as the people in the castle falling asleep, in slow motion, multiplied by video effects.
11 *From Being Jealous of a Dog's Vein* was originally written in 1969, and then published in 1976 by Yukawa Shobo in a collection of 16 different short-to-medium essays under the same name as the fourth publication in the series *Sosho tokeru sakana* [*Melting Fish Series*] (Hijikata 2006, p. 28).

References

Banes, S. (2003). Gulliver's Hamburger: Defamiliarization and the Ordinary in the 1960s Avant-Garde. In S. Banes, ed., *Reinventing Dance in the 1960s: Everything Was Possible.* Madison: University of Wisconsin Press, pp. 3–23.
Barbe, F. (2011). *The Difference Butoh Makes: A Practice-Based Exploration of Butoh in Contemporary Performance and Performer Training.* Thesis (PhD). University of Kent, Canterbury.

Boyd, M. (2006). *The Aesthetics of Quietude Ota Shogo and the Theatre of Divestiture.* Tokyo: Sophia University Press.

Hemming, S. (2010). What Playing Lear Does to an Actor. *Financial Times,* 26 February. Available at: www.ft.com/cms/s/2/547d6d10-2262-11df-a93d-00144feab49a.html [Accessed 5 January 2016].

Hijikata, T. (2000). To Prison. Translated by N. Kurihara, *The Drama Review,* 44(1), 43–48. Originally published as Keimusho e. *Mita Bungaku,* 1961 May.

Hijikata, T. (2006). *From Being Jealous of a Dog's Vein.* Translated by Elena Polzer. Berlin: Mori-Ōgai-Gedenkstätte der Humbolt Universitat zu Berlin. Originally published as *Inu no jomyaku ni shitto suru koto kara (Bijutsu Technō,* 1969 May).

Kurihara, N. (1996). *The Most Remote Thing in the Universe: Critical Analysis of Hijikata Tatsumi's Butoh.* Thesis (PhD). New York University.

Mikami, K. (1997). *Tatsumi Hijikata: An Analysis of Butoh Techniques.* Thesis (PhD). Ochanomizu University, Tokyo.

Nagatomo, S. (1992). *Attunement Through the Body.* Albany: State University of New York Press.

Nakajima, N. (1997). Ankoko *Butoh.* Unpublished Paper Presented at *Feminine Spirituality in Theatre, Opera, and Dance,* Fu Jen University Decade Conference, Tai Pei.

Royal Shakespeare Company. (2010). *King Lear Feature Trailer.* Produced by Dusthouse. Available at: www.youtube.com/watch?v=uvA_gUDGKik [Accessed 5 January 2016].

Spencer, C. (2009). The Winter's Tale. *The Telegraph,* 13 April. Available at: www.telegraph. co.uk/culture/theatre/5148528/The-Winters-Tale-the-RSC-Stratford-Upon-Avon-theatre-review.html [Accessed 5 January 2016].

Suzuki, D. T. (1959). *Zen and Japanese Culture.* New York: Pantheon Books.

Viala, J. and Masson-Sekine, N. (1988). *Butoh: Shades of Darkness.* North Clarendon, VT: Tuttle Publishing.

Zarrilli, P. (2009). *Psychophysical Acting: An Intercultural Approach After Stanislavski.* London: Routledge.

Zinder, D. (2009). *Body, Voice, Imagination: ImageWork Training and the Chekhov Technique.* London: Routledge.

4

STEPPING OUT OF THE FRAME

contemporary *jingju* actor training and cross-cultural performance in Taiwan

Jasmine Yu-Hsing Chen

Much recent performance-studies scholarship explores intercultural confluences in theatrical productions (Schechner 1990; Pavis 1996; Zarrilli 2009). However, as Erika Fischer-Lichte (2009, p. 399) notes, "the transfer of non-Western elements into Western theatre is dealt with in the main body of research on so-called intercultural theatre", whereas the use of Western elements in non-Western theatre "are generally seen within the purview of modernization, which is largely equated to Westernization". This chapter repositions this understanding of change in traditional Asian theatrical forms by analysing a Taiwanese stage adaptation of *Macbeth*, titled *Kingdom of Desire* (1986), probing into its interweaving of Western and non-Western performing elements. I focus on the cultural contexts that gave rise to the use of modern dance, cinematic slow motion, and dramatized facial expression in *jingju* (Peking/Beijing "opera"), and transitions in the understanding of self-definition underpinning Wu Hsing-Kuo's practice. In tracing the various factors shaping actors' style and artistry, this article argues that cross-cultural training needs to be viewed in relation to its specific social, cultural and historical contexts.

I provide a detailed case study of how cultural adaptation occurs via mediating local contexts and highly nationalized theatre. In Taiwan, *jingju* functions as the critical medium for such mediations. This article begins with exploring the fundamental training methods of *jingju*, and how it shapes actors' body language and understanding of performance. It then looks at cross-cultural inspiration, examining how the humanistic spirit of Cloud Gate Dance Theatre of Taiwan, a modern dance troupe, inspired Wu to "step out" of *jingju*'s psychophysical frame. It then demonstrates how *Kingdom of Desire*, an experimental practice, changed *jingju* in Taiwan. My analysis considers both visible aspects during performance and performers' interactions during rehearsals. Through drawing on performers' biographies, descriptions, interviews and the author's own physical practice of *jingju*, this article considers both the processes of production and the final stage performance.

Beyond *Jibengong*: cultural shock from modern dance

The premiere of *Kingdom of Desire* in 1986 was a turning point in the history of Taiwanese *jingju*, during which the newly founded Contemporary Legend Theatre (CLT) presented a whole new version of *Macbeth*. In the last scene, Wu Hsing-Kuo, the CLT's founder and the play's protagonist, performed a magnificent back-somersault off an eight-foot-high rampart, landing in full view of the audience. Wu's backward falling reads as a symbolic enactment of *jingju*'s decline and subsequent revitalization in Taiwan. The performance successfully revitalized the audience's impression of *jingju* and kick-started the use of innovative aesthetics in contemporary Taiwanese theatre.

Wu's career as a leader revolutionizing *jingju* demonstrates how the strict performing conventions of *jingju* became unsettled. Having trained professionally in *jingju* for eight years, Wu declares that it had seeped into his very bones, but he did not know how to fully interpret a character until he became involved in "retraining" at Cloud Gate (Wang 2005). Cloud Gate is a modern dance troupe, whose training system incorporates the Graham Technique, *Tai-ji*, and Chinese martial arts. Cloud Gate recruited and trained male *jingju* actors to be dancers, who were few in number during 1970s Taiwan. A scene in Cloud Gate's rehearsal room during 1974 concretely depicts the troupe's impact on Wu:

> Lin Hwai-Min, the founder and choreographer of Cloud Gate, was in the midst of directing *Wu Long Yuan*, a modern-dance piece adapted from *jingju*. Wu Hsing-Kuo, as a professional *jingju* actor and modern dance novice, was to perform the movement of clasping a female dancer's leg. In *jingju*, even in flirting scenes, actors should not touch each other. Wu, an outstanding young *jingju* actor, uncomfortably tried again and again until Lin impatiently stopped him and yelled, "Are you an actor?" Lin asked Wu to arm-wrestle with him and then demanded Wu to use the same force to clasp the female dancer's leg. Wu felt extremely ashamed and resentful. Though he had been a leading actor for a decade, he still could not meet Lin's requirement. Outside the second-floor rehearsal room was a crowded market. Lin roared at the people, so everyone stopped, curiously looking up at the window. Lin asked Wu, "Now, your turn!" After roaring, albeit with embarrassment, at the people, Wu felt that it was the first time a knot in his mind untied.
>
> *(Lu 2006, pp. 114–15; my translation)*

Wu's embarrassment illustrates how modern dance inspired him, releasing him from the constraining framework of traditional *jingju* techniques. Whether a handclasp or seemingly crazy roaring, both implied the importance of "letting go". "Letting go", the cornerstone of modern dance, involved body, mind and soul. Modern dancers perform more according to feelings than to performance strictures. Since modern dance has no sole criterion, each dancer connects experimentation with different movements while exploring the body's limits. Rehearsals become crucial, during which each actor personally interprets a character to create a comprehensive performance. Nevertheless, "letting go" contrasts entirely with *jingju*, which emphasizes precision in every movement. In such a tradition, all movements should be based on conventions derived from *jibengong* (fundamental performing techniques), which consequently discourages varying patterns or subjecting genuine emotion in performance.

Without considering how *jibengong* shapes an actor's body language and consciousness, it is hard to understand how *Kingdom of Desire* was a breakthrough in *jingju*. Traditional *jingju* requires mastery of *jibengong*; literally, *jiben* means basic, essential and fundamental, whereas *gong* refers to time, effort, work, ability and meritorious deeds. *Jibengong* training revolves around highly standardized patterns, each with its specific term. Broadly speaking, *jibengong* includes three basic training categories. The first is *yaotuigong* ("core and leg work"), which hones an actor's flexibility and coordination, emphasizing basic stepping, walking, kicking and dance movements. The second is *bazigong* ("handle work").[1] Having evolved from martial arts, this aspect focuses on using weapons with handles, including holding, dancing and sparring with weapons. The third is *tanzigong* ("carpet work"),[2] which involves somersaults and gymnastic movements. In a narrow sense, *jibengong* concentrates on the first category, *yaotuigong*.[3]

Undoubtedly, *jibengong* is the foundation of *jingju*, functioning as the framework of an actor's physical style. Yet, paradoxically, *jibengong* cannot be directly performed on-stage. Even though the evaluation of *jibengong* is based only on an actor's manifestation of it, what audiences see instead is the expression of *jibengong* rather than *jibengong* itself. Whereas classical ballerinas for instance, are expected to perform movements on-stage exactly as practised in the studio, *jingju* actors do not perform *jibengong* on-stage. How successfully an actor embraces the practice and philosophy of *jibengong* is judged through their standing poses, the angle of their arms, their palms and finger gestures, and other subtle details of movements.

This mandatory training aims to develop strength, balance and fine motor control while emphasizing the physical ability to generate movements at optimal angles. *Jibengong* requires extreme repetition of the same movements as well as motionless positions. An actor is often expected to maintain the same pose to increase flexibility and strength. Motionless states are in fact the core of the training. This is reflected in the Chinese verb for *jibengong*, which is to hold/endure (*hao gong*) and to practise (*lian gong*). The Chinese meaning indicates how *jibengong* involves prolonged and reiterative training, not only to cultivate physical endurance, but also to gradually transform the actor mentally. The physical training eventually becomes internalized, forming the foundation of the actor's inner prowess – the *gong*.

Given that *jibengong* is a long-term process, with actors receiving meticulous training at an early age, *jibengong* consequently encompasses more of an attitude than mere physical training. Practising *jibengong* refers to the mindset and ideas accumulated in order to approach a paradigm of performance and precisely accomplish established patterns. With constant, repetitive training, an actor develops the ethos, characteristics and the capacity to perform characters through a specific style.

While *jibengong* is thus a type of acting constructed and instilled through physical training, its main purpose is, in fact, the systematic cultivation of actors' abilities to respect and sustain performing conventions.

Role-types (*hangdang*), which can be seen as "specializations" for each actor, further secure *jingju* conventions. Particular *jibengong* varies with these role-types, whose categories and subcategories are differentiated through make-up and performance skills. For example, many heroic characters are categorized as *wusheng* (male martial artist), a role-type based on martial arts skills. Actors represent characters according to set role-type descriptions, and personal interpretation of characters is always secondary. Wu's master, Chou Cheng-Jung, an archetypical *jingju* actor, once admonished him, "We (*jingju* actors) do not analyse the characters; as long as your *gong* is strong, the character can be formed" (Lu 2006, p. 133). Hence, the first instruction Wu gave his actors was to forget *shanbang* (a common *jibengong* movement).[4] Only if actors forget or "let go" of these conventions could they get into the characters' psychological situation (Lu 2006, p. 168).

Wu admits that although he has acted in lead roles since his youth, he could not empathize with the historical emperors, officers or generals he performed until he took Chinese literature and Western drama college courses. This, in addition to the inspiration he received from Cloud Gate, suddenly made him realize that the world of performing arts was wider than he thought. He became dissatisfied with remaining within his previous training, and attempted to combine canonical Western works, such as Shakespeare's plays, with *jingju*. On one level, Wu hoped to apply his confidence in *jingju* to integrate what Richard Wagner has termed *gesamtkunstwerk*,[5] therefore expanding *jingju's* boundaries. On another, he believes his practice will always remain rooted in and benefit from his *jibengong* training. Wu thinks that his background in rigorous *jibengong* training developed his determination and strong mental willpower, subsequently allowing him to persist in experimenting with different performance styles (Wu 2015). As such, he believes that *jingju* actors must have a solid physical and mental grasp of *jibengong* before being able to enrich their performances through adopting transcultural elements.

Without a complete mastery of physical techniques, a resolute will, mental endurance and self-discipline, Wu believes that it is impossible for actors to perfectly perform *jingju* and psychophysically inhabit their character roles. *Jibengong* appears to emphasize the physical aspect of *jingju*, but it is actually a holistic process pushing actors to strengthen their mental capacities. Unlike Western realist theatre, in which actors first analyse the character's subjectivity before developing movements embodying their interpretation, *jingju* actors learn how to perform character by accurately imitating detailed *jibengong* movements and gestures through self-discipline. While Wu observes that not many *jingju* actors progress beyond the first stage of technical mastery, he nonetheless believes that the more solid their *jibengong* capacities are, the more capable actors will be in portraying a character's feelings, because they will be better positioned to focus on character interpretation and understand the character's psychological subjectivity (H.K. Wu, personal communication, 27 January 2016).

The desire for change: searching for a new definition of *Jingju*

To grasp the significance of cross-cultural inspiration for young *jingju* actors, it is necessary to understand how *jingju* was initially nationalized in Taiwan. Under nationalization, *jingju*, a theatrical form originating from northern China, was assigned to symbolize Chinese cultural heritage. In 1949, when the Nationalists/*Kuomintang* (KMT), emigrating from China to Taiwan, brought over one million military men, they also brought *jingju* performers due to the preferences of high-ranking military officers and the soldiers' nostalgia (Guy 2005, pp. 1–10). *Jingju* became known as "national opera (*guoju*)". The nationalization of *jingju*, however, meant that *jingju* was expected to promote only official ideology, thereby restricting creativity and innovation. The so-called national opera strictly maintained *jingju* traditions from the late Qing and early Republican period. Nationalization thus turned *jingju* in Taiwan into a vehicle for conserving "Chineseness", especially the morals of filial piety and loyalty.

As noted above, actor training is not limited to physical performance, but also includes intellectual cultivation. Whereas *jibengong* furnished the mindset for traditional *jingju*, I suggest that the young intellectuals' preference for theatrical experimentation renovated *jingju*. Wu entered the Chinese Culture University in 1973, and the academic environment made him aware of how isolated traditional *jingju* was from contemporary society. Since 1970, the Chinese Culture University has annually held the Theatre Exhibition of *Huagang*,[6] which, because it provided audiences with a rare chance to see Shakespeare's works performed on-stage, was a grand yearly occasion for young intellectuals. Wu was struck by the full house of young theatregoers and their vibrant reactions, which were similar to those when he performed for Cloud Gate; it contrasted strongly to when he performed *jingju*, as most of the audience there was in or beyond their fifties, and largely cheerless (Lu 2006, p. 128). This contrast stimulated Wu to create a Shakespearean *jingju*.

As Taiwan's "national opera", *jingju* kept most of its traditional repertoires. Original *jingju* scripts were rare, and the concept of playwriting almost non-existent. Therefore, writing a new *jingju* play was considered "experimental" in 1980s Taiwan, and adapting a Shakespearean play even more so. Identity politics had become more pronounced during that period. Enquiring into one's personal style when confronted with being in an in-between situation was exactly the spirit of challenging existing authorities and searching for a new self-definition. *Kingdom of Desire* encouraged young performers to redefine the meaning of being a Taiwanese *jingju* actor. The transcultural elements in the play were therefore a theatrical manifestation representing the anxiety of in-betweeness and the desire to create a distinctive, Taiwanese *jingju* style.

Wu believes that creativity generated from an actor's innermost heart rather than politically correct themes is the most valuable aspect of Taiwanese *jingju*. In contrast to Chinese *jingju*, which was reshaped during the Cultural Revolution (1966–1976), Taiwanese *jingju*, due to KMT efforts, maintained Chinese cultural traditions, shielding it from change. This cultural protectionism caused *jingju* to lose its appeal to younger audiences, becoming a decadent artistic form. To keep *jingju* alive and profitable, young actors in the 1970s had to discover new practices. Fortunately, Taiwan had opened up to the world earlier than China, so actors had more opportunities to enrich their multicultural knowledge and had a strong ambition for Taiwanese *jingju* to be recognized worldwide (H.K. Wu, personal communication, 27 January 2016). Unlike Chinese *jingju* troupes founded, funded and censored by the government, the CLT is wholly independent, run by its own actors. Consequently, the CLT has more freedom to experiment with themes and styles. In 2001, the China National Peking Opera Company (CNPOC) invited Wu to direct *Kingdom of Desire*. This experience in Beijing raised Wu's confidence in the irreplaceability of the CLT's style. Because CNPOC actors did not experience, as the Taiwanese actors did, the decline of *jingju* and subsequent efforts at revival, Wu found that CNPOC actors were unable to perform creatively. For instance, in the play's last scene, when soldiers learn that the forest is moving, the ideal performance should portray panic and flurried movement. However, CNPOC actors could not vividly perform this chaos, since their training had not exposed them to such techniques (Lu 2006, p. 179). In contrast, Wu's method, combining *jingju* training, modern dance, and Western theatre, enabled him to visualize and artistically perform chaos. Indeed, because Wu and the CLT did not have previous models of *jingju* that incorporated multicultural aspects to follow, they were forced to experiment with themes and mixed performance methods that eventually represented their own style. Thus, what is perhaps most distinctive about Taiwanese *jingju* is each actor's persistence in finding creative ways of performance combining traditional training with new, multicultural methods. Since Taiwanese actors faced more crises in the history of Taiwanese *jingju* than Chinese actors, they were motivated to continually expand their acting skills and identities and could think beyond rigid traditions.

The CLT's establishment points to the attempts of Wu and other young actors to transform *jingju*. Having received professional training for a decade, they were disappointed to find that, when they began performing, their productions hardly attracted young theatregoers. This crisis spurred them to create a novel production enticing to both a younger and larger crowd.[7] Wu, as director, joint playwright and lead actor, took on some of Shakespeare's authority to "shake up" "national opera", avoiding Chinese ideological doctrine in *Kingdom of Desire*. Although *Macbeth*'s plot was slightly similar to the *jingju* play, *The Punishment of Zi-Du (fazidu)*, with which Wu was familiar, *Kingdom of Desire* nevertheless portrayed a whole new topic: the struggle of fulfilling individual desire.

Kingdom of Desire directly highlights desire in its title. Aoshu Zheng (*Macbeth*'s counterpart) is depicted as an ordinary person constantly battling human vulnerability. Aoshu Zheng's murder of the king completely subverts the doctrines of filial piety, loyalty and integrity embedded in "national opera", as it would have been considered absolutely politically incorrect to overthrow a superior. *Kingdom of Desire* was thus not merely a Taiwanese interpretation of Shakespeare, but also, a revolutionary literary creation for its audience.

FIGURE 4.1   Wu Hsing-Kuo performing Aoshu Zheng (Macbeth)'s desire on-stage

Reproduced with permission from the Contemporary Legend Theatre (CLT).

In addition to the intellectual stimulation received at college, Wu joined Cloud Gate, and his experience there was pivotal in his career. The humanistic spirit of Cloud Gate expanded Wu's horizons, and the founder, Lin Hwai-min, encouraged Wu to rethink the meaning and responsibility of being a performer. In Cloud Gate, the courses went beyond dance to include literature, music, painting, calligraphy, movies and fieldwork investigating folk arts and outdoor *kua-a-hi* (traditional Taiwanese "opera"). After conducting fieldwork, everyone was required to share their opinions on indigenous Taiwanese culture (Lu 2006, p. 139). The CLT's producer, Lin Hsiu-Wei,[8] also a dancer at Cloud Gate, recalls working with Lin Hwai-min:

> The schedule at Cloud Gate was very rigorous. Lin Hwai-min introduced cross-cultural training since the 1970s. Everyday at 7 am, we practiced *Tai-ji*, which asked dancers to sink low in their positions; at 9 am, we had ballet classes, both American and Russian style, which asked dancers to pull up their bodies. In the afternoon, we learned the basic movements of *jingju*, and rehearsed modern dance from 3pm until night. After each rehearsal, Lin would gather dancers and give a speech. He insisted that Cloud Gate has no idols, no stars, but only social and cultural workers. Everyone here should be concerned with the history of this island and care about its people. To expand the dancers' vision, he demanded all dancers to visit art museums when performing abroad.
>
> *(H.W. Lin, personal communication, 26 May 2015)*

This experience was dissimilar to that in the Dramatic Arts Academy, where practising *jibengong* was the only routine. At Cloud Gate,

> Dancers did not have to be under so many limitations. Dancers were always encouraged to represent themselves on stage, and they are really free and rich in spirit. It is unlike the actors of *jingju*, where even if you dropped your prop once, you failed. Everything there counts severely.
>
> *(Ibid.)*

The ideal of being an artist, rather than merely a dancer or actor, inspired Wu to ask all the CLT actors to identify themselves as artists at work, rather than merely people singing *jingju* (*changxide*). Thus, the CLT's initial production, *Kingdom of Desire*, represents the desire to rebel against themes of piety and loyalty in traditional *jingju*, challenging what was believed to be unchangeable principles.

Surpassing conventions: cross-cultural performance in *Kingdom of Desire*

Kingdom of Desire demonstrated theatrical ideas distinct from traditional *jingju* in its very first scene. Conventionally, *jingju* was performed on a relatively empty front stage, with no physical separation between audience and actors. This allowed audiences to easily see star actors and admire their graceful figures. However, *Kingdom of Desire* added a gossamer-like front-layer curtain during the first scene. After raising the gossamer, the audience saw the Mountain Spirit (*shangui*) and the background landscape, a dark forest.

The modelling of the Mountain Spirit challenged the *jingju* tradition of maintaining an actor's beautiful on-stage image. *Kingdom of Desire*, similar to *Throne of Blood*,[9] replaces *Macbeth's* three witches with an old female forest spirit, signalling a double recreation of Shakespeare and Japanese *noh*. The Mountain Spirit has a shrivelled, prune-like face, dishevelled hair and bare feet, which went against the specific ideals of *jingju* beauty that emphasizes an actor's graceful – albeit standardized – image on-stage. In traditional *jingju*, all make-up changes are executed by the professional prop man to guarantee these ideals of beauty. Thus, for instance, Mei Lanfang (1894–1961), the most famous cross-dressing *jingju* artist, mentions that even when he played a madwoman, it was still necessary to maintain these ideals. As a young lady who suddenly faced an emergency and was supposed to act "crazy", he insisted on performing the part in an almost unrealistic way. He merely pulled a strand of hair loose and smeared two streaks of rouge on his face to symbolize that the character's hair was in disarray and her face scratched (Xu 1979, pp. 106–17). Mei's case illustrates how *jingju*'s dictums affect actors' opinions of their appearance on-stage: no matter what character or emotional circumstance, they should appear neat, good-looking, and graceful.

Furthermore, the Mountain Spirit character also forced the actress to rework her physical training. Few female nature spirit characters exist in *jinju*, but a representative example is the Spider Spirit in *Pansidong* (*The Cave of Silken Web*), a traditional *jingju* work. The Spider Spirit is often played by performers who are skilled in martial arts. The Spider Spirit's customary costume has extremely bright colours, which catch the audience's attention, and *jianxiu* (narrow sleeve-cuffs), which allows the actor to perform nimble martial arts' movements. Colourful tassels on the shawl's fringe and the hip scarf symbolize the Spider Spirit's spinning instinct. All together, these elements function to make the performer appear light and lively on-stage. Conversely, the Mountain Spirit's costume in *Kingdom of Desire* was a loose, dark grey frock with wide sleeves. The heavy fabric affected the performer's physical movement; accordingly, she had to walk with bare feet, maintaining a low centre of gravity and stepping slowly. This lower stance, which does not exist in the traditional portrayal of spirit characters, was adapted from *Throne of Blood*. Kurosawa drew on stylistic elements from *noh* plays, which "typically presented the confrontation of a wandering priest with a ghost or spirit drawn back to this world" (Prince 1991, p. 144). Each step in *noh* involves a careful shift of body weight from one foot to the other, whereby "one leg is slightly bent and holds the weight while the other one is kept straight" (Moore 2014, p. 54). Stepping with a slight bend leads *noh* actors to hold their weight in the lower half of their body when walking on-stage. This method, however, contrasted with *jibengong* training; actors must keep their legs entirely straight while walking, kicking and stepping. The portrayal of the Mountain Spirit, who would point with orchid-shaped fingers (*lanhua zhi*) with its body leaning forward on the left, thus fused this lower stepping movement with *jingju* twisting gestures. Although this stance contradicts *jingju* conventions – a spirit character is never portrayed as humpbacked – Wu envisioned this movement to symbolize the twists of desire in the character's mind.

The changes to make-up, costume and physical movement caused the actress, Ma Chia-Ling, to be extremely uncomfortable during rehearsals. For her, it was hard to perform the Mountain Spirit, as the image was entirely new to *jingju*;

FIGURE 4.2 The Mountain Spirit in *Kingdom of Desire* (performed by Chang Chin-Ping)

Reproduced with permission from the CLT.

indeed, she also had to redefine both the role-type and standard of beauty (Lu 2006, p. 169). Ma could not accept that she was an "unsightly spirit", and all her *jibengong* training never included walking humpbacked. She was also upset at being unable to perform a beautiful *liangxiang* pose[10] because of the dark lighting. These elements challenged the actors' original understanding of what *jingju* should be. Ma Pao-Shan recalls that sometimes, when actors could not meet Wu's expectations, he would scold them irritably, and question them the way Lin Hwai-Min did to him by demanding, "Are you still an actor?" (P.S. Ma, personal communication, 27 May 2015).[11] The young actors rehearsed *Kingdom of Desire* with such anxiety, because they could not imagine their future success, given that the last generation's models had been cast aside.

The extent to which *Kingdom of Desire* reworked *jingju* norms is evident in the arrangement of chaotic scenes involving soldiers. All the soldiers, despite being minor characters, had distinctive movement trajectories and individual emotions. This challenged the lead-actor centrism of *jingju*, in which minor actors were merely foils to the lead. Consequently, minor characters' responses and movements were performed only according to role-type conventions; their individuality was not important, and their function, merely walking on-stage or standing back. However, in *Kingdom of Desire*, each role's significance was maximized. Each soldier represented human desires through body language. Wu states that when he did not know how to arrange the soldiers, he repeatedly watched *Throne of Blood*, and envisioned similar arrangements in his play (Lu 2006, p. 172). He insisted that every actor should have all the details necessary for a complete character. For example, when soldiers hear the forest moving, they displayed their fear of death through distorted stretching. This enactment gave the soldiers more significance, allowing minor characters to actively contribute to the scene. To instruct the soldiers on performing fear, Lin Hsiu-Wei applied her Cloud Gate experiences, offering modern dance courses. She asked all soldiers to form a human pyramid, letting them experience the panic and shouting. Another game relied on improvisational skills: each soldier had to clash with another, while simultaneously avoid being clashed with. Since no one knew another person's direction of movement, one had to think on one's feet (H.W. Lin, personal communication, 26 May 2015). But because there were only twelve soldiers in the cast to represent a magnificent army with thousands of men, the soldiers had to move in diagonal lines. As Wang Kuan-Ching[12] suggests, the movements thus actually contained a specific order within the apparent disorder, transforming *jibengong* (K.C. Wang, personal communication, 27 May 2015). These rehearsal practices cultivated an actor's improvisational skills and the mindset of "letting go", demonstrating how the production of *Kingdom of Desire* differed from the rigidity *jingju* traditionally required.

Furthermore, *Kingdom of Desire* diversified performing conventions previously based on role-types. Wu, as director, mentions how the play's psychological interrogation of guilt forced actors to think more profoundly (Wu 1987, p. 50). When directing, he not only paid attention to the cast's specific body-movement arrangements, but also motivated them to mentally challenge the performance framework learnt during *jibengong* training. Hence, actors were expected to include personal interpretations of their characters. As actor, Wu drew on his experience in modern dance and movies. His role-type is originally a *wusheng* (male martial artist). However, to more accurately represent Macbeth's inner struggles and desires, and along with his desire to renovate *jingju*, Wu's performance surpassed role-type boundaries. Wu mentions that he combined three role-types: *wusheng*, *laosheng* (old man), and *dahualian* (painted face) (Hu 1996, p. 25). Additionally, in the final scene, when

FIGURE 4.3 The soldiers' performance of fluster in the last act

Reproduced with permission from the CLT.

Macbeth returns to the forest looking for the Mountain Spirit, Wu used a horsewhip to imply that he was riding a horse. Wu combined this traditional *jingju* movement with cinematic slow-motion techniques. He exaggerated the height of his arms and relied on modern dance movements, creating the visual impression of cinematic slow motion on-stage. Slow motion allowed him to dramatize his facial expressions, similar to Toshiro Mifune's performance in *Throne of Blood*. When performing Macbeth's suffering after being stabbed, Wu also applied the Graham technique of "contraction and release" (Bannerman 1999, p. 38), reworking the "straight spine" convention of *jingju*. Thus, while the creation of new *dramatis personae* that were unique individuals from traditional role-types caused initial difficulties for actors (Diamond 1994, p. 124), *Kingdom of Desire* nonetheless demonstrates Wu's efforts in creatively incorporating modern dance concepts and effectively using visual images to renovate *jingju* for contemporary Taiwanese audiences.

Conclusion

In this article, I have demonstrated how *Kingdom of Desire*'s cross-cultural elements, at rehearsal and performance levels, redefined *jingju* as Taiwan's "national opera". By integrating modern dance, Shakespeare and Japanese play and film techniques, *Kingdom of Desire* challenged *jingju* conventions and undermined the forced identification of *jingju* with Chinese nationalism. The young performers' efforts challenged authoritative views of what theatre is, and how it should function. The play's success reflected the audience's approval of redefining *jingju* and its role as a symbol of government-defined Chineseness. Retrospectively, this work is arguably the transitional point for Taiwanese actors and audiences to begin imagining an identity beyond state-imposed Chinese nationalism. It mirrored the Taiwanese identity of being a hybrid, caught in between classical Chinese doctrines, Anglo-American orthodoxies, Japanese influences and local cultures.

Modern dance enriched the vocabulary of body movements for contemporary *jingju*. The highly standardized *jibengong* of *jingju* had structured the paradigms of psychophysical embodiment on-stage. Because traditional *jingju* actors were expected to strictly obey rigid, standardized *jibengong* performance criteria, *jingju* was not a genre that deeply explored metaphysical sensibilities. Instead, whatever portrayed emotion was only performed according to specific modes and symbolic gestures; actor-led renovations were extremely difficult. The whole basis of a performance founded on *jibengong* is merely imitation; no innovation or questioning was allowed.[13] The improvisational facets of modern dance in *Kingdom of Desire* thus allowed a whole new way for portraying an actor's personality on-stage.

The desire to search for a style representing the cultural diversity of contemporary Taiwan challenged filial piety and loyalty beliefs embodied in *jingju*. Traditional *jingju* masters had insisted on preserving patriarchal relationships while passing on their craft. Since it was believed that all performing crafts were "inherited" through hands-on teaching, the socio-cultural atmosphere in *jingju* training schools accentuated the authority of teachers. Arguably, it was never the CLT's purpose to entirely *abandon jingju* traditions; instead, it aimed to "extract the origins"[14] (Chiang 1993, p. 70) of the genre while enabling creative innovations.

Far beyond the CLT's expectations, *Kingdom of Desire* helped young actors find their identity in *jingju* and take pride in being Taiwanese actors. After its premiere, this play received invitations from different countries, including Shakespeare's homeland, the United Kingdom, and *jingju*'s birthplace, China. These international experiences deeply encouraged the young actors. The play thus brought opportunities for Taiwanese *jingju* to appear on international stages based on its artistry. With worldwide recognition, the CLT actors gained confidence in the uniqueness of Taiwanese culture. They applied their experience to creating other *jingju*-styled productions such as *King Lear*, *Medea* and *Waiting for Godot*. Their subsequent works prove their intentions to coordinate *jingju* with various cultural resources and theatrical manners. These works, highlighting the CLT's potential to create a brand-new genre based on and beyond *jingju*, have in fact reinvented *jingju* by decentralizing it from mainland-based conceptions of the genre. The process of localized creation thus has another by-product – the global recognition of Taiwan as a productive place for old and new theatrical forms.

Notes

1 *Bazi* (handle) refers to the classical Chinese weapons used on-stage, divided into three groups: the long handle (knives, spears, halberds, sticks, etc.), the short handle (knives, swords, axes, hammers, etc.), and the unarmed (pugilism and *kung fu*) (Pan 1987, p. 231).

2 While practising *tanzigong*, actions must be performed on a carpet to minimize the impact of falling and to protect the trainee. Actions are roughly classified as turning, rolling, tumbling, falling and fluttering (Pan 1987, pp. 229–30).

3 My discussion adopts both narrow and broad definitions of *jibengong*.

4 *Shanbang* (literally meaning "mountain arms"), as Li Ruru explains, emphasizes "strength as if the arms had the power to hold a mountain", providing "the foundation for all the elaborate *jingju* gestures and arm movements" (Li 2010, p. 62).

5 *Gesamtkunstwerk*, according to Richard Wagner, is a manifestation of a disposition to "think big" and to plan all-embracing enterprises on a titanic scale, and refers to a work of art that makes use of all or many art forms, or strives to do so (Young 2014, p. 56).

6 *Huagang* is the name of the college's location.

7 The name "Contemporary Legend Theatre" demonstrates the young actors' ambition of departing from tradition. "Contemporary" denotes the present times and generation; "Legend" refers to the origins of traditional opera while including the creation of new agendas; "Theatre" indicates a modernized performance space (Lu 2006, p. 153).

8 Lin Hsiu-Wei is a dancer as well as Wu's wife. She helped Wu found the CLT and has served as its producer for 30 years.

9 *Throne of Blood* (1957) is a Japanese film directed by Akira Kurosawa. The film transposes *Macbeth* to feudal Japan, with stylistic elements from *noh* drama.

10 *Liangxiang* means striking a signature pose on the stage.

11 Ma Pao-Shan has been a core member of the CLT since it was founded.

12 Wang Kuan-Chiang has been a core member of the CLT since it was founded.

13 Though the "master" actors did make innovations, those successful at it numbered only a handful each generation and their innovations in turn became the paradigm that later generations had to imitate.

14 "Origins" for *jingju* refers to *jibengong*.

References

Bannerman, H. (1999). An Overview of the Development of Martha Graham's Movement System (1926–1991). *Dance Research: The Journal of the Society for Dance Research*, 17(2), 9–46.

Chiang, S. F. (1993). From Tradition to Legend: The Contemporary Legend Theatre's Innovation of *Jingju*. *Performing Arts Review*, 9, 66–71.

Diamond, C. (1994). Kingdom of Desire: The Three Faces of Macbeth. *Asian Theatre Journal*, 11(1), 114–133.

Fischer-Lichte, E. (2009). Interweaving Cultures in Performance: Different States of Being In-Between. *New Theatre Quarterly*, 25(4), 391–401.

Guy, N. (2005). *Peking Opera and Politics in Taiwan*. Urbana: University of Illinois Press.

Hu, H. C. (1996). A Decade of *Kingdom of Desire*: Wu Hsing-Guo Talks About His Non-Traditional Creation. *Performing Arts Review*, 48, 24–25.

Li, R. (2010). *The Soul of Beijing Opera*. Hong Kong: Hong Kong University Press.

Lu, C.Y. (2006). *The Contemporary Legend of Wu Hsing-kuo*. Taipei: Commonwealth Publishing Co.

Moore, K. L. (2014). *The Joy of Noh: Embodied Learning and Discipline in Urban Japan*. New York: Suny Press.

Pan, X. (1987). *The Question and Answer for Jingju Art*. Beijing: Wenhua Yishu Press.

Pavis, S. (1996). *The Intercultural Performance Reader*. New York: Routledge.

Prince, S. (1991). *The Warrior's Camera: The Cinema of Akira Kurosawa*. Princeton: Princeton University Press.

Schechner, R. (1990). *By Means of Performance: Intercultural Studies of Theatre and Ritual*. New York: Cambridge University Press.

Wang, I. F. (2005). Wu Hsin-Kuo Caused the Tempest of Theatre. *Global Views Monthly*, 224, 250–253.

Wu, H. K. (1987). From Tradition Walking to the World of Shakespeare. *Chung-Wai Literary Quarterly*, 15(11), 50–51.

Wu, H. K. (2015). Interview, *The Celebrity's Bedside Books*. TV, CTi News (Chung T'ien Television in Taiwan), 5 June.

Xu, J. C. (1979). *Mei Lanfang's Career on Stage*. Taipei: Liren.

Young, J. (2014). *The Philosophies of Richard Wagner*. Idaho Falls: Lexington Books.

Zarrilli, P. (2009). *Psychophysical Acting: An Intercultural Approach After Stanislavski*. New York: Routledge.

5

RE-CONSIDERING INTERCULTURAL ACTOR TRAINING IN SOUTH AFRICA TODAY; "BORROWING ON OUR OWN TERMS"

David Peimer

The context

The past

After apartheid, after colonization, after the Truth and Reconciliation Commission period of the Mandela years in the late 1990s, this article reconsiders the notion of intercultural performer training in the current South African context and how it found expression in the studio and curricula at the University of the Witwatersrand, Johannesburg (where I taught for many years). To do so, requires a brief outline of the historical context, not only of apartheid and the colonial project, but the city of Johannesburg itself.

I will explore these issues in relation to the university studio experience and curricula during apartheid and the changes that took place during the 1990s, especially after the first democratic elections in 1994. Finally, I will track how we chose to implement changes in the curricula in early 2005/6 based on questions around interculturalism and actor training.

During apartheid, the university theatre curricula can broadly be categorized as being dominated by Western notions of actor training, with UK and US approaches most important. I must also note that at that time the student body was almost entirely comprised of white students. Echoing Leavis' notion of the "Great Tradition", pedagogical structure and content focused on Stanislavsky, Grotowski, Brecht, Strasberg, Michael Chekhov and others – without critique or reference to the apartheid or colonial context.

Ironically, the world renowned, innovative and politically motivated anti-apartheid theatre being devised in the black townships bore little relationship to this pedagogy which largely emerged from the influence of Gibson Kente's[1] work and teaching in Soweto, e.g. performances including *Woza Albert!, Sizwe Bansi is Dead, The Island, Gangsters, eGoli-City of Gold, The Hungry Earth, Bopha, Asinimali, Sarafina*. In the university, pedagogical practice was hegemonic without reference to the potential for inter-, intra-, trans-, or cross-cultural work or process.

After apartheid ended in 1994, the changes in curricula in the 1990s aimed to inculcate South African and African approaches to actor training such as: ritual storytelling, Township-made theatre, a focus on physicality and orality rather than only the literary text. Student classes were 75% black and this approach to curricula involved questioning the appropriation of indigenous forms of actor training and history.

But this was less an intercultural dialogue or negotiated space and more of a hasty "need to put Africa in syllabi". For the most part, white students clung to Euro-American training approaches, and black students combined this with Township-made theatre which had a political content and entirely different aesthetic style. As a result, two pedagogical approaches, reflecting a simplistic binary sat uneasily side by side and notions of how to begin a possible intercultural endeavour were not really engaged. It was a naïve approach to pedagogy.

The twenty-first century

In 2005/6 a number of seminal developments occurred. These included the following objections and assertions from black students:

- It was ethically debatable whether traditional ethnic rituals led to or influenced a South African theatre
- What, if any, role might such study benefit pedagogy?
- Was the inclusion of traditional black ethnic rituals a result of a colonial perspective?

The process began with taking a multiracial group of students for a long walk through the city. They were then asked to write about this experience as "performance". Students objected and, echoed Zarrilli's (cited by Shepherd and Wallis 2004, p. 87) later statement that: "*To say everything is performance is ultimately to say very little*". Students and staff argued that Schechner's later notions of Performance Theory – anthropologically, everything is a variation of performance – could lead to an absurd situation and reflect an area where an inappropriate influence of the post-modern spirit was being proposed.

Finally, the ethics and content of what "intercultural actor training" actually meant needed to be completely reconsidered within the university curricula. Through discussions with students, staff teaching in cultural studies, African Literature and philosophy, we decided to focus on the following notions and argument for a university studio-based curriculum within the new South African context: *Borrowing on our own terms.*

"Our own terms" included:

- The context of the city (noting the apartheid and colonial past)
- South African Township-made political theatre that would inform the core approach to acting pedagogy
- The concept-driven curriculum would interact with an intercultural ethos, but always in dialogue with historical and global approaches

Our plan that all actor training be reconsidered by *incorporating it on our terms*, was intended to resist the ethics of appropriation of past hegemonic and pedagogical practice. Therefore, training would be informed by the above premises, and de facto, imply a resistance to the centuries of appropriation by the colonial and apartheid project. As a colleague stated:

> We have our traditions, our uniqueness; now what do we wish to incorporate from the world; in this way we will reconfigure the ethical debates of inter-culturalism and borrow what we want.
>
> *(M V Norman, Discussion, Johannesburg, 2005)*

Of course, this statement raises further ethical questions to be addressed in a future essay.

It is this approach and how it was experienced in both the studio and university curriculum at the University of the Witwatersrand, Johannesburg that I focus on in the remainder of this article. In a broader sense, the South African context provides an opportunity to investigate a reconsideration of intercultural actor training in general and of the ethical implications of such an enterprise.

Context: the city of Johannesburg

Johannesburg is arguably the most global and cosmopolitan city in Africa. Just over 100 years old, its population is 6 million and situated on the harsh, unforgiving gold fields. Lured by its wealth, people from all over Africa and beyond have migrated there to find work or escape from poverty and wars. In Tswana, Johannesburg is called *eGoli* – "City of Gold", and in its brief history, more than 30% of all the gold discovered in human history was found in this area. The primary image for Johannesburg is the miner – a symbol for enforced cheap, black labour, enormous wealth and poverty.

The apartheid regime created the "townships" of Soweto (acronym for South Western Townships), Alexandria, Lenasia and Westbury – all for millions of brutalized labourers living in abject poverty. From being a "frontier town" to the city of today, Johannesburg is characterized by the ethos of lawless, streetwise gangs, a murder rate greater than Iraq and Afghanistan combined, corruption and mining lords. It is a city with eleven official languages and eleven official ethnic groups – an urban sprawl dedicated to the singular aspiration of gaining wealth.

In short, a clichéd but "true" microcosm of ethnic, religious, racial, class, traditional/ post-modernist collision of experiences which mostly takes place in the streets. To mention but one example of this: important roads were named Empire Road, Queen Elizabeth Road, etc.

These historical and ideological constructs do not imply that historical/contemporary forces are being "performed"; rather, they are lived in the liminal spaces where, given the multitude of colliding influences, the liminal becomes the "norm". This "norm" frames lived realities, with actor training being a minor but significant player as it must function in dialogue with the immediate environment.

The city, curriculum, classroom

In the curriculum for 2005–2006, we began by isolating selected elements of actor training and identified Township-made theatre (including orality and physicality) as the core South African urban-oriented approach to training. The syllabus also included sections on ritual to stimulate the debate over their appropriation/resistance to contemporary performance theory. We also chose a selected range of Western and African historical and global influences on topics such as: storytelling, dance and physical movement, voice (including singing, vocal exercises), character, genre, language, rhythm, politically influenced themes and the ethics of interculturalism.

From its beginnings as a mining camp (with forced cheap black labour) the city today exhibits an African and international diversity, rampant consumerism, continental African influences – much more than Cape Town or Durban, the two other major South African cities – a distinctive lawlessness, extreme inequality in the wealth-poverty divide and collisions of aspects of intercultural articulations which resist tempting notions of trans-, cross- or multicultural definitions.

With regard to actor training, a few simple examples may suffice to suggest contextual connections between the city and interculturalism. The university is located in the inner city where most strikes with attendant police action take place. The strike is known as the "toyi toyi" and includes marching, dancing, singing and chanting. From time to time students break from classes and participate in the strikes. In addition, crime including robbery, assault, rape and murder affect most students in classes, and any training needs to be mindful of these everyday realities when selecting training exercises.

A brief example: For one class, three black students arrived two hours late. All the other students, and especially the white students, were angry. I calmly enquired why they were late. They answered that they had been attacked and held up by a gang with guns who had eventually left having stolen their mobile phones. Had I reacted with anger before checking the facts, I would never have gained the trust needed for any training class.

Black trainees enter the studio as the stereotyped violating and violated body, while white trainees enter with the stereotype of guilt and fear inscribed in skin colour. Thus, interculturalism in this context must aim to battle with the legacy of binary-constructed stereotypes inculcated over the centuries through the colonial and apartheid eras. This is crucial since the studio cannot ignore social context. This is a country-wide reality but is heightened in urban Johannesburg.

Another example was when class was due to begin and four black students entered with no shoes, no sweater. It was winter. The other students were scared as they saw the vacant, hopeless stare in their eyes. I gently enquired how they were. They replied that aside from not being able to buy shoes or a sweater, they had not eaten for two days. In silence the other students knew we were facing a small example of the 45% unemployment amongst black youth, especially in the city. It was evident that class and not only race problematized the notion of "interculturalism"; how do you begin intercultural approaches to training when faced with these realities?

Without a word, the middle-class students went and bought these students some food. I cancelled class and appropriated some of Brecht's notions as we all related stories of living in the city in relation to our socio-economic class backgrounds. I quietly told the class how, one day, during apartheid, I was rehearsing one of my plays in the theatre before the 1994 democratic elections. It was late at night and we had both black and white actors on-stage. The apartheid police burst in, shouting that we were a "terrorist group". They did not know the building was a theatre. They began shooting at our feet, making us all dance. As usual, most of the group were arrested. Again, the city had forced its reality on our modest attempt to create an "intercultural (rehearsal) space".

The city was and still is the contested space where attempts at intercultural activities are being experienced and ruptured daily. This process of fracture cannot be ignored when teaching a studio class. In addition, in South Africa one in six people are HIV positive and studio-training classes needs to be mindful of this fact of life as well.

A final brief example: a colleague and I were conducting an actor training class in the theatre. A PhD student stormed in, gun in hand, and began firing wildly, shouting that my colleague had marked his last assignment unfairly. Everyone tried to flee and the police were called. They arrived two hours later.

Among others, these experiences inspired the following idea: what if, in our training, we incorporated the aspirational intercultural context of an emerging post-apartheid Johannesburg? What effect would that have on the learners' training experience and the notion of intercultural training? We proposed that interculturalism needs to include the very culture and city in which the educational experience occurs.

> The everyday impact of South Africa's urbanisation in the years since apartheid, the daily struggles that the poor urban infrastructure imposes, the expanding social and spatial inequalities that fragment the city, and the architecture of anxiety that determines so many ordinary urban habits . . . (create narratives . . .) as uneven and diverse as the cityscapes themselves'.
>
> *(London School of Economics and University of Cambridge 2016; conference programme)*

But Johannesburg the city also demands innovation, improvisation, satire and a streetwise creativity to navigate daily urban survival. The context of the city in relation to notions of interculturalism is best characterized as a paradigm of *colliding interactions* – fracturing fault lines which are the result of juxtaposing the studio space/the city; ethnicity (and gender, race, class) and history and geography; Western/African; historical/contemporary; apartheid/postcolonial projects. Whatever the fault lines, the city flourishes, especially when compared to the crime of apartheid, of the police state with forced removals, mass political killings, forced "living, working, socialising, racially dictated apart-ness".

Ultimately, I propose that discussions of intercultural actor training should always include consideration of the immediate so that the aspirations of training engage with immediate realities. There should be no naïve ambition or "purity" in considering training. The reality of the city/studio interface produces a creative fracturing of pedagogical processes. This was echoed in the way we found that engaging with Western and African teaching and learning could work when rooted in a pedagogy of Township-made theatre along with physicality and orality, and selected actor training notions from non-South African sources.

Seen from this perspective, pedagogy becomes a process of appropriation (*on "our own terms"*) and a reconfiguration of historical and global training approaches in terms of what will benefit the student process. This of course opens up another debate about a re-imagined notion of ethics.

The curriculum

Thus, we began the Year 2 curriculum with Township-made theatre for the first six weeks. This involved nine hours per week of training, including body and voice. Township-made theatre is a term used to clarify theatre made in the township; it reflects theatre made by black South Africans which emerged from their forced removal into townships and to work cheaply on the mines. It is partly influenced by traditional African song, dance, call and response, one performer transforming to become numerous characters structured as social types with minimal psychological "inner life", storytelling as narration, sudden changes in space and time as narrative structure, a few props, an empty space, an appropriation of the notion of the Poor Theatre made for economic rather than aesthetic reasons.

The *physicality* and *orality* of the performer focused on exercises embodying rigorous African training rooted in the body (usually dance), voice (usually singing, chanting, call and response, sound not just word), the physical virtuosity of the storyteller (exploring ancient African and contemporary characteristics), encouraging the actor to make sudden, imaginative leaps in space and time using body and voice only as opposed to using props or linear concepts of narrative with a psychologically informed training. Later, the transformation of the actor into portraying multiple roles using only body, voice and a few simple props (a pipe, shoes, a hat, a jacket, etc.) was incorporated into classes.

We also encouraged this physicality to engage with an audience that is participatory and spectating. The emphasis on the body and orality of the performer enables barriers of language/the literary to be contested and is rooted in African storytelling, and perhaps, traditions of African religious rituals. It is important to note that the often-assumed link between anthropology, ritual and theatre is inconclusive and led to many interesting debates amongst students. They had of course been stimulated by Soyinka's well-known work articulated in *Myth, Literature and the African World* (2008).

From a postcolonialism point of view, as Rustom Bharucha (1993, p. 34) explains:

> What happens to faith in rituals when its actions are performed in a theatrical context? . . . For instance, if a . . . Mass . . . had to be reproduced in an Indian theatre, . . . it would be imperative to know the meaning of Christ's death to those "actions" of . . . (the Mass) . . . and can they resonate in the larger structure of the Mass, . . . congregration, . . . priest . . . church.

In class we debated Bharucha's important question in relation to African rituals and their appropriation, not just for Western tourism, but the fatal fascination they might hold for Western consumption if framed as an aesthetic of theatre. Either way, it is a clear example of appropriation and questionable ethics.

Just as the Mass requires a context, African ritual has similar demands. In many African religions, the focus of rituals is on man's/woman's relationship to the gods (*Moremi*) and metaphysical questions, and not as a fictional theatre experience.

To illustrate the problematic ethical assumptions about African ritual, I included an exercise based on an ancient Xhosa ritual. This involved the students getting "in touch with pre-cerebral ways of being". The group went through lengthy imagined physical and vocal experiences of starvation, drought, rain, agricultural regeneration of land, birth of a baby, learning to walk. After nearly two hours the task ended. In the discussion after, black students voiced the group's concern and said; "We feel like we have been on a walk to Soweto and back 4 times! Please, no more rituals"!

Ritual, Artaud and religion were discussed as possible origins of theatre and acting. Needless to say, most students rejected this premise. They were exhausted and questioned what it had to do with acting. They were right, and, through this experience of Western appropriation they learned that it had nothing to with actor training and had no meaning when taken out of its religious context.

Interestingly, some years later, I did the same exercise with a group of graduate NYU and Goldsmiths students. They responded very positively as they felt "in touch with primal and spiritual feelings necessary for acting". I then told them how the African students had responded. In the ensuing debate, we noted the blurred boundaries to the very notion of intercultural experience/training and ethics. Was this an experience of intercultural training or was it merely doing a decontextualized African ritual to exotically pose as "getting in touch with primal roots for actors"? If the latter, the question of ethics needed to be acknowledged and the experience then seen as the politics of cultural appropriation sans meaning and being for Western "training consumption".

More notes on the curriculum

Our year of intercultural actor training began with eight intensive weeks of Township-made theatre work. This is the most significant of all South African acting styles that emerged from the black workers in the mines in the city during the twentieth century. It incorporates some aspects of song, call and response, ethnic Zulu, Xhosa, Tswana, Pedi, Sotho dance, but it is important to note that these traditional forms of performance have been radically altered and barely relate anymore to these traditional forms of performance, except for the notion of physicality as the one performer, using their body, adopts multiple characters in a heightened/exaggerated non-realist style. The body is transformed into a range of social bodies and the dominant influence is forms of performance which emerged from the depths of the mines and the city streets, far from an idealized colonial gaze or indigenous past.

Davis and Fuchs (1996, p. 53) cite Fleishman's summary of Township-made theatre's acting style which formed the core of our course:

> Each performer plays a variety of parts as the stories of the streets of South Africa's cities and townships come to life on the stage. The transformation of the performers into this multiplicity of characters is not aided by complex make-up, designs or elaborate costumes. Most transformations take place in front of the audience with perhaps a single item of clothing, a hat, a coat, a simple prop, a pipe, a newspaper, a pair of spectacles to aid the actor. It is the performer's body that changes most to suggest the age, the build and the essential quality of the character. The physical transformations are visible to the audience. These transformations refashion and re-invent the material body into extraordinary and often grotesque forms by which they subvert and parody aspects of the society. The transformed body contains its own logic which can unsettle "given" social positions and interrogate the rules of inclusion, exclusion and domination which structure the social body.

Given the context of the improvisational way of life in the city of Johannesburg/Soweto, the historical legacy of colonialism/apartheid and attendant fracturing of ethnic groups, language, race, religion, class, inequality and the life of miners forced into hostels, in structuring our Year 2 Acting curriculum we then asked what aspects of global actor training we might appropriate for the course. Perhaps naïvely, perhaps arrogantly, we chose the phrase *"productive misreadings"* when we selected notions from these acting theorists.

Given the context outlined above, we noted this as a wish rather than as an act of resistance to the Western canon of theoretical informed practice. The very lives and aspirations of our students, the daily reconfigurations of the city, and the fast-changing post-apartheid world could not ignore the global era and this led us to appropriate, perhaps misread, and not imitate or "try to copy" certain Western training notions.

To help trainees with exercises to develop their abilities as a single actor playing multiple roles with a few props in any space and with a narrative as leaping in
space and time, we appropriated some of the exercises of Grotowski which focus
on physicality. We also utilized his notion of "Poor Theatre" for economic rather
than aesthetic reasons. But, it was important to also incorporate Blau's observation
(cited by Zarrilli 1995):

> "Training! Training!" . . . cried Meyerhold. "But if it's the kind of training
> which exercises only the body and not the mind, then no thank you! I have
> no use for actors who know how to move but can't think. If it becomes easier
> for actors . . . or shamans, . . . to be possessed, it becomes harder for them to
> be intelligent . . . especially in the act of performance . . ."

This part of the course also appropriated from Stanislavsky and others, the notion
of the need for "intelligence, imagination – intention or motivation or the 'magic
if'". Line readings, exercises and improvisation were employed to help inculcate
this aspect of training. It was also important to dispel the vague notion of "inspiration" without rigour. As Barba (1994, p. 28) states, "energy, or rather, the thought",
were vital no matter how much physicality was focused on.

Later in the year we incorporated Barton's *Playing Shakespeare (1984)* in the
class to guide students in the need to utilize intelligence along with physicality
and imagination at all times. We appropriated Barton's use of "intention". For four
weeks, the students for whom English was a first, second, or often third language
responded enthusiastically to the kind of "release" Barton encourages. We primarily
focused on conscious "intentions" – a much more helpful concept than "motivation, objective".

The students responded strongly to playing with the rhythms of the Sonnets and
then moving to theatre scenes. They noted that the language gave them the sense
of "who am I talking to, and why"? Character emerged from language, intention
and imagination (the "if"). There was no need to "invent character". The iambic
combined with the above, were sufficient to inspire. It is important to note that
during colonization and apartheid, black students were made to read the *Bible,
The Pilgrim's Progress* and other religious texts and barely ever Shakespeare. For the
colonizer, religious control was of course more effective than reading Shakespeare.
Perhaps ironically Shakespeare has a less jaded, certainly less familiar presence in the
consciousness of the colonized than the colonizer.

Much debate was stimulated by Welcome Msomi's Zulu version of *Macbeth*
("*Umabatha*") from the apartheid era. This production included Zulu witchdoctors,
impepe (Zulu incense), ritual and dances. Students critiqued it as cultural piracy
for Western commercial consumption. Indeed, no resistance to Western imperial
appropriation was noted in the West when it toured.

I shared with the student my own experience of directing *Macbeth* professionally.
The urbanized, black South African actor performing Macbeth lived with his uncle
in Soweto. Two weeks before the opening of the production, he received a phone

call from the village his father came from. His father had died and the village elders were calling to tell him to return to take up his father's role as the local *sangoma* (wise man) of the group. He called me and we met. Although he did not identify with *sangomas*, ancient cultural traditions, and the elders,[2] he felt torn. I told him he must do whatever was in his heart.

He was an upcoming, excellent stage and screen actor in the country, but had to make a life-changing decision. The students noted that this experience captured much of the essence of the year's course on intercultural training and questions of ethics and the fractured intercultural reality of life in the country. Some years later, I went to see him in the village. He was suffering from alcoholism and cried in my arms. This of course captures the lived experience of the colonial narrative in contest with the conquered, indigenous narrative. In terms of the course, it was important to note what it obviously meant in terms of intercultural debates and training.

We felt it important to test/observe if Stanislavsky's notion of "emotional memory" might be helpful to students. What we discovered was that the only time when it helped was when the memory was banal or simple and not painful. As one student stated: "The city is hard, death is easy; the more banal the memory, the easier it will be". For this, students were given the example of a cat. Rehearsing on a humid city summer day, I had tried many ways to use emotional memory to help an actress who had to murder her husband in the play. After a week of trying, I found that some years back, she had come home to her flat, hot, bothered, sweating. Her cat jumped down from a bookcase, scratched her arm, drawing blood. In a flash, she picked it up and threw it hard against the wall.

From that one impulse to kill, she could then employ the "magic if" rather than try to "recall" the emotion. We incorporated similar banal examples in the class, and to be honest, found minimal interest. When it did help, rather than employing tragic examples of loss, grief and death, this kind of banal memory helped the students much more.

For many black trainees, emotion memory was seen as "strange, indulgent", whereas for the white trainee it was much more useful. The racial division was interesting to note as an intercultural and ethical clash, and overall, we concluded that racial clash was the intercultural aspect of the learning space. The banal examples were more an interpretation of a Stanislavsky exercise than an intercultural collision.

For four weeks of the course, we attempted to make use of "Method Acting". We took the students (and professionals) of all races to the Kalahari Desert to rehearse a new play I had written about a farm, the exploits of the apartheid army, the desert, the descent into madness of an apartheid soldier and his wife. After a glorious day watching massive herds of wild animals roam the desert, we settled down on the first night to improvise some scenes by candlelight. Within a few minutes, every mosquito from the continent seemed to descend on us. Needless to say, we were bitten to shreds and I was soundly cursed!

The next day we left. After two days' drive, we were back in Johannesburg, red and bloodied from scratching. We went to the university rehearsal room, and with coffee, closed doors, rehearsed. We agreed: no more Method Acting South African style! The other mistake was we had filled a truck loaded with red Kalahari Desert sand. When we placed it under the theatre lights, it had a pink glow! We threw it all out, went to a city building site, loaded up sand, and under the theatre lights, it looked like the red Kalahari Desert sand; our lesson was learnt!

We observed how interculturalism is *not* attempting to be transcultural or universal as in Peter Brook's performances. But it also does not mean ignoring the imagination and the varied, culturally nuanced media used to make theatre.

A "productive misreading" of Brecht enabled us to appropriate aspects of Brecht – primarily, to focus on the socio-political aspects of character, narrative structure and theme. This is essential in South African theatre and training: actor training as it engages with the notion of character as a physically heightened social type driven by socio-political events, rather than driven by a detailed psychology.

In the great anti-apartheid plays such as *Woza Albert!*, *The Island*, *Sizwe Bansi*, *eGoli*, etc., as well as other Township-made theatre, this style is a very South African approach to the rough, often semi-improvised mode of acting and creating text. The "productive misreadings" of Brecht provided a language and some exercises for students to engage the most significant (Township) acting style to have emerged from South Africa during and after apartheid.

Our misreading of Brecht's epic theatre included fantastical leaps in space and time, a focus on injustice, dialectical structures of historical forces shown, character as a social position, actors playing multiple roles, breaking the fourth wall, montage, fragmentation and juxtaposition.

Appropriating some of Brecht's ideas also enabled students to gain both an actor's "language" that made sense to them, and in their words, "empowered" them as they chose from Europe what they wanted and were not simply passive recipients of colonial thought. The ethical question becomes inverted.

Training included discussions of these ideas in relation to Township-made theatre, a few of Brecht's exercises being done, much improvising/devising around student-chosen themes to hone the skills was needed for this approach to acting, and looking at given texts from South African theatre and other countries which might relate in some way to student concerns.

We also appropriated Brecht's street accident scene in the form of a "structured improvisation". To further training, and moment-to-moment concentration, we developed the idea of a four-part narrative structure: four "plot" points around which students improvised.[3] Improvisation can lead to remarkable discoveries or boredom. The four-point plot structure aimed to focus on the former and limit the latter. Whatever theme or style the students chose they had to find four major plot points which would tell the simple story and engage with the relational elements of the training that are "believable". We appropriated Yoshi Oida's (1992, p. 1) comment at the beginning of his book, *An Actor Adrift* to define "believable" as follows:

"When I am onstage and pointing to the moon, all that matters to me is that the audience believe I am pointing at the moon".

When the four-step narrative structured improvisation was repeated many times, the next step was to introduce the *transformations* of the actor into a *multiplicity of roles* to achieve the direct link to the specific South African tradition of acting. One storyteller is the core of this technique, but it was applied to numerous actors in numerous structured improvised situations or stories somewhat like Brecht's street accident scene with the multiplicity of roles possible. The inner psychological life of a character's "journey" is minimized and a physicalized series of socially framed roles actualized. The society is seen as informing the individual and societal processes, rather than a character's specific psychology. This exercise led students to propose an "inter-training dialogue within an intercultural context" as perhaps a way forward for training. The danger here of course is that it could lead one back to a "general unified theory" (universalist) rather than noting specific acts of "inter-training dialogue".

Over the year, students were given a fairly large choice of plays from which to select scenes to perform. Their choices might seem surprising, but only when viewed from a stereotypical perspective of colonial/post-colonial binaries. Students often chose scenes from Beckett, in addition to plays by African-American authors. With *Waiting for Godot*, they often used to say: "We have been waiting for ages for the white man to leave, so we know about waiting!"

It was further interesting to note the connection with authors such as George C. Wolfe, August Wilson, Lorraine Hansbury, and how they would adapt scenes from the work of Richard Wright, C.L.R. James, Toni Morrison and ideas from James Baldwin, Fanon, Appiah, West and other cultural thinkers. Very few chose "naturalistic" plays demanding a detailed, psychologized "inner life of character" and many interesting discussions centred around this. It was proposed that the history of centuries of injustice, poverty and being constructed according to pigmentation was overwhelming in relation to internal concerns of an individual.

The influence of African-American jazz was expressed in the desire to begin classes with a "jazz circle". Students developed a technique of starting in a circle with basic foot movements, and call and response singing. The 30-minute warm-up would evolve into making a jazz-influenced circle of sound/use of voice rather than formal singing, and finding physicality in movement/dance to link body and voice.

Rhythm is probably the most ideologically loaded term when thinking of a performer from Africa, but it needs to be stated that rhythm of body movement/dance and voice would direct the jazz circle warm-up. The Western gaze was, at times, encountered when students from Europe would visit and comment on the rhythm without knowing the context or history of the South African students – an "improvisational jazz" approach to surviving and living in the city was expressed by students as part of the "rough, improvisational" experience of city life combined with so many post-colonial/apartheid forces. For the year, almost every class began with this exercise as the warm-up of choice.

The warm-up was seen as an intercultural act and ethically welcomed – African at core and borrowed from African-American jazz. It was also a vital part of training. It was not only about "bonding" or actors "warming-up", but reflected a more profound contemporary South African cultural expression in dialogue with a part of American culture.

Conclusion

It is important to note that we had briefed the students on a fairly large number of possible theorists to study, and plays and scenes to choose from around the world. It was an exciting pedagogical experiment. The key question was always the relationship between interculturalism and actor training and ethical questions. We wished to learn and develop further, rather than try to quantify data reflecting a so-called "proven result". What began with Turner, Schechner, Carlson and others, then evolved by Zarrilli, Pavis and others, now perhaps requires a humble look from an African perspective.

In this short essay, it is not possible to include many other areas of important work from Carol Martin (2010), to other local and African trainings, to Eastern approaches and beyond. By *borrowing on our own terms*, we hope to have contributed to a vital debate of our times in our own small way.

To adapt Paul Gilroy (2015, keynote paper), in the face of increasing global "groomed ignorance of education" to negate the "other", we all may, just may, help cast an eye on our charged times, and the eternal hope, naïve yet yearned for, is the disappearance of the "colonized man" (Fanon 1967, p. 86).

Notes

1 Gibson Kente (1932–2004) was a playwright, director, theatre maker and teacher based in Soweto. In South Africa he is regarded as the "Father Black Theatre" focusing on life in the townships.
2 Given the importance of oral rather than literary traditions, devising is very popular in South Africa training and theatre making.
3 The *sangoma* is also the mediator and interpreter between the material and metaphysical world, between the living and the ancestors, gods and spiritual world.

References

Barba, E. (1994). *The Paper Canoe: Guide to Theatre Anthropology*. Routledge, p. 28.
Barton, J. (1984). *Playing Shakespeare*. A&C Black Publishers Ltd.
Bharucha, R. (1993). *Theatre and the World: Performance and the Politics of Culture*. London: Routledge, p. 34.
Davis, G. V. and Fuchs, A. (1996). *Theatre and Change in South Africa*. Amsterdam: Harwood Academic Publishers, p. 53.
Fanon, F. (1967). *The Wretched of the Earth*. Penguin, p. 86.
Gilroy, P. (2015). Europe Otherwise: Mare Nostrum and the Banality of Good. *Postcolonial Studies Association Convention*. University of Leicester. Keynote Paper.

London School of Economics & University of Cambridge. (2016). *Writing South Africa Now: A Colloquium*. Conference Programme.

Martin, C. (2010). *Dramaturgy of the Real on the World Stage*. New York: Palgrave Macmillan.

Oida, Y. (1992). *An Actor Adrift*. Methuen Drama, p. 1.

Schechner, R. (2006). *Performance Studies: An Introduction*. New York: Routledge, p. 46.

Shepherd, S. and Wallis, M. (2004). *Drama/Theatre/Performance*. Routledge, p. 87.

Soyinka, W. (2008). *Myth, Literature and the African World*. Cambridge University Press.

Zarrilli, P. (ed.). (1995). *Acting (Re) Considered*. London: Routledge.

6

THE ACTOR'S PROCESS OF NEGOTIATING DIFFERENCE AND PARTICULARITY IN INTERCULTURAL THEATRE PRACTICE

Sunhee Kim and Jeungsook Yoo

Introduction

This chapter is a two-part case study of "intercultural" acting written by two Korean actors from our unique perspectives within a completely new, co-created performance, *playing "the maids"*.[1] The production was created through a process of interweaving diverse artistic skills and cultural references by a group of nine inter-national artists from Wales, Ireland, Korea and Singapore as a creative response to – but *not* a production of, Jean Genet's modernist play, *The Maids*.[2] Our performance was created to explore the dynamics of power and servitude, wealth as privilege and the politics of intimacy in a globalized world . . . [T]wo pairs of sister-maids (Irish and Korean), a Chinese "madame", a sound artist, and a cellist weave together a rich web of music, new text, movement and gestural languages.[3]

Issues of difference and particularity in intercultural theatre practice

In his 2010 essay "Intercultural Theatre Today", Patrice Pavis (2010, p. 5) asked "what does the term 'intercultural theatre' mean today?" He answered his question by observing how:

> The question seems paradoxical, or even provocative, as all kinds of cultural exchanges regulate our daily life and any artistic adventure goes back to the most varied sources and audience.
>
> *(Pavis 2010, p. 5)*

He concluded that this once "contested notion, has become a very common thing" (Pavis 2010, p. 5) – a fair observation considering the number and diversity of productions that aesthetically or dramaturgically take an "intercultural" approach. It seems even truer when viewing the interculturalness that pervades our everyday lives, especially in larger cosmopolitan cities of the world. Despite the increasing interculturalness in our globalized world, we witness and participate in the struggles amongst "different" cultures, ideologies and identities.

The issue of how to view, engage with and negotiate cultural particularities and differences informs a wide range of responses to past intercultural theatrical practices "ranging from the celebratory to the highly critical" (Lo and Gilbert 2002, p. 39). At one extreme intercultural theatre is seen as exploring the creative possibilities of fusing different cultural elements beyond national and ethnic boundaries without asking "whether or not this interculturalism . . . was a continuation of colonialism, a further exploitation of other cultures" (Schechner 2006, p. 19). At the other extreme is an ethical critique that views (Western directors') intercultural theatre as an invasive globalization. In both, the main issue still relates to the differences in the use of selected elements, techniques and symbols of a specific (foreign) culture and the socio-political/historical specificities from which they arose in the first place.

The negotiation of differences is also central to Lo and Gilbert's more complex theorization of intercultural theatre practice.[4] Within their categories the question remains one of the negotiation between home and foreign or of self and other. Even Rustom Bharucha's notion of intra-cultural wherein differences and particularities are not between different nation states but regions within a nation, the focus remains on "confronting [these] specificities" (Bharucha 1993, p. 92).

But how do actors co-creating/performing an "intercultural" production negotiate their specific particularities and differences from within their own cultural/identity positions and trainings? What follows are two analyses of our processes of negotiating the particularities and differences encountered not only between Korean and non-Korean cultures, but also within our own hybrid-but-not-exclusively Korean perspectives.[5] Each contribution examines how particular elements – an expressive form or a sentiment marked as "Korean" – are interwoven or juxtaposed with different particularities to create and put into dynamic tension specific moments of performance. Each also examines whether and how specific training experiences have helped us as actors to negotiate this process of intercultural creation and embodiment of "character".

As the "Korean" sister-maids in *playing "the maids"*, with our Irish sister-maids we "shared" Solange (Kim/Cronin) and Claire (Yoo/Crowley). In our creative process, we did not wish to erase differences or particularities; therefore, although the text co-created was primarily in English, we made strategic use of Korean, Mandarin and Gaelic. Only when necessary was there translation via subtitles. As discussed below, in our mutual exploration of Solange's and Claire's position of servitude, Korean and Irish perspectives were not erased or reduced, but put in dialogue/creative tension with one another. As Koreans we each drew upon the culturally specific sentiment/emotion of *han*, and put this into "play" with our Irish sisters' inhabitation of Catholic notions of guilt.[6]

FIGURE 6.1 *Playing "the maids":* Jing Hong Okorn-Kuo surrounded by her two sets of maids

Photo courtesy of The Llanarth Group: Kirsten McTernan Photography

When creating our individual performance scores and the dramaturgy of the performance, we stylistically and technically utilized culturally specific performance concepts/styles/traditions/languages unique to each particular performer's train-ing/experience, as well as the shared experience of the five actors who had all trained in Zarrilli's intercultural, psychophysical approach to performance (Zarrilli 2009).

Intercultural aspects of acting in *playing "the maids"* – an aggregate of relationships (Jeungsook Yoo)

Between ways of life

In this case study, I examine selected intercultural aspects in the process of co-creating/performing the shared role of Claire from my point of view as an actor. Following Longhurst et al. (2013, p. 10), I understand "culture" as "a particular way of life".[7] When culture is defined as a way of life, then "culture is also a matter of age, gender, class, status – so that any such culture bloc, defined in terms of nation, tribe or society, will be made up of many cultures" (Longhurst et al. 2013, p. 10). This opens up our understanding of intercultural theatre practice beyond generalized concepts of national or ethnic culture and invites us to consider culture in the context of an individual's life where both identity and practice are multifaceted, complex and located "between".

An intercultural process of actor training

The contemporary actor's body-mind could be considered as a dynamic field – a process of learning where diverse cultures can meet and interact. Since all five actors are based in cosmopolitan cities, we have all been exposed to a wide range of actor/voice/movement/dance training methods such as Stanislavski, modern dance, traditional Korean dance, Linklater voice training, etc. Our trainings have all been interdisciplinary and intercultural. Through a never-ending process of mediation among the approaches we have experienced, each of us has shaped their *unique* approach and professional identity. Our practices like our "cultures adapt, change and mutate into new forms" (Longhurst et al. 2013, p. 10).

While the five of us are each unique, we also have a shared experience of extensive training in Phillip Zarrilli's (2009) approach to the psychophysical training of the actor. Our mutual experience of this training and approach became the common intercultural ground for our work together. We shared the value of body-mind preparation, mutual awareness in space, and discovery through improvisation. We shared "a way of working" which formed an important part of both our rehearsal room and pre-performance culture.

Keeping this sense of mutuality, we enriched our process by offering individual specialities: Regina Crowley's expertise in voice training and my body-mind exercises based on *DahnHak*, a form of Korean meditation. One reviewer observed:

> The fruits of Zarrilli's methodology are clear to see (and hear) in *playing "the maids"* – it has been a long time since this critic has observed a cast that is so evidently and intensely listening to each other. They make the act of listening palpable, and imbue the performance space with a concentrated energy that is utterly riveting, especially during moments of silence and stillness.
>
> *(Morris 2015)*

Having practised *DahnHak* meditation since 1999 for my personal well-being, Zarrilli inspired me to re-examine the potential of *DahnHak* and the traditional Korean/East Asian perspectives on the body-mind that inform its practice for actor training and acting. *DahnHak* training is assumed to cultivate *ki*. In East Asia the substance called *ki* forms the universe including all things, living and non-living. It informs traditional East Asian culture from philosophy to religion, medicine, meditation, as well as martial arts and performing arts. The paradigm of *ki* contributes to the formation of body-mind monism since *ki* is a linking state between the body and mind.

The *DahnHak* principle of *simkihyuljung* (Mind, *Ki*, Blood, Body) may be explained as "where consciousness lies, energy flows, bringing blood and transforming the body" (Lee 2002, p. 62). This does not imply a hierarchical order among the four elements. Rather, it describes different states of one's phenomenal life according to the degree of materiality. Consciousness is the most intangible phase, and the body is the most material manifestation. *Ki* is in between. Once there is a change in any state, other states are influenced. A change can start either from consciousness or from the body; that is, the directions among the phases can be one direction or the other. *Simkihyuljung* monism may be understood as the body-mind awareness as it expands through practice.

DahnHak training aims to sensitize, refine and reinforce the body-mind and *ki*. It helps practitioners deepen their awareness and sensitivity of themselves: the state of their body-mind and subtle sensations of *ki*. For example, the *Jigam* exercise in *DahnHak* training guides a practitioner to develop *ki* sensitivity. The practitioner sits in a half-lotus position, spine lengthened, hands on the knees with the palms facing the sky, eyes closed, breathing comfortably and relaxing the body. Then the practitioner slowly raises their hands to chest level, with the palms facing each other, putting about 5–10 centimetres of space between them. They start to pull the hands apart and push them closer in while concentrating on the hands and/or *Jangsim* (an acupuncture point at the centre of the palms) and the space in between the palms. The practitioner is encouraged to observe the slightest sensation or change in the hands and the space around them in this state of relaxed concentration.

Sensing *ki* in the *Jigam* exercise begins with the hands because the hands are known as the most sensitive part of the body, allowing the practitioner to experience a sensation of *ki* most easily. The sensation of *ki* varies depending on the emotional state or bodily condition of the practitioner at the moment – exemplifying the *simkihyuljung* principle. A tingling or ticklish sensation, magnetic attraction and repulsion between the palms, a pulse in the fingertips, warmth or coldness of the hands, a bright ball of light between the palms etc., are commonly reported by beginning practitioners. These sensations expand and become subtler as the practice deepens. Once the *ki* sensation is developed in the hands, it is easier to expand the sensation throughout the body and around the body.

Through long-term training, *ki* has become my creative asset along with the body and mind. *Ki*, the intermediary between the psychical realm and physical domain enriches my acting experience as a flexible and fine net to capture the subtler sensations and feelings in the grey area which escapes the illusion of the clean-cut boundaries of the body or mind. These sensations become an inseparable part in the totality of the "design" of a psychophysical acting score – more precisely a "psycho-*ki*-physical" acting score.

The "I Can Not" scene

Using "design" to mark an acting score might give the impression of careful pre-planning; however, in the process of creating/devising/acting, the "design" emerges out of the fertile, thick chaos of improvisational discovery and experience. As the structure of a performance becomes more settled during rehearsals, the design of an acting score is elaborated and becomes clearer. I will analyse my score in the "I Can Not" scene in *playing "the maids"* as one example of how my acting process is interfused with my pre-performative *ki* training.

The germination of the "I Can Not" scene began before I met the text. On our first development day, we worked with 10 Japanese *haiku* poems authored by our cellist, Adrian Curtin, in response to Genet's play. Zarrilli distributed sections of the poems to each performer. I was given the following:

No, don't tell me that!
Sudden, terrible panic –
Flight into terror –

Zarrilli asked us to create a physical vocabulary as a response. While experimenting, he provided additional instructions, such as repeating certain phrases or speaking some lines together. He suggested I delivered the lines in Korean. The outcome of my encounter with the poem was an abrupt, angry shout while thrusting my right palm into the air as if to block someone's mouth. My body was tense. The quality of my *ki* was direct, intense, violent and heavy. The sudden high vibration of the action shook me. It was an interesting discovery in terms of my character development. It aligned with the quality of the maid, Claire, that I imagined based on Genet's text. Although I was not developing the exact Claire in *The Maids*, she was a useful departure point for my *playing "the maids"* Claire.

Although this poem did not become part of the performance, the quality of my body-mind and *ki* that I had discovered became central to my encounter with the text Zarrilli wrote for the two Claires, "I Can Not". He suggested that I sat on a chair, with Crowley on the floor beside me. My right hand and her left hand were joined tightly on my right knee. We faced front.

Without permission,
I can not look.
I can not drink.
I can not touch.
I can not speak.

I can not whinge.
I can not watch.
I can not make a sound, open the shutters, slam the door.
(*I repeated the above lines three times in Korean. Regina then repeated it three times in English.*)
Regina/Jeungsook (*together*):
I can not piss.
I can not shit.
(*2 beats . . . quietly*)

Regina: I can not express my anger.
Jeungsook: My rage.
Regina: It is expected that I smile. (*Bernadette/Sunhee, kneeling, both smile*)
             It is expected that I speak when spoken to.
Jeungsook: It is expected – [8]

My repetition of the above lines in Korean progressed from a low murmur to full roaring. I immediately recognized that the same psychophysical quality from the previous day reappeared and intensified with the new words, especially the repetition of the phrase "I can not". Dramaturgically, this structure was eventually placed between a non-verbal structure entitled "Dark Play", where madame revealed her darkest side, and a section of performance entitled "Release of *Han* Dance and

FIGURE 6.2   "I Can Not" (Jeungsook Yoo with Regina Crowley)

Photo courtesy of The Llanarth Group: Kirsten McTernan Photography

Vocal Duet". As explained below, this placement of "I Can Not" allowed me to fully elaborate, shape and reshape my *ki* within the dynamic context of each of these three sections of my performance score.

The non-verbal structure, "Dark Play", began when madame "entered" the upstage centre area where Korean Solange, Sunhee Kim had been sitting in madame's chair while I had been trying to "tend" to her. Madame's entrance interrupted our interaction, and we both immediately stood to her left in a position of servitude. After madame was seated, Kim stepped in front of me to "attend" to madame's left hand, so I circled behind madame – kneeling beside her to touch and admire her feet. Madame began to draw me to her breast, and pulled me closer and closer until I was almost suffocating as she squeezed me tighter and tighter. As she pulled me up, my legs floundered, sliding on the floor. To escape being suffocated, I finally went flaccid in madame's merciless embrace. Madame released her arms and then placed her hand on my head and slowly pushed my head away – shaking me off from her.

Standing from her chair at centre stage, she slowly walked downstage. Her right hand and arm seemed to possess a will of their own as they moved erratically – betraying her demonic underbelly. She eventually retrieved her poise and slowly walked around the edge of the performing area. All four maids were dispersed on the floor – not moving, but acutely sensing madame's presence and trying to avoid further cruelty. When madame eventually disappeared from our peripheral vision, we slowly released our breath and began to move.

On the floor, I looked at the downstage right corner where Crowley had placed a chair: a space for Claire to go, to be alone – perhaps the maids' shabby attic or her inner world. I slowly stood and crossed there. The Irish Claire, Crowley, held my hand and helped me sit. She sat on the floor beside me.

When I crossed to the chair, my *ki* was dispersed and trembling. It didn't have a specific direction. It was just around me without a distinctive boundary or core. This hazy/scattered quality continued as I began to speak: my breath subdued, my voice low, my eyes open/looking out, but my focus inward and rather vacant. My body was frail. It was like talking to myself – an attempt to regain my senses and recover from the shock caused by madame's crushing rejection through recitation of the familiar routine of a maid. However, this did not work. It highlighted the fetters of the maid's life again and again.

While repeating the text, *ki* intensified in and around me. It became a sphere containing me with a clear border and high density. Its core was my lower abdomen. It then found its direction straight ahead: my eyes became focused and pierced the open space ahead; my voice assumed a strong, hard, direct quality and poured out following the direction of *ki*; my body became more and more tense at each repetition of "I can not".

With the final repetition, my body-mind/*ki* blasted forward like "shooting a cannonball". The quality was straight, strong, dense, massive, heated and direct. My lips, tongue, cheeks and jaws laboured with the explosion of the words. The muscles of my mouth vigorously articulated each syllable. Tension ran through my lower body, with the soles of my feet and toes digging into the floor as if I would jump out into the space following the flying cannonball of my *ki*. My upper body, hands and fingers were pressing down my knees into the ground, resisting the impulse to spring out from my position. This dynamic opposition fuelled the forceful movement of my voice and *ki*.

Shooting *ki* and voice forward was the main design of the psycho-*ki*-physical score throughout this section. As described above, this apparent "design" was accompanied with the vertical opposition of the *ki* flows of my upper body (downwards) and lower body (upwards). Another stream of *ki* was moving backwards, tautly counterbalancing the *ki* running forward. It anchored me down. The centre of all these dynamic *ki* streams was my lower *dahnjon*.[9] The vertical clashed there. The horizontal was pulled away towards the opposite directions there. My *dahnjon* and lower abdomen were compressed – vibrating high with all that energy.

This acting score could be identified as a state of "rage". The vibration of "rage" arose and it found its way in my words. In the dramaturgical flow, madame's behaviour in "Dark Play" directly affected this scene. However, the object of the rage was not specific. My eyes glared out into the space ahead, but there was no specific target. They pierced the black void. From my perspective "inside", this was the condition of a maid who would never escape her servitude, or "touch" in some way the position of a madame who was out of her reach despite her constant adoration, or reach a god who was never there. The rage was a reaction to repetitive "deprivation" where there was no possibility to be and act freely.

"Rage" is a name of an emotion that is general and abstract – a label to put on what I experienced through my body-mind and *ki*. When performing, the name was not important. What was meaningful were the body-mind sensations and *ki* unfolding in specific time and space: the increasing tension in my body and eyes, the heat in the strained muscles of my mouth and neck creating the strong voice, the violent vibration in my lower *dahnjon*. Rage arose from those clear sensations tied to each specific embodied moment.

Crowley was kneeling beside me throughout the scene – another element holding me down. Her left hand was situated between my right knee and right palm, and physically linked us – feeling the pressure of my *ki*, in a discussion Crowley explained how "I felt I was a conduit to your words and anger . . . I allowed them to echo in me" (R. Crowley, personal communication, 2015).

Her repetition of the same text in English had a different texture from my Korean version. Her delivery was like the compulsive chanting of a mantra which was getting faster and out of control – as if she was repeatedly whipping her own back. She was being punished, but would not give in. Crowley explains how "I felt like a deep well where the words could resound. . . . Allowing the pain of each line to strike hard on the nervous system but never flinch or to put up any defence" (R. Crowley, personal communication, 2015).

It was pain rather than rage – a bitter confrontation with the maid's condition. While listening to Crowley, the quality of my body-mind and *ki* cooled, settling backwards and downwards. It became less dense. My *ki* formed a bigger sphere and included Crowley. Our togetherness became stronger, and flowed into "Release of *Han* Dance and Vocal Duet".

The Korean imagination – salpuri *dance and* han

I was intrigued by the emotional intensity of the characters in *The Maids*: the sister-maids' yearning for madame's lifestyle, their frustration from knowing their position as maids, their desperate fantasy to "be madame", and the resulting volcano of emotions – desire, excitement, love, hatred, bitterness, jealousy, despair, sadness, etc. Knowing that Genet's text was our initial stimulus gave me the freedom to explore the emotional layers of the maids from my Korean perspective. The maids' suffering in their stifling situation triggered my imagination about the Korean sentiment, *han*, epitomized in *salpuri* dance.

Salpuri originated in Korean shamanism. "*Sal*" means a curse, misfortune or evil. "*Puri*" means to untie, release or resolve. The compound word *salpuri* has several meanings. *Salpuri* is a shamanic term for an exorcism driving out bad luck or evil. In the field of music, *salpuri* is a name for the basic rhythmic pattern of "*sinawi*" – shamanistic music from the southern region of Korea (Jeong 1999, p. 225). *Salpuri* dance is performed to *salpuri* music using a long, white silk cloth, and traditional everyday dress – usually white. Following the flow of *sinawi* music, *salpuri* dance begins with a sorrowful slow tempo, then progresses into faster, dynamic rhythms, and eventually calms to serenity.

Salpuri is considered an archetypal Korean dance due to its origins and thematic matter, *han* – the quintessential Korean sentiment. *Han* is commonly described as an entangled knot in the heart. Yeolkyu Kim (1980, pp. 26–7) lists the exemplary emotional experiences of *han* as being lonely, sorrowful, empty, painful, sad, sentimental, miserable, lacking, desperate, remorseful and resentful. *Han* usually refers to an old, deeply rooted, long-suppressed sentiment rather than a raw emotional response.

Han is both an individual emotional experience and a significant foundation of Korean culture. *Han* culture is shaped through a long historical process of internalization of Korean history: numerous wars, Japanese colonialism, poverty, oppression of women, etc. *Han* is caused by "unfair discrimination and injustice", "unfortunate deprivation" and "one's own irrevocable mistake" – circumstances beyond one's control (Choi 2012, p. 75).

Koreans are not the only ones who experience war, poverty, etc. and the consequential emotions. *Han* is the Korean way of dealing with these emotional consequences. Yidoo Cheon (1993) categorizes the dark attributes of *han* as "aggressive grudge" and "submissive lamentation", but also notes the transformation of the negative into positive features – human empathy and indomitable hope. The deconstructive aggression towards others or oneself sublimates into positive values of maturity in character and artistic grace by "digesting, purifying and fermenting" the negativity.

Cheon focuses on this ceaseless process of "digesting, purifying and fermenting" as the mechanism of qualitative transformation of *han* – known as "*sakim*". *Sakim* literally means to digest, age, repress and ferment – the process of *han's* transformation. *Sakim* as fermentation is a process of acquiring its "flavour" just like *kimchi* acquires its full taste by being fermented. It needs to be "well" fermented or else it goes bad or rotten.

Although in reality not all individuals experience this process of transformation, it is nevertheless central to traditional Korean values and artistic achievement. In this case, *han* reaches the state of "aesthetics of endurance and sorrow" (Choi 2012, p. 13). *Han* and *sakim* have shaped traditional performer training and development in Korea as an artistic ideal.

In the process of co-creating *playing "the maids"*, while experimenting with the sentiment of *han* and *salpuri* dance, comparable cultural references emerged, such as a traditional Irish *sean-nós* song and a traditional Korean singing style called *gu-eum*.[10] This particular cultural exploration found its place in the structure of the performance and became a scene, "Release of *Han* Dance and Vocal Duet".

The "Release of Han Dance and Vocal Duet" scene

On the third day of rehearsals, I demonstrated *salpuri* for the group. An active discussion about the dance and its underlying sentiment of *han* followed. Kim and I talked about our understanding of *han* in Korean culture derived from the history of suffering. It resonated with the pain in Irish history due to British imperialism. When *han* was explained in terms of its influence in the formation of our Korean identity, the Irish sense of guilt was brought up as a unique but comparable element in the shaping of "Irishness".

Crowley responded to the dance and *han* by sharing a song of lament in Gaelic, *An Raibh Tú ar an gCarraig* (Were You at the Rock?) from the *sean-nós* singing tradition and her account of the sense of Irish Catholic guilt.

> The feeling of being a sinner is very much part of being an Irish Catholic – at least it was in the past. Also the celebration of sacrifice is fundamental. As an Irish child I was steeped in these beliefs. My mother warned that it offended Our Lady if a girl whistled – that if you ironed on a Sunday you would burn a soul in Purgatory. This feeling of guilt and sacrifice – of offering yourself up to pain and sorrow was in your dance and in your explanation of *han*. There seemed to be a celebration of the pain. Of letting go of your own agency and allowing the world to whip you as it desired.
>
> I think there is a special quality and persona in Irish *sean-nós* singing. There is a feeling of longing never satisfied. So often it tells the story of a girl left bereft but she languishes in her sadness and usually will not blame the person or incident that did her wrong.
>
> *(R. Crowley, personal communication, 2015)*

Crowley's description exemplifies the nature of our cultural exchange. We found similarities and differences in our "national" cultures. However, what we shared in our

FIGURE 6.3 "Release of *Han* Dance and Vocal Duet" (Jeungsook Yoo)

Photo courtesy of The Llanarth Group: Kirsten McTernan Photography

practice were not generalizations, but specific cultural examples that we as individuals interpreted and embodied. The *sean-nós* song that I heard for the first time in my life was not a general *sean-nós* song but a song that was internalized specifically by Crowley.

During rehearsals, my *salpuri* dance underwent internal and external changes according to the dramaturgy of *playing "the maids"*. First, the length of the dance was shortened for the overall flow of the performance. The *salpuri* music was introduced several beats later than my usual practice, creating a dynamic moment of silence between my movement and the beginning of the music. I wore Claire's black costume – *not* changing into a white traditional Korean dress. I wore white leather dance shoes rather than traditional Korean socks.

Situated in the middle of the performance, the *salpuri* dance was affected by the other performers and what had cumulatively happened up until the moment of my dancing. That is, in my usual practice of *salpuri*, I dance between the choreography, music and myself. In *playing "the maids"*, I was surrounded by other performers, their actions and the specific state of my body-mind, which had been living the life of the performance thus far. It all situated my dance within a specific/loaded context. The dance became something else as a result of my relationship with these stimuli.

When Crowley and I finished the "I Can Not" text, we faced each other. This eye contact gave me a sense of solidarity. We were together in this situation – now. It was not personal rage or pain but shared. Her eyes were understanding and supportive. We recognized the common wound we shared. Crowley gently put white dance shoes on my feet. We stood up. She handed me the long white cloth of *salpuri* dance. I received the cloth. She opened her left arm guiding me to the centre stage.

While turning away from Crowley towards centre stage, my awareness and *ki* expanded into the theatre space sensing all the performers. They surrounded me – not moving. I stopped walking and stood facing stage left. Before I began my dance, there was a sudden burst of silence. Our sound artist, Mick O'Shea, and cellist, Curtin, had been continuously producing their unique soundscape from the beginning of the performance. I realized that there was no sound. The sound had been carefully moulding the "temperature" and density of the air – shaping the environment. The silence felt extremely loud and strange like fish deprived of water. The silence and stillness were filled with listening and waiting. The moment was full and taut.

I began my dance moving through the thick air of silence. After several dance units, O'Shea introduced the *salpuri* music. The music was familiar but also strange since it was not the usual way of coordinating dance/music. The mixture of the familiar and unfamiliar sharpened my senses. Then the cellist added a deep thud by hitting the wooden body of the cello with his hand. His intuitive addition of the sound gave me a sudden pang in the heart – a sense of irrevocable loss or foreboding of loss.

This heavy sound resonated with a way of expressing *han* in *salpuri* dance. My *salpuri* dance teacher, Myung-Yeon Kim, teaches a particular quality of certain movements in *salpuri* dance by using a term, "*dulkerdung*". It is an imitative word referring to the sound of clattering. However, her usage is more linked to another Korean adverb, "*dulkuck*", which means suddenly, unexpectedly. It is commonly used to imply a sense of the heart sinking through shock or fear. She uses the word for a sudden dropping of one's breath and body especially in the chest. It is not a big movement, but a subtle choreography which evokes a powerful emotional reaction. The cellist's sound caused a similar effect in me – the sound of my heart sinking.

As the musicians' sound began to fade, Crowley began her song in Gaelic. I could sense the quality of sadness, pain and suppressed anger in her beautiful

FIGURE 6.4   Creating the soundscape: Adrian Curtin (cello) and Mick O'Shea (sound artist)

Photo courtesy of The Llanarth Group: Kirsten McTernan Photography

strong voice – similar to the flying silk cloth in the air as I danced, asking the desperate question –"why" – or seeking a handful of solace. The cloth inevitably fell down to the floor due to both gravity and the heavy burden of the maid's life. Kim joined the aural soundscape by humming an impromptu low-pitched *gu-eum* delivered with Solange's heavy/dark heart.

When I finished the dance, I was sitting in front of the fallen cloth. I looked at the cloth. It had been with me throughout the dance. It was something special: my soul, my dignity. And now it was spread on the floor, not different from the white rag that I used in previous scenes to clean the floor. This image gave me an ineffable feeling. Maybe it was pain, but this word is too small. It felt like a hard knot of heavy *ki* at the centre of my heart. I collected the cloth and held it closely to my chest.

A transitional scene, "Dust the Flowers", followed as our cellist narrated the action. We maids put a smile on our faces and began to pick up our aprons as we recited all the varieties of "maids":

> maid: maiden's maid, housemaid, parlour maid, serving maid, lady's maid, chambermaid, nurse-maid, hand-maid, domestic maid.[11]

We returned to our mundane life – waiting and attending as if nothing had happened. We moved into the next scene, "Dressing Madame", as the maids' lives continued.

The absence of sound, the heavy thuds of the cello, Crowley's singing, Kim's humming, Bernadette Cronin's painful kneeling, the white *salpuri* cloth on the floor – these were stimuli to which I responded. My body-mind, which formed relationships with these stimuli, was a specific body-mind "prepared" by the previous scenes. My reactions filled the external score of the *salpuri* dance. It became Claire's *salpuri* dance. The sentiment of *han* was the sum of the sensations of my body-mind reacting to each stimulus.

In the moment of performance, the national cultures of Irish *sean-nós* singing, Korean *gu-eum* and *salpuri* dance became Crowley-Claire's singing, Kim-Solange's humming and my-Claire's dance. The nationalities of each cultural practice disappeared from my awareness in the microscopic moments of acting, leaving only the specific qualities of the practices embodied by the specific actors on-stage.

Acting – an aggregate of relationships

In my creative process, the encounters between different cultures turned into the relationships between me and the stimuli. The nature of an actor's work requires this subjective, intimate approach to whatever one encounters and relates to. The phenomenological question –"what it is like for me to experience" – determines my performance, i.e. the character's development and the specific choices I embody in the here and now. The aggregate of relationships and reactions builds my acting that is, in this sense, intercultural by nature.

Creating an intercultural maid; one actor's perspective from "inside" *playing "the maids"* (Sunhee Kim)

Dongyilon: an alternative approach to considering (cultural) differences

As discussed in the Introduction, discourses and responses to intercultural theatre practice have been primarily concerned with issues of difference between cultures. It is important to examine how cultural differences and particularities are negotiated in *the actor's* performance, especially for actors whose cultural identity is *already* hybrid. Moral critiques, while absolutely essential to the politicizing of interculturalism, risk instigating a kind of paralysis insofar as they suggest that virtually no form of theatrical exchange can be ethical. This position is clearly untenable for a number of practitioners, especially those whose art is derived from (and aims to explore) experiences of cultural hybridity. (Lo and Gilbert 2002, p. 44)

The notion of hybridity calls for reconsideration of intercultural practice and the framework through which cultural differences are considered.

An alternative approach to viewing differences can be found in Wonhyo's (617–686 CE) notion of doubleness of a being. Doubleness points to the absence of any self-elements that are separate from and independent of other non-self-elements in the manifestation of a being. *Dongyilon* (same-different theory) on the whole can be examined through two broad approaches: one is to look at the way it is written and the other way is to examine how seemingly opposite concepts are paired and paralleled within a being such as "*dong il yi bul yi*" (one does not mean not-two). In *dongyilon*, the same and different are not positioned as two polar opposites but are considered to be an interdependent pair in the manifestation of a being.

When viewed through this specific Buddhist perspective, the relationship between "different" (or "particular") cultural elements can be approached beyond both essentialist and reductionist frames of reference. Furthermore, this view allows an alternative way of negotiating cultural and individual particularities without the risk of being reductive or a sense of insensitivity since they are not-two. In order for the dynamic interweaving of *dong* and *yi* as both not-one and not-two to be possible, any controlling interference on the individual's part is unnecessary, if not problematic. Instead, Wonhyo suggests that the phenomenal "distance" between not-one(s) and not-two(s) be viewed like a gate: when open, it is the expansion/continuum of the not-two and when closed, it is the manifestation of one. In other words, *dongyilon* is the simultaneousness of the non-simultaneous nature of a being manifest as a whole.

From this perspective, the question for the actor then becomes how Kim can simultaneously open her awareness to the multiple stimuli in performance, some of which may seem culturally distant, and then how she negotiates these stimuli to create an intercultural performance score.

Ji-gwahn *practice and a meditative mode of acting*

The Buddhist notion of *gwahn* (to look) is helpful in conceptualizing the actor's process of encountering and negotiating multiple stimuli in each moment of a performance. According to Buddhism, this mode of looking enables one to see the object of one's perception without imposing upon it preconceived ideas or concepts, regardless of whether the object is a "real" being in the world, an image, or thought. What is revealed through this "looking" is the interdependence between perceiver and perceived; and therefore the insubstantiality of both. Thus, the principle of *gwahn* can shed light on the relationship between the actor and various stimuli to which the actor is exposed in each moment of performance.

As described in *Sandhinirmocana Sutra* according to Woncheuk's Exposition (Woncheuk 2009, pp. 308–487), – among others – the principle of *gwahn* is paired with the principle of *ji*, which can be translated as "the meditative practice of calming the mind in order to rest free from the disturbance of thought" (Seogwang 2003, p. 436). Over time, the assiduous practice of *ji-gwahn* meditation enables the practitioner to attain both concentration and insight, and ultimately "the union of tranquility of mind and penetrative insight" (Seogwang 2003, p. 438). Although the focus of different meditation methods varies, it is most common for the practitioner of *ji-gwahn* to begin by focusing attention on and sustaining her breath. As she progresses in this practice over a lengthy period of time, she develops a heightened awareness, which allows her to develop multiple awarenesses without compromising the sustained focus and clarity of awareness. Gradually, the practitioner reaches a state wherein the body is seen in relation to the world around it. In the following section of this chapter, I discuss a specific moment of performance in *playing "the maids"* where I applied this "meditative mode of acting" to my performance process. My discussion focuses on the underlying states of desire and oppression that inform the social position of servitude for both Solange and Claire. I then examine how different cultural elements have been interwoven in the creation of my "intercultural" Solange.

Solange's weeping of han through gu-eum

Before discussing the specific moment of performance, I must introduce both the Korean performance tradition of *gu-eum* and the sentiment/emotional state *han* in the Korean context. In the context of traditional Korean music, *gu-eum* may be translated/defined as signs – i.e. the marks that are used to make the sounds of traditional Korean musical instruments such as *janggu* (a traditional Korean percussion instrument) through onomatopoeia.[12] *Gu-eum* refers not to the pitch or notes played, but rather to the sound of an instrument. Today *gu-eum* is used primarily in teaching so the student learns not only to play the instrument, but also *gu-eum beop* (the method, or system, of *gu-eum*, i.e. reading and/or making sounds of *gu-eum*). Used both in court and folk music, *gu-eum* has also long been used in shamanistic rituals through the onomatopoeia of *sinawi* – improvisational (instrumental) music accompanying the rituals. *Gu-eum sinawi* can be "sung" by the shaman leading the ritual or by a highly regarded performer of *pansori*, a form of traditional Korean singing/performance.

Typical to *gu-eum sinawi* is – among others – a performance of *gu-eum salpuri*. *Salpuri* is a form of dance performed either by a trained dancer and/or danced by an audience member typically at the end of the shamanistic ritual. Central to *salpuri* in both contexts is the act of release of *han* – i.e. misfortune or ill luck. Regarded typically as a uniquely Korean emotion, *han* can be roughly characterized by a mixing of sorrow and joy, and grief with hope.[13]

In the remainder of this section I provide a phenomenological account of my performance process during a section of *playing "the maids"* where *han* informs my process of creating and experiencing both the performance score and sub-score for Solange.

I am sat on the floor with my hands clasped on my lap and with a smile on my face. This smile is forced and my mouth is tightly closed, the edge of my lips slightly upturned. At the periphery of my visual field, I can see Bernadette Cronin (my Irish-sister-Solange) diagonal to my left, while the two musicians are seated diagonal to my right just out of our actors' playing area. As I am sat angled towards the downstage right, I can see the two Claires (Crowley/Yoo), who have just finished their shared two, and are now slowly beginning to move. Also within my visual field are the flowers hanging suspended in the air that frame the acting area and the audience – a dark mass in the dim lighting.

I sense the tightness of my hands and my lips in the form of a smile, and sense the sweat in my palms. I can sense the stillness of Bernie, who has been kneeling on the floor for some time now. I also sense the stillness of my body as I remain in this physical shape, and through this mutual stillness shared with Bernie, everything feels so "quiet" even though I hear the sounds produced by our sound artist and the Claires as they continue moving (slowly).

Although I am not looking directly at the Claires, I can "see" Regina putting a pair of white shoes on Jeungsook's feet, one by one . . . They are getting up and have turned to face each other. The space is still so quiet even with the sound still being played (at low volume), and the sweat and heat in my clasped hands and my breathing are growing in intensity in my still body. Bernie is so still, and from where I am I cannot hear or see her breathing.

As I see Regina handing a piece of white cloth to Jeungsook, I release my hands and the tight smile and "come down" to sit on my bottom on release of an exhalation. My external focus has also come down and is now on the floor. The floor feels cold and I sense the momentary chill through my palms as the sweat touches the floor. But the exhalation still carries the heat. My right hand is on my right ankle and my left on the floor. I am literally in touch with the floor and at the same time with flesh, and this mixture feels strange.

As Jeungsook moves to centre-stage, I still have a strong sense of "strange-ness" – the mixture of living and "non-living". I want to break out of this tension. . . And I realize that there is complete silence. . . My desire to break the tension grows in this silence. Does anyone else whose presence I am sens-ing not see that it is so strange? Why is Bernie so still and not responding? Momentarily, a piece of text comes back to my mind from the Claires: "with-out a permission, I cannot move. . ." Then I hear Jeungsook's breathing. I can see her start to move. Is she going to break this silence? At last, is someone going to break this claustrophobic stillness and we are going to be "freed"?

To my dismay, Jeungsook remains where she is and starts dancing. I am thinking, "I would have left, had I been able to move". Since I am to remain, as little as might be, I can do as much as I can in the given situation. . . so I breathe in sync with Jeungsook as she dances salpuri. I hear a piece of music at a high volume. Jeungsook continues dancing and I continue my inhalation and exhalation taken and released – not only Jeungsook's dance, but by the music (traditional Korean music accompanying *salpuri*, amplified by the cellist and sound artist's elaborations) as it resonates through me. I don't know how much time has passed but it feels like a long time. And during this time I am breath-ing. . . which is all I can do. Then I hear a voice. Regina has started to sing (in Gaelic). I don't understand what she is saying, but its addition to this world I inhabit makes the intensity of my desire to break free stronger and stronger.

Then there is only Regina's voice. Jeungsook has stopped dancing and the music has stopped, too. I am back in the same place – the quiet and cold place in which I am stuck. Despite what just happened and of my desire to leave (again and again?), I am back in the same place. Claire (Regina) is still singing, and I start my *gu-eum*.

I am a woman who is asking "were you at the rock" looking at the sea afar but on a Korean land faraway in time who is seeing her memory of dancing at the periphery of her eyes. As our voices travel through each other and through the space, and as I see Jeungsook's feet and the cloth move and the shadows it draws, I am all three: the voice of sorrow, the silent dance, and a woman always in the black stockings that she wears every day . . . every day of servitude which she so hates but from which she cannot break free . . . Then I am reminded of the jobs that need to be done as our cellist, Adrian, reads "stage directions" over his microphone in a quiet/amplified voice: "Dust the flowers. Ensure there is no human hair amongst the petals. Dust the ledger with madame accounts . . ."

The actor's experiential/sensorial work

Rather than a description of my work on Solange from the audience's perspective the above description is a phenomenological account of my *experience* of that section of the performance where a sense of *han* informed my Solange. Although recorded after completing the premiere run of our performances, it provides a fairly complete account of what was happening; however, as detailed as it may seem, the above cannot and does not exhaust every aspect of my experience. The account is of my experiential world as it was being enacted – a "world" of actions that arose through the complex web of:

- rehearsed, predetermined blocking
- sensorial stimuli perceived simultaneously from both within and outside of my body, including the space, other actors/performers, and the audience; and
- the felt stimuli and any associations, memories, imagination, thoughts and/or emotions arose simultaneously

As Colombetti and Thompson (2008, p. 55) argue, "meaning and experience are created by, or enacted through, the continuous reciprocal interaction of the brain, the body, and the world". Solange's identity and world are enacted through my experience in each moment of playing. My experience of being the Solange who is "all of the three" – the voice of sorrow, the silent dance and a woman always in the black stockings that she wears every day – arose from the following complex web of constitutive elements, stimuli and actions:

- *The execution of my minimal performance score*: coming down onto my knees from sitting on my knees so that I sit on my buttocks, and then remaining in this physical position – not frozen but no overt physical movement – as I improvise *gu-eum* sometime after Regina starts singing, and finish *gu-eum* sometime after the end of Jeungsook's dance

- *Inter-subjective interaction with the environment while sensing that environment:* While executing the above score, I am acutely aware of the interaction between the internal milieu and physiology of my body in action (e.g. the internal space my breath travels, the movement of my heartbeat) and the external environment (e.g. the quietness of the space, the hardness/rigidity of the floor, others in the space)
- Accompanying images, memories, thoughts and emotions: I feel the felt sensations (e.g. the coldness and/or the quietness), I see the images (e.g. the sea), I think/ask (e.g. who is this person stuck in the black stockings and in unbreakable condition?)

All three aspects above that constitute my performance interact reciprocally, and it is through this interaction that the (theatrical) world of *playing "the maids"* and my Solange are brought forth – not as pre-given abstracts, but as the phenomenal world and "character" that I live and that I am in that particular time and space. The relationship among these three constitutive aspects of my Solange is neither hierarchical nor linear.

Enabling the type of experience and sensorial actualization of character to be embodied as discussed above, the actor needs to possess the ability to enable and sustain a heightened sensorial awareness and a high degree of focus throughout the performance. For example, while I am doing *gu-eum*, I need to be able to simultaneously hear both my voice and Regina's. Or it could be explained as hearing the two voices in one sound *and* at the same time "listening to" the quietness of the space after the music has stopped. If I lose my awareness of the sensorial field as a whole, or if my sensorial field "shrinks", would I have the experience that I had as described in the above account? The point of this question is not whether and how the actor can (re)produce the same experience every time she performs. It is rather a practical question as to whether and how the actor can enrich the complexity of the web that her (experience of) performance is by opening to the performance environment. An additional question that arises is how an actor's heightened awareness can be enabled *and* sustained.

Through focusing her attention, the actor opens her sensory awareness to the available possibilities among the constitutive elements of the performance score for creative interaction. The act of focusing on selected stimuli within the environment does not necessarily mean I "lose" what I am not attending to. When hearing my own voice while doing *gu-eum* I inevitably hear the other voice (Regina's singing). Since my focus is primarily on the soundscape of the environment, this inevitably opens my auditory awareness also to the "quietness" or "emptiness" of the space that enabled the sound to be made in the first place. The same is true also for my visual awareness: seeing Jeungsook's feet move as she dances, I am "seeing" my feet "always in the black stockings". The act of focusing in this sense actually enriches my experience rather than limits it and sustains my openness in the same way. In short, this type of "inclusive focus" can enable the actor to experience more complex textures.

The next question for the actor is how the focus itself can be sustained. In the context of the Buddhist *ji-gwahn* and the meditative mode of acting discussed earlier, as the actor in the moment of playing I know where my external focus is as a part of the performance score; but ideally I do not know what my looking as such will actually "see". According to a Buddhist view, this is only possible if and when the practitioner is highly focused on sustaining the act of looking, but not on what her looking does. To do so shrinks the sensorial field. If and when I am able to sustain my sensory awareness through "inclusive focus" as such, the three constitutive aspects of my experience discussed earlier can bring forth both the world and the sense of identity of my Solange (as supposed to the one performed by Bernadette). In a contemplative context, this type of "looking" does not only apply to visual awareness but also to the other four sensorial awarenesses – i.e. the auditory, olfactory, tactile and the sense of taste. The Buddhist mode of *gwahn* (looking) can enable the actor's experience of the performance environment to be multisensorial, thereby enriching the actor's performance and the character she embodies.

In this chapter focused on my process of creating an intercultural Solange, I have suggested that a meditative mode of acting as informed by Buddhist *ji-gwahn* principles and its training can be helpful both in conceptualizing the actor's process and as a way of negotiating cultural differences and particularities. Neither my Solange in *playing "the maids"* nor I, the author/actress, can be reduced to a single culture, be that nation-specific or "post-national". By considering acting as an enactive process through which a "character" becomes manifest within a theatrical world, the meditative mode of acting provides a helpful way to reconsider the notion of the relationship between self and Other in performance and within our globalized world(s).

Notes

1 *playing "the maids"* premiered on 19 February 2015 at the Chapter Arts Centre (Wales).
2 The nine co-creators included: director Phillip Zarrilli and dramaturg Kaite O'Reilly (The Llanarth Group, Wales); performers Bernadette Cronin/Regina Crowley and sound artist Mick O'Shea (Gaitkrash, Ireland); performers Jeungsook Yoo and Sunhee Kim (Theatre P'yut, Korea); cellist Adrian Curtin (Ireland) and performer Jing Hong Okorn-Kuo (Singapore). For a trailer, visit https://youtu.be/stWcbtqN6kQ. Also see another written reflection on the production by Adrian Curtin. 2017. Recomposing Genet: Analysing the Musicality of *playing "the maids"* in *Contemporary Theatre Review*, vol. 27. issue 2. pp. 177–94.
3 This description was written for production flyers by the co-creators to reflect key issues based on our diverse cultural backgrounds and experiences, and the performance textures "between" sound, music, performance, dance, movement, gestures.
4 Lo and Gilbert (2002, p. 32) differentiate between intercultural, multicultural and postcolonial categories under their umbrella term of cross-cultural practice. They then differentiate the transcultural, intra-cultural and extra-cultural as subcategories of the intercultural.
5 Along with other members of the creative team, Sunhee Kim and Jeungsook Yoo are "hybrid". Both have lived and worked internationally and have been outside Korea as

much as inside it. Both were in the UK for many years, and both collaborated with Jing Hong Okorn-Kuo at Theatre Practice in Singapore on – *ing*. Kim recently had an extended residency as a director in Hong Kong, and Yoo was acting in a major intercultural production of *The Water Station* in Norway.

6 Although not discussed below, a second example of juxtaposition related to the construction and social pressures around ideal cultural forms of female "beauty" – the type of "beauty" a "madame" possesses or can purchase from her privileged position. Here the pressure on Korean women generated by Seoul's position as arguably the world's leading location for cosmetic surgery is juxtaposed with Catholic responses to "beauty" embedded in "The Story of Saint Mary Magdalene" from the children's book series, *Miniature Stories of the Saints*.

7 Longhurst identifies three meanings of culture: artistic activity; learned, primarily symbolic features of a way of life; and as a process of development (Longhurst et al. 2013, p. 2).

8 From the unpublished script of *playing "the maids"*.

9 *Dahnjon* is a name for a centre of *ki* located in the body. There are three inner *dahnjons*: upper, middle and lower *dahnjon* which are located in the head, chest and lower abdominal region respectively. The centre of the palms and soles of the feet are four outer *dahnjons*.

10 Its literal English translation is "mouth sound" – a type of humming imitating sounds of instruments or nature, for example, birds, wind, waterfall and so on.

11 From the unpublished script of *playing "the maids"*.

12 Encyclopedia of Korean Culture. Available at: http://encykorea.aks.ac.kr/Contents/Index?contents_id=E0005967 [Accessed 18 March 2016].

13 For further discussion of the history and socio-political context of *han* in the Korean socio-cultural context, see Kim (2013).

References

Bharucha, R. (1993). *Theatre and the World: Performance and the Politics of Culture*. London: Routledge.

Cheon, Y. (1993). 한의 구조 연구 *Hanui Gujo Yeongu [A Study on the Structure of Han]*. Seoul: Munhakgwa Jiseongsa.

Choi, S. (2012). 한국인의 심리학 *Hangukinui Simrihak [Korean Psychology]*. Seoul: Hakjisa.

Colombetti, G. and Thompson, E. (2008). The Feeling Body: Towards an Enactive Approach to Emotion. In W. F. Overton, U. Muller and J. Newman, eds., *Developmental Perspectives on Embodiment and Consciousness*. New York: Erlbaum, pp. 45–68.

Jeong, B-H. (1999). 한국의 전통춤 *Hangukui Jeontongchum [Korean Traditional Dance]*. Seoul: Jipmundang.

Kim, S. (2013). *'Han' in Emotion and Performance Processes: From a Korean Buddhist Perspective*. Thesis (PhD). University of Exeter.

Kim, Y. (1980). 원한, 그 짙은 안개 *Wonhan, Gue Jiteun Angae [A Grudge, the Dense Fog]*. Seoul: Bummunchulpansa.

Lee, I. (2002). *Brain Respiration – Making Your Brain Creative, Peaceful, and Productive*. Las Vegas, NV: Healing Society.

Lo, J. and Gilbert, H. (2002). Toward a Topography of Cross-Cultural Theatre Praxis. *TDR*, 46(3), 31–53, Autumn.

Longhurst, B. et al. (2013). *Introducing Cultural Studies*. London: Routledge.

Morris, P. (2015). Playing 'the maids': Austerity, Inequality and the Tyranny of Glamour. *Wales Arts Review*, 10 April. Available at: www.walesartsreview.org/playing-themaids/ [Accessed 10 October 2015].

Pavis, P. (2010). Intercultural Theatre Today. *Forum Modernes Theater*, 25(1), 5–15.

Schechner, R. (2006). *Performance Studies – An Introduction*. New York: Routledge.

Seogwang. (2003). 한영불교사전 *Hanyeong Bulkyo Sajeon [Korean-English Buddhist Dictionary]*. Seoul: Bulkwang Chulpanbu.

Woncheuk. (2009). 원측소에 따른 해심밀경 *Woncheuksoeh Ttareun Haeshimmilkyeong* [Samdhinirmocana Sutra according to Woncheuk's Exposition]. Translated by Jiwoon. Seoul: Yeongothosuh.

Zarrilli, P. (2009). *Psychophysical Acting – An Intercultural Approach After Stanislavski*. London: Routledge.

7

THE ROLE OF "PRESENCE" IN TRAINING ACTORS' VOICES[1]

Tara McAllister-Viel

In 2007, master voice teacher, Patsy Rodenburg, OBE, released her fifth book, *Presence*, offering the field of training actors' voices a way of conceptualizing energy as "Three Circles of Energy™," the basis for training towards "presence". Rodenburg defined her understanding of "presence" through her experiences teaching in UK voice classrooms: She taught student-actors to become "audible, coherent and interesting to listen to, yet that wasn't enough . . . I couldn't understand why some actors did everything right yet didn't engage me" (Rodenburg 2007, p. xiii). When she discussed this with colleagues, she was told that the thing she was seeking was "it", "talent", or "presence". She was told "presence" was something that couldn't be taught. However, she found the opposite to be true. She wrote, "Once in a while, a student in one of my classes who initially didn't seem to have 'it', would suddenly get 'it'. And if I acknowledged this transformation some would keep it. . . . I had somehow enabled a student to find their true energy and this true energy was their presence" (Rodenburg 2007, p. xiii). Eventually, she "began to know that presence is a universal quality that we all have but is somehow flattened out of us . . . What I discovered was that it wasn't a miracle that students found their presence, it was a tragedy that they had lost it in the first place" (Rodenburg 2007, p. xiii–xiv). For Rodenburg, "presence" is described through a lost/found, or absence/presence binary (Rodenburg 2007, p. 13). Thus, the aim of her training is to "reinstate presence into your life" (Ibid.). The way she thinks, talks about and trains towards "presence", particularly her application of universalism as a key principle in her work, links her methods with a larger branch of training, which I am calling the "natural" or "free" voice approach.

Like Rodenburg, I have also had certain experiences in my voice classrooms that have led me to investigate the link between "energy" and voice. But there are key differences in our teaching experiences which inform differences in our approaches. While teaching at The KNUA, School of Drama (Seoul, The Republic of Korea) my students would bring into my voice class other ways of thinking and talking about "energy" as *ki* based on mappings of body from Korean traditional medicine. Lee Seung-Heun understands *ki* (energy) as three types. The first type, *won-ki*, is vital energy received from the mother *in utero* via the blood through the umbilical cord before breathing is possible. After birth, the blood of your parents is part of the *won-ki* energy you "inherited". To this, a second type, *jong-ki*, is now possible through breathing air via the lungs. Lee wrote, "[*Jong-ki*] is acquired energy from nourishment. The energy source is replenished through diet and respiration". The third type, *Jin-ki*, is "accessed through deep mindful concentration of the breath. . . . Wherever in the body that you focus that is where the *Jin-ki* goes" (Lee 1999, p. 33).

From this worldview, "energy" is not singular but plural. Also, *won-ki* and *jong-ki* cannot be "flattened out of us". Thus, the purpose of training is not to "reinstate" what has been lost. The materials of training (body, voice, breath, "energy") are not stable, universally agreed concepts reducible to "human" experience. When designing my voice curriculum at KNUA or in my current post in the UK, I often negotiate differing ideas of what a voice is, what it can/should do, and how voice can/should to "it".[2] Within this mix are varying understandings of what makes a voice "engaging", and how "presence" may emerge through different understandings of "energy".

Using my experiences teaching actors' voices at KNUA as case study, how might an intercultural approach which places multiple traditions along a continuum of training offer other ways of conceptualizing and training "energy" and/or "presence" in relation to voice? What new models for training the voice of today's intercultural actors in a globalized world have emerged and how are they different from the iconic mainstream voice approaches used in many US and UK acting conservatoires? With *Presence* as a departure point, this article offers a comparative study between the two main traditions I use in training, the "natural/free" voice approach and a Korean traditional vocal art called *p'ansori*. The aim is to demonstrate some of the areas of training I negotiate in preparing the way for different techniques to interact in studio. Here I focus specifically on the techniques of "centring", adapted from the "natural/free" voice approach and "*dahnjeon* breathing", adapted from *p'ansori*. Ultimately, this chapter hopes to offer a perspective that reframes a discussion of the role of "energy" and "presence" in contemporary voice training by displacing universalism as a primary explanatory position and offering instead an alternative paradigm to understand the interior/inner processes and potential of the voice as embodied phenomenon and process.

Conceptualizing "energy" and "presence" through the "natural/free" voice approach

Rodenburg wrote that her fifth book *Presence* was part of a "quest for positive energy started thirty years ago" (Rodenburg 2007, p. xi). Simultaneously, Rodenburg was developing her understanding of a "natural" or "free" voice approach. A quick comparison of key principles between her first book, *The Right To Speak*

(1992), and her fifth book, *Presence* (2007), evidence the ways her concept of "presence" is intimately linked with her concept of a "natural" voice.

- The first premise in conceptualizing "presence" is that "the state of presence is your birthright" (Rodenburg 2007, p. 17), similar to the concept of a "natural voice" which is "what we came into the world with at birth" (Rodenburg 1992, p. 19).
- The second premise is that the learner lost their "presence" like they lost their "natural" voice, in part, through the act of others or "life", e.g. "life batters and restricts us" (Rodenburg 1992, p. 19); "As life and its pressures infiltrate the infant and then the child, habits grow and take control. The natural voice begins to slip away . . . " (Rodenburg 1992, p. 23); "some people . . . don't want your presence, so it has been knocked out of you" (Rodenburg 2007, p. 13) and "[presence] is somehow flattened out of us" (Rodenburg 2007, pp. xiii–xiv) or "you are knocked out of your Second Circle presence by life's unwholesome forces" (Rodenburg 2007, p. 97).
- Universalism remains a key principle. "Voice work is for everybody. We all breathe and the vast majority of us speak . . . 'the right to speak' is a right we all have" (Rodenburg 1992, pp. x–xi). In *Presence* she wrote, "I began to know that presence is a universal quality that we all have . . . " (Rodenburg 2007, pp. xiii–xiv).
- The fourth premise is that one's "natural voice" and "presence" can be regained through the exercises she offers in her training texts. Thus, the aim of the training is to "reinstate presence into your life" (Rodenburg 2007, p. 13) or "reclaim what I have since called the right to speak" (Rodenburg 1992, p. xiii).

The Right To Speak (1992) built on concepts developed twenty years earlier with the publication of Cicely Berry's first book, *Voice and the Actor* (1973) and Kristin Linklater's first book, *Freeing the Natural Voice* (1976). These three master voice trainers have established the predominate approach to training actors' voices in mainstream US and the UK acting conservatoires.[3] They pioneered methods, emerging from the politically turbulent 1960s, and broke from the "voice beautiful" approach, popular in the 1940s and 1950s. They each discarded "rib reserve" breathing (Berry in Boston and Cook 2009, pp. 11–12; Linklater 1976, p. 122; Rodenburg 1992, p. xii) and repositioned or questioned the use of "bone prop" (Berry 1973, pp. 49–50; Linklater 1976, p. 162; Rodenburg 1992, p. xiii) and mimetic training practices in favour of approaches to voice training described as more "natural" or "free" and "individual" (Berry 1973, p. 16; Linklater 1976, p. 185; Rodenburg 1992, pp. 131–3, 183).[4]

All three master teachers share certain fundamental approaches to their methodologies, perhaps as a result of their training; all three were trained in London-based acting conservatoire programmes[5] and Berry and Rodenburg were influenced by the teaching of Gwynneth Thurburn[6] (Rodenburg 1992, pp. xii–xiii; Berry 2001, pp. 33–4). All three master trainers follow a similar pedagogical design, which seem to be influenced by practices that predate their publications, such as the work of F.M. Alexander, founder of The Alexander Technique (Rodenburg 1992, p. 63; Berry 2001, p. 287; Linklater 1976, p. 2; also refer to McAllister-Viel 2007, p. 101). Exercises are grouped in a similar linear training progression (body, breath, sounding, speech) like that discussed in Thurburn's *Voice and Speech*, "Relaxation – Posture – Breathing – Vowel Formation – Tone – Consonant Formation – Audibility" (Thurburn 1939, p. 127).

All three have knowledge of each others' teachings[7] or have close professional associations; Rodenburg worked with Berry for nine years at the Royal Shakespeare Company (Rodenburg 1992, p. xiii). All three have worked extensively between the UK and the US, creating a strong trans-Atlantic link between Anglo-American voice pedagogies.[8] Additionally, they each have extensive teaching experience internationally, contributing significantly to shaping contemporary voice pedagogy globally through their books, workshops, teacher-training certification programmes and participation in teacher-training Masters courses which attract international students.[9]

Rodenburg's observations about "energy" in her first two books were organized into "circles of concentration" in her third book *The Actor Speaks* (2000). Here "energy" was conceptualized as actors' "tools, placing you in the here and now"(Rodenburg 2000, p. 226) in order to "help actors focus and energize their voices and place their imagination directly in service to the characters' words" (Rodenburg 2000, pp. 225–6). Seven years later "circles of concentration" became "Three Circles of Energy"™ in *Presence*, and marketed to a broader demographic, beyond actor training, through her book, her TED talk, her workshops and her website.[10]

The first circle of concentration is "speaking to yourself" (Rodenburg 2000, p. 226) similar to First Circle energy which represents the "circle of self and withdrawal" (Rodenburg 2007, p. 17). The third circle of concentration "is addressing many people or the universe. The speaking imagination is very generally distributed" (Rodenburg 2000, p. 226), whereas Third Circle energy represents the "circle of bluff or force" (Rodenburg 2007, p. 19). The second circle of concentration "is speaking very directly to one other person. You might shift rapidly between several people, but your imagination is focused on one person at a time" (Rodenburg 2000, p. 226). Second Circle energy represents "the energy of connecting" (Rodenburg 2007, p. 21). Second Circle is characterized as a state in which "your energy is focused. . . . The art of being present is the art of operating from Second Circle" (Rodenburg 2007, pp. 21–2).

There is a noticeable shift of purpose from the second circle of concentration to Second Circle energy. In *Presence*, non-performers are encouraged to "stay[ing] in Second" (Rodenburg 2007, p. xvii) as a means of "return[ing] to the positive presence you were born with" (Rodenburg 2007, p. xi). But in *The Actor speaks*, "certain professional types fall into a specific circle of speech . . . such as receptionists, air stewardesses or telephonists" who are "required to be friendly, which needs Second, but that would be impossible to maintain . . . To sustain Second all day long would result in a breakdown!" (Rodenburg 2000, p. 227). The aim shifts from using "your imagination" for the purpose of "creating canny moments on stage" (Rodenburg 2000, p. 226) to "make[ing] you more successful, more joyful and loving" (Rodenburg 2007, p. xi).

Presence, released in the US under the title, *Second Circle*, makes no explicit attempt to delineate how "circles of concentration" for actors differs from embodying "presence" as a non-actor.[11] Current discussions surrounding "presence" point out the importance of conceptualizing "presence" specifically for theatrical representation (Fischer-Lichte 2012, pp. 106–7; Goodall 2008; Jaeger 2006, pp. 122–41; Power 2008, p. 142; Zarrilli 2012, p. 122).[12] Many of the exercises Rodenburg used to train actors' voices are similar if not the same as exercises used to train the voices of non-actors. This is not to say that voice exercises for actors cannot be adapted to train non-actors. However, a given context asks the voice to perform in a particular way. Also, the relationship to the listener changes, and this becomes especially important in performer/audience relationships.

Universalism works in several ways here. First, it becomes the foundation of a pedagogical model to democratize voice training from the exclusivity of apprenticeships and conservatoires to "anyone who breathes and communicates sound to the world" (Rodenburg 1992, p. ix). This was part of a larger movement in voice pedagogy emerging from socio-political changes in the US and UK during the 1960s (Martin 1991, p. 170–1). Voice training sought to "free" the voice from social conditioning as part of a larger political act, giving voice to disenfranchised groups.[13] Rodenburg and Berry, among others, took their work into UK prisons. In *Presence*, the demographic includes ". . . business people, teachers, physicians, police, politicians, even convicts" (Rodenburg 2007, p. xvi). In teaching these other learners, *Presence* constantly refers back to Rodenburg's work with actors as the basis for conceptualizing "presence" for non-actors and is one of the main selling points of the book and her workshops.[14] Thus, universalism becomes not only a pedagogical model but also a business model, broadening the scope and application of her training. Finally, universalism is also the means by which techniques, based on *human* anatomy and physiology and training towards a "natural and free" voice (Rodenburg 2007, p. 90; also Rodenburg 2007, pp. 85, 87), can be used to train towards "presence". Here, the human body is understood as the common denominator that links all of the learner demographics. However, anatomy-based exercises reinforce the assumed universal application of the practice without allowing for a more complex discussion of the ways in which different cultures understand body and voice within a specific cultural context.

Case study: The Korean National University of Arts, School of Drama

From 2000–2005, I trained actors' voices at KNUA, School of Drama, in both undergraduate and postgraduate actor training programmes. The actor training at this conservatory included an "integration of fusion techniques" in "both external and indigenous methods and traditions", in order to develop "a contemporary national culture and Korean artistic 'voice'" (KNUA prospectus 2000, p. 14).[15]

The "integration" of techniques included "[Kristin] Linklater voice technique, Alexander movement, Asian martial arts . . . and traditional Korean singing" (Ibid.). To this mix, I added the approaches of Cicely Berry and Patsy Rodenburg because the similarities of their training approaches create a significant branch of training useful to my students. Also, I was asked to develop a systemized voice-training curriculum based on the curriculum found in leading US and UK institutions and the "natural/free" voice is a popular, widely respected training approach which dominates Anglo-American voice pedagogy. During my tenure at KNUA, "traditional Korean singing" meant two years of training in adapted *p'ansori*.

P'ansori is a traditional Korean vocal art form in which a single vocalist performing on a straw mat [*p'an*] tells a story using sung passages [*ch'ang*], and spoken passages [*aniri*], along with dramatic gesture [*pallim*].[16] The single vocalist is accompanied by a seated drummer playing a double-barrelled drum [*puk*]. At certain points during the performance the drummer and/or the audience will shout calls of encouragement [*ch'uimsae*] to the storyteller, which is vital to the energy and spirit of the performance. (I will return to this when discussing *p'an* in *p'ansori*). One traditional *p'ansori* story may take several hours to perform with the storyteller embodying multiple characters and character voices. Vocal endurance, strength and flexibility is paramount to the *p'ansori* performer, as is the unique sound [*songgum*]. These elements are directly related to breathing from the lower *dahnjeon*, located two inches below the navel and two inches inside the body. Within the School of Drama at KNUA, breathing from the *dahnjeon* was one of several *p'ansori* techniques considered beneficial to Korean actor training.

In back-to-back timetabled classes, students travelled from their two-hour *p'ansori* class into my two-hour voice class, transferring skills, ideas and vocabulary from one mode of training to understand and embody the practice from another tradition. For example, a student asked, "When you talk about 'centring' the breath do you mean using the 'dahnjeon'?" The word "centre" or the act of "centring" the breath/voice within the body is language and training particular to the "natural/free" voice approach. This student was attempting to understand "centring" by relating it to the practice of breathing from the *dahnjeon*, which she was learning in her *p'ansori* classroom.[17]

In order to better understand what my KNUA students may be experiencing in their bodies/voices through learning techniques in both traditions simultaneously, I trained with Human Cultural Treasures Han Nong Son (until her untimely death) and then Song UHyang intensively over the course of several years. When multiple training traditions bringing different cultural understandings of voice meet on a muscular level through the learning of technique, not only are techniques interacting but also cultures are interacting. Teaching and learning different traditions side-by-side offered me multiple embodied knowledges that could develop different aural/oral experiences in training and performance. It also offered "a strategic way of rethinking the local and context-specific through the global and vice-versa"

(Lo and Gilbert 2002, p. 48). In this way, I understood training as embodied cultural exchange and thought of it as a form of "interculturalism", a "way of working" as well as a "state of mind" (Marranca and Dasgupta 1991, p. 11).

"When you talk about 'centring' the breath do you mean using the 'dahnjeon'?"

Although sometimes *dahnjeon* as a word and concept is translated into English as "centre", Korean *dahnjeon(s)* includes a system of knowledge that is different from the understanding of "centre" or "centring" in the "natural/free" voice approach.

There are three internal *dahnjeons* and four external *dahnjeons*. The "lower *dahnjeon*" also referred to as *dantien* or *tan-den* [Japan] or *nabhi mula* ["the root of the navel"],[18] is located two inches below the navel and two inches inside the body. The "middle *dahnjeon*" is located two inches inside the body behind the sternum, and the "upper *dahnjeon*", is located roughly between and just above the eyes within the forehead. In my experiences of hatha yoga, seated meditation and martial arts I have also heard this area referred to as the "mind's eye", the "inner eye" or "third eye". There are four external *dahnjeons*, one located in the palm of each hand where the centre fingernail touches the palm while fisting [*jangshim*], and one located on the bottom of each foot, just below the ball when the foot is flexed [*yongchun*].[19]

In the practice of *p'ansori* the lower *dahnjeon* can be understood as the musculature that prepares the breath for sounding. *P'ansori* scholar Um Hae-Kyung wrote:

> The principal technique in vocalization is *t'ongsong* (lit. straight voice) or *chungangsong* (lit. central or principal voice), which the pressure is exerted on the diaphragm in combination with *dantian* respiration to push out the vocal sound more powerfully. The *dantian* respiration makes the most of the breathing energy supported and controlled by the abdominal muscle around the umbilicus and lower abdomen.
>
> *(Um 2013, p. 76, italics in the original)*

Um's description of "*dantian*" details intra-abdominal pressure exerted on the diaphragm to create a well-supported breath stream, part of "*dantien* respiration". But her description also includes "breathing energy" cultivated in the lower *dahnjeon*. This "energy" is integral to an understanding of the way the *dahnjeon* functions, not only in *p'ansori* but through other Asian modes of training. The lower *dahnjeon* is part of Eastern body knowledge, integrated into Eastern medicinal practice and is fundamental to the way the body functions. This body knowledge then becomes fundamental to the transmission of embodied practices.

As an embodied practice, the term "*dantien*" in *p'ansori* describes not only the process of breathing ("abdominal muscle" + "breathing energy") but the resultant sound itself. According to Chin Pong-gyu "*tanjonsong* (dantian voice)" comes from the *dantian* and can be identified by its sound as different from "*poksong* (lit. abdomen voice)" which comes from the abdomen (Chin 1984, pp. 42–5; Um 1992, p. 28).

Voicing from the *dahnjeon*, not only for performers but also for the drummers who accompany them and the audience when offering *ch'uimsae*, helps create the performative "energy" of *p'an* in *p'ansori*.[20] *P'an* can be understood not only as the physical playing area ["straw mat"] but also as the emerging feeling of "connection" between performer and audience during performance. Chan Park described *p'an* as the "flow" (Park 2003, p. 233) of a performance and Um Hae-kyung described emerging "*p'an*" using Victor Turner's term "communitas" (Um 2008, p. 41). By specifically referencing Abraham Maslow, Victor Turner, and Mihaly Csikszentmihalyi, who are also often referenced in discourses surrounding "presence", their descriptions could be understood as the beginnings of theorizing "presence" in *p'ansori* performance. Lee Cheol Yoo (Cheol-u I) suggests the "art of pan" creates a relationship between "drama and p'ansori" through "the benefit of presence as a principle of art", although noting the differences between the ways actors embody character and "the character of [the] singer in p'ansori" (Lee 2003, pp. 35–6).[21]

In comparison, "centre" can be understood as the body's centre of gravity (Benedetti 1990, pp. 28–9). But as a concept used in the transmission of embodied practice "centre" is understood differently between disciplines and/or practitioners within disciplines. Linklater wrote, "Center means one thing to Martha Graham, another to Michael Chekov and other things to others and to me" (Linklater 1976, p. 136). "Centre" shifts between biomechanical functions ("centre of gravity") and more conceptual functions. Linklater conceptualized both a "centre" and multiple "centres" with the additional understanding of "centre of energy". Linklater wrote:

> I want to suggest two paradoxical approaches to the center. One is to pin down more precisely where it is, and the other is to say that it can be any-where. . . . Thus, pragmatically, it must be stated that the center is moveable. As a purist, however, I would argue that there is an immutable center, one primary center of energy from which all movement and sound springs.
>
> *(Linklater 1976, p. 135)*

This "paradox" set up a kind of oppositional relationship in which they ultimately chose "as a purist" the idea of "one primary centre". I argue that using both "centre" and multiple "centres", like *dahnjeons*, does not have to be seen as paradoxical or oppositional but instead can co-exist on a continuum of training, allowing the student to shift how they see their body by applying different mappings to the body.

Unlike a moveable centre, the *dahnjeons* do not move around the body but are specifically located either inside or on the body. What does move around the body, in/through/between the *dahnjeons*, is a kind of energy called *ki* [Korea], *chi* [China] *qi* [Japan], *prana* or *pranavayu* [India]. But like "*dahnjeon* breathing", "centring" as a technique also has an effect on the resultant sound. Linklater wrote, "The strict, physiological benefit of centering the voice is that the more economically the breath plays on the vocal folds, the better the tone" (Linklater 1976, p. 136).

In *Presence*, Rodenburg begins the practical training towards "presence" with a centring exercise (Rodenburg 2007, pp. 49–50). She wrote that the student "will relearn how to centre and place your body naturally, giving you access to your physical presence . . . " (Rodenburg 2007, p. 39). This centring exercise is part of a larger series of exercises to train Body (chapters five and six), Breath (chapters seven and eight) and finally Voice (chapter nine) as part of the "first stage work" in which "you have exercises and techniques that can place your body, breath and voice into present connection to your world" (Rodenburg 2007, p. 97). According to Rodenburg, "even if you don't read on further and merely do this first stage work, your life will be transformed and your presence will be felt more powerfully and humanely. You will feel better and more alive on a daily basis . . . " (Rodenburg 2007, p. 97).

Her centring exercise in *Presence* is based on earlier exercises found in her first book training the "natural" voice. Rodenburg instructed:

> Stand with feet directly underneath the hips taking the full weight of support, knees unlocked, spine up, back unbraced, shoulders unheld and head balanced on top of the spine. As you gently rock in this position you will feel the weight of the body find and return to its center.
>
> *(Rodenburg 1992, p. 126)*

Commenting after the exercise, Rodenburg added, "Being centred (and what is more and more coming to be called 'in the zone') is fundamental to concentrated expertise in sports and martial arts" (Rodenburg 1992, p. 127). Breathing into the centre is part of her understanding of "rooting" the breath in which the "lower part of the body has to be balanced" with "proper even distribution of the weight over the feet" (Rodenburg 1992, p. 129). This sense of balance (what I understand as a kinaesthetic feeling of one's centre of gravity) gives the practitioner a "state of readiness . . . You are standing alert and ready to begin" (Rodenburg 1992, p. 129). In the same exercise in *Presence*, Rodenburg notes, "Do this and you will begin to feel more alert and on your toes! More ready for life" (Rodenburg 2007, p. 50). What Rodenburg has described is a kinethestic awareness in which proprioception enables the practitioner to sense body in relation to itself and the space around it. The description of "centring" in Rodenburg's exercise in *The Right to Speak* (p. 126) as well as its adaptation in *Presence* (p. 50) instructs the learner using an anatomical description – it tells the student what to do with their body – then follows with an explanation of what this experience aims to accomplish. Like many training texts, Rodenburg's instructions are written in an order; once the act of finding one's centre is accomplished then another task, the idea of "readiness" is possible. This suggests that the body as object is instructed to complete an action, following from which mental preparation, "readiness" results. Instruction, written in this way, is a kind of Cartesian description in which body and mind are related but separate. The limits of written instruction do not capture an understanding of "energy" voice trainers identify with the experience of "centring". Linklater asserts that, "working from it [center] clears the mind and focuses energy" (Linklater 1976, p. 136).

In my experience, these two events happen simultaneously. The body-mind task of finding one's centre is the act of "readiness". To be "ready" is to anticipate, to be "present" to perform a task, whatever that task might be. "Presence" and being "present" are different but related.[22] Being "present", mentally and physically "here and now" in the training studio, makes the transference of skills possible between the bodily co-presence of teacher and student.[23] Also, a "state of readiness" (Rodenburg 1992, p. 129) creates a heightened state of awareness in the studio which focuses both teacher and student on task(s).

Sometimes, the focus on task can become intense, in part through a kind of mindful repetition which asks the learner and teacher to constantly reinvest in this focus through an ever-becoming embodied awareness of the task. At other times, this co-created "awareness" can lead to an energy exchange in which the teacher and learner become so involved, or using Drew Leder's term "absorbed" (1990) in the task that they may forget about time and place; they are able to feel "connected" not only to the task but to each other in the doing of the task. The doing of the task becomes a nuanced level of understanding action between teacher and student in which stepping out of task to give instruction and reflection would interrupt this "flow". If this "flow" and "connection" is understood as a kind of emerging "presence" in studio then it is founded on being "present" in the exchange of learning/teaching for both student and teacher.

Perhaps such experiences in studio become the embodied reference points for young performers as they perform for audiences? If the student during training was able to create with her teacher this feeling of "connection" then this could become a guiding experience used to try and "connect" with an audience in performance. In this way, moments of "community" in studio during the training of technique can possibly become employable moments of "community" with an audience, reliant on the deployment of technique in performance. I am not suggesting that "presence" can be reduced to technique but instead am interested in teasing out how "energy" as actors' "tools" (Rodenburg 2000, p. 226) in voice training "engages" (Rodenburg 2007, p. xiii) the listener, or how "presence" works in training to develop "connection" (Rodenburg 2007, p. 97). Also, I am interested in how different techniques can interact to create "connection" and how, perhaps, doing so creates different kinds of "connection" or understandings of "presence". I am not arguing that this exchange of "energy" in studio between student and teacher can or does happen universally.[24] I will return to this later.

The way the "natural/free" voice understands the location of "centre" differs from *dahnjeon* but the larger notion that working through a "centre" can "clear the mind and focus energy" (Linklater 1976, p. 136) or suggests a way to prepare the body to be "ready" (Rodenburg 2007, p. 50) offers the potential to place "centre" and "*dahnjeon*" on a continuum of training practice within the same voice studio.

"Mind" and "energy"

In many Asian modes of training, breathing through the lower *dahnjeon* trains the mind through the body, creating an intense body-mind relationship and cultivates *ki* [energy]. Unification of *ki*/mind/breath must be achieved in order to execute a task well (Yuasa 1993, p. 76). This means that for many Asian modes of training one does not train the breath only but simultaneously trains *ki* and mind. The training does not begin by trying to create a relationship between mind and body but assumes mind and body are already related.[25]

In *Presence*, Rodenburg's chapter thirteen, Mind, briefly discussed her understanding of "mind". Here, "mind" is a place of reflection, "idea" (Rodenburg 2007, p. 127), and "thought" (Ibid.). A Second Circle mind is "listening and connecting to new ideas" (Rodenburg 2007, p. 128). In this way, "mind" is understood through a traditional Cartesian split in which "mind" is located in the head and is the source of logic and reason.

In contrast, *p'ansori* practitioner/scholar Chan Park wrote, "Cartesian dualism falls short of explaining the conceptual mind-body collaboration in the materialization of . . . sori" (Park 2003, p. 199). For her, "Voice is acoustic reflection of the mind" (Park 2003, p. 189). When asked during interview to clarify what she meant by "mind", she said that "mind" was everything including mind and body together.[26] Translating from the Confucian *Book of Rites*,[27] Park wrote:

> Music rises as the mind is moved. First, the mind moves as it is touched by things external. The mind, touched, moves and it creates sound. Sound is distinguished in clear turbid, slow and fast, high and low, and these qualities interact with one another creating changes. The changes create melody, called *um*.
>
> *(Park 2003, p. 189)*

In Park's translation of the *Book of Rites*, "mind" is essential to the process of training of the voice. Other writings of Eastern practice also refer to the importance of "mind" (Nearman 1982, p. 347).[28] What the passage above suggests goes beyond the idea of training the actor's body as one might train an athlete, embodying a set of skills well-executed during performance (Berry 1973, p. 44). The muscles of the body are not simply being trained through "conscious bodily movement" (Yuasa 1993, p. 28) but the body-mind is being trained. Japanese philosopher Yuasa Yasuo wrote:

> In short, the mind that is subject dominates and moves the body that is object, and this is conscious bodily movement. In the state of body-mind oneness, the mind moves while unconsciously becoming one with the body. That is, there is no longer a felt distinction between the mind qua subject and the body qua object; the subject is simultaneously the object, and the object is simultaneously the subject. The movement of the object that is the body is such that it is wholly the movement of the mind that is subject. . . . Zeami calls this state "no-mind" [*mushin*] or "emptiness" [*ku*].
>
> *(Ibid.)*

The mind and the body become one through the practice of training the body – through the process of embodying a practice. The practice itself, whether in my various experiences training in *p'ansori*, cultivating seated meditation at *Wa gye sa* [temple], *taiqiquan*, or "moving" mediation in martial arts, the set of skills being developed are dependent upon body-mind oneness. It is the fundamental means by which other skills in each of these various practices can be accomplished.

In my teaching practice, I am interested in cultivating *jin-ki* which cannot be understood by the daily practice of breathing but is acquired through long-term, rigorous breath training. In biomedical terms, *ki* can be felt as heat or vibrations in the performer's body. Through the manifestation of the breath as *ki*/mind, the performer can understand breath as "awareness" or "consciousness" (Zarrilli 1997, pp. 103–16), a heightened state through which the practitioner functions in the world, or (depending on the variables of training and performance) through which the performer behaves in the "world" of the play.

The "consciousness" that can be seen or felt by performer and audience is also a "consciousness" that can be heard. The sound has a kind of "strength" that does not come from muscularity alone. There is a concentrated focus in the sound that affects tonal quality and intensity. This contributes to what makes a voice "engaging" and links voice with perceptions of "presence".

Conclusion: the "problem" with "presence"

In the Introduction of *Presence*, Rodenburg wrote:

> Here's the problem with the word "presence." Many people believe it is something you have or don't have . . . I don't agree: you might not have the make-up, clothes and lighting effects that enhance the stars but you can learn to find your full charisma. All it is, is energy. Present energy – clear, whole and attentive energy.
>
> *(Rodenburg 2007, p. xi)*[29]

Although she rejected the idea of "presence" as a thing one does or does not "have", she offered in substitution other binaries, "to be or not to be" (xii) and a few pages later lost/found binaries (xiii and xvii). As mentioned in the Introduction, such absence/presence binaries are difficult to integrate with understandings of *ki*; *won-ki* and *jong-ki* are linked to blood inheritance and diet/respiration which cannot be "lost" in the way Rodenburg means. "Presence" is also essencialized as a human quality outside of a given cultural or discipline-specific context.

When placing different traditions within the same studio, often I ask the student to see and hear their voice from different perspectives, different mappings of body, different value systems. This creates within one student, many possible voices and other possibilities for understanding what makes a voice engaging or how "presence" might function in relation to voice. Instead of emphasizing a singular, "natural" voice I am interested here in students investigating multiple voices.

Zarrilli argues for a notion of "multiple presences". For him, "presence" is "an emergent state of possibility" in which "from the performer's perspective inside the performance 'presence' should only exist for the actor as a question – is it possible on *this* night with *this* audience to attain an optimal mode of engagement of awareness, deployment of energy, and embodied consciousness appropriate to the aesthetic and dramaturgy of *this* performance score?" (Zarrilli 2012, pp. 120–1, italics in the original). This "emergent state of possibility" (p. 121), from moment to moment, can be understood as manifesting "multiple presences". The conditions under which multiple presences emerge rely on "the quality, valence, and intensity of the actor's ability to generate an inner 'energy', to engage one's entire embodied consciousness in each performance task, to command space and hold attention is always shaped by one's training/experience, as well as the dramaturgy and aesthetic of a specific performance" (Zarrilli 2012, p. 122).

If the ability to "hold attention is always shaped by one's training/experience" can multiple "presences" also result from multiple trainings? When multiple trainings are placed along a continuum of ways of doing, they may offer different results in sounding. As the sounding voice is heard, does a perception of voice as it becomes "present" also lay along a continuum of ways of listening to and eventually perceiving "presence"? And, how does the ability to "hold attention", or a voice that "engages" the listener, function once formed into speech? What is the relationship to the semiotic meaning of sound and words with any perceived "presence" that the voice carries?

As the "natural/free" voice continues to enter into cultural contexts outside of the ones that initially developed its foundational principles, I suspect trainers, like me, will find it necessary to (re)consider not only how to adapt the techniques this approach offers but negotiate the belief systems that underpin the practices.

The benefit of training in two different traditions simultaneously means the student can call upon different training techniques depending on the performance task. The student can think and talk about "energy" and "presence" using different concepts of breath and different vocabularies. In my experience, having multiple worldviews in the voice studio enriches the experience of training and designing interactions between worldviews helps address the many ways my students understand their bodies and voices and the potential of voice as it is trained. This approach also offers an alternative understanding of "presence(s)" and voice(s) which could benefit the ways voice trainers and scholars think, talk about and train towards "presence(s)" and relationship(s) to actors' voices.

Notes

1 This work was supported by the International Research Centre "Interweaving Performance Cultures" Freie Universät-Berlin, Germany, through a generous research fellowship (2015–2016).
2 Ben Spatz asks in his 2015 publication, "What can a body do?" which is a similar investigation of "technique as knowledge" that I am interested in here. However, my question, "What can/should a voice do?" includes the recognition of a value system. "What can a voice do?" is not a neutral question, simply testing the possibilities of a voice in training. Inherent within training is an idea of what should be done that guides the training. Refer

to the discussion of vocal fold "damage" and *sankongbu* ["mountain training"] in p'ansori, Tara McAllister-Viel. (2007). Speaking with an International Voice? *Contemporary Theatre Review*, 17(1), p. 98.

3 American Theatre Magazine (January 2010) wrote that Rodenburg, Linklater and Berry comprise three of the five "pillars of voice work" in American theatre training, describing them as "innovators in the craft" in which "there can hardly be an actor, singer, or voice specialist who has not been touched directly or indirectly by [them.] (p. 33)".

4 Also refer Jane Boston. (1997). Voice: The Practitioners, Their Practices, and Their Critics. *New Theatre Quarterly*, 51, August. "For example, some of the socio-cultural indicators contained in the practitioners' texts reflect aspects of the revolutionary fervour which spread throughout western Europe in the late sixties and early seventies. It is my contention that it is essential to examine the effects of these socio-political and psychological movements on the individual practitioner and thus bring out the unconscious as well as the conscious processes involved in their writing (p. 249)".

5 Both Berry and Rodenburg graduated from what is now called The Royal Central School of Speech and Drama. Linklater graduated from London Academy of Music and Dramatic Art.

6 Thurburn trained at Central and after graduation taught there from 1922, becoming head of all voice work in 1935, Vice Principal in 1937 and Principal in 1942, taking over from the school's founder Elsie Fogerty. During this time the school was named Central School of Speech Training and Dramatic Art, but is now known as The Royal Central School of Speech and Drama (Susi 2006, p. 85).

7 At the 2007 Performance Breath conference at the Royal Academy of Dramatic Art, in London (UK) Linklater and Rodenburg participated in the final panel discussion which also referenced Berry's work. One conference outcome, the publication *Breath in Action* (2009) includes a Forward by Berry and chapter by Linklater. The 2009 Voice and Speech Trainers' Association conference in NYC, New York, USA. "Vocal Methodologies from the Source: Lessac, Linklater, Fitzmaurice and Rodenburg" www.vasta.org/history-of-conferences Linklater and Rodenburg sat on a panel discussing their work and referenced their work alongside Berry's work.

8 Rodenburg is Head of Voice at Guildhall School of Music and Drama, London, UK and has had a long-time association with Michael Howard Studios in New York, New York, US in which she recently established The Patsy Rodenburg Centre for Voice and Speech offering The Rodenburg Master Teacher Certification Program; Cicely Berry maintains her post as Voice Director of The Royal Shakespeare Company (UK) while working extensively with Theatre for New Audiences in NYC (US); Kristin Linklater is professor Emeritus at Columbia University, NYC (US) and established the Linklater Voice and Speech Centre, NYC, New York, US offering a teaching certification programme in Linklater technique, but also lives and works within the UK, specifically in Sandwich Orkney, Scotland (UK) where she has recently opened the Linklater Voice Centre.

9 www.patsyrodenburg.com/PatsyRodenburg.com/Home.html; www.linklatervoice.com/kristin-linklater-voice-centre; Berry has taught workshops to voice teachers-in-training at The Royal Central School of Speech and Drama, through the MA/MFA Voice Studies course, London, UK which graduates "leading practitioners in the field in Britain and abroad" specifically trained through the methods of Berry, Linklater and Rodenburg (MA/MFA Voice Studies Course Specification, version 3 2015–2016: 2 online). Also, as Voice Director of the Royal Shakespeare Company she is in contact with students from the Birmingham School of Acting's MA Professional Voice Practice, a teacher-training course "developed hand-in-hand with the Royal Shakespeare Company's voice department" www.bcu.ac.uk/acting/courses/professional-voice-practice-ma

10 www.ted.com/talks/patsy_rodenburg_why_i_do_theater, and www.patsyrodenburg.com.

11 When addressing non-actors, which includes a wide range of vocal users, there is also no explicit attempt in the training to address the unique ways these learners use their voices

within a given context and how that context might influence access and implementation of "presence" for the voice user as well as the receiving listener.

12 "The question arises as to who is present and perceived by others – the actor or the dramatic figure?" (Fischer-Lichte 2012, p. 106).

13 Also refer Tara McAllister-Viel. (2009). Voicing Culture: Training Korean Actors' Voices Through the Namdaemun Market Projects. *Modern Drama*, 52(4), pp. 432–3, Winter.

14 www.patsyrodenburg.com/PatsyRodenburg.com/Teaching.html. Rodenburg 3-day workshop in Portugal emphasizes a connection between her theatrical background and training participants' voices in other areas like presentation skills and leadership along with "presence". Her website advertizes, "Patsy Rodenburg's intensive 3-day course on voice, presence and ethical leadership is based around her extensive knowledge of classical texts. The aim of the course is to engage in not only connected speech and presence, but to provoke meaningful debate on the good use of power (a concept which lies at the heart of all Classical Greek and Shakespearean text) and to reflect upon how these principles should be applied today".

15 KNUA is not the only South Korean school to develop a curriculum based on combinations of indigenous arts with Western actor training. Nor is this way of working isolated to South Korea. For instance, Theatre Training and Research Program in Singapore trains performers in voice, movement and acting through combinations of Western acting training with Japanese *noh*, Indian *kutiyattam*, and Beijing Opera.

16 Practitioners and scholars define *p'ansori* in a variety of ways. Also refer to Marshall R. Pihl. (1994). *The Korean Singer of Tales*. Cambridge: Harvard University Press, p. 3. Um Hae-Kyung. (1992). *Making P'ansori: Korean Musical Drama*. Unpublished PhD in Ethnomusicology at Queen's University of Belfast, June: Introduction; Also, Um Hae-kyung. (2013). *Korean Musical Drama: P'ansori and the Making of Tradition in Modernity*. Surry: Ashgate, pp. 11–6. Sung-Sook Y. Chung. (1998). *The Impact of Yin and Yang Ideology in the Art of Korean P'ansori Tradition: An Analytical Study Based on the Late Mme. Pak Nok-Ju Version of P'ansori Hungbo-ga*. Unpublished PhD in Ethnomusicology at University of California-Santa Barbara, December: Introduction. Woo Ok Kim. (1980). *P'ansori: An Indigenous Theater of Korea*. Unpublished PhD in Theatre at New York University: Introduction. Chan Park. (2003). *Voices from the Strawmat*. Honolulu: University of Hawai'I Press, pp. 2–3; Yeonok Jang. (2014). *Korean P'ansori Singing Tradition*. Toronto: The Scarecrow Press, p. xv.

17 I will return to discuss "centring" and "*dahnjeon*" later in the comparative analysis.

18 Refer Zarrilli 2009, pp. 71–2. Difference in the spelling of *dahnjeon* (and *ki* as well as *p'ansori*) into English has been influenced by the South Korean Government's adoption of a new spelling system July, 2000. The Ministry of Culture and Tourism [MOCT] introduced the MOCT Hangeul Romanization System to replace the formerly used McCune-Reischauer system. Also, different spellings in English are sometimes adapted from other languages using various other spelling approaches.

19 My understandings of *dahnjeon* are based on Korean practices. Yuasa Yasuo provides other understandings of *dantian* [Chinese] or *tanden* [Japanese] meditative and self-cultivation practices, refer to Yuasa 1993, p. 79.

20 Refer Yeonok Jang 2014, p. 153. "According to Kim Yongja, *ch'uimsae* must come from one's abdomen, and should not be made with a light, "flying" voice. This is why *ch'uimsae* from drummers who have previously learned *p'ansori* is the best (Interview with Kim, Yongja, 23 April 1997, Seoul)".

21 It is not my aim here to argue that *p'an* = "presence'" and then attempt to merge Rodenburg's understanding of "presence" with an understanding of "presence" from *p'ansori*. Instead, I am interested in how two techniques (specifically "dahnjeon breathing" and "centring",) which already concern themselves with different understandings of "energy" from within their different traditions can bring their shared interest in "energy" as a material of training and performance, finding a relationship within the same voice studio. How "energy" works to cultivate what might be understood as "presence" in

p'ansori or "presence" in Western-style theatre performance would need an extended discussion not possible here.

22 For larger conversations about the relational difference between "presence" and "present" refer Power 2008, p. 3; and Fisher-Lichte's "weak concept of presence" in Giannachi et al. 2012, p. 106.

23 This understanding of "present" may shift in future as more conservatoires are under pressure to devise ways of training through "distance learning", live or recorded workshops offered online to enrolled students who are not or cannot be physically in the classroom, disrupting understandings of "present" as being in the same place at the same time.

24 The power relationships in studio as well as time, the space of the studio and resources enabling training are all factors helping to determine if both teacher and student can be "present", allowing for an intensive focus on task or "energy" exchange, as conditions for "connection" or emerging feeling of "community". This is similar to the necessary conditions by which "presence" may emerge through the conditions of performance; here I am adapting Zarrilli: "is it possible in *this* [class] with *this* [student(s)] to attain an optimal mode of engagement of awareness, deployment of energy, and embodied consciousness appropriate to the aesthetic and dramaturgy of *this* [training task] (2012, p. 120)?" I will discuss Zarrilli's quote in the next section, the "problem" with "presence".

25 I have already argued in (Re)considering the Role of Breath in Training Actors' Voices: Insights from Dahnjeon Breathing and the Phenomena of Breath," Theatre Topics, 2009, pp. 165–80 the difference between the aim of a "psycho-physical" approach in the "natural/free" voice and the aim of training towards body-mind in Asian modes of training. Also, refer to Thomas Kasulis. (1993). The Body-Japanese Style. In Thomas Kasulis, Roger Ames and Wimal Dissanayake, eds., *Self as Body in Asian Theory and Practice*. Albany: State University of New York Press, p. 303. Kasulis wrote, "Rather than asking how the mind and body are related, the Japanese have more often asked how the mind and body become increasingly interrelated".

26 Personal interview, August 2007, Columbus, Ohio, USA. I had the opportunity to receive intense *p'ansori* training and talk with Dr Park when she graciously invited me to stay with her family in Ohio for ten days during my research leave, August, 2007.

27 The book of rites (Liji), is another of the Chinese Five Classics, compiled by Confucian scholars and came into existence around the same time as Shu (the Book of History). It offers a very comprehensive picture of highly developed theory and practice of musical performances before the Qin Dynasty came into being in 221 BCE. Refer, Faye Chungfang Fei. (2002). *Chinese Theories of Theatre and Performance from Confucius to the Present.* Ann Arbor: University of Michigan Press.

28 Refer Zeami Motokiyo (1364–1443), in his treatise *Kakyo,* trains the Nō actor's voice using ki, "First the Key; Second the Activating Force [*chi*], Third, the Voice", in Mark Nearman. (1982). Kakyo: A Mirror of the Flower. Part One. *Monumenta Nipponica*, 37(3), pp. 343–74, p. 347, Autumn.

29 In *Presence*, Rodenburg sometimes used the word "charisma" interchangeably with "presence".

References

Benedetti, R. (1990). *The Actor at Work*. Englewood Cliffs, NJ: Prentice Hall.

Berry, C. (1973). *Voice and the Actor*. New York: Collier Books.

Berry, C. (2001). *Text in Action*. London: Virgin.

Boston, J. (1997). Voice: The Practitioners, Their Practices, and Their Critics. *New Theatre Quarterly*, 51, 248–254, August.

Boston, J. and Cook, R. (2009). *Breath in Action: The Art of Breath in Vocal and Holistic Practice*. London: Jessica Kingsley.

Chin, Ponggyu. (1984). P'ansori ŭi Iron kwa Shilche [Theory and Practice of P'ansori]. Seoul: Susŏwŏn.

Chung, Sung-Sook Y. (1998). *The Impact of Yin and Yang Ideology in the Art of Korean P'ansori Tradition: An Analytical Study Based on the Late Mme. Pak Nok-Ju Version of P'ansori Hungbo-ga*. University of California, Santa Barbara, Unpublished PhD-Ethnomusicology.

Deutsch, E. (1993). The Concept of the Body. In Thomas P. Kasulis, Roger T. Ames and Wimal Dissanayke, ed., *Self as Body in Asian Theory and Practice: SUNY Series, the Body in Culture, History and Religion*. Albany: State University of New York Press, pp. 6–8.

Faye Chungfang Fei. (2002). *Chinese Theories of Theatre and Performance from Confucius to the Present*. Ann Arbor: University of Michigan Press.

Fischer-Lichte, E. (2012). Appearing as Embodied Mind–Defining a Weak, a Strong and a Radical Concept of Presence. In Gabriella Giannachi, Nick Kaye and Michael Shanks, eds., *Archaeologies of Presence*. London: Routledge, pp. 103–118.

Gener, R. (2010). 'Pillars of Voice Work,' in 'Special Section: Approaches to Theatre Training'. *American Theatre Magazine Special Issue*, 27(1), 33, January.

Goodall, J. (2008). *Stage Presence*. London: Routledge.

Jaeger, S. M. (2006). Embodiment and Presence: The Ontology of Presence Reconsidered. In David Krasner and David Z. Saltz, eds., *Staging Philosophy: Intersections of Theatre, Performance and Philosophy*. Ann Arbor: University of Michigan Press, pp. 122–141.

Jang, Y. (2014). *Korean P'ansori Singing Tradition*. Toronto: The Scarecrow Press.

Kasulis, T. (1993). The Body–Japanese Style. In Thomas Kasulis, Roger Ames and Wimal Dissanayake, eds., *Self as Body in Asian Theory and Practice*. Albany: State University of New York Press.

Kim, Woo Ok. (1980). *P'ansori: An Indigenous Theatre of Korea*. New York University, Unpublished PhD–Theatre.

Korean National University of Arts, School of Drama Prospectus. (2000).

Leder, D. (1990). *The Absent Body*. Chicago: University of Chicago Press.

Lee Cheol Yoo. (2003). *The Character of Singer for Pansori*. Unpublished Thesis, Master of Pedagogy, Kunsan National University, Graduate School of Education.

Lee, Seung-Heun. (1999). *Dahnhak*. Seoul: Dahn Publications.

Linklater, K. (1976). *Freeing the Natural Voice*. New York: Drama Book Publishers.

Lo, J. and Gilbert, H. (2002). Toward a Topography of Cross-Cultural Theatre Praxis. *The Drama Review*, 46(3, T175), 31–53, Fall.

Marranca, B. and Dasgupta, G. (1991). *Interculturalism and Performance*. New York: PAJ Publications.

Martin, J. (1991). Voice in Modern Theatre. London: Routledge.

McAllister-Viel, T. (2007). Speaking with an International Voice? *Contemporary Theatre Review*, 17, 97–106.

McAllister-Viel, T. (2009a). (Re)Considering the Role of Breath in Training Actors' Voices. *Theatre Topics*, 19(2), 165–180, September.

McAllister-Viel, T. (2009b). Voicing Culture: Training Korean Actors' Voices Through the Namdaemum Market Projects. *Modern Drama*, 52(4), 432–433, Winter.

Nearman, M. (1982). Kakyo: A Mirror of the Flower. Part One. *Monumenta Nipponica*, 37(3), 343–374, Autumn.

Park, C. E. (2003). *Voices from the Straw Mat: Toward an Ethnography of Korean Story Singing*. Honolulu: University of Hawaii Press and Center for Korean Studies.

Park, C. E. (2007). Personal Interview, August, Columbus, OH, USA.

Pihl, M. R. (1994). *The Korean Singer of Tales*. Cambridge: Harvard University Press.

Power, C. (2008). *Presence in Play: A Critique of Theories of Presence in the Theatre*. New York: Rodopi.

Rodenburg, P. (1992). *The Right to Speak*. New York: Routledge.

Rodenburg, P. (2000). *The Actor Speaks: Voice and the Performer*. New York: St. Martin's Press.

Rodenburg, P. (2007). *Presence: How to Use Positive Energy for Success in Every Situation*. London: Michael Joseph.

Spatz, B. (2015). *What a Body Can Do: Technique as Knowledge, Practice as Research*. London: Routledge.

Susi, L. (2006). *The Central Book*. London: Oberon.

Thurburn, G. L. (1939). *Voice and Speech*. Digswell Place: James Nisbet and Co. Ltd.

Um, H. K. (1992). *Making P'ansori: Korean Musical Drama*. The Queen's University of Belfast, Unpublished PhD–Ethnomusicology.

Um, H. K. (2008). New P'ansori in Twenty-First-Century Korea: Creative Dialectics of Tradition and Modernity. *Asian Theatre Journal*, 22(1), 24–57, Spring.

Um, H. K. (2013). *Korean Musical Drama: P'ansori and the Making of Tradition in Modernity*. SOAS Musicology Series. Aldershot: Ashgate.

Yuasa, Y. (1993). *The Body, Self-Cultivation, and Ki-Energy*. Translated by Shigenori Nagatomo and Monte S. Hull. Albany: State University of New York Press.

Zarrilli, P. B. (1997). Acting . . . 'at the nerve ends': Beckett, Blau and the Necessary. *Theatre Topics*, 7(2), 103–116.

Zarrilli, P. B. (2009). *Psychophysical Acting: An Intercultural Approach After Stanislavski*. London: Routledge.

Zarrilli, P. B. (2012). '. . . presence. . . ' as a Question and Emergent Possibility: A Case Study from the Performer's Perspective. In G. Giannachi, N. Kaye and M. Shanks, ed., *Archaeologies of Presence*. London: Routledge, pp. 120–152.

Websites

www.bcu.ac.uk/acting/courses/professional-voice-practice-ma
www.cssd.ac.uk/course/voice-studies-ma-mfa
www.gsmd.ac.uk/acting/staff/staff_biographies/department/16-department-of-acting/669-patsy-rodenburg/
www.linklatervoice.com/kristin-linklater-voice-centre
www.patsyrodenburg.com/PatsyRodenburg.com/Home.html
www.ted.com/talks/patsy_rodenburg_why_i_do_theater
www.vasta.org/history-of-conferences

8

TRAINING A PERFORMER'S VOICES

Electa Behrens

Introduction

Using the voice in diverse ways is a primary aesthetic and practical vehicle for communicating with audiences in many emergent forms of intercultural performance. The aim is to subvert singular narratives of a dominant culture, and to give voice to the multiplicity within any retelling. Are there trainings that support this approach? What gaps exist between what is offered and what the performer requires in order to "speak with the voices of the now"? How can voice be a driving dramaturgical force rather than aesthetic icing on the cake? This chapter is a studio-based analysis of pedagogical strategies for working "between" cultures in the context of an international conservatoire. Uncovering limiting assumptions and offering proposals in the form of teaching strategies and conceptual models, this chapter aims to be a "tool" for the pedagogue and deviser.

The research took place at the Norwegian Theatre Academy (NTA).[1] Participants were from the UK, Norway, Denmark, Lithuania, Romania, Switzerland, Italy, France, Bosnia, Czech Republic and Russia. Significant work has already been conducted on the subject of how to adapt voice exercises to be more culturally inclusive. I focus here on an area of pedagogical practice overlooked in most training programmes: vocal composition.

An alternative academy

The NTA offers a unique context in which to explore questions of interculturalism. The students are international, the groups are small and the study lasts three years. Most significantly, the NTA actively works against giving students a singular narrative of "what performance is". Gordon (2006, p. 2) writes:

> Most actors today are trained according to the one method favoured by
> their . . . school. Most often the specific approach is not taught in a conscious

or critical process, but is absorbed *experientially* by the student . . . Problems occur when . . . actors are asked to create performances utilizing techniques and stage conventions other than the ones in which they were schooled. These problems arise not merely because actors are unfamiliar with the alien conventions and techniques, but also because their performing identity has already been formed by the aesthetic they have unself-consciously absorbed in training.

At NTA, the curriculum is curated, tailor-made to each class. There is no singular lineage of training which is favoured. The syllabus is rather made up of workshops held by active international artists whose methods counterpoint each other. The philosophy is that the "contradictions" between workshops stimulate critical reflection and autonomous creativity. In an arc of student-led devised projects (Independents), the students' ability to apply skills learned in reflected and original ways is evaluated.[2] Voice practitioner McAllister-Viel (2009a, p. 174) describes this approach as a comparative intercultural methodology.

> Principles and practices inside of my body/voice can be understood in reference to each other; each tradition becomes an embodied context for learning the praxis of another tradition. Through trial and error as well as strategically designed interactions, the different trainings inside of me can interface. These combinations create different body knowledges from which I am able to develop alternative methods and models for training.

This approach also forms the basis of my voice-centred research. In this subject, students are taught by three pedagogues, each with their own method.[3] My research is thus continuously challenged through a process of student and collegial questioning and through application within a wide aesthetic range in Independent projects. This application is significant. The results of solely studio-based studies can be misleading. Voice practitioner Bryon (2012, p. 83) reflects:

> What was interesting, especially when leaving training and conditioning and approaching rehearsal, where performance values would be a concern, was what was considered important by each practitioner as the aesthetic goal shifted. Many returned to the values of their primary disciplines.

For this reason, the study of voice methods within the context of composition is key.

Intercultural theatre = physical theatre?

I will examine some ways in which intercultural voice training is approached. Historically, Barba's 1991 book *The Secret Art of the Performer* can be seen as a starting point. As significant as it was, it had a far-reaching consequence for how the voice is viewed. Barba coined the term "pre-expressivity". He suggested that in all performance forms there is a level which is pre-expressive and "independent of the director's poetics and/or aesthetic choices" (Barba and Savarese 2006, p. 173), and that these principles constitute a "culture-less" common ground. The book focuses primarily on the body. Hands and eyes have a limited number of ways in which they can move and were perhaps more accessible in terms of the cross-cultural comparisons Barba was looking to make. The voice, conversely, if one includes the spectrum of world languages, non-linguistic sounds and song traditions, has a range that is daunting. One symptom of this body fascination is a deafness to the vocal aspect of intercultural work. An example is Brook's famed *Mahabharata*, which was, when it premiered, embraced as a triumph by many Western reviewers, though at the same time it was critiqued by authors such as Rustom Bharucha (1993, p. 4). All of the actors (who came from a variety of cultures) spoke a kind of heightened British English, despite the fact that few of them were British. It goes without saying that this limits the performer's expressive range and supports a kind of colonizing dynamic. The argument, when cultural voices are thus silenced, is often: "but we need to understand what they are saying". This justification still persists today. The trend has been for intercultural theatre to be a subset of physical theatre. As Keefe and Murray (2007, p. 200) rightly describe the situation: "The theatre forms most likely to serve the impulse of transculturalism will be those which are highly visual and which employ and explore vocabularies of movement and physicality". How can the voice and its space as a communicator which is not bound to language gain the visibility it has the potential to demand?

A universal voice?

There are of course, pedagogues looking to develop intercultural voice trainings. Many of them start from Barba's idea of pre-expressive principles to unite diverse performers. On closer inspection, these methods appear theoretically unsound. McAllister-Viel (2007, 2009a, 2009b, and her essay in this book) looks to uncover the cultural specificity and historical roots of Western approaches to voice. One argument she dissects is the universality of anatomy:

> Mainstream contemporary voice training for actors has been heavily criticized for privileging anatomy over cultural influence and has therefore been characterized as an "effacement of cultural and other kinds of difference" that attempts to "transcend cultural conditioning" in favour of "universal" anatomical experience.
>
> *(McAllister-Viel 2009b, p. 426, quoting Knowles)*

The privileging of this biological "reality" has been the justification for a narrative of "broken voice" as the starting point for the performer; the performer begins with blocks, created by social and/or cultural habits that are considered negative and which they must unlearn in order to return to the efficient functioning of the "universal" mechanical body.[4] McAllister-Viel compares the duality in Western voice methods with the polarity[5] in Eastern approaches. This has a direct effect on how voice trainings are structured.

> Because Western Voice assumes the body begins training with unnecessary 'tension' . . . the majority of the training focuses on 'release' exercises. In contrast, *p'ansori* [traditional Korean singing] trains the body/voice using a muscular contract/release cycle . . . because one cannot have release without 'tension', and one cannot have 'tension' without release.
>
> *(McAllister-Viel 2007, pp. 103–4 my insertion)*

In the East, the practitioner does not train the breath, but trains the united body-mind, cultivating *ki* (energy), which then manifests itself as breath. She concludes:

> Concepts are dependent on cultural and discipline-specific concepts of the body. Breath is not a universally understood physiological process able to be reduced to lung function (object-body). Also, breath understood subjectively (subject-body) is equally problematic, in part because the 'lived body' is heavily influenced by the sociocultural understandings of self and the place of body as self within praxis.
>
> *(McAllister-Viel 2009a, p. 173)*

If breath is not universal, then a training which supposes it is, is culturally bound.

McAllister-Viel provides some new directions. However, her research participants and methods came from two specific cultures, both with clear approaches to voice: at the KNUA she integrated Western voice approaches with traditional Korean methods. The first-year students at a European university/conservatoire do not often have such a common base of prior knowledge: they are more diverse in background and not as aware of the world-views that underlie their practice. In addition, employing Eastern methods in the West, methods which were developed in contexts of long-term in-depth study and are based in conceptual models of the self that are difficult for many Western practitioners to grasp, is a challenge, especially within the relatively short duration of university programmes. In this sense, McAllister-Viel's approaches, like many of those which come from cross-cultural voice studies, are perhaps most successful in contexts of professional practice or intensive workshops. I argue that as a basis for university/conservatoire training, we need an approach that is simultaneously wider and more specific to the individual performer.

Bryon is another practitioner who aims to create methods which cross cultural borders. She works on an anatomically exacting level to create impressive results, such as singing upside down. However, her work shows traces of aiming at a singular, Western truth. In Barba's time, he looked for underlying principles that united across culture. Bryon (2012, p. 82), instead of looking to where the principles came from, looks to where they can be applied. If they can be used in a variety of contexts, she argues, that justifies them as useful "skills" for the performer. She asks:

> How far can we go in integrating voice and movement without compromising either on its own terms? Can one sing and dance without compromising the vocal line, pitch, articulation or intonation; without the loss of upper harmonics, resonance or timbre?
>
> *(Bryon 2012, p. 82)*

She assumes that this desire to be able to dance without the movement affecting the song is a universal wish. She writes that many singing methods train singing while in static positions that allow "proper" breathing and that her method allows the performer to take this "architecture of support into dynamic movement" (Bryon 2012, p. 95). I would argue that this desire for a voice unaffected by movement is an aesthetically and culturally specific value. In West African traditions, in contrast, voice and movement have always been connected, hence no need for a method to unite them or contrasting requirements of each discipline. Here, it is the dialogue between voice and soft repeated dance movements and gestural improvisations that help the performer unlock their vocal resonance.[6] Bryon's movement vocabulary, I would suggest, is not universal, but rather closely connected to the trills and extended melodies of the ariettas she uses in training. Moreover, although she argues that these methods are applicable in various aesthetic contexts, this claim is not supported by a wide variety of practical example in either her article (Bryon 2012) or her book *Integrative Performance* (Bryon 2014).[7] Due to the time it takes to develop such principles, as Bryon discovered, it is understandable that the study of these methods in diverse application is deprioritized. She is not alone in this. I would however argue that this lack allows certain culturally bounded value judgements that are embedded in the work to go unexamined.

Let us return to the "broken voice" metaphor. Embedded within it is the assumption that the Western performer's goal is to release blocks in order to return to a "free" voice. This emancipated voice is cleansed of its quirks, and one might even say its uniqueness, its stories. Neutrality is very important to the performer looking to transform themselves into different characters, or to sing arias "as they should be sung". However, for the performer looking to use their own personal experience as the source of stories, this "cleansing" can actually be counter-productive. The individual and imperfect voice is here the effective storyteller. This is a political as well as artistic question. What dramatist Ludvig Uhlbors (personal communication, 2015) writes about the body is even more apt for the voice:

> Theatre schools have been given a task by society: select the people who will represent humanity ... As long as we maintain the idea of neutral bodies, a desire for bodies which are able to become anyone and then return to neutrality, we will exclude large parts of our population from the right to discuss what it means to be a human being.

It is not by mistake that traditions of devising which develop the performer's creative voice do not often promote voice training in a traditional sense.[8] Behind this de-prioritization is a residual distrust of the voice as a mere function of text-based performance. For example, in *Devising Theatre: A Practical and Theoretical Handbook* (Oddey 1994), the voice is mentioned only 14 times in 272 pages. In *Making a Performance: Devising Histories and Contemporary Practices* (Govan et al. 2007), it is mentioned only nine times in 215. Most of these instances reference the idea of the performer's creative rather than physical voice. In UK university drama departments, which often aim to teach a devising performer, voice training is minimal or non-existent. Instead, voice work is found primarily within the walls of conservatories, which cater mostly to text-based theatre; the deviser's voice remains technically weak, the "trained actor" lacks a training for how to craft creative thought into vocal output.

Pedagogical proposals

Voice training consistently remains connected to more traditional modes of performance, and the body is prioritized as the main communicative channel in intercultural work. The existing voice trainings which claim universality are actually culturally or aesthetically limited. I argue for a re-visioning of voice training, which moves it from the realm of supplementary coursework focusing on a limited range of technical skills, to a central subject related closely to physical and conceptual composition courses.

While this research is conducted at NTA, the aim has always been that these methods have wider application. The exercises aim to be deceptively simple "rough and ready" approaches which are easy to understand regardless of previous knowledge, as they are based in concrete instructions/games for the body-voice. They are intended to be void of unexpressed aesthetic-specific "goals" and stripped of mystical language. The hope is that the theoretical writing which accompanies the practice provides the core ideas and that students/artists can adapt exercises and principles as needed. The paradigm shift I am suggesting is, after all, most significant as a mental shift. My practice is one manifestation. However, these ideas can also be explored within an artist's existing practice as a series of attitudinal shifts. Figure 8.1 can serve as an example of the transparency I look to promote, as well as being a checklist against which performers can reconsider their own practice.

Vocal composition

As far as I know, there are no existing trainings which integrate embodied voice work with vocal composition training in a comprehensive way. Within traditional theatre, there is "speech" training, working with, but not creating, text. Outside theatre, there are several composition traditions for the voice: musical composers and music theory, writers and literature, jazz singers and improvisation, etc. Except in the case of folk singers/pop musicians, the one who composes is rarely the

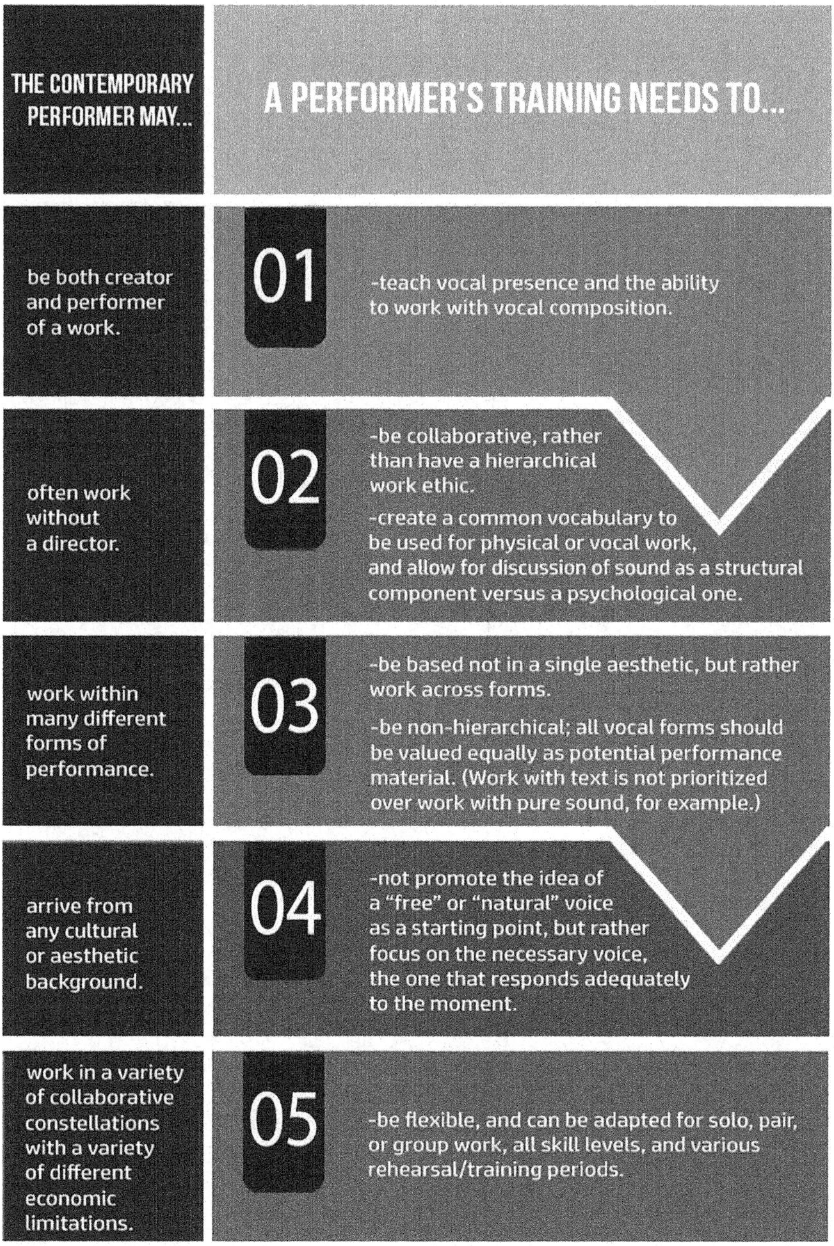

THE CONTEMPORARY PERFORMER MAY...	A PERFORMER'S TRAINING NEEDS TO...	
be both creator and performer of a work.	**01**	-teach vocal presence and the ability to work with vocal composition.
often work without a director.	**02**	-be collaborative, rather than have a hierarchical work ethic. -create a common vocabulary to be used for physical or vocal work, and allow for discussion of sound as a structural component versus a psychological one.
work within many different forms of performance.	**03**	-be based not in a single aesthetic, but rather work across forms. -be non-hierarchical; all vocal forms should be valued equally as potential performance material. (Work with text is not prioritized over work with pure sound, for example.)
arrive from any cultural or aesthetic background.	**04**	-not promote the idea of a "free" or "natural" voice as a starting point, but rather focus on the necessary voice, the one that responds adequately to the moment.
work in a variety of collaborative constellations with a variety of different economic limitations.	**05**	-be flexible, and can be adapted for solo, pair, or group work, all skill levels, and various rehearsal/training periods.

FIGURES 8.1A These graphs originally appeared in my article "Manifesto in Praxis" in *Responsive Listening, Theater Training for Contemporary Spaces*. Eds Karmenlara Ely and Camilla Eeg-Tverbakk, Brooklyn Arts Press, New York, 2015. Published with permission

"VOICE TRAINING SHOULD..."	WHY SHOULD THIS ASSUMPTION BE AVOIDED?
teach vocal skills such as range, resonators, articulation, pitch, blending, etc. as the *only* set of vocal values	-Concepts of skills are culturally bound. -"I saw some highly educated King's College choirboys demonstrate their aural acuity by repeating with their voice complex chromatic phrases played once at the piano. The same talented group was then presented with some "simple" tunes learned by novices in Java [...] The choirboys were confounded by a division of the scale that evaded the concept of both tones and semitones, although found simple by Javanese children of half their age [...] what may seem apt vocally in Cambridge may seem inept in Java." (Barker 3-4)
"warm-up" the voice	This idea artificially isolates one part of the work from the rest and places it in the fictional space of "not being the real thing"; an idea which has limited validity in many performance forms today. Secondly, it often results in performers not committing fully to the warm-ups and doing them automatically.
train one to "breathe correctly"	In most Western voice trainings, the breath is conceptualized and trained as a biological process. Breathing is thus seen as a skill which you can get good at. As McAllister-Viel made clear, this approach is culturally limited.
work to "free" or "open" the voice and promote the concept of a "good" voice	"Free," "open," and "good" are culturally bound concepts. An extreme example is *The Diagnosis and Correction of Vocal Faults*, where McKinney defines "good" and "bad" voices into very narrow technical boxes. This search for *openness/goodness*, which guides many of the leading vocal techniques in a Western context, leads to a great amount of stress put on realigning actors, fixing postural habits, and correcting breathing. This is, however, based on a Western concept of body-mind duality and the metaphor of the voice as machine (McAllister-Viel, "Voicing Culture" 427). Both of these images constrict the creation of voice exercises as well as the range of expressive choices the practitioner perceives as available to them.

FIGURES 8.1B (Continued)

one who performs. Within body-based practices, a range of terms has emerged to describe underlying principles of movement: balance, weight and tempo–rhythm etc., as well as categories of elements, such as walks, runs, movements with the core of the body/limbs, movements which are curved/straight. It is this kind of awareness I am trying to develop for the voice. Judita from my Kent team remarked, "in movement classes, you learn to sense how what you do looks from the outside. What you are trying to get us to do is to understand how to *see* our voice" (personal communication, 2011).

The elements of vocal composition must be taught coupled with an understanding of how they function communicatively, as the elements of a dramaturgy. Zarrilli (2009, p. 113) writes:

> The term "dramaturgy" refers to how the actor's tasks are composed . . . that constitutes the fictive body available for the audience's experience in performance . . . Post-dramatic performances often require the actor to develop a performance score that has multiple dramaturgies.

Regarding the particular challenge of working with the voice, Barker (2004, p. 72) asserts:

> The presence of both speaking and singing on stage . . . provokes a series of . . . questions. . . . the question of the relationship between song and speech . . . the presence of both leads us to necessarily provide an answer as to why one is appropriate at one moment, while the other is more appropriate at the next.

Composing with our voices

Let's turn the discussion to how this approach manifests in the studio. I begin year one with the exercise shown in Figure 8.2.

Exercise: My Voices

You have no single 'true' voice. We all have a variety of truths living within us to which we can give voice. These voices may be your mother tongue, the language you speak daily, a childhood nonsense language, the language of Shakespeare, your telemarketer voice, your stand-up comedian voice or your singing voice, to name a few. Create a short score, maximum 5 minutes, which includes 3 of these. You will perform them – in the dark. The audience will sit, blindfolded in the centre of the space. Make clear choices about how you enter, exit and where you are in space during your score.

FIGURE 8.2   Exercise: My voices

The exercise provides space for unlocking the transformational power of the voice; in the dark, a small Indian woman can sound like a large white male, an African man can be a French woman, or a lion. This is a "getting to know you" exercise, allowing groups to quickly form an aural picture of "who they are". Importantly, this happens from a place of individual agency: performers themselves choose what aspects of their cultural material they wish to share. For the pedagogue, it can speak volumes about where each individual and group are, both anatomically and compositionally. Performed, the structure is an embodied spectrum, allowing individuals' "talents" to be heard, but constantly reminding us that "talent" is content- and aesthetic-specific. I will here discuss three concepts which underpin this work: (1) rethinking the vocal score, (2) flow training and (3) composer's vocabulary.

Rethinking the vocal score

Fixed vocal scores are often privileged as "better" than other forms of vocal output. In the West, improvisational sound work is often only an "exercise": "although you work with the actor, moving through the room with them to free the voice, that actor will then, of course, always be working towards being able to say that speech standing up straight" (Cicely Berry, personal communication, 2011). In singing, a pre-written score's importance is even greater: "the singer's only recourse to 'truth' lies in an understanding of the score. . . . The singer's motto is 'In score we trust'" (Barker 2004, p. 79).

This prioritization is standard in many trainings; the skills they train are focused towards the needs of these limited forms. This is not enough for the contemporary performer. Training someone in listening for Western melodic structures can actually hinder their ability to perform more "free-form" modes of singing, or speaking impromptu to the audience, as they unconsciously judge their vocal output on the values of the fixed form: it should be as eloquent as Shakespeare, as melodic as Vivaldi. Today the performer needs to be able to inhabit vocal acts which are both highly pre-structured and those that are "improvised". I would suggest that both the opera singer and the jazz musician are looking to make communicative acts of great complexity. It is not that the improviser does "simple" things and the opera singer complex things. The difference instead is *when* this complexity is made. The jazz musician's work only looks less difficult if you judge it for what exists prior to the performance. If we examine sonic events *at the performance moment* (the aria does not exist without the singer), it becomes easier to see the variety of vocal forms as points on a spectrum rather than rungs in a hierarchy.

The nature of this form/flow relation determines how the voice communicates (acts) in the moment. It is not a principle such as "energy" which, though seemingly universal, can be tinged with many cultural complications. Instead, looking for this relationship is something which is possible to do across forms. As a pedagogue, it allows you to engage with individuals from different backgrounds without either adapting their "voices" to the aesthetics in which you are skilled or needing to be versed in their cultural tradition. As a performer, being aware of what is the composition of your vocal output helps you communicate with co-devisers about

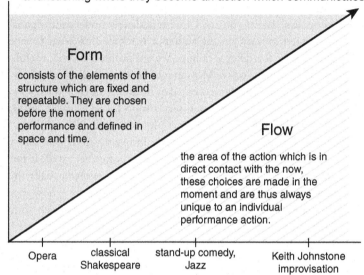

Action = Flow + Form

Without flow, a form is an empty activity, without form, flow is unarticulated and incomprehensible viewed from the outside. As a functioning whole they become an action which communicates.

Form

consists of the elements of the structure which are fixed and repeatable. They are chosen before the moment of performance and defined in space and time.

Flow

the area of the action which is in direct contact with the now, these choices are made in the moment and are thus always unique to an individual performance action.

Opera   classical   stand-up comedy,   Keith Johnstone
              Shakespeare   Jazz   improvisation

FIGURE 8.3   Action = flow + form

how this form might be an element of composition. Most importantly, it is not aiming to unite methods of East and West, but rather asking performers to relate to what is the one thing they necessarily have in common: the NOW of performance.

I suggest that vocal forms include those: (1) based on fixed scores,[9] (2) based on task/game structures[10] and (3) metascores.[11] (These may occur within the fields of sound, text or song). In terms of the performers' embodiment of form in the moment, Shakespeare and opera are actually more similar than Shakespeare and stand-up comedy, even though the latter both work with text. The listening for form one develops in Shakespeare will help one approach opera, while training for listening in jazz can assist one when developing an ability to speak impromptu to the audience.

Any of these vocal forms can be used dramaturgically to create meaning in a variety of ways. How does the exercise allow one to focus on this? There are two significant aspects. Firstly, within each score there is a juxtaposition of three different ways of making meaning; the voice as text cannot remain sovereign. Moreover, the difference of how each "voice" engages with the moment becomes evident: the performer is in a constant negotiation of how much they are "acting" or "listening" within each "voice". Secondly, as pauses are not filled with visual input and performers can move wherever they wish, an awareness of time and space are heightened. What is really "happening" in the voice becomes clear. Using these two parameters (space and time), the performer can analyse the vocal composition (how something is communicated) and avoid the trap of speaking only of the content (what is said).

I divide the spectrum of how sound makes meaning roughly into three categories: informational, associative, instinctive.[12] Within text-based performance (as an example of the first), performers communicate with the text. This can take little time: someone says "I love you" and we immediately understand. Spatially, the "voice" does not need to move, as the audience is focused on what is happening ("moving") in the story the teller is telling. A fixed position is often useful, so the audience can tune in to the voice. Movement can be added when this is established. Functioning *associatively*, the voice makes meaning much as it does in music: it gives associations, provokes memories, sets a mood. For example, in Handel's Halleluiah chorus, the voices repeat the same phrase, building to a glorious frenzy and accomplishing the action of metaphorically lifting the audience. This way of making meaning can take more time and material is often repeated. It functions on principles like vertical layering rather than linear progression. Spatially, shifts can be necessary; the material itself is a repeated phrase so movement – how the sound approaches or retreats – can be the element of the composition which communicates. Movement can also destabilize the sense of listening to a single voice (which is easily associated with the image of a single person/character), and direct the audience instead to listen to the interaction of sound with the room. The last way that sound makes meaning I call *instinctive*. This is when whatever the performer does with the voice communicates viscerally. Here, extreme use of time (very fast or very slow) can be effective, as can similar movements in space. Sound performed very close to the audience provokes, for example, a completely different experience than the same sound performed at a three-metre distance. To sum up, vocal composition is about learning how to direct the ear of the audience; what element of the sonic event should they listen to, the words of text, the echo in the ceiling or the vibration of breath on their arm?

Flow training

Although I promote the idea of performer as composer, I will argue that the way towards form is always through flow; focusing on flow keeps the act of composition as a subset of communication rather than concept. Csikszentmihalyi, a positive psychologist studying happiness, describes flow as a graph.

The channel of flow is represented as a 45-degree diagonal corridor between the increasing axes of skill and challenge. When the challenges of a situation are too great the individual feels anxiety. When the challenges are not great enough for the skills at hand, boredom ensues. To remain in flow, the individual must make choices that challenge them enough to stimulate the development of new skills but not enough to arouse panic. Remaining in flow is a constant re-evaluation of the present moment and a successful assessment of how you, with your specific skills and blocks, can act. Significant when examining this as a model for performer training, is that in it the individual develops new skills not as a result of the goal, "I want to

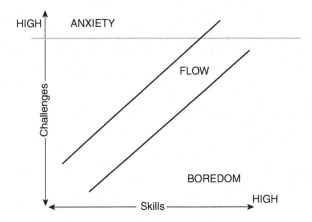

FIGURE 8.4   Flow graph. A diagram representing the relationship between a person's levels of skills in a specific activity, the level of challenges the activity provides and the resultant experience of the person. Specifically, flow is experienced whenever there is a match between skills and challenges; when the challenges are larger than the skills, anxiety is likely to be felt, when the skills are greater than the challenges, boredom is likely

Credit: Mihaly Csikszentmihalyi. Published with permission

learn a new skill", but rather as a *by-product* of being in flow (in the process of making creative material). Moreover, as flow is by necessity individual, a training which begins here, in essence starts from each person's unique voice. Individuals develop a unique skill set which is directly related to their creative process; how they use the voice is directly related to what they want to say artistically.

Csikszentmihalyi (1990, p. 97) describes staying in flow as a detailed process which leads to continuous refinement of the action:

> (a) to set an overall goal and as many subgoals as are realistically feasible (b) to find ways of measuring progress in terms of the goals chosen (c) to keep concentrating on what one is doing, and to keep making finer and finer distinctions in the challenges involved in the activity (d) to develop the skills necessary to interact with the opportunities available (e) to keep raising the stakes if the activity becomes boring.

In my PhD thesis I argue that this description of flow is similar to Stanislavski's *method of physical actions*, simply updated in a non-theatrical context; it is a description of how to ACT-REACT in "real life" (Behrens 2011). Basing an understanding of, "what we do on stage", on the cycle of Action–Reaction can be a valid metaphor across aesthetics. To act and react, to breathe in and out, is as universal a principle as it is possible to find. Working on intercultural material not as fixed aesthetic "things", but rather as *a cycle of actions and reactions in a NOW*, can be a functional and freeing model which creates a common ground for performers from various cultures. As Merlin writes, in a world of multiplicity the Action–Reaction cycle can be a universal translator, helping us decipher performances in many languages, without appropriating them, but simply reading the action underneath.

> [W]hen it comes to TRUTH, what we're really looking for is a *context* for what we're seeing, some rules which determine our expectations, some kind of LOGIC AND COHERENCE ... the key to this sense of TRUTH is the *ongoing sequence* of Action – Reaction.
>
> *(Merlin 2007, p. 114; my italics)*

Composer's terminology

It is useful to have a compositional language for the whole performer, rather than one for body, another for voice. Viewpoints, a training methodology originated by Mary Overlie and developed by director Anne Bogart, has become widely applied over the past 20 years, proving themselves one of the easiest to use and most democratic systems available in the field of actor training.[13] Significantly, they also provide a terminology for both the flow aspect of the performance event (kinaesthetic response) and the form (the other Viewpoints), and exercises for how these two pieces combine in order to communicate. Bogart gives kinaesthetic response equal weight with the others, but I contend that she actually trains it *within* them; I read Viewpoints as an exploration of impulse (kinaesthetic response) within Space and Time. Traditionally, voice training has occurred in small rooms with little consideration of where the performance will take place. One could say that the voice is trained from the centre of the performer to the level of their lips. Interestingly, the "new" ways that the voice is used, in site-specific work for example, are greatly dependent on an interaction with space; the voice as it moves from the lips towards the audience/room. Viewpoints help the performer speak about the structure of sound in space, rather than structure simply as words and notes. Although not exhaustive, Viewpoints can serve as a starting point for performers to talk about vocal composition.

Composing from pre-existing material

Two main modes of work for the contemporary performer are devising from nothing/theme/idea (as explored in the previous exercise) and the adaptation of existing material. In year two, I introduce how to read form (play text) and hear flow (action – reaction). I begin from Chekhov, and Stanislavski's *method of physical actions* (see Figure 8.5). Stanislavski wrote that the words of the text are the outer expressions of inner actions. In his rehearsal method Active Analysis, his actors began without saying the text. They worked with their own words and eventually came to the original text through rehearsal (Merlin 2007, p. 196). This idea of returning to what is underneath the text is highly functional for the intercultural performer. It means working "before" language – on the level of impulse. The performers begin from the need to communicate and therefrom find the vocal forms which

Exercise: exploding Chekhov

Divide the scene into bits.

> 'A bit is simply a piece of text lasting anything from about six lines to maybe a page. A typical 3-page piece of dialogue may consist of between two and five BITS of action.' (Merlin 2007:71)

Find out what happens in each bit and what you want in the scene.

Together, the partners find a spatial relationship for each bit. Individually, they create a repeatable sound which is the essence of what their character is/wants in each bit.

Improvise the scene using only the sound and relationship. Note: neither sound nor position in space are frozen statues, they can and will mutate. It is through this negotiation of sound in space that the performers communicate to each other.

Improvise the scene again adding 1 line of text to each bit. (As the sound, the word can be used at will, repeated, twisted, deconstructed etc).

Improvise the scene adding a larger piece of text.

Improvise the scene with all the original text and the spatial relationship.

Improvise the scene choosing yourself whether to work with sound or text or some hybrid.

Continue to improvise, searching for a dramaturgy that is unique to the two performers and makes clear choices about what you are looking to communicate with the scene. Note: it does not have to communicate the events of the original scene.

FIGURE 8.5   Exercise: exploding Chekhov

communicate to their partner and eventually the audience; this is composing from the starting point of action, not concept. In my exercise, beginning from sound allows the performers to start on a kind of shared territory, and allows them to decide together the level of inclusion of language and/or song as fits the evolving scene, rather than text (in the dominant language) being added to explain movement, or illustrative movement being added to explain dialogue spoken in a minority language. This exercise should be workshopped over several weeks.[14]

"Centring" is physical, cultural, dynamic

Concepts of breath are diverse from culture to culture. However, modern voice methods continue to speak of "returning to the breath" as an act which centres one in some kind of pre-expressive place of pure impulse. The air one draws in is never described – it is "just air"; neutral. Yet it is not. The air is full of the culture, even temperature, of the current moment and it is the source of impulse for action. Most specifically, the air is full of what just happened. As Merlin says, this is how the audience will hear what happens next – based on its relationship with the event before. Instead of training voice in a "neutral" studio, outside of space and time, many cultures have this idea of the voice being born from something specific in the world around it. Natalka Polyvynka, a Ukrainian singer, speaks about how she takes the first note of song from other sounds occurring around her where she sings; her pitch and tone are in relation to the stream and the birds. Grotowski (1997, p. 297) understood this approach within a theatrical context:

> there is also a jet plane passing over the work building. And you, with your song, your melody, you are not alone . . . The sound of the engine is there. If you sing as if it is not, that means that you are not in harmony. You must find a sonic equilibrium with the jet plane and, against everything, anyway keep well your melody.

Slowly, this awareness of how "loaded" our actions and each moment of performance are, is becoming more common in a post-dramatic reality. Zarrilli (2002, p. 3) asserts:

> Every time an actor performs, he or she implicitly enacts a "theory" of acting – a set of assumptions about the conventions and style which guide his or her performance, the structure of actions which he or she performs, the shape that those actions take (as a character, role, or sequence of actions as in some performance art), and the relationship to the audience.

He goes further to suggest that a change in "theory" alters the very "nature of the self" and that different training models are created to help the "process of actualizing a particular mode of embodiment or inhabitation of action within an aesthetic form" (Zarrilli 2009, p. 41). In different aesthetics, and even more in different cultural forms, the inner world of the performer is closely connected to an outer world: the inner air is in relation to the outer air. Centring is thus a process of relating the inner part of the voice event to the outer in both a physical and associative sense. Bryon speaks of dynamic alignment being physical, how to keep the breath free within a moving body. I take it one step further to suggest that it includes a conscious awareness and choice of how you relate to the space (physical, conceptual, political, spiritual) around you: for the performer who is also composer, flexibility and hence freedom of the voice requires agility of the conscious mind as an integrated part of the instinctive body-voice.

Action-Reaction

When it comes to composing, one common approach is that the composing is a brain task which takes place "at the table" and is then explored "on the floor".

I propose a version of Stanislavski's Action–Reaction cycle updated by Merlin (2007, p. 92), as a tool that helps the performer be both the embodier and composer at the same time; an action linked on the level of breath (Figure 8.6).[15]

Many voice methods train the performer to respond instinctively with voice. This is often described as body-mind integration or psychophysicality. This is an important aspect of the work and all that is needed when the next ACTION (i.e. the words the performer will say), is predetermined – the performer's relation to the moment needs only to help them choose how to shape the words, not what the words are. For the composing performer, the fact that the moment of REAC-TION is made up of two parts (body and mind) has significance. This moment of the mind is the moment in which the performer is composer. During the in-breath and out-breath, the performer *must be* the embodier, the one who does, with full belief in what they do – it is a moment "inside" a single culture of performance. The moment of the mind, however, is the moment of choice, the moment when the performer decides to sing instead of speak the next line, or to look to the audience silently. This happens in the moment of suspension between one breath and the next. Like a pendulum which is difficult to push off-course during the down-swing but easily diverted to a new path when it is at the apex, this is the moment of release and listening in which a gentle thought can redirect an action.[16] This is

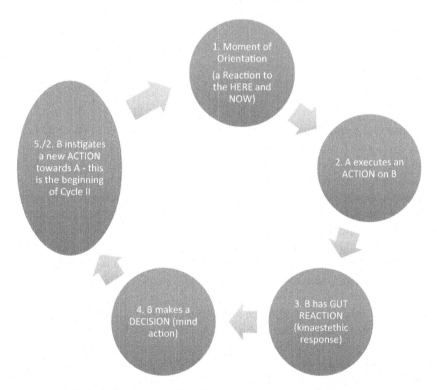

FIGURE 8.6 Action–Reaction cycle

the moment which most voice trainings do not train and the moment my training focuses on integrating.

In order for the brain to get fresh oxygen so as to create a new direction of work, the performer needs to widen their awareness (in this moment of suspension), to increase the field within which they search for impulse. To understand this as an image, I have updated Stanislavski's metaphor of Circles of Attention (1937), a spotlight which can widen to include the whole room, or narrow to include only a hand. In a Stanislavskian world, this circle does not cross the footlights and includes the inner imaginary world the performer has created through rehearsal. Widening these circles to include various inner realities and outwards into the metatheatrical space of interaction with the audience and performance site, these renamed "Circles of Awareness" can allow the performer to visualize the various "worlds" they inhabit and the relationship of these worlds to each other. In this way, by widening and narrowing their awareness and choosing "what air to breathe", the performer enters into different worlds in which to perform. These "worlds" take different amounts of time to manifest for the audience, and they do not disappear the minute the performer stops to focus on them. Rather, they become the NOW into which the next action of performance is born. This exercise promotes the idea that "saying something" is not just about figuring out what to say, but rather finding out how to create the world in which that "saying" resonates: it acknowledges the role of context/culture in how a "signifier" and "signified" make meaning. It challenges performers to create dramaturgies that mindfully embrace the culture of each moment and consciously open the audience's awareness of and journey through, different "worlds".

Conclusion

For the voice to fulfil its potential as dramaturgical force and become a mode of expression which can develop new trends, shifts are needed. Voice training must be re-envisioned: composition work should accompany traditional voice classes, most beneficially within a single course. The studio must be understood as a culturally charged space rather than one of neutrality. Student-driven practice rather than top-down learning must be implemented. Exercises need to be introduced which allow different aesthetics and voices from different cultures to live alongside each other. The metaphor of action – reaction, as described in Csikszentmihalyi's flow research, can be a functional and culture-flexible vocabulary from which to build and listen to voice work. Research on psychophysicality has made clear how linking body and mind can enhance the performer's ability to embody material. In order for the performer to be both embodier and composer of work, what really needs to be integrated is the conscious mind with all of its cultural histories and ability to structure. Listening must be an act which includes both. This integration must occur on the level of breath. When this is successful, the voice can reach beyond the body, telling stories with a range of subtlety that only comes from the voice's nature as vibrating air, which has the potential to "touch" us in a way nothing else can. Combining this sensual power with an ability to compose, the range of stories which the performer can tell and where they can reach is significant.

> In the twenty-first century we have the entire panoply of methods and sounds available to us . . . Today we have a chance . . . to be in charge of how our music is to be created, how we communicate it to other people. We can experience the liberating value of being at the origin of our creative acts.
>
> *(Nachmanovitch 2005)*

Notes

1 The initial phase was conducted at the University of Kent during my PhD studies. Some main ideas are outlined in the book *Responsive Listening: Theater Training for Contemporary Spaces* (Eeg-Tverbakk and Ely 2015).
2 There are an equal number of "Directed projects", in which guest artists function as directors/concept developers.
3 One of the other voice teachers has a curriculum based on Western methods focused towards text-based theatre. The other pedagogue is a classically trained singer who also has worked with song heritages from indigenous peoples. My work concerns both what is normally called "voice work" and vocal composition.
4 Kristin Linklater's *Freeing the Natural Voice* (1976) is an iconic example of this notion that the voice needs to be "set free" from blocks.
5 McAllister-Viel (2009a, p. 174) quotes Roger Ames's definition of polarity: "I want to claim that mind and body are polar rather than dualistic concepts, and as such, can only be understood by reference to each other".
6 The Workcenter of Jerzy Grotowski and Thomas Richards, as well as other practitioners in this lineage, are prime examples of this approach within a performance context.
7 While the book does contain more examples than the article, they are all from distinctly Western aesthetics.
8 When I use the word "traditional", I am referring to the tradition of dramatic performance in the West, a tradition which still dominates how theatre is taught within many European institutions.
9 Fixed scores: the sounds which the performer emits have been structured to a high degree before the performance moment. Common examples of this are working with pre-existing text or song. Scat singing in jazz has a lot of technical form to it, but it is not a fixed score, as the sounds and melodies were not set before the performance moment.
10 Tasks and game-structured scores: these are more common in the realm of physical scores. This consists of the performer (pre-performance) deciding on some tasks or structuring principles which determine how they will sound (e.g. to greet all the audience one by one and then to scream until some of them start to cover their ears).
11 Metascores: are largely improvised, based on interaction with the audience and/or autobiographical material. They are "meta" in the sense that they actively point to how they are created out of the "real" of the performance moment.
12 These categories are suggestions, helping the performer to visualize the variety of ways in which meaning-making can occur. Many vocal events are a combination of these.
13 The Viewpoints of Time are: Tempo, Duration, Kinaesthetic Response and Repetition and Space: Architecture, Topography, Spatial Relationship, Shape and Gesture (Bogart and Landau 2005).
14 Within the context of a BA course, I find it relevant to ask the students to take their scene through the experience of saying the complete original text. This step is however not essential and in certain contexts this step could easily be skipped.
15 Merlin makes the distinction that the moment of REACTION is articulated as two smaller actions, that the instinctual reaction and the decision, though infinitely close

together in time, are actually separate actions. My addition is to reassert the importance and complexity of the "Moment of orientation", especially in relation to voice within contemporary performance.

16 This moment is significantly longer in some performance forms than in others.

References

Barba, E. and Savarese, N. (eds.). (2006). *A Dictionary Guide to Theatre Anthropology: The Secret Art of the Performer.* 2nd ed. London: Routledge.

Barker, P. (2004). *Composing for Voice: A Guide for Composers, Singers and Teachers.* New York: Routledge.

Behrens, E. (2011). *Vocal Action: From Training towards Performance.* Thesis (PhD). University of Kent.

Bharucha, R. (1993). *Theatre and the World.* London: Routledge.

Bogart, A. and Landau, T. (2005). *The Viewpoints Book: A Practical Guide to Viewpoints and Composition.* New York: Theater Communications Group.

Bryon, E. (2012). From Walking and Talking to Cartwheels and High Cs: An Examination of Practice-Based Laboratory Work into Physio-Vocal Integration. *Theatre, Dance and Performance Training,* 3(1), 81–98.

Bryon, E. (2014). *Integrative Performance: Practice and Theory for the Interdisciplinary Performer.* Abingdon: Routledge.

Csikszentmihalyi, M. (1990). *FLOW: The Psychology of Optimal Experience.* New York: Harper and Row.

Eeg-Tverbakk, C. and Ely, K. (2015). *Responsive Listening: Theater Training for Contemporary Spaces.* New York: Brooklyn Arts Press.

Gordon, R. (2006). *The Purpose of Playing: Modern Acting Theories in Perspective.* Ann Arbor: University of Michigan Press.

Govan, E., Nicholson, H. and Normington, K. (2007). *Making a Performance: Devising Histories and Contemporary Practices.* London: Routledge.

Grotowski, J. (1997). Tu es le ls de quelqu'un [You Are Someone's Son]. In R. Schechner and L. Wolford, eds., *The Grotowski Sourcebook.* 1st ed. London: Routledge, pp. 294–305.

Keefe, J. and Murray, S. (eds.). (2007). *Physical Theatre – A Critical Introduction.* Abingdon: Routledge.

Linklater, K. (1976). *Freeing the Natural Voice.* New York: Drama Book Publishers.

McAllister-Viel, T. (2007). Speaking with an International Voice? *Contemporary Theatre Review,* 17(1), 97–106.

McAllister-Viel, T. (2009a). (Re)Considering the Role of Breath in Training Actors' Voices: Insights from Dahnjeon Breathing and the Phenomena of Breath. *Theatre Topics,* 19(2), 165–180.

McAllister-Viel, T. (2009b). Voicing Culture: Training Korean Actors' Voices Through the Namdaemun Market Projects. *Modern Drama,* 52(4), 426–448.

Merlin, B. (2007). *The Complete Stanislavski Toolkit.* London: Nick Hern Books.

Nachmanovitch, S. (2005). *'On Teaching Improvisation': A Talk with College and University Conductors.* New York, 24 February, College Band Directors National Association. [online]. Freeplay. Available at: www.freeplay.com [Accessed 21 November 2011].

Oddey, A. (1994). *Devising Theatre: A Practical and Theoretical Handbook.* London: Routledge.

Stanislavski, K. (1937). *An Actor Prepares.* Edited by E. H. Reynolds. London: Methuen.

Zarrilli, P. (2002). *Acting (Re)Considered: A Theoretical and Practical Guide.* London: Routledge.

Zarrilli, P. (2009). *Psychophysical Acting.* London: Routledge.

9

GRASPING THE BIRD'S TAIL[1]

Inspirations and starting points

Christel Weiler

The following chapter ponders the question whether learning and practising Taijiquan is a sensible and useful tool for actors, both in their initial training and later in their professional life.

As its starting point, it takes the personal experience as a performer on stage, as well as a practitioner of Taiji (Yang style) – the former only occasionally and as a laywoman, the latter on a continuous basis for more than 20 years. In addition, the text is inspired by the following remarks, which I heard only recently in one of my Taiji classes:

> In practising Taiji I found everything that I expected to discover as an actor.
> *(JM, former actor, now practising and teaching*
> *Taiji for more than 20 years).*

> In practising Taiji now I discover how little I know about my body.
> *(ML, former actor, retired and beginning with his*
> *Taiji practice at the age of 70).*

Finally, as a theatre scholar, I am also interested in finding out more about and reflecting on this special state of being, which characterizes the process of acting. What does one need to become an actor? What are the challenges and specific demands of this profession? What is transmitted in movement classes? What does it mean to be present, to "think" with the body (to quote Eugenio Barba)? What would be an ideal system for training actors' bodies? Is there anything like that? All these questions have somehow accompanied me in my private life and while teaching at Freie Universität Berlin. It became apparent to me that there is neither a strict border or time for thinking nor for what it means to become/be an actor.

I have encountered these questions in my everyday life, with my own body, my way of moving and teaching, my being in the world and being with other people in and outside the university.

Histories

It was in the late 1970s that I first encountered an intended joining of Taiji and theatre. Frieder Anders, former disciple of Chu King-Hun and currently "master/ head" of Germany's exclusive Taiji Academy, together with a group of enthusiastic students (the author among them) started his Tai Chi Schule (Taiji school) in Frankfurt/Main and at the same time initiated quite an interesting and fascinating experiment: linking Taiji with experimental theatre and thus injecting some fresh stimulus into German independent theatre of those days. The ambitious project tried to combine the physical and mental abilities of a Taiji-player with a creative, but not lest due to its amateurish character, risky psychoanalytic-oriented search for personal "true" stories.[2] Although Anders' career as a Taijiquan master evolved into a track record, the experiment was unfortunately short-lived and brought to an end in 1981. Nevertheless, it has left its traces and sown its seeds, as could be seen in the biographies of its participants.

As far as the knowledge of Taiji in Germany and its spread to actor training in general is concerned, it all started with Zheng Manqing's practice and teachings, which were received already in the 1970s by Petra and Toyo Kobayashi, Christel Proksch and others. Whether Taiji already then made its way into actor training is difficult to determine. To the best of my knowledge, starting with 1980 Taijiquan has been taught for future actors at Berlin's former Hochschule, now Universität der Künste (University of the Arts), by Anna Triebel-Thome, who studied among others with W.C. Chen in New York.

The story of Taijiquan, how it travelled from China to Europe and the US, how it was transported from China, Hong Kong, Taiwan to other parts of the world, how it was transmitted, and how it was interwoven with actor training remains as a whole somehow enigmatic up to this day. There are some clear traces; others appear to be highly obscure. It seems that there is still a lot of research to be done regarding the topic.[3]

After the experiment initiated by Frieder Anders had come to an end and I – now as a theatre scholar – started reflecting on how cultures interweave by means of theatre and performance art, I came across Herbert Blau and his essay "Shadow Boxing: Reflections on the T'Ai Chi Chuan" (Blau 1973). I also learnt that Taijiquan had already been introduced in the US in the 1940s by a dancer named Sophia Delza, and popularized by Zheng Manqing. Accordingly, it could be that Taijiquan was brought into the country either directly by Chinese immigrants or was mediated through visitors to China to theatre people like Herbert Blau and A.C. Scott, Phillip Zarrilli's teacher. Especially these three men saw its value to theatre, in particular to actor training. Blau and Zarrilli have been writing about their practice more or less extensively. It is not accidental that they both are/have been interested in a kind of theatre that leaves psychological realism behind and instead seeks to discover the distinctive features of the art, not least in the body of its protagonists. I will come back to that later in detail. First, I would like to take a closer look at the present German situation.

At present

Although Taijiquan has been popularized in Germany – there exists meanwhile an expanding body of related literature, even a special magazine, which is exclusively dedicated to Taijiquan and Qi Gong – there is hardly any scholarly discourse, especially in what we call "Theaterwissenschaft" or "Tanzwissenschaft", about its use for actor or dancer training.[4] In almost all related publications, one can find a strong emphasis on its constitutional and health benefits, its philosophical aspects and meditational qualities. It is accepted by the general health insurances as a kind of treatment for a variety of indispositions, such as balance problems, spinal and back disorder, tensions, stress symptoms, depressive mood, etc. It is offered in public educational institutions as well as in private schools, people could aspire to a teaching career, strive for different ranks, specialize in practice with weapons like sword or sabre, participate in competitions, etc. In short, it seems that there exists a differentiated field of procedures that make Taijiquan an integrated part of social and cultural life. Most probably, the same applies to Yoga, which has become a lifestyle feature par excellence in Germany today. Although I see some fundamental differences in learning as well as practising the one or the other, it is especially this concept of practice as a kind of lifestyle habitus that should lead to careful consideration. Without any doubt, one has to agree with what Maria Kapsali has explained in detail regarding ideological implications, in which not only theatre making and performances but also actor training operates equally. She is also absolutely right in claiming that Yoga, Taiji and Feldenkrais – to name only a few – could be instrumentalized for everything from individual self-development and self-optimization to consumerism, idealization of specific body images and the exclusion of others, etc. (Kapsali 2013). The same goes for practising mindfulness and all kinds of meditation, which seem to become indispensable components for neo-liberal business-management these days.

However, actors are human beings who live their lives, and on the level of practice and learning it would be of little help for them to consider all these critical objections. In the end nothing would withstand its utilization for various affirmative reasons, functions and claims. Although I see Kapsali's point, I would like to elaborate on the different aspects of this subject and also stress some oppositional features, which make me sympathetic towards the practice of Taijiquan.

With regard to actor training, I am aware of all the subtleties that go along with the exclusive focus on one single body technique in the context of acting schools/ actor training (which could be a lifelong task, even desire). Nevertheless, I am convinced that it is less the technique, the movements, poses and gestures as such, and more their use and way of transmission that renders them ideological. Of course, they correspond to a special concept of the body (less to an image), but they also meet different bodies in different spaces and thus also could lead and contribute to diversity. I would also like to stress the self-reflexive potential, which is inherent, without denying that there could always be an affirmative aspect to it. However, one should not burden these arts and techniques with claims that they would never satisfy. In any case, the practice and use of a martial art or a body technique like Yoga could contribute to unfolding empowerment, refined sensory awareness for others, combative as well as respectful, accepting and supportive qualities – provided that they are taught with the goal of pursuing these aims. Yet the optimal way of teaching and practice would be to leave the outcome and result open to the practitioner's curiosity and capability for lifelong learning.

Before I go into more detail with regard to the possible benefits of practising Taijiquan for actors, I would prefer to take a closer look at how they would actually be judged and seen within their own professional field and what seem to be the demands and requirements that they are subjected to at drama schools.

The 2018 ideal

The annual German Theatertreffen, which takes place every year in May in a variety of Berlin venues, not only presents what are considered to be the top ten German-speaking productions but also includes an award ceremony for the Actor of the Year. In his 2018 elegy[5] for Benny Claessens, actor Fabian Hinrichs – well known for his outstanding performances in René Pollesch productions, among other things – stressed that with Benny Claessens "in the midst of all these alienated, replaceable, not completely socialized servants, mere supporters of necessity" a human being enters the stage, "someone with presence – presence to be experienced as distinctive from alienation [...] tangible in an almost dangerous sense ..." Hinrichs goes on with his praise: "There has been a voice of one's own, a body of one's own and feelings/sensations of one's own. And thinking, thinking of one's own". For Hinrichs, all these qualities – speaking, moving, feeling, thinking and all at the same time – is what makes a great artist/actor. For him, Claessens is a promise, "the promise of a sovereign actor, who could save the theatre by making it a place for alternative worlds, a place which is rich of content because it allows to be worldly innocent" (Hinrichs 2018).

I have quoted Hinrichs at length, as he not only praises Claessens's qualities but at the same time delivers an admittedly personal critical assessment of what it could mean to be an actor these days, as well as expresses his strong desire or even utopian vision for/of a different future theatre, a theatre that would be more than "Prussian barracks, no bad-tempered critical theory, no prison of direction [...] but a window in all these prisons [...] " (Hinrichs 2018). If we take this not as highly idiosyncratic but at least as partially agreed judgement, if we therefore take it seriously, then it would be of less importance whether I share this praise for Claessens or not – what then becomes the crucial question here is: what would an actor need in order to embody these Claessens-qualities on a practical level? How to reach this ideal? How to approach it?

Drama school movement

In all German drama schools – be they private or public institutions – movement classes are an integral part of the respective curriculum. If one takes a closer look, if one wants to find out what kind of concept or philosophy provides the ground and the reason for these classes, one would find hardly anything substantial. For example, a renowned institution Theaterakademie August Everding in Munich offers on its website under the heading "BodyWork" the following details for interested applicants (Theater Akademie 2018):

• Darstellende Bewegung, Fechten, Tanz (descriptive movement, fence, dance)
• Akrobatik (acrobatics)
• Bewegungslehre und Kampfkunst, Bühnenanwendung (kinematics and martial arts, application for stage)
• Individuelle Körperarbeit (individual bodywork)

A bit more precise would be Hochschule für Musik und Theater "Felix Mendelssohn Bartholdy" in Leipzig. The first-year module "Körper und Bewegung I/ Body and Movement I" aims at getting to know one's body and its potential for movement; intensifying perception and awareness of oneself and others; development of new bodily experiences and ways of expression. All this would be achieved by means of "development of basic attitudes, presence, understanding tension and release, coordination of breathing and movement, Tai Chi Chuan, flexibility and energy, coordination and rhythm, stage fight" (HMT-Leipzig 2018). Similar general remarks could be discovered on other websites. Looking upon this with favour one could see it as general openness to a variety of concepts; the actors-to-be are offered different techniques, at some time they could make a choice of their own and probably stay with what they think to be most useful. It admittedly also highlights indirectly the still ongoing focus on psychological approaches, the dominance of work with texts and respective development of characters in the German schools.

From a more critical point of view, one could say that this seeming openness invites consumerism, superficiality and disorientation. For the majority of German drama schools, it seems to be of utmost importance that their students are prepared to meet the market, know a bit of everything, and in the end are willing to do what they are asked to do. Especially two long-term observations, one of them already some years behind, which were published as documentary films, support this assumption to a certain extent.[6]

Coming back to Fabian Hinrichs's complaint, especially his characterization of his colleagues as "alienated", "not completely socialized", one could not help but compare young actors to birds thrown out of their nest prematurely. To stay with this image: what then could be offered by drama schools to enable/empower the actor-to-be to use their wings adequately and playfully in accordance with experience and age? It goes without saying that experience comes with practice and age, and that learning – ideally – never ends. And without any doubt, it would make sense to have a kind of signpost. Maybe a different kind of education would be an option, a different concept of acting-culture, one that – in an admittedly old-fashioned, Humboldtian sense – provides the person with more than skills and information. This would allow the person to conceive of themself as "not complete" in a positive sense, as someone who gets to know themself constantly. It would also mean to conceive of actor training as something that does not only serve the stage but also reaches out beyond, something one could refer to beyond aesthetics, beyond theatrical fashion. And in today's world it would be most desirable to step out of one's confines, to try to find one's place between what seems to be the natural and the unknown. As regards the German educational system, it would also mean widening the horizon and taking the richness of other actor training systems into account. Then Taijiquan would also become more than "slow movement".

Here comes Taijiquan

Of course, this should be taken with some humour. I am far from suggesting that practising Taijiquan would solve all problems; it should not be burdened with such a heavy load. I would rather like to take it as one example, one possibility to think through a different model of intercultural actor training that, on the one hand, supports the actor-to-be on various levels and, on the other hand, could be a signpost for their life in general, i.e. something that keeps its value after graduating from drama school. Becoming/being an actor should not be understood as something that draws to a close once drama school has ended. It could rather be seen as a lifelong, constantly dynamic process, as an ongoing change and transformation that embraces the person as a whole. Not only are actors' bodies aging, they are also going to meet a variety of environments in the course of their career, different spaces, theatrical "fashions", multiple demands and challenges by colleagues and directors. Last, but not least: being an actor neither starts on-stage nor stops once the performance has come to an end. If we take into account that training systems are meant to develop and improve "the actor's expressive and imaginative freedom through the discipline of physical structure" (Hodge 2000, p. 4), or, as Phillip Zarrilli writes, to "attune one's body-mind, to open one's sensory awareness, to learn how to be attentive, focused and able to concentrate, etc." (Zarrilli 2016), then it seems to be necessary to demand of a training system to operate on three levels: on the level of practice, ethos and spirituality. Then it would not only be pre- but also post-performatively in operation. In the best sense, it would be nourishing for the actor's life as such, not only for their profession. There would not be a split between individual life and life as an actor.[7] Creativity, expressive and imaginative freedom, sensory awareness, all these demanded qualities are less actor- or theatre-bound, but rather connected to living a full and rich life. When Fabian Hinrichs talks about "alienation", not being "completely socialized", when young actors complain about being out of touch with reality, they refer to this lack of connectedness, this void. Seen from that perspective, actor training needs to shift its focus from preparing for the stage and performance exclusively to providing something that also helps in creating a distance to the very field. It could then be an "open window", to quote Fabian Hinrichs once more.

In which way Taijiquan (or any other similar system) might be a possible aid or source for actor training will be outlined below.

Nourishing life

As mentioned above, to include Taijiquan[8] with all its richness in an actor training system would mean for it to operate on three levels: the practical, the ethical and the spiritual.

Starting with the practical, i.e. learning the choreography, the various movements, steps, poses, etc. serves not primarily in fulfilling a formal task. Serious Taijiquan players stress that the outer appearance of the form is only one part of the business; the other part is using one's mind and sensory awareness to follow certain basic principles and reach out in order to be precise, to know where and how to find oneself in space, to coordinate one's steps and arm movements, upper and lower body, to know what makes the difference between full and empty, to raise the head, relax the tendons, joints, shoulders and elbows – to name only a few.[9] This way one learns to know one's body. Additionally, inner qualities are required and trained accordingly: to become calm, be alert, empty one's mind, be focused, raise the spirit, and give oneself completely to practice. At the same time, one should not overstrain oneself, but find an appropriate measure in spending effort and energy. This does not mean being lazy and less committed; it means treating one's body kindly and leaving a space to meet obstacles carefully.[10]

All in all, one could say: you are engaged in creating a new or additional habit.[11] Or, to quote the German Taijiquan pioneer Christel Proksch, it becomes a "Lebensmuster", a design for life (Proksch 2009, p. 191).

As far as breathing is concerned, there are different opinions. Practice of Yang-style Taijiquan, for example, does not focus on breathing, but starts from the assumption that it will deepen in the course of training without paying too much attention to it. Breathing will develop naturally, as long as you focus on your lower abdomen – one of the three energy centres that the Daoists call *Dantian*. Last but not least: the slowness of the movements suits the purpose of training. It is of course possible to perform Taijiquan at different rates, but it makes more sense to start with a slow and moderate pace. It allows the practitioner to pay more attention to the quality of performance as described above. This also goes for practice with weapons (sword, sabre, fan, stick) and exercises with partners. On the level of performance, you also learn how all these movements, steps, etc., could function once they are conceived as strategies and applied in a fight. Taijiquan – this must not be forgotten – is a martial art, or at least it could be practised as such and thus also implies the use and handling of more than soft vital energies. Seen from the right perspective, one could say that it shows and leads to a respectful and controlled use of one's aggressive and violent forces. This also means to feel the flow of one's vital energy/energies (in a broad sense what is called "*qi*"), to get an understanding about their flow, their different ways of coming up and how to make use of them. In particular, the practices with sword and sabre contribute to the initial understanding of what this could mean.

One must of course bear in mind that taking these basic steps and their further refinement does not happen without a teacher. Not only should one keep in mind that body techniques are relational techniques – they include a relation to oneself as well as a relation to other bodies – they are also taught and transmitted by bodies; they are taught with the use of words, on the basis of knowledge, with a special conduct. As Grotowski already detected, "the attitude with which (these techniques) are discovered, researched and performed, that is of primary significance" (Hodge 2000, p. 195). There is no teaching, learning, discovering without an implicit ethical dimension.

The ethical dimension of training and practising Taijiquan not only becomes evident in the above-mentioned relationships but also very clearly in exercises with partners, so-called Push Hands or *Tuishou*. The prime concern of respective exercises would not be to learn the variety of movements, but to "listen to the energy" of your opponent. This means that the quality of a relationship would be at stake. The experience might relate to touch, resistance, pressure, togetherness, following, losing touch, too much pressure, absent-mindedness, wanting the other to be different, to behave in a different manner, so that you or your partner would feel more comfortable. It also might relate to not knowing anymore who started and who followed, but being together in something happening that does not function according to mechanisms of cause and effect. To train with various partners also means to clearly feel that people are different, that one could "listen" to a broad range of energies and thus see oneself, one's own energy, as only one possibility among many. What you learn about others, your partners may find out about you. There is no need to feel superior, better, more advanced; it is just that people are different and this includes everybody. Thus, not to judge is of prime importance, and recrimination becomes difficult. That this would be something that goes against narcissism, and also possibly against the politics of drama schools seems to be obvious. But whenever it comes to self-reflexivity, it might be a strong tool. Correspondingly, it is there where one learns to be with the other and at the same time present, i.e. in a self-reflexive state of being in the truest sense of the word. To engage with others in the context of Taijiquan practice demands flexibility, softness. Only then could what Brecht formulated in his poem "Taoteking" become true: that in the long run "the softness of water would overcome the toughness of the stone". He added: "you understand: the hard would be defeated".

As already mentioned above, acting – like learning and teaching – always bears on a special attitude or composure. Camilleri – with a reference to Grotowski – calls it "something that occurs beyond technique: a quality in the actor's work that is unplanned and which occurs beyond or despite intentionality and voluntary action" (Camilleri 2016, p. 46). It could not only be related to the energy of the other, which in practising *Tuishou* should be listened to. It applies to the same extent to the teacher. It is highly dependent on "what techniques the teacher uses, how each teacher engages the student and approaches the specific process of transmission in a specific context" (Zarrilli 2015, p. 123). It all should be based at least on mutual respect and responsibility.[12]

Regarding the spiritual dimension of training and practice, this is quite a difficult topic to discuss. One could read in the *Oxford Research Encyclopedia of Religion* that when it comes to spirituality in the arts, there are potentially "as many interpretations of spirituality as there are viewers", and that it "is a term that is often used vaguely to refer to an attitude or approach toward life that involves a search for meaning" (Arya 2016.). In a very broad secular sense, spirituality could mean, accordingly, to see oneself as part of something more extensive, as part of what obviously could be experienced but not be proved, dealing with questions that are inevitable, but would never be answered satisfactorily, such as: why are we here on earth? What would be the deeper meaning of being alive? What is the secret of charisma/radiation? And so on. Quite a number of Taijiquan practitioners, and without doubt many artists, refer to the realm of spirituality as something that is constitutive for what they do, but they rarely work out carefully what it means in detail. It certainly seems to be less a question of belief than a vehicle for searching, for questioning and what might be called self-cultivation, as it does not go without a special kind of practice, without intended self-conduct, or at least serious attempts to honestly perform certain qualities.

Taijiquan pioneer Gerda Geddes made a comment in an interview that she always "was more concerned with a kind of spiritual connection through [. . .] Tai Chi", and that it has always been her strong point of interest (Taiji Forum 2018). Frank Camilleri, when referring to the work of Grotowski, mentions that there could be an unplanned quality in the actor's work, "which occurs beyond or despite intentionality and voluntary action" (Camilleri 2016, p. 46). In the course of his essay, and again in connection with what Grotowski understood as "grace", he points to the dual quality of habits, with ease, facility and power on the one hand, and repetition on the other. The grace of movement, for instance, could be seen as resulting from endless repetition – the latter understood as surrendering, as devotion to practice and self-cultivation at the same time. The English translation of Stanislavski's seminal book says: "preparation of an actor", while in German it says: "Arbeit an sich selbst". It is largely this aspect of Arbeit an sich selbst/self-cultivation, which would make a strong point in actor training. Because of that, I would like to look at actor training and the practice of Taijiquan in more detail, and ask where the hints and traces of the art's spiritual dimension could be.

Without any doubt, Taijiquan needs commitment, a devotion to continuous practice, the willingness to sacrifice time, to do all simultaneously would be gratuitous. Neither health, nor beauty, nor grace would be guaranteed – nevertheless, repetition and the need for refinement are to be maintained. It would not even be visible on-stage, but rather shown as a hidden quality. Experienced Taijiquan players agree with the canonical literature when they express that in the end one should forget the form, the outer appearance, and instead freely move according to the underlying principles. Then, after endless moments of research, you would have reached the state of Kleist's bear, the grace of the animal (Kleist 2007). Practising then would be nothing but a vehicle with which one could reach a point of 'being-moved' rather than move intentionally. It would show that one's vital energy, one's liveliness and creativity, are not tied to special appearances, but are things that could be nourished in different ways in order to fully develop.

It is quite evident that this does not correspond to the current code of practice in drama schools, particularly not with regard to the requested usability of skills. What could be strengthened, however, might be a habit that provides a kind of inner freedom or independence from arbitrary demands. Alienation then could become a foreign word but unity a desired destination.

In drama schools, a warmer welcome of course could be given to the meditational qualities of Taijiquan practice, the quiet, the empty mind – this would correspond to the actual overall stress on mindfulness and the ideologies that come along with it.

Finally, practising Taijiquan means to give oneself up to a never-ending process of learning, searching and transformation. Insight and intuition could only be reached by doing, by acting in the double sense of the word; they would neither be the result of rational knowledge nor correspond to skills or tricks. What would be embodied or rather revealed, what would reappear, is one's animal spirits as they emerge and vanish.

In conclusion

All this may sound quite idealistic and limited at the same time – not only with regard to a possible component of actor training, but also with regard to the practice of Taijiquan itself. I am quite aware that no single system could satisfy all the requirements of actor training, that no single system could be applicable to all kinds of theatre and, above all, be suitable to all kinds of students. I agree that it is necessary to learn something about breathing, how to use one's voice, how to dance, how to move in more exaggerated ways, how to be present, etc. What I nevertheless have tried to think through here is how at least one element of an educational system could contribute to a different kind of subject-formation, how practising Taijiquan might contribute to a kind of self-cultivation that opens a window – to stay with Fabian Hinrichs's utopian wish.

Notes

1 "Grasping the bird's tail" is the name for a very complex sequence of movements in Taijiquan. Although it has to be performed at the beginning of the course, it is difficult to master.
2 Early Taiji pioneer Gerda Geddes also tried to combine psychoanalysis and movement (see Taiji Forum 2018).
3 About the history and dissemination of Taijiquan in the US, see Frank 2003.
4 Which is different from the US, UK and only recently also Romania; see Lese 2014.
5 All translations from German to English by Christel Weiler.

6 See *Die Spielwütigen* 2004; 13 *Schauspielschüler* 2018.
7 See also Kapsali 2014.
8 There are different styles to be distinguished: e.g. Yang, Chen, Wu, Wu Hao, Sun. As a rule, they are so-called "family-styles", and thus differ slightly from each other with regard to their appearance.
9 See for example Tai Chi For Health 2018; or Yang Family Tai Chi Chuan 2018.
10 Compare Wayne and Fuerst 2018.
11 The issue of habit is discussed at length in Camilleri 2016.
12 See also Camilleri 2009.

References

13 Schauspielschüler. (2018). Germany: Karoline Wirth.

Arya, R. (2016). Spirituality and Contemporary Art. *Oxford Research Encyclopedia of Religion.* [online]. doi:10.1093/acrefore/9780199340378.013.209 [Accessed 24 September 2018].

Blau, H. (1973). Shadow Boxing: Reflections on the T'Ai Chi Chuan. In J. Schevill, ed., *Break Out: In Search of New Theatical Environments.* Chicago: Swallow Press, pp. 360–362.

Camilleri, F. (2009). Of Pounds of Flesh and Trojan Horses: Performer Training in the Twenty-First Century. *Performance Research*, 14(2), 26–34. doi:10.1080/13528160903319232.

Camilleri, F. (2016). On Habit and Performer Training. *Theatre, Dance and Performance Training*, 9(1), 36–52. doi:10.1080/19443927.2017.1390494.

Die Spielwütigen. (2004). Germany: Andreas Veiel.

Frank, A. D. (2003). *Taijiquan and the Search for the Little Old Chinese Man: Ritualizing Race Through Martial Arts.* (PhD). The University of Texas at Austin. Available at: http://citeseerx. ist.psu.edu/viewdoc/download?doi=10.1.1.135.5392&rep=rep1&type=pdf [Accessed 29 August 2018].

Hinrichs, F. (2018). *Die Kunst sitzt im Kerker, Tagesspiegel.* [online]. Available at: www.tagesspiegel. de/kultur/laudatio-auf-benny-claessens-die-kunst-sitzt-im-kerker/22586896.html [Accessed 2 October 2018].

HMT-Leipzig. (2018). *Modulordnung.* [online]. Available at: www.hmt-leipzig.de/home/ fachrichtungen/schauspielinstitut-hans-otto/studiendokumente_schauspiel/fileac- cess_item_939192/view/mo/ma_sp_mo_160707.pdfwww.hmt-leipzig.de/home/ fachrichtungen/schauspielinstitut-hans-otto/studiendokumente_schauspiel/fileaccess_ item_939192/view/mo/ma_sp_mo_160707.pdf [Accessed 24 September 2018].

Hodge, A. (2000). *Twentieth Century Actor Training.* London: Routledge.

Kapsali, M. (2013). Rethinking Actor Training: Training Body, Mind and . . . Ideological Awareness. *Theatre, Dance and Performance Training*, 4(1), 73–86. doi:10.1080/19443927. 2012.719834.

Kapsali, M. (2014). Psychophysical Disciplines and the Development of Reflexivity. *Theatre, Dance and Performance Training*, 5(2), 157–168. doi:10.1080/19443927.2014.914968.

Kleist, H. (2007). *Über das Marionettentheater.* Frankfurt: Wilfried Nold.

Lese, A. (2014). The Contribution of Biomechanics and of Tai Chi Exercises to the Psycho- logical and Development of Training Actors. *Procedia – Social and Behavioral Sciences*, 149, 495–502. [online]. Available at: https://ac.els-cdn.com/S1877042814050101/1-s2.0- S1877042814050101-main.pdf?_tid=dd93480e-0dde-4097-a4a3-d658ff38ada7&acdn at=1537796293_452aca5cb3a666d2443ce5cf384b0d03 [Accessed 24 September 2018].

Proksch, C. (2009). *Die Kunst der natürlichen Bewegung.* Schiedlberg: Bacopa.

Tai Chi for Health. (2018). *The 10 Essential Principles of Tai Chi Practice.* [online]. Available at: www.taichiforhealth.net/10-essential-principles/ [Accessed 17 September 2018].

Taiji Forum. (2018). *Tai Chi Interview – Gerda Geddes.* [online]. Available at: https://taiji-forum.com/tai-chi-taiji/tai-chi-interviews/gerda-geddes [Accessed 29 August 2018].

Theater Akademie August Everding. (2018). *Bachelor of Arts.* [online]. Available at: www.theaterakademie.de/studium/ausbildungskonzept.html [Accessed 24 September 2018].

Wayne, P. and Fuerst, M. L. (2018). Tai Chi's Synergy with Sports and Creative Arts Such as Dance, Music, Painting and Writing. *TaiChiChuanBerkley.* [online]. Available at: https://taichichuanberkeley.com/tai-chi-synergy-sports-creative-arts-dance-music-painting-writing/ [Accessed 24 September 2018].

Yang Family Tai Chi Chuan. (2018). *10 Essential of Tai Chi Chuan.* [online]. Available at: https://yangfamilytaichi.com/documents/wallpapers/wp-10-essential-1600x1200.jpg [Accessed 17 September 2018].

Zarrilli, P. (2002). 'On the edge of a breath, looking': Cultivating the Actor's Bodymind Through Asian Martial/Meditation Arts. In P. Zarrilli, ed., *Acting (Re)Considered.* London: Routledge, pp. 181–199.

Zarrilli, P. (2009). *Psychophysical Acting: An Intercultural Approach After Stanislawski.* London: Routledge.

Zarrilli, P. (2015). 'Inner movement' Between Practices of Meditation, Martial Arts, and Acting: A Focused Examination of Affect, Feeling, Sensing, and Sensory Attunement. In M. Bull and J. P. Pitchell, eds., *Ritual, Performance, and the Senses.* London: Bloomsbury, pp. 121–136.

Zarrilli, P. (2016). Training. *Phillip Zarrilli.* [online]. Available at: https://phillipzarrilli.com/training/2017/5/1/pre-performative-psychophysical-training-for-performers-through-asian-martial-arts-and-yoga [Accessed 24 September 2018].

10

EMBODYING IMAGINATION

Butoh and performer training

Frances Barbe

Introduction

Butoh and *butoh*-based processes inform and expand how we understand the way in which the performer works with imagination and embodiment. The process of embodying imagination is something all performers do to some extent. Actors, dancers, singers, performance artists might all be called upon to embody an idea, thought, image or emotion by manifesting it in physical form. The focus here is how to cultivate or train this capacity for embodying imagination using *butoh*-based approaches. A series of *butoh*-based exercises and their rationales will be articulated here as an exploration of embodying imagination in performer training. The exercises are organized into three sections: 1) training through **distillation** and the use of stillness; 2) training **receptivity** (not moving, but *being-moved*); and 3) training for **transformation** (embodiment of *butoh-fu* imagery).

The practice is framed by a discussion of the language of the training studio with particular attention to challenging limiting binaries. Language can liberate or inhibit performers. Frank Camilleri (after Matthews) asserts that the battle over body-mind discourse has been won and we are enjoying "the spoils" and therefore it is time to "ventilate a new set of questions" (Matthews 2011 as cited in Camilleri 2013, p. 37) in order to "surpass the embedded dichotomy in compound[s] . . . such as 'bodymind' and 'psychophysical' whose linguistic morphology reinforces the discursive split they seek to avoid" (Camilleri 2013, p. 31). How we *talk* about performance impacts how we *think* about and, in turn, how we *do* performance. The intention here is to consider the language of performance practice so as to provide performers with precise language that is expansive not reductive. Part of this involves interrogating the way acting approaches have been categorized as either outside-in or inside-out, and how *butoh* is discussed in terms of a tension between inside feeling and outer form. The project discusses alternatives to such binaries that can perpetuate an opposition between mind *over* body, inside versus outside, and intellect versus emotion.

The intercultural performer training approach outlined here was developed through ongoing dialogue with Japanese *butoh* and *butoh* artists over twenty years (from 1992 to the present) in Australia, Japan, the UK and Germany. It is inherently intercultural, arising as it does from a conversation between Japanese and European artists and approaches. It is part of ongoing research into intercultural performer training in the Bachelor of Performing Arts (BPA) course at the Western Australian Academy of Performing Arts (WAAPA) in Perth where a *butoh*-based approach complements Euro-American approaches to training to provide an international perspective on performance. The intention here is to contribute to knowledge in performer training around embodying imagination in the context of the diverse performance challenges facing contemporary performers from movement-based performance to text-based acting. Most training institutions in Australia, the UK and the US still prioritize a Euro-American view of performance, with a few exceptions. The inclusion of approaches like *butoh* at conservatoires like WAAPA helps to ensure a more international and intercultural outlook on training to prepare performers for a dynamic landscape of performance. This chapter focuses on Japanese *butoh's* unique potential to contribute to international performance practice outside of Japan and outside of *butoh*.

There is a well-known anecdote about "form" and "spirit" in *butoh* dance that was discussed in numerous *butoh* workhops I attended. Apparently Hijikata said "find the form and the spirit will come", whereas Ohno said "follow the spirit, and the form will take care of itself". While difficult to trace to an origin, it is significant and useful and therefore continues to be discussed in *butoh* rehearsal rooms. The apparent contradiction focuses the performer's attention on the pathway between spirit and form, rather than either of them as the confirmed origin of *butoh*. Similarly, acting approaches have been categorized as either inside-out, epitomized by Konstantin Stanislavski, or outside-in, epitomized by the work of Jacques Lecoq or *Commedia dell'arte*. While such categories have been useful, this study challenges such binaries that set the internal aspects of performance (feeling, psychology, imagination) in opposition to the external aspects (form, action, shape).

> Dualistic concepts of mind/body, self/character, reason/emotion, and knowledge/imagination have led to a situation in which approaches to acting are characterized as either physical or psychological.
>
> *(Kemp 2010, p. 186)*

It will be argued here that *butoh* is neither an "outside-in" approach prioritizing form, nor an "inside-out" approach prioritizing internal psychological work. *Butoh* provides a unique opportunity to experiment with what it means to embody imagination and how it is not limited to flowing in one direction or another. Something far more complex and interesting is at work. It is necessary to move beyond the idea of a single pathway between inside and outside, spirit and form or even beyond the idea of a two-way street between these two. A more complex, multifaceted model for thinking about what the performer does is required and with that a more expansive language is needed to talk about the practice of embodying imagination.

In training I experiment with different words and instructions and note the effect of my choice of words on individuals and groups I work with. Words can be subjective so that what liberates one performer can confuse and immobilize another. This conundrum keeps me alert to each individual I encounter. New vocabulary arises as I seek to elicit a different response from a particular performer or group and as I try to invite greater creativity and range. In what follows, I communicate the exercises and the kinds of language I have found useful, at times problematizing my own language as binaries sneak back in even when one commits to overcoming them. Practical trial and error combines with performance theory and interdisciplinary knowledge from neuroscience in my interrogation of language. In particular I have drawn on Phillip Zarrilli's exploration of "psychophysical acting", the terminology of Eugenio Barba especially "pre-expressivity" (Barba 2006, pp. 216-234) and interdisciplinary knowledge from neuroscience through the work of Antonio Damasio, particularly *Descartes Error* (Damasio 1994) and *The Feeling of What Happens* (Damasio 2006).

The practice described here developed in conversation with numerous Japanese *butoh* masters, particularly Tadashi Endo, whose Butoh Mamu Dance Theatre company I joined from 1997 to 2008. My practice also developed through teaching in conservatoires and university theatre departments including the University of Kent (2001–2010), London International School of Performing Arts (LISPA), Central School of Speech and Drama, Exeter University, Rose Bruford and East 15. My practice has largely applied *butoh* in a Western theatre and performance context in Britain and Australia with non-Japanese performers. This means there has been particular emphasis on the translation of ideas from one context or culture to another. Working with actors tended to frame the work in relation to or in contrast to the conventions of Euro-American acting, and required explicit articulation of how it was useful to actors. More and more, I was working with people who did not want to become *butoh* performers per se, but rather who saw *butoh's* unique contribution to a performer's skill set. Katsura Kan saw it as a positive thing that Western performers were less interested in trying to become a *butoh* dancer, but rather were interested in engaging with *butoh* processes amongst other approaches.

My decision to call my work *butoh*-based rather than *butoh* is intended to acknowledge the debt owed to *butoh* while also foregrounding the inevitable translation and evolution of *butoh* that has occurred. *Butoh* has mixed with my particular background in Western dance and theatre and my particular artistic concerns. I foreground the process of translation whenever I teach this work in order to undercut any assumption of my work being pure or authentic *butoh*. It is my evolution of *butoh* that makes it interesting and gives it integrity. Tadashi Endo encouraged his company, including me, to find our own dance through *butoh* and this cultivated a deeper and more nuanced relationship with *butoh*. "Paradoxically, the more 'butoh' your process is, the more deeply your own the work becomes"

(Barbe 2011, p. 27). The term "*butoh*-based" therefore refers to an interaction with the structures and processes at work in *butoh* without claiming that the product arising from that process is *butoh*.

Lineages other than *butoh* inform my perspective on training including Tadashi Suzuki's Method of Actor Training as evolved by John Nobbs and Jacqui Carroll into Nobbs-Suzuki Praxis. I trained as a Yoga teacher 1998–2004 and in Viewpoints with SITI Company, all of which affects what I do and how I talk about performance and performer training. I trained initially on ballet and modern dance, the drama and theatre which also affected why I turned to *butoh*.

Performing *butoh* led me to create exercises that cultivated the skills I needed but didn't feel I had from previous training. I now describe my work as "movement-based performance", existing between the categories of "dance" and "theatre". It is theatrical, yet often non-verbal. It is physical, bodily movement yet not what most would call dance. I value visual and physical analogy and metaphor and the performer's ability to "act" through non-verbal action. I am interested in the quality of a performer's presence and not only *what* the performer is doing but *how* they are doing it, the quality of actions.

This study builds on the training chapter in my doctoral dissertation *The Difference Butoh Makes: A Practice-Based Exploration of Butoh in Contemporary Performance and Performer Training* (Barbe 2011, Chapter 4 'Preparing Performers', pp. 113-143). The section on transformation below particularly builds on my contribution of an exercise to the book, *Hijikata Tatsumi and Ohno Kazuo* by Sondra Fraleigh and Tamah Nakamura (2002, pp. 133–8). The exercises that follow are organized around three categories important in *butoh*-based work: distillation (stillness, slow motion and simplicity); receptivity ("not moving, *being-moved*"); and transformation using embodied imagery. The exercises and the language used to discuss them have been refined over more than 20 years in the studio which is framed by contextual analysis and research. I am trying to put on the page the complex conversation that occurs in the studio while avoiding language that upholds binaries that no longer serve performers in training. As Richard Kemp outlines in a recent doctoral thesis:

> cognitive science shows that dualistic concepts of process are inaccurate. Approaches to acting that are based on those dualistic concepts reduce the potential of the actor rather than expand[ing] it, and narrow the possible scope of meaning in performance. An approach that acknowledges the holistic and inter-related nature of the expression of meaning would support the actor in integrating all the cognitive and expressive features of the body.
>
> *(Kemp 2010, p. 187)*

Brief historical background to *butoh*

Butoh is particularly interesting as an intercultural model because it is not a traditional form such as *Noh* (traditional Japanese drama) or *Nihon Buyo* (traditional Japanese dance). *Butoh* carries with it some knowledge, values and attributes of traditional

Japanese theatre and aesthetics without being limited by their inherited form. *Butoh* found a way to avoid throwing the baby out with the bathwater, so to speak. *Butoh* also drew on European sources such as German Expressionist dance and the writing of Antonin Artaud and Jean Genet, while rejecting Western ballet and modern dance.

Butoh is something of an umbrella term for diverse practices. "For some it is brutal and for others, therapeutic. *Butoh* can be grotesque or serenely beautiful; it can refer to improvisational dance, choreographed pieces, or work similar to durational performance art" (Barbe 2011, p. 2). Each practitioner of *butoh* has emphasized or elaborated some aspects over others contributing to the diverse range of practices identified as being *butoh* or *butoh*-based. As Susan Blakely Klein has stated, "[. . .] the large number of people influenced by [butoh] and the wide range of styles that have evolved from it conspire against coming up with a single all-inclusive definition" (Klein 1988, pp. 2–3). Despite the broad spectrum of colours within *butoh*, there are discernible, recurring qualities or values common across different artists.

Butoh emerged in the late 1950s in Japan with Tatsumi Hijikata and Kazuo Ohno acknowledged as its founders. Viala and Masson-Sekine refer to Kazuo Ohno as the "soul of butoh" and Tatsumi Hijikata as its "architect" (1988, p. 62).

> To Hijikata's dark and powerful charisma, butoh's co-founder – Ohno Kazuo – provided a stark contrast. He brought to the dance the qualities of illumination and tenderness. Through twenty years of collaboration, the two men formed what might be thought of as the yin and yang that constitute the totality of butoh.
>
> *(Whelan 2006, p. 2)*

As noted in the Introduction, the seemingly opposing forces between form and spirit assigned to Hijikata and Ohno are relevant to this project's intention to expand beyond a dualistic understanding of the performer through *butoh*.

Butoh developed significantly in the 1960s and 1970s as more artists and companies started to align themselves with it. The period of the 1970s is of particular relevance here because in that decade Hijikata withdrew from performing and started to explore the use of dense, sensual imagery as a way of eliciting new dance vocabulary. The 1970s also saw the emergence of what would become signature *butoh* movements, such as the low crouched walking style, the painfully slow movements, the white eyes and extreme grimacing faces, among others.

Hijikata's work in the 1970s on formulating a kind of method for embodying imagery or *butoh-fu* is a contested area of *butoh* scholarship.

> Hijikata's desire to create new forms had led him away from the original vigour of butoh, dance of "being", whose truest expression is found in the freedom of improvisation. In his desire to enrich butoh, had he somehow lost its prime energy, its vital strength? Had the forms destroyed the being; had he closed behind him the very doors he had once opened?
>
> *(Viala and Masson-Sekine 1988, p. 92)*

Some consider that an over-emphasis on form in this period is misleading, particularly given that what is known of this period comes from the notes and memories of the dancers of the time. While contested, it is exactly this controversial period of formulation that is of most interest in relation to embodying imagination. At the heart of the debate is whether it is possible to formulate while maintaining freedom to invent. That is a tension at work in most performance practice.

There are a number of good historical overviews for a more detailed history of *butoh* than is possible here including the Jean Viala and Nourit Masson-Sekine 1988 publication *Butoh: Shades of Darkness* and the publications of Sondra Fraleigh. Key performance works relevant to this study are Tatsumi Hijikata's *Hosotan* (*A Story of Small Pox*, 1972) and *Natsu No Arashi* (*A Summer Storm*, 1973), made available on DVD in 2004. The solo, *A Girl*, evidences Hijikata's delicacy, control and the craft of his transformations. It maintains an unnerving or uncanny quality consistent with his earlier work, but without the overt violence and self-conscious intent to shock. He emerges from shadowy darkness to dance with delicacy, detail and specificity. Dynamics are compressed into tiny motions of intense volume. His body jangles like chains one minute, and falls like soft fabric in another. His face dances throughout, not in a self-conscious grimacing way, but integrated fully into the tensions and desires of the whole body. He rises as if gravity has no effect on him, and falls as if he lacks the strength to stand. His gaze is other than human; it is animal, puppet and child all at once, but this is more than just parody or comic drag.

Butoh was highly successful when exported to Europe and America in the 1980s. Japanese artists based abroad, such as Sankai Juku and Ariodone as well as Kazuo Ohno who toured regularly, were invited to the world's top festivals. Sankai Juku is recognized for bringing *butoh* to a very wide audience. Whether this represents a "watered-down version of *butoh* [. . .] or its greatest achievement" (Viala and Masson-Sekine 1988, p. 109) is debated. Some of Sankai Juku's work seems far removed from the "dirty avant-garde" associated with the early *butoh* pioneers (Barbe 2006, p. 41).

Training through distillation and the use of stillness

Butoh's emphasis on distillation, particularly stillness, highlights that a performer can exist more strongly in stillness than in motion and certainly that stillness is instructive as part of performer training. The focus of this section is on the use of stillness or "distillation" in training to cultivate skills, heighten awareness and access creativity.

Distillation is reduction that intensifies. A distilled saline solution has excess water removed and the result is a stronger, more potent solution. In performance, ideally reduction should produce stronger work, but that is not always the case. The skill and awareness of the performer determines whether doing less, using stillness and slow motion, engages or disengages audiences. Stillness is not just a case of nothing happening. Slow motion is not just taking a long time to do something. Distillation relies on and therefore cultivates attention to detail and self-awareness so that the smallest shift in a finger or the use of the eyes or quality of the gaze are attended to. Distillation, particularly stillness, is instructive because it renders any areas of weakness highly visible.

Butoh training commonly uses the slow motion walk for extended periods to train performers' awareness. Walking in slow motion affords the performer an opportunity to notice what is happening with the transference of weight, the connection to the ground, with their posture, gaze, mental fluctuations and physical tensions. Often they are assisted with images like imagining the pelvis is a container of water, an image that gives weight, grounding and a sense of the centre along with a fluid potential. Slow-motion walking is a rich foundation to build on. I have used it effectively to create work including as a base for chorus work and "flocking". Another simple structure that can be instructive and revealing is asking performers to move on the breath, on the exhale for the duration of the exhale, then to remain still for the inhale. In such simple structures there is an opportunity for the performer to observe themselves and for the trainer to sidecoach points of awareness. In my practice I use this structure of moving on the breath to guide performers in noticing habitual movement choices to expand range. I also use it to introduce the idea of the body having six limbs: two arms, two legs, spine and head and the gaze as a sixth limb. Performers are encouraged to first notice the gaze, then to work more deliberately with the quality of the gaze as part of their creative choices. The gaze and eyes are often left unattended by inexperienced performers who benefit from training in this area. All of this lays important foundations for later work on training for transformation and the embodiment of imagery. Until a performer is attentive to the gaze as another "limb" they cannot use the gaze as a vital ingredient in their transformation, as will be explored in the section on training for transformation.

Stillness is a dynamic process and not just an absence of motion. Distillation requires that the performer expends excessive amounts of energy that is heightened through compression or opposition. Eugenio Barba uses the term "dilated body [. . .] a glowing body [. . .] [and] its complementary image; the dilated mind" (Barba 2005, pp. 53, 196) a state that utilizes excessive, or "extra-daily" energy. It is useful to precede stillness or slow motion with a period of dynamic action that charges the performer's organism with kinetic energy. Aerobic dancing, shaking, jogging, or jumping works well. Images such as "moving through mud" or "dragging a heavy weight" or carrying water in the pelvis can also charge or energize the performer's presence. Such images affect the tonicity of the body and energetic presence of the performer. Different practitioners have their own images through which to discuss this quality of energetic, mental and imaginative engagement, or animating energy, as Phillip Zarrilli points out:

> Whether identified as the idling engine, the flame beneath the stew pot, the inner action that is manifest when one 'stands still while not standing still', or in the more culturally specific Asian terminologies as ki/qi/prana-vayu, the first point of reference for the *psycho-* within the compound term,

psychophysical, is not psychological per se, but rather the actor's complete engagement of her energy, sensory awareness, and perception – in-action in the moment.

(Zarrilli 2009, p. 21)

The exercise called "Circles" uses the contrast of dynamic, continuous flowing action with an abrupt arrest into stillness to interrogate the performer's understanding of stillness.

Exercise: "Circles"

Move in circles. No stopping, no lines. Move the joints of the wrists, shoulders, hips and ankles in circular, spiralling or figure-of-eight motions. Other parts of the body will follow.

Move continuously, don't stop. Continuous, sustained motion is important. Find a speed that can be sustained.

Use music that helps keep the flow.

Try not to plan your movement. Just move. Set the body in motion then experience and observe the flow of motion and energy.

Stop when the music is stopped or when the leader claps. Stop as soon as possible after the cue.

Stay exactly as you find yourself in that very moment. Avoid dissolving into a neutral or more general position. Don't just "freeze" and wait. Think of "arresting" motion rather than cutting or stopping it. Find yourself caught, arrested between two moments. Energy continues through the stillness.

Investigate the detail of form as you inhabit stillness. Notice physical detail (muscles and bones). Notice your contact with the floor. Consider the gaze, its quality, direction and what it contacts. How is the spine? The breathing?

Imagine that you were a sculpture or work of art and consider what material might this sculpture be made from – stone, sticks, ash or ice? What are you? Who are you? Allow associations or memories or images to arise and inform your experience of this form in stillness.

This exercise is a highly effective warm-up that serves to introduce important principles for later work. It also affords the opportunity to introduce different terms or language that will have an impact on the work. For example, introducing the performer as an organism, not as a mind and a body provides an opportunity to talk about movement that is not planned or deliberated, movement that is not repeating patterns, but rather movement that is abandoned and seeking fresh new physical pathways through access to flow or chaos (within safe parameters). The movement in circles in itself does not matter, there is no wrong or right way to move in circles so long as it is continuous to emphasize flow. I find that the more abandoned or undeliberate the movement improvisation in circles, the more likely it is that a performer will find themselves in fresh new forms in the stillness that follows. The quality of the process determines the quality of the product. Stopping immediately after the cue is important to finding oneself somewhere new. Even a few seconds is enough time for the body to fall into familiar habitual patterns.

When done in two groups, the stillness in this exercise provides an opportunity for one group to be asked to observe then copy the shape or position of another performer. This explores the performer's ability to take on and inhabit form that is not of their own creation. Moments spent interrogating imaginative phenomena that arises in a state of charged stillness allows performers to experience the way in which ideas or imagination can seem to arise from the shape of a finger, a twist in the spine. Ideas do not always have to come from intellect. It is an opportunity to observe the nervous system, the embodied brain, in action, and to notice how attention to detail positively affects the imagination. The implication is that students who feel they are not creative or imaginative can cultivate creativity by cultivating attention to detail. Detail fires the imagination.

Stillness renders the subtle detail of the performer's work more visible and palpable – both to themselves and to the spectator. Reduction can be revelatory because it requires greater awareness of the complex, internal processes at work that become more evident in stillness. This work gets performers thinking beyond *what* they are doing to consider more deeply *how* they are doing. There are different qualities of stillness. One stillness might have an intense, fast vibration or inner rhythm. Another has the quality of time stopping. There is stillness with the quality of a sustained intake of breath and stillness that feels like a violent slice in time. Attention to *how* things are done helps performers be more convincing in *what* they choose to do.

In devising work, understanding distillation helps the performer to discover more out of less material. Typically, I see actors who make ten movement choices during a speech when selecting three would do. Once they attend more fully to the *how* of their actions, they tend to need less material. Distillation can help performers overcome rhythmic habits and broaden their creative palette since it encourages them to work at the extremes of their range. Ellen Lauren, performer with Tadashi Suzuki's company in Japan and the Saratoga International Theatre Institute (SITI) Company in the US, says in her article "In Search of Stillness" that as she "matured under Suzuki's direction, [she] gradually understood that all the energy expended in the studio was a pragmatic way to arrive at the confrontation between habit and objectivity" (Lauren 2011, p. 63).

In performance, stillness can function as a framing device. I do not remember any of my *butoh* teachers talking about stillness in these terms, but I know I learnt of it from watching them. I often speak to actors about using stillness as a "frame" for the movement of voice and text. As an example, I was co-directing *Tender Napalm* for WAAPA students to perform at the Asia Pacific Bureau of Theatre Schools conference in Singapore in 2015. In a speech of heightened emotion, I used stillness to frame a particularly emotional monologue by asking actor Angus McLaren to lie in a carefully sculpted form, and to speak the text in absolute stillness, without any movement at all – not even tiny gestures of the head while speaking. The distillation or reduction made that performance moment stronger. This is an example of the application of my *butoh*-based work in contemporary theatre. The influence was detected by reviewer Sarah Miller who commented on the production for Real Time Arts:

> WAAPA's intensely athletic contribution was UK playwright Philip Ridley's *Tender Napalm*, co-directed by Andrew Lewis and Frances Barbe. The emphasis on Butoh and Suzuki training for the actors was evident in the virtuosic performances, and an indication of the potential of WAAPA's new degree in performance-making.
>
> (Miller 2015, para 10)

In leading the Circles exercise described above, I often found myself saying: "just move, don't think". It troubled me that I was reinforcing the kind of binary that I sought to overcome. My request to "just move, don't think" sets moving and thinking in opposition which excludes the possibility of moving as a way of thinking. I found neuroscientist Antonio Damasio's term "deliberation" useful. I think when we ask performers not to think, what we are actually asking is for them to avoid planning, deliberation or judgement. So "don't think, just move" could usefully be replaced with "don't plan, don't judge, just move".

Training receptivity: not moving, *being-moved*

Butoh typically requires a particular mode of operating often referred to as *not moving, being-moved*, or *not dancing, being-danced*. The quality of *being-moved* cultivates receptivity in the performer. It demands that they listen, respond and follow rather than lead. I often feel that movement in *butoh* has the quality of a question rather than a statement. Receptivity requires alertness without rigidity. It requires a soft, listening exterior around a firm core. Awareness of distillation explored in the previous section helps performers cultivate receptivity and is an important preparation for training receptivity.

The "Sculptor and Clay Exercise" introduces receptivity by literally having one person move another as a research into what it means or what it feels like not to move, but *be-moved*.

Exercise: "Sculptor and Clay-Performer"

PREPARATION: Decide who is clay-performer and who is sculptor. The clay-performer stands in front in a state of readiness. The vertical core, their spine, should be enlivened. Extremities such as arms, fingers and face should be soft, receptive.

PASSIVE: Sculptors check that the clay-performer can be "passive" in the arms. Lift and drop the arms one at a time so that the arm of the clay-performer surrenders. Keep the elbows safe. The passive arm can be floppy but the vertical core in the spine should not also be floppy.

RECEPTIVE: Sculptor moves the arms of the clay-performer into different shapes and gestures. The clay-performer follows where they lead until they stop, and clay-performer takes control to hold the position as the sculptor no longer holds them. Clay-performer in that moment moves from passive to receptive. Observe the sensation of being-moved, attend to the experience of moving. Really feel the body moving as it's being-moved. Sculptor offers a range of shapes, dynamics and qualities of action to the clay-performer.

SOLO BEING-MOVED: Sculptor steps back to observe. The clay-performer moves alone in a short solo keeping the quality of being-moved in silence or with music. The music is a kind of partner or wind to move the clay-performer.

The sculptor partner is a device to help cultivate the quality of *being-moved* but ultimately the performer aims to move with that quality alone, without the help of a partner. Receptivity requires alertness alongside letting go. Receptivity draws on the qualities of the active and passive modes but is distinct from both. Adding music to the final stage can give a more performative context in which to observe this quality of *being-moved*, allowing a consideration of what the quality has to offer an audience.

A number of *butoh* practitioners, including Yumiko Yoshioka, Katsura Kan and Stuart Lynch, have their own version of this exercise. Another influence for my approach is the work of David Zinder, a theatre practitioner drawing on the work of Michael Chekhov who I met at the 2003 Changing Bodies Symposium at Exeter University. Zinder's "Statue Exercises" focus on training creativity through the body and his approach has informed and extended my *butoh*-based work with receptivity. Zinder uses questions to elicit a creative response. The person *being-moved*, the clay-performer in my version, should answer the question as quickly as possible whatever comes to mind. Like in my "CIRCLES" Exercise where stopping as soon as possible was important, answering as quickly as possible is important to ensuring access to more unconscious creativity, as opposed to a more deliberated idea. A full discussion of how Zinder works with questions in partner work can be found in his book *Body Voice Imagination* (2002). Zinder's work references "the engaged imagination" and "training your creative instrument so that it will be able to transform [. . .]" (2002, p. 198) which intersects with the current study of embodied imagination. Contact with David Zinder's "Statue Exercises" made me realize that in *butoh*, I was tracking unconscious firing in my imagination but had never made that explicit for the performers I worked with. Zinder modelled a far more explicit and specific way of guiding performers into an engagement with imagination from detailed observation of sensations and phenomena arising from their activity and experience. Zinder constantly returns to the idea of "input from the physical position" (Zinder 2002, p. 200). "For the trained performer, even the tiniest change in physical posture has an enormous impact on what the performer radiates to the audience" (p. 198). His example encouraged me to elaborate on some of the *butoh*-based exercises I had and how they explored embodiment and imagination.

Another exercise that explores not moving, *being-moved* is imagining the body as a puppet which formed a large part of my work with Tadashi Endo, particularly as we worked his choreographic work, *Kimera* in which I performed in 2008. We improvised as a puppet, then as a human dancer. We then learned choreography and experimented with performing it first as a dancer, and then imagined we were a puppet. It was a fascinating study of the performer's experience of inner feeling and outer-form performer as we were asked to carve a face and not to change it, yet we were experiencing feeling and emotion. I became interested in the way in which watching each other as a puppet with the compressed or resisted expression was often more moving than watching us perform as a human. Why that might that be? There is a connection between the effect of the *butoh* dancer "not moving, but *being-moved*" and the actor's ability to be affected.

Training for transformation (embodiment of *butoh-fu* imagery)

The ability of the performer to transform is one of the defining features of *butoh*. The very best *butoh* performers possess a rare capacity to transform convincingly and on cue, instantaneously or over a long, sustained duration. Yoko Ashikawa is one of those renowned for her ability to transform not just into characters, but into different substances. One of Hijikata's original dancers and part of the all-female group, Hakutobo, she is seen in *Butoh: Piercing the Mask* (Moore 1991, 35 mins) dancing as a tree. Every fibre of her is in transformational process to reveal a humanity that only a dancer imagining themselves as a tree might reveal. Yumiko Yoshioka in *Before the Dawn* is another example of great craft in transformation. Much of my training exercises arise from a desire to understand how I might transform reliably and convincingly. Transformation is an area of rich intersection between the *butoh* practitioner and the Western actor as both seek to become something or someone "other". This section explores training for transformation using the embodiment of imagery. Distillation and receptivity are important preconditions to working effectively with transformation. First, I will outline a series of three exercises: *Sour Lemon*; *Nina Simone* (after the song used); and *Eyes of a Lion*. Then I will focus on the embodiment of *butoh-fu* or *butoh* images.

The exercise *Sour Lemon* was created in 1993 at the very start of my work with *butoh* and remains a central part of my training approach. It is a *butoh* evolution of Suzuki's "Standing Statues" Exercise. *SOUR LEMON* works with the idea of "face-as-mask" – a feature of *butoh*.

Exercise: "Sour Lemon"

Stand with feet shoulder-width apart, to create a good foundation for the work. Simplify the body by removing unnecessary tension in shoulders, arms, hand and face. Let the extremities be soft and receptive. Hold the spine – the vertical core – upright, enlivened, prepared.

There will be two triggers: an image and a clap. For example, "sour lemon", "cold shock" or "happy baby". On the clap, quickly make a face mask in response to the image trigger. The priority is to use the face. The body may also respond, the fingers might curl, the toes shift in shape or the spine may change, but make sure the face responds.

On a clap. Transform as instantaneously as possible. When the command is "sour lemon in 10 counts" use all the counts to gradually transform.

When sustaining a state over time, pay attention to the moment you feel the state starting to die, when it seems to drain away. Interrogate how to keep the state alive in stillness, how to inject life into it through breath, energy and imagination even as you feel it dwindling. Keep reconnecting to the image.

This tests the performer's ability to commit to transforming either in an instant or slowly over time. Extreme face work was a signature of many early *butoh* works in which silent screams tear across the face and body. Such extreme face work can become empty caricature or grimace unless it is sustained internally and energetically. As *Noh* master Zeami said, the performer should feel 100%, but show 70%: "What is felt in *the heart* is *ten*; what appears in movement *seven*" (Masakazu 1984, p. 75) Huge silent screams or crying masks are fertile grounds for interrogating the craft of transformation. This work can be misunderstood as "emotional expressionism". It is not a case of conjuring an emotion and then expressing it physically. Initially I wrongly assumed *butoh* performers were conjuring and experiencing deep emotions to express, but if that were the case, they would not be able to snap out so immediately and convincingly. Something more complex is going on when a performer embodies imagery. Part of its power is exploiting the particular and profound connection between facial muscles and the nervous system, which the next exercise also utilizes.

The *Nina Simone* also works with the idea of face-as-mask, but is a more open, improvisational exercise than Sour Lemon. It is done to Simone's song "My Baby Just Cares for Me", thus the title. The music provides a playful tone which assists inexperienced or self-conscious performers to release into it. It provides a rhythmic structure for the improvisation that helps to use a range of rhythmic choices to expand range.

Exercise: "Nina Simone"

Sit or kneel comfortably. The position should allow the spine to be energized and the body to be simple. Calm and simplify the face.

With the music, begin an open improvisation moving only the face.

Work with expressions that can be named, like "sour", "surprise" or "growl". Or work more abstractly, imagining the face as clay or plasticine and bounce on the beat. At times sustain stillness across several bars of music. Trace the line of the melody with your dancing face muscles.

When the music stops, arrest the state in which you find yourself in stillness. If you are in neutral when the music stops, quickly, instinctively pop into a facial expression – you need something to work with for the next section.

Sustain the final face mask. Listen to it. Observe sensations, associations and imaginations that arise. Inhabit this mask. Notice the details of physical form. Notice sensations arising such as temperature, weight, texture.

Now, slowly rise to stand, building a body in response to this face mask. Create a sculpture inspired by the face mask. Move slowly and observe keenly as you sculpt legs, feet, torso and arms for the mask. "Discover" don't "decide".

What material might this body be made of? Ice or paper? Woodchips or stone?

Now you have not only a face mask but also a full body mask. "Listen to" the mask and its resonance in the organism. Name the state, give it a kind of nickname, to help to recall it later.

Practise coming into neutral gradually over 10 counts, then back into the sculpture over 5 counts. Try the journey to neutral in 3 and back again in 10 counts.

What are the eyes of this mask, creature, or character? What is the perspective? Look at others in the space. Take the perspective of this body mask.

Moving into and out of the state through neutral tests and strengthens the craft of transformation and the ability to change on cue. Being asked to walk or to waltz checks that the performer is capable of responding and acting within the state and are not held rigid there. Using both nameable and unnameable expressions is important to broadening range and accessing more unpredictable, less habitual material. Finding unnameable states can give access to states in between or across the obvious ones like happy, sad, or shock. Faces emerge that cannot easily be named but nevertheless have a strong resonance in the organism. Like work on distillation, face work emphasizes the importance of detailed observation and the ability to "discover, not decide".

Butoh face work is powerful and useful because performers are often discouraged from using the face. Overusing the face can rob the body of expressivity but so too can underuse of it. I have seen contemporary dancers so afraid to overuse the face that they develop a cold, detached face that is equally limiting. Rather than focusing on whether to use or not to use the face, it is important to find a more nuanced and detailed control of the face as part of the whole organism allowing just enough, no more no less of feeling and experience to resonate on the face without it becoming demonstrative or illustrative. In this regard, working deliberately and extremely with the face in *butoh*-based training can be revelatory.

For transformation to be complete and convincing, performers must attend to the eyes. The "Eyes of a Lion" Exercise arose to address the importance of the eyes and gaze in the performer's work with transformation.

Exercise: "Eyes of a Lion"

Kneel on the floor or sit on a chair. Sit simply, take the focus away from the body.

Observe the breath moving in and out of the body. Imagine breathing through the eyes so that energy is felt to flow on the breath and also through the eyes and gaze.

When prompted with "eyes of a lion", "eyes of a drunk", "eyes of a baby" or "neutral", change the quality of the gaze, the energy and the breath accordingly.

Focus on eyes and gaze only. The head can move, just enough to allow the gaze to fall on objects in the space.

The strategy here is to isolate the eyes and gaze by taking away the body including the face as much as possible. The head can move just enough to allow energy or life force to flow. If the head is held too rigidly, the energy does not flow and it is hard to transform the quality of the gaze. If the head moves in such a way as to demonstrate the lion, drunk or baby, for example through rhythmic movement, that tends to detract from the focus on the gaze. The focus is on the capacity of the performer to transform only by changing the quality of the gaze. This is subtle, difficult and often frustrating work. But it is possible to detect transformation using only this small part of the organism; the eyes and gaze. As a training, it is intended to ensure that when performers transform, the eyes are not forgotten. Phillip Zarrilli discusses the relationship between breath, face and eyes in *Psychophysical Acting* (2009):

> The training begins with the breath because it offers a psychophysical pathway to the practical attunement of the body and mind. Attentive breathing provides a beginning point toward inhabiting an optimal state of body-mind awareness and readiness in which the "body is all eyes" and one is able to "stand still while not standing still."
>
> *(Zarrilli 2009, p. 25)*

This exercise originated with a specific moment working on Katsura Kan's *Curious Fish* at the 2001 Edinburgh Fringe Festival. I felt unconvincing in a particular scene and tried a strategy of imagining that I looked at the audience with the eyes of a fish. Suddenly that imagery dropped me into full inhabitation as I embodied the image and transformed. Of course, the audience would not have guessed what I was imagining, but they would detect that I was altered. "Eyes of a Lion" was created to interrogate this revelatory moment to understand and later share it. My interrogation of transformation was further elaborated through contact with John Dean and Bianca Mastronomico of the mask company, Organic Theatre. As John coaxed my eyes to change inside a mask, suddenly I felt a shift noted also by him. It was as if a lens slid over my eyes. It was me, but looking through different coloured glasses.

The final section explores a process for embodying imagined imagery, known as *butoh-fu*. *Butoh* is well known for using transformational imagery in a very particular way.

> Hijikata trained his dancers and choreographed works using words. His dance was notated by words called *butoh-fu* (butoh notation) [. . .] But Hijikata's words are not easy. Often his writings are strange, equivocal, and incomprehensible even for Japanese people [. . .] He freely coined his own terms, such as "ma-gusare" (rotting space) and "nadare-ame" (dribbling candy). His writings are like surrealistic poems [. . .] Hijikata's language implies meanings and feelings that logical language cannot convey [. . .].
>
> *(Kurihara 2000, pp. 14–5)*

Aspects of the process are documented by Yukio Waguri in *Butoh Kaden* published as a CD Rom in 1998 and as a DVD in 2004. Most dance or acting work uses imagery to some extent, but *butoh* does so in a highly distinctive way. It is not so much the fact that imagery is used, but the kind of imagery used in *butoh* and the manner it is used that is significant. *Butoh-fu* elevates sensation and the senses, they are not purely visual phenomena. Sensual and textural information is important including qualities of sound, temperature, motion, shape or taste that they suggest. *Butoh-fu* often refers to paintings such as those by Francis Bacon, Henri Michaux and Aubrey Beardsley or figures from well-known Japanese art works like the Ukioe woodblock prints but the expectation seems to be to inhabit or live within those paintings, not to imagine them purely visually. *Butoh-fu* should not so much be expressed through the body as they should be considered a process to enter into. That process transforms the organism, the space, and ultimately hopefully the spectator. The images are not to be acted out or demonstrated, but to be entered into as a process or inhabited. Phillip Zarrilli uses the term "active images" to stress that the image is an "activating force" and not something purely visual.

> Active images are not static pictures. [. . .] They are active in that each provides a simple but clear point of entry into developing and sustaining a relationship to the exercise. [. . .] The mind [. . .] is active as one enters and embodies the image.
>
> *(Zarrilli 2009, p. 90)*

Here is a well-known *butoh-fu* made available by Waguri's CD Rom *Butoh Kaden* (1998, unpaginated). (Change of gender is my own emphasis.)

Wall: You Live Because Insects Eat You

A person is buried in a wall.
S/he becomes an insect.
The internal organs are parched and dry.
The insect is dancing on a thin sheet of paper.
Trying to catch falling particles from its body.
It makes rustling noises.
The insect becomes a person, who is wandering around.
So fragile, s/he could crumble at the slightest touch.

How do we prepare the body to embody such images? Into what kind of body or state of attention do we invite these words? It is ineffective to invite *butoh-fu* into a daily or pedestrian body or state of attention. *Butoh-fu* requires highly receptive flesh, heightened senses and an activated imagination.

"BUTOH-FU: PREPARATION"

Come to a simple standing position with your eyes closed.

Consider the space between your arms and your torso. Expand it. Consider the space between your fingers, behind your ears, between your thighs, under the arch of your foot. Allow the awareness of these spaces to expand the spaces "in between", to expand the body.

Consider the body as a kind of container. Imagine it as something empty and allow the space inside the container to expand. Or imagine it being full of clear transparent liquid. Whether it is full or empty, it is potent potential, awaiting the drop of inspiration – the image.

Charge up your nervous system. Imaginatively, peel off your skin to expose the nerves to the air, to touch, to imagined stimulus. Consider the body as a "kingdom of nerves", as Hijikata said.

Into this container, this space, this liquid, this kingdom of nerves, drop one image at a time. Let the image be like ink dropped into water, swirling at first in shifting patterns in a finger, a face, a foot, before colouring the whole. Investigate the image as a gradual process of change.

Allow physical form or shape to arise. Allow internal energy, vibration or presence to alter. Taste the image.

Considering the body as a "kingdom of nerves" after Hijikata is useful for working with *butoh-fu* (Waguri 2004 *Butoh Kaden* unpaginated DVD). Imagining a body without its skin and with all the nerves exposed immediately brings a heightened sense to the performer's nervous system. It prepares the performer's sensibility both imaginatively and physically to work with imagery that is dripping with sensual information. Considering the body as a container of clear water primes the body as a transparent state of potential.

Having thus prepared the performer, I invite performers to improvise as I speak the *butoh-fu*. I speak one line at a time leaving space for the performer to embody the image in bodily shape, energetic presence and the use of the gaze. What precisely is being asked of performers when we say "embody this image"? What assumptions are at play? What do we expect them to do? What is best avoided?

"BUTOH-FU: EMBODYING IMAGES"

As I speak each image, continue to explore one image until you are given the next.

Don't literally mime, act out or demonstrate the images. "Take written matters as things actually happening to your body" (Waguri 2004, unpaginated DVD). Try to "become", allow the images to act on and change your body. Be moved.

What form and figuration is suggested? What connection with the ground? What spinal orientation? What internal rhythm or vibration?

Take time with each image. When a new image is given, don't quickly drop the current image to move on. Enjoy the process of change from one image to the next.

You can choose to dissolve the first image in order to embody the second, or to layer one image onto another. Enjoy the moment in between one image and the next, when you might experience being both at once.

Consider the implications of these words and images for the senses. As Waguri says: "Focus on words relating to the sense of touch and nerves and awaken the memory of your sensations" (Ibid).

Notice recurring verbs like cramp, entangle, crumble, wander, float, smoulder, tremble and sink. These suggest more than action, providing information for texture, quality and rhythm.

Consider changes of perspective, where subject becomes object. In one moment you can contemplate a bird above you and in another become the bird.

Work intuitively. There is no single, correct response. Avoid judging or analysing the work, at least initially.

Butoh-fu also often uses substances such as smoke, pollen, a falling pillar of ash, smouldering coal or tissue paper. Through such images, the familiar human body is made strange and therefore captivating. Embodying tissue paper gives performers access to a powerful sense of vulnerability. In my recent work, *Exquisite*, tissue paper and the act of folding or being folded became a way to explore the physicality of grieving. One benefit is that performers are not overly demonstrative with strong emotions like grief. Instead they are attending to the image of being tissue paper. This can be more affecting for the audience. For some performers, this distancing is frustrating, for others it is liberating and provides a safe way to work with strong emotion. This study makes a case for expanding the approaches available to a performer to choose from for any given context.

It is important that images are embodied and not simply contemplated mentally. The transformation must go beyond the body and skin of the performer. The accomplished performer will affect a change in the space, as if the temperature or texture of the space changes as a result of their embodiment of imagery. I often quote Akaji Maro from the documentary film, *Butoh Piercing the Mask* (1991): "It's not the bodies that dance. Something else crawls up onto the stage as a result of their bodily movement" (Moore 1991, unpaginated).

Hijikata's "kingdom of nerves" resonates with the emphasis on the nervous system that I have drawn from Antonio Damasio's definition of the brain as nervous system (Damasio 2006, p. 86). The term nervous system in place of body or brain helps avoid a brain/body dichotomy. The nervous system is necessarily embodied extending from brain stem to fingertips, from intercostal muscles wrapped around lungs and heart to the genitals or guts. The nervous system is the web of interconnecting highways we should be working on in training, not inside feeling or outside form. As neuroscience opens up the study of consciousness even further, now more than ever performance can draw on more precise terms of reference to articulate what we do with greater clarity. Substituting body or brain with "nervous system" or "organism" has the power to change how a performer thinks about themselves and the act of performing. It changes how they interpret the task or invitation.

Conclusion

Butoh provides a unique opportunity to experiment with what it means to embody imagination. It is neither an "outside-in" approach prioritizing form, nor is it an "inside-out" approach prioritizing internal psychological work. *Butoh* informs our understanding of how performers manifest or embody physically the kinds of mental ideas, thoughts and images they encounter as part of their training or creative process.

> Transformation of the actor occurs when she engages with a fiction to the extent that it affects unconscious neural patterns of empathy, of imagination, of emotion. When audience members, through empathic processes, experience the actor's emotional state, it is a lived experience because of a mirror mechanism firing in one part of the brain. At the same time they know with another part of the brain that they are witnessing a fiction. This is an embodied paradox, a sensually experienced paradox, a paradox that feels magical.
>
> *(Kemp 2010, p. 190)*

The *butoh*-based approach discussed here utilizes distillation, receptivity and embodying images to develop skills, cultivate creativity and broaden range. Distillation sensitizes and heightens awareness. Distillation makes more out of less. Performers often do not fully utilize the potential of one moment or one gesture and therefore feel they need more material, when in fact they need less material, more fully experienced or processed or utilized in a more nuanced manner. Distillation challenges acting skill. It makes highly visible any lack of connection. Receptivity tunes performers to the signals coming from their own or their partners' organism and it prepares them to respond. "Not moving, *being-moved*" or receptivity is particularly useful for strange, heightened or supernatural characters like ghosts in *Macbeth* or the grieving people in *Exquisite*. But even outside of these obvious examples, "not moving *being-moved*" relates to an actor's ability to be affected, to allow, to yield. The physical experience of *being-moved* can help facilitate an actor's ability to be affected by text and ideas in a scene. Being physically touched as in the clay sculptor activity described above sensitizes and prepares the actor to be affected or moved by words or ideas in text-based acting. To be moved is to be affected and exploring that as a physical sensation is useful preparatory work for the actor.

Transformation through the embodiment of verbal imagery, particularly highly sensory, nonsensical imagery as is used in *butoh*, is a powerful tool for training directors as well as performers. It demands that a director provides a specific stimulus or image for the actor or performer to respond to without having preconceived or prescriptive expectations of what that stimulus might lead to. This process places the emphasis on preparing experiences or structures for the performer to enter into as process. The director needs to be prepared, specific, inspiring and attentive. The performer needs to be responsive, receptive and capable of transformation. They need to be connected to self, text and fully inhabiting action. They need to be nuanced in listening and highly skilled at embodying imagery in their organism. Ideally, they have access to a broad range of actions, gesture, energetic states, use of space, or tone of voice. *Butoh* makes space for more unconscious instinctive processes that have value alongside the deliberating, analytical or intellectual processes that are also vital to rigorous art-making. Listening to more unconscious responses in the body and imagination when confronted with some of the more nonsensical *butoh-fu* imagery can give performers access to a broader range of material and start to move beyond a habitual use of the whole organism in performance. As Richard Kemp asserts:

> The discoveries of behaviour [for performance] can arise both from spontaneous responses to the imagination and from voluntary control of muscular activity, acknowledging the reflexive relationship between the two. This . . . is accurate for the actor who adopts the traditional posture and mannerisms of Pantalone in Commedia. It is also accurate for the actor who plays a character close to herself in age, experience, and personality in the style of psychological realism. The model is also applicable to both scripted and improvised material.
>
> *(Kemp 2010, p. 188)*

"Broadening range" means a performer has access to more variation in their choices. *Butoh's* emphasis on *how* an action is done gets performers looking beyond *what* they are doing to the quality of their actions or presence. A performer is more "creative" when they have access to greater range and more variation in their choices or responses. Creative performers have access to more unpredictable, unusual, surprising or rare choices. In my work, a creative performer can also work beyond the literal and descriptive to make choices that are metaphoric or associative which can give work more layers. The *butoh*-based work introduced here helps performers cultivate this capacity. Sustained engagement with *butoh*-based work sharpens awareness, heightens the senses, cultivates creativity and works holistically on all the aspects of the performer. The more heightened and nuanced the performer's awareness becomes the more proficient and creative they will be.

Butoh-based approaches gave me a more complex experience of the performer's organism as a system which in turn demanded a more nuanced and complex use of language to communicate to performers. Careful choice of language can shift understanding because how we talk about what we do to some extent determines how we think about it, what our expectations are, and what we look for in our work as performers, directors and choreographers. Language indicates assumptions, values and expectations of the one who is speaking. The careful choice of words by a director, choreographer, teacher or collaborator can open up or close down creative possibilities for the performer. How we speak about the work determines what we are looking for and therefore what we will find. How we speak about and to performers has an impact on how they think about themselves, their work and what is expected of them. Language affects how performers interpret what is being asked of them. "Don't think" tells a performer that "thinking" is bad, dangerous or detrimental to their work.

> This is an important issue [because] one's conceptual understanding of the body defines what one believes it to be capable of, and this has implications for theatrical style. The ubiquity of the style of psychological realism in Western theatre leads to a literalism that encourages actors to "type" themselves in order to gain work, which is necessarily restricting. I hope that, as more practitioners become aware of the ways in which meaning can be communicated through embodied metaphor, a greater diversity of styles can flourish.
>
> *(Kemp 2010, p. 190)*

The performer is a complex living organism engaged in activity that demands suitably nuanced and precise language and terminology that moves beyond limiting binaries of body and mind, outside and inside.

Butoh, particularly its use of imagery, is effective as a complementary, supplemental training that can work alongside other approaches. *Butoh* is highly effective as a complement to text-based approaches to acting and traditional dance training. At WAAPA I am not teaching people to "do *butoh*" but rather utilizing *butoh* as part of an intercultural approach to performer training that provides students with the skills and creativity training required to meet the diverse challenges of twenty-first century theatre. Ultimately, institutions like WAAPA have a duty to ensure their training offers a global perspective on performance through intercultural practice. Concerns over cultural appropriation must ensure intercultural work is undertaken ethically and with due care, but everyone is poorer if a fear of appropriation stops intercultural performance from taking place. Rather than shutdown intercultural work for fear of appropriation, my intention is to continually interrogate how to do it with integrity.

References

Barba, E. (2005). *A Dictionary of Theatre Anthropology: The Secret Art of the Performer*. 2nd ed. London and New York: Routledge.

Barbe, F. (2006). Barbe's Workshop Words on Butoh-fu. In S. Fraleigh and T. Nakamura, eds., *Hijikata Tatsumi and Ohno Kazuo*. London: Routledge.

Barbe, F. (2011). *The Difference Butoh Makes.* (PhD). University of Kent.

Camilleri, F. (2013). 'Habitational action': Beyond Inner and Outer Action. *Theatre, Dance and Performance Training,* 4(1), 30–51.

Damasio, A. (1994). *Descartes Error: Emotion, Reason and the Human Brain.* New York: Penguin.

Damasio, A. (2006). *The Feeling of What Happens: Body and Emotion in the Making of Consciousness.* London: Random.

Hijikata, T. (1972). *Hosotan (A Story of Small Pox) YouTube.* Posted by subbodycobodybutoh 6 January 2009.

Hijikata, T. (1973). *Natsu No Arashi (A Summer Storm)* filmed by Misao Arai.

Kemp, R. J. (2010). *Embodied Acting Cognitive Foundations of Performance.* (PhD). University of Pittsburgh.

Klein, S. Bl. (1988) *Ankoku Butō: The Pre-Modern and Post-Modern Influences on the Dance of Utter Darkness, New York.* Cornell East Asia Series.

Kurihara, N. (2000). Hijikata Tatsumi: The Words of Butoh. *TDR: The Drama Review,* 44(1), 10–28. The MIT Press.

Lauren, E. (2011). In Search of Stillness. *American Theatre,* 28(1), 62–63. Arts Premium Collection.

Masakazu, Y. (1984). *On the Art of the Noh Drama: The Major Treatises of Zeami.* Translated by J. T Rimer. Princeton, NJ: Princeton University Press.

Matthews, J. (2011). *Training for Performance: A Meta-Disciplinary Account.* London: Methuen.

Miller, S. (2015). A Generous Learning and Sharing: Sarah Miller: The 8th Asian Pacific Bureau Theatre Schools Festival. *RealTime Magazine,* issue 128, August–September, p. 5. Available at: www.realtimearts.net/article/issue128/11996 [Accessed 19 August 2018].

Moore, R. (1991). *Piercing the Mask.* Ronin Films.

Viala, J. and Masson-Sekine, N. (1988). *Butoh: Shades of Darkness.* Tokyo: Shufunotomo.

Waguri, Y. Hijikata, T. (2004). *Butoh Kaden.* Tokyo: Kohzensha (Dance) and JustSystem (Film DVD).

Whelan, C. (2006). *Butoh: Theatre of the Soul. Introductory Talk at Zero Arrow Theater in Boston (November 8th) and Bowker Auditorium in Amherst (November 9th) before GooSayTen's butoh performance of "To the White, To the Sky".* Cited in http://www.ne.jp/asahi/butoh/itto/

Zarrilli, P. (2009). *Psychophysical Acting: An Intercultural Approach after Stanislavki.* London and New York: Routledge.

Zinder, D. (2002) *Body Voice Imagination: A Training for the Actor.* London and New York: Routledge.

11

ARIFIN AND PUTU

Teater Modern acting in New Order Indonesia

Kathy Foley

This chapter discusses two important Indonesian author/directors – Arifin C Noer (1941–1995) and Putu Wijaya (1944–)[1] – who helped develop "New Tradition" (*Tradisi Baru*) performance, which mixes indigenous movement and comic depiction with Western script-based performance, using proscenium staging, sets, tickets, programmes, and related conventions. Modern performers, unless in film/TV, seldom live off art, and while production subsidies come from *Dewan Kesenian Jakarta* (Jakarta Arts Council) or other groups, theatre does not provide a livelihood. Traditional theatre by contrast, is normally improvised based on a scenario, staged outdoors, using little or no set, subsidized by a single patron (free to other viewers), and personnel live off performance fees.[2] In defining Arifin's and Putu's work as intercultural theatre I follow Julie Holledge and Joanne Tompkins: "The meeting in the moment of performance of two or more cultural traditions" as quoted by Ric Knowles who sees intercultural theatre's potential as "a site for continuing renegotiation of cultural values and the reconstitution of individual and community identities and subject positions" and potentially fostering equality "across difference" (Knowles 2010, pp. 4–5). Intercultural dimensions for this paper are three: Indonesian language theatre requires negotiation between makers' first language/culture (for Arifin Cirebon-area Muslim Javanese, and Putu Hindu Balinese) and national language (Indonesian) with a multi-ethnic urban culture. Prior to Independence no common language or culture evolved in the archipelago, though nationalists had already proposed Malay-Indonesian (a trade pidgin) for the common language. As Indonesia won independence after the Second World War declared in 1945 and won by 1949, it adopted Indonesian rather than using local languages. Hence, writing and performing in Indonesia since 1950 has been an intercultural project to define a new joint culture. Secondly, all Arifin's and Putu's works shows hybrid influences in theatre – Western and local. Thirdly, I reference intercultural experiments as Arifin and Putu directed American actors.

Arifin and Putu emerged in modern drama in the 1970s and each developed a strong group of actors-collaborators. Acting training for Arifin and Putu is delineated by Gillitt (2001) who gives insight from stage-managing Putu's *Teater Mandiri* ("Self-standing"/ Independent Theatre) and interviews with Arifin's *Teater Kecil* (Little Theatre). Rafferty (1989) edited an account of Putu's 1986 intercultural project at the University of Wisconsin in which Putu, Phillip Zarrilli, and Kathryn Braun reflected on working with Putu's style in American educational theatre.[3] I additionally rely on seeing productions, meeting directors and actors at *Taman Ismail Marzuki* (TIM), the Jakarta government arts complex which, due to protection of Mayor Ali Saidikan from its 1968 opening until at least the late 1970s, was seen as the "only place in Indonesia with true freedom of speech" during Suharto's regime. I also reference my collaboration with Arifin for *Ozone: Okes Madiun IV* (Ozone: Street Performers of Madiun IV, hereafter *Ozone*) that he directed at University of California Santa Cruz (UCSC) (1991).

Points that I will make are that the acting methodologies of the two show congruence (though artistic outcomes are divergent); both are hybrid artist drawing selectively on local resources joined to Western models, especially theatre of the absurd, Brecht, improvisational techniques of the 1960s–1970s, and, to a lesser extent, American Method acting; traditional ideas mixed with evolving literary theories (the "roots" movement, postmodernism and post-colonial studies). Indigenous group formation, where a strong author-director becomes the central figure under whom *murid* (students) develop themselves, pertains, as do aspects of local philosophies (specifically, Javanese and Balinese spiritualism), but remodelled as an urban secular artistic practice. While groups tap local genres, stagings are not from the deeper "classical" aspects of traditional genres[4] that involve long, precise training – for example, *wayang* (traditional puppet or dance drama) or *topeng* (mask dance). Older forms are usually only used in modern theatre for referential purposes, something I call "quoting", with clowning often emphasized. Urban hybrid theatres and clowning are both designed to be close to the audience. Classical dance, music and aristocratic characters build distance – directors have seen such genres and selected actors have background or done short-term studies of these arts,[5] but rather than involving the groups in detailed practical training of regional performance, short-term borrowing for the specific production is the norm.

For each director, I will give background information, address training, cite sample productions and note some common features in both directors' practices. I highlight work during New Order Indonesia because, in this period, *teater modern* was a core site of political-social "thinking in public" – hence theatre served as a megaphone for expression of students and intellectuals when there were few public venues to contest bad governance. This made watching TIM performances breathtaking: artists attacked issues at a level that no village *dalang* (puppetmaster) would dare – similar points were raised for rural viewers but much more metaphorically.[6] In a TIM audience I experienced a group that felt it *could* bring on the revolution: abuse of the people and the defeat of the dictator were the focus of many stagings. Since the fall of Suharto in 1998, *teater modern* has persisted, but theatre (as in post-glasnost Eastern Europe) is no longer the front line of resistance and youth identity formation. With the fall of the regime, the strengthening of the Islamic Revival, and post-2001 global dynamics, *teater* has yet to reclaim centre stage.

Background

Both directors emerged during the 1960s when Cold War dynamics prevailed. On 18 February 1950 with Independence achieved, Indonesian artists delivered their "Testimonial of Beliefs": "We are the legitimate heirs to world culture and we are furthering this culture in our own way" (Lindsay and Liem 2012, p. 10). However, which international and local sources were to be used caused disagreements. Eastern block socialist realism, with arts judged for political orthodoxy, was espoused by LEKRA (*Lembaga Kebudayaan Rakyat, People's Cultural Association*), including artists associated with the PKI (Indonesian Communist Party). The counter group sought universal humanism and these Western-leaning humanists devised their "Cultural Manifesto" ("*Mankebu*", 1963) stating, "For us, culture is the struggle to improve the human condition. We do not prefer one [i.e. communist ideology] over the cultural sector . . . Each sector together [has the right] to fight [for] the culture in accordance with his nature".[7] "*Mankebu*" signers were persecuted by Sukarno's leftist government, but soon – after widespread bloodletting as those labelled "communists" were killed or arrested (1965–1967) – "*Mankebu*" created the frame for *teater modern* artists to come of age.

In high school and college literature studies, poetry declamation contests were held. Young authors read their verses in stentorian tones and teachers staged plays (often translated Western works). In urban centers like Yogyakarta and Jakarta, the same students entered college and formed "study clubs" performing dramatic literature for audiences. W.S. Rendra's (1935–2009) Yogyakarta-based study club (founded 1961, later *Bengkel Teater*, 1967) was where first Arifin and later Putu were initiated into *teater modern* – commonalities stem from Rendra's influence. Groups initially staged Western works. French absurdists and existentialists (Ionesco, Sartre and Camus) and Euro-American realists (Chekhov, Ibsen, Williams) were explored using Boleslavsky's (1966) *Acting* and Stanislavski's (1936]) *An Actor Prepares*.[8] Brecht, Artaud, Brook, Grotowski and Schechner became associated readings by the 1970s.

Western authors and techniques, including realism, were tools for developing interiority that students felt was lacking in local theatre. As in Meji Japan when Koaru Osanai (1881–1928) did only foreign scripts during national self-strengthening – so too Western scripts from 1950–1970 were ways for actors to absorb realism (Stanislavski Method), stylization (Brecht's alienation), or Artaud's transcendence. These, it seemed, could model future Indonesian theatre. Foreign languages, especially English, gave access to international discourses on theatre. Travels to study abroad, in the US (Rendra, Putu, Arifin), and Europe (Rendra, Putu, Arifin) were common. Group leaders could then introduce their actors to selected innovations in Western performance melded with their own materials. In each group actors worked under a charismatic leader and this teacher's house/practice site often became the place actors debated, ate communally, and some slept. Ideologically, rather than creating performances, leaders cultivated training sites where the actors could expand body, voice and mind in a society where challenging the status quo was not the norm.[9]

Arifin C Noer

Arifin C Noer is unusual among Indonesian artists in that his background is not middle class. His parents sold *satay* (skewered meat) in Cirebon and as strict Muslims (*santri*) avoided the rich traditional arts of the region. Few with this class background work their way to the middle class and seldom do *santri* become theatre directors. He began writing and declaiming poetry in high school and read for radio plays at the state radio in Cirebon. When he faltered at school, his father sent him to an Islamic boarding school (*pesantren*). Among modern dramatists, he is one of the few grounded from youth in observant Islam.[10] He imbibed religious inclinations with the Sufi mystical leanings of Pasisir (north coast Java) culture. In Yogyakarta he also worked with Mohammad Diponegoro's *Teater Muslim* (Muslim Theatre 1961), a company that strove for realism. Seeing Rendra perform, Arifin begged to become his student, initiating Rendra's study club group established in 1961 where actors lived together. Arifin read avidly at the American library (US Information Service) and continued script-exploration exercises with other study club actors after Rendra left to study in the US from 1964 to 1967. Arifin eventually finished a degree in administration at University of Cokroaminoto in 1967 and moved to Jakarta. Impoverished, he would sleep along with other penniless actors at *Balai Budaya* (Culture Centre) after rehearsals. His *Teater Kecil* (Little Theatre, 1968) was developed as an experimental lab for small audiences. Actors would work together doing *gerak indah* ("beautiful movements", free improvisation, adapted from Rendra) as Arifin created sounds with gongs and other percussion. Actors would hit rocks to improvise group music. Association games built concentration, imagination and emotive skills (see Gillitt 2001, pp. 243–4).

An early *Teater Kecil* performance was a happening. During the opening of TIM, with its three theatres, art gallery, and hostel, Arifin's group paraded in, interrupting. Artifin announced:

Friends, audience, we, who represent that which cannot be put into words will now proceed with the baptizing of all events that will take place in this Arts Complex . . . [which] is a jungle,

> From out [of] Indonesia, which is still a jungle
> And from the edge we pledge
> Forcefully: we want to cut it down
> – arrogantly like rowdy youths drag racing on the highway
> What is there?
> What?
> What there is, is what.

(Gillitt 2001, p. 214)

Arifin presented Mayor Ali Saidikan with his "portrait" (an empty frame), a shattered mirror, and letter written in invisible ink.

Arifin observed Jakarta's method-trained actors of Teguh Karya's *Teater Popular* exploring emotional memory and flailing their hands. Arifin felt most Western plays were too far from Indonesian realities (Gillitt 2001, p. 245).[11] Arifin used association games and movement-word improvisations for expressive bodies, rehearsing the group from 5 pm to 11 pm daily at *Balai Budaya* and later TIM. Arifin wrote material suffused with poetry and abjured Aristotelian structures. For example, *Moths (Kapai-Kapai* performed in 1970) explores mytho-poetic landscapes alternating with realistic scenes showing the cruelty of Boss towards Abu, the impoverished protagonist. Abu's mother tells him tales of the Prince (identified with Abu and both played by Balinese actor Ikranagara [1943–]), and the healing magic mirror at the edge of the world. The Prince scenes were presented in an *Arabian Nights* mode, using *lenong/stamboel* styles, popular urban theatre styles.

Actors recounted to Gillitt (2001, pp. 230–55) how Arifin quickly typed scenes after his day as a journalist. Actors rehearsed with no idea where the material would end up in *Moths*. Ikranagara suggested lively Balinese *kecak* (monkey chant) to explore a scene where Abu looks for the mirror, encountering all sorts of animals. Ikranagara also used his Marceau style mime to open doors at the "end of the world" where Abu meets Darkness, who hands Abu the mirror as Abu's mother crowns and then shoots him, then Darkness intones: "It is now 1980 . . . It's time you were dead" and the play starts again (Arifin 1974, p. 81).[12]

At UCSC Arifin found auditioning alien; his company was whoever appeared and worked seriously daily. Plays were written for known actors. His group ate together, discussing politics and art as part of their process.

At UCSC Arifin introduced Rendra's freestyle movement exercises using percussion to give actors rhythm. All students were to be present all the time. As we started with text, Arifin sought a strong, deep voice, supported from the diaphragm. I recognized this as the sound cultivated for poetry declamations, which can draw thousands in Indonesia. Such vocalization was standard in theatre groups and also resembled the style adopted by Muslim preachers for circumcisions or weddings (lectures were increasingly popular for feasts by the 1980s as Islamic Revival took audience share from *wayang* performances). The American students initially found this voice "stagey" compared to the "natural" voice of their Linklater training. Deep resonance was crucial in Indonesia where theatres lacked refined acoustics.

As Operation Desert Storm began (17 January 1991), Arifin shifted the script overnight. Agitation on campus was anti-war, but graffiti on bus stops said, "Kill all the Kuwaitis". Arifin, seeing anti-Muslim sentiment, adapted his 1989 production, *Ozone* featuring Waska, "Saint of Crime", with his buffoonish followers Borok and Ranggong. Waska is:

> Roaming the universe
> from one galaxy to another
> With rooted anger
> With unwavering vengeance.
> (Arifin 1991, p. 1)

Like Flying Dutchmen, the three wander through space seeking release. They "hope for death/in the beauty of the moon" (Arifin 1991, p. 2). Doffing space helmets, they await a "bliss-filled" demise:

> But how strange, how mysterious
> All of a sudden they were uncertain.
> Were they truly dead?
> It turns out you see, that Waska and Borok could still pee.
> Can the dead still pee?
>
> (Arifin 1991, pp. 2–3)

Disappointed, they return to post-Armageddon earth, "Where combat warplanes were still fighting with all their might" with bullets flying and "New York, London, Paris Moscow, Jakarta, Cairo, Tokyo all cities . . . gone" (Arifin 1991, p. 5). They seek for Wiku (Hermit) and his wife Nini (Grandmother).

Arifin often trusted his well-trained actors, including Ikranagara and Arifin's wife Jajang Noer, to develop movement, energy and context. He worried UCSC undergraduates would lack intensity of stylized voice and movement. He summoned Ikranagara to play Waska.

Brusque, booming voices and abrupt, rhythmic dialogue showed characteristics of the clowns in Balinese *topeng* masking (the characters Panasar and Wijil) or *wayang* (the characters Delem and Sangut, the "left/ogre" side clowns in shadow theatre). Ikranagara's modelling probably determined the Balinese flavour. Yet this energy/style is shared with all clowns in popular theatre. Arifin aimed in *Ozone* for a *gara-gara* ("world in chaos"/*wayang* clown scene) where clowns link the epic world with the mundane reality of viewers. Unlike *wayang*, however, we had no refined characters, all movement was large and angular. Voices had the staccato sound of gunfire, echoing our world at war. Because in Santa Cruz we were better prepared to do traditional Sundanese (West Javanese) *gamelan*/dance drama than *teater modern*, Arifin worked with Undang Sumarna, my *wayang* drummer adding percussion. Arifin, as narrator, used his wooden hammer on the slit drum, cuing energy shifts for drummer and actors. Students matched their energy to Ikranagara's acting and Arifin's hammer. The dynamic style would have suited *Ubu Roi*, but few pieces done at UCSC. My notes from the postmortem state "overall successful, the most puzzling process that I have been through on a play; a workshop with both pluses and minuses". Arifin found working with the students "interesting, perplexing, and delightful" and noted the actors were "rational, talented, young, and alien" (K. Foley, Production Notes, 1991). Yet, not having his customary team to address design issues, lacking the ongoing collaborative training with all members continually present, had created challenges.

The play, with its mixture of buffoonish characters seeking death "quoted" popular/*wayang* clowning and challenged our actors. *Waiting for Godot's* vaudeville combined with Balinese clowning and physical acting. Refined elements were confined to poetry delivered by a narrator/*dalang*; as Waska comes to Earth he intones:

> Only crumbled and cracked land everywhere.
> And dust filling the air.
> And bodies and corpses ...
> (Arifin 1991, p. 5)

Then immediately the bodies on stage were discussing constipation.
   Arifin stated in 1992:

> In the Stanislavsky system, I become Hamlet. With Brecht, I perform Hamlet. With my concept of *teater tampa batas* [theatre without limits], the actor sometimes becomes Hamlet, sometimes performs Hamlet, sometimes performs performing Hamlet, sometimes is someone talking about Hamlet, or sometimes is someone associated with Hamlet.
> (Gillitt 2001, p. 224)

Students rose towards intensity. But this was their first encounter with "world in chaos" where the farting clown is a divine fixer (Southeast Asian clowns are actually gods). This experience pushed them to rethink farce, force and infinity.

Arifin was always looking for ways beyond the colonialization of the mind that could make third-world theatre a replica of Western "isms": realism, absurdism, postmodernism. An alternative he advanced was arts of mystical Islam – religion provided a foundational metaphor for much of his work (i.e. *Moths*, with Sufi imagery of moths burned by flame/light). An encounter with the ultimate/death, which was both nothingness and apotheosis, was a recurring theme.

In his essay *"Teater Indonesia Masa Depan"* (Indonesian Theatre's Future), Arifin called for moving beyond Western models "not only because my skin is brown, but also because clearly the landscape of Cirebon is different than the landscape of Iowa or Nancy (Arifin 1983, p. 19, my translation)". He stated the predicament – artists are emerging from a Westernized education, wear Western clothes, communicate with Western technology in cities where Western architecture and living are engrained. For the modern urbanite, traditional theatres of feudal/agrarian pasts are not a viable option. As a possible way forwards he suggested Quran recitation, noting, "It is different from the standards of beauty in Western singing (drummed into us from grade school), and certainly provides a different method" (Arifin 1983, p. 19).[13]

Putu Wijaya

After collaboration on *Geez!* Phillip Zarrilli noted: "Putu views acting as 'total football', or 'total war', where each act is infused with total commitment, with Eugenio Barba's sense of a 'decided body'" (in Rafferty 1989, p. 44). Rather than creating psychologically rounded characters of realistic narratives, Putu asserted in his 1986 interview with Zarrilli (in Rafferty 1989):

> My manuscripts and my style of directing are neither anti-psychological nor do they support psychological reality . . . Sometimes the actor is a character but he is also frequently a thing, a color, or a shape in the structure of the performance.
>
> (p. 44)

These comments are comparable to Arifin's statement regarding playing in *Hamlet*, but add Putu's interest in the visual/spatial. The Wisconsin production evoked a mixture of surprise, delight and puzzlement: Putu's work is similarly received in Jakarta. His theatre is "conceptual from the start" (Gillitt 2001, p. 249), illustrating his various manifestos (*Teater Luka* [Theatre of Wounds], *Teater Bodoh* [Stupid Theatre], *Tontonan* [Spectacle], *Teater Masturbasi* [Masturbatory Theatre]).[14] Teater Mandiri seeks self-sufficiency, as a mode of being for author/director, co-creators, and audiences. Major critic Goenawan Mohammed, editor of the journal *Tempo* (Time) where Putu works, stated:

> Putu Wijaya came to the scene with his imaginative tragi-comic depictions of nonsensical realities of everyday life. His works – I think Putu Wijaya is the most original of all Indonesian playwrights – reflect the cultural mood of the time [New Order Indonesia].
>
> (Goenawan 1991, p. 3)

Rather than outward forms of traditional theatre, Putu seeks its spirit. He uses Balinese concepts of *desa-kala-patra* (place-time-situation) to gauge what he presents, and trains actors so they can develop a secular variant of *taksu* (divine inspiration or charisma). Balinese dance or other markers are abjured, but the principle of *ramai* (busy, exciting) is cultivated.

Putu comes from a princely (albeit economically declining) family from Tabanan, Bali. In high school he performed a Chekhov play, then started writing. Escaping the patriarchal nexus of home, he studied law (Yogyakarta's Gadja Mada University) and took additional classes at the Academy of Dramatic Arts and Film (ASDRAF), and studied painting. He sees the stage as his canvas, which, as in Balinese painting, should approximate one plane and be completely filled. In 1967 Putu joined *Bengkel Teater* as Rendra returned from the US.[15] Putu absorbed Rendra's techniques (*gerak indah*, association improvisations, voice and sound exercises). Moving to Jakarta in 1969, Putu worked temporarily with Arifin's *Teater Kecil* and Teguh's *Teater Popular*. Writing for newspapers and *Tempo* by day, Putu also acts, directs and writes (plays, fiction, film scripts, essays and manifestos). He is prolific.

He formed *Teater Mandiri* in 1971 with *Tempo* co-workers. Members contribute to all aspects. There are no auditions and membership comes of being there in mind, body and spirit: Gillitt (2001, Chapter 4) notes the company members can range from movie stars to street cleaners who sleep in the rehearsal space. Performers see the group as "family", eating and socializing together with Putu as leader/teacher. Work is not about money. Subsidies pay for production costs and, if something is left, it is divided according to seniority/commitment (Gillitt 2001, p. 258). Putu is the team coach – he evaluates his bench, deploying players as needed. He does not set blocking; he helps performers themselves become conscious of composing the stage picture. Meanings are not defined for actors or audiences, yet many read his work as attacking injustices in Indonesia and advocating radical freedom.

In "swarming", the group moves as close together as possible without touching. In "drunk", actors career through space without colliding. In "bats", the group moves with eyes closed, first slowly, then accelerating, to develop intuition to avoid contact and simultaneously fill the stage.[16] Putu compares his spatial use to the busyness of Balinese painting – no perspectival lines angle the "chorus" to point out the "hero". His theatre is *tontonan* – something watched. Gillitt recounts movement explorations by the group at night in a field, experiments akin to Grotowski's paratheatrical exercises. Putu's stagings routinely break the fourth wall: in *Lho* performed in 1976, he led the audience out of the theatre to a TIM fountain where nude actors mimed defecation, interpreted by many as representing the political "crap" of the government (prompting one of the first moves toward censorship at TIM).

Putu sees scripted and pre-planned director's theatre as *teater pintar* (smart theatre) and his work as *teater bodoh* (stupid theatre); the actor begins from their body responding to peers, and then audience in lived, spontaneous interaction.

Geez! in Wisconsin was judged both comic and thought-provoking. The play starts with two gravediggers who note: "The only capital we got in life is hanging between our legs" (Putu in Rafferty 1989, p. 62). Grandmother, Father, Mother and Wife lament the death of the protagonist Bima, as the gravediggers comment comically, hoping the family will hurry away. Their noble speeches reference the Indonesian revolution and the uselessness of protest against death/fate. But the youngest Child unmasks everyone: "Of all of them not one is sad" (Rafferty 1989, p. 82). Bima's parents want his money; his wife wants to remarry. During his funeral, Bima's corpse returns to life, causing relatives to coach him back into the coffin. Only the clownish gravediggers show compassion, but only after affirming Bima is actually alive by bashing him with a shovel:

Bima: Ouch! OWW! What was that for? . . .
Gravedigger: Craazzy! I don't think he is dead yet.

Zarrilli notes the character and staging "'force' at least some in the audience out of their accustomed indicative frame of reference" (in Rafferty 1989, p. 49) in a carnivalesque performance of surprise. "Whether in the liminal world of tribal ritual or the liminoid world of postmodern performance, this experience of pure potentiality itself holds within it a "subversive flicker", the (illusory?) release from structure itself" (in Rafferty 1989, p. 50).

Katherine Braun detailed warm-ups where an actor created sound or touch stimuli for a prone partner with their eyes closed. This promoted intimacy and intensifed awareness (in Rafferty 1989, p. 132). Braun noted the emphatic voice, needing "breath support coming from energy centered below my abdomen" (in Rafferty 1989, p. 135). In Wisconsin *gamelan* and Javanese dance assisted (certainly a rare moment when classical Javanese dancers represented maggots). Putu used puppetmaster-hammering to control performance rhythm.

Braun found developing a character biography or choosing a Stanislavsky style acting *Superobjective* to define what the character wants or needs was pointless. Instead, "By playing it [the moment] in a direct, straightforward manner, without the actor's emotions getting in the way, the audience is more likely to endow what they see and hear with their own emotions" (in Rafferty 1989, p. 136).

Gillitt (2001, p. 295) asserts Putu's intent was shock therapy "to wake up his peers, to take them by the shoulders and give them a swift shake . . . [to] see where they were headed". Putu demands strong actors with *taksu* or *tenaga dalam* (spiritual energy) (Putu 1999, p. 131). But *taksu* is no longer coming from traditional religion. It is a force built via the performers' self-development.

Putu, commenting on the University of Wisconsin process, noted auditioning and designers' meetings were new. He wanted the whole group present continually, collaborating fully. Instead, "In Madison everyone waited for my instruction" (in Rafferty 1989, p. 152). Eventually, actors put on make-up on-stage talking to the audience: for Putu nothing on stage is hidden. Performers wanted rational explanations for his script – but Putu knew the only answer was in the group work. In a late run-through, actors found the rhythm. He applauded: "That is *Geez!*; skillful, direct, harsh, yet comical and intimate . . . This is war. This is a total performance. This is life and death" (in Rafferty 1989, p. 155).

Congruencies

In conclusion, I will note some similarities that Arifin and Putu share and which correlate with other groups in *teater modern*. This is a movement undertaken by outsiders from traditional arts circles, redefining roots and offering resistance to the status quo, using actor-based theatre to achieve self-actualization.

Outsiders

The people drawn to *teater modern* are "outsiders" born or made. Arifin is from *santri* roots: in embracing theatre he chose hybridity that included the West, going beyond a Cirebon Javanese frame. Putu started from Balinese royalty, but dropped parts of his name denoting caste, and is now Muslim.[17] Other directors are Chinese Christians (Teguh Karya and Nano Riantiarno), and Catholics/Christians turned Muslim (Rendra and Ratna Sarumpaet, respectively). Directors' life processes are not about being something traditional but about becoming something new: all move to Jakarta and modify their culture of birth. They are the "heirs of world culture" that the 1950 manifesto heralded. They make arts collaboratively with actors and designers of diverse language-ethnic groups, using materials sourced from various genres. They build towards a joint performance language in their common tongue, Indonesian, to process urban Indonesian realities.

Roots

Roots-seeking is part of a wide post-colonial effort. By the late twentieth century urban artists in India, throughout Southeast Asia and Northeast Asia were rethinking their Western orientation as part of decolonialization. Great innovations took place from Indian experiments of Girish Karnad and Ratan Thiyam, through Japanese *butoh* and Suzuki work, to Korean efforts of Oh Taeseok. Arifin and Putu are part of an Indonesian branch of this wider roots movement, but the looping back to tradition comes in a postmodern moment. Tradition is never traditional, and the genres used may not stem from ones' own ethnic group. The actors rarely have normative training in a tradition. Arifin points out that, as urban, Western-educated artists with significant international experience, modern theatre artists are already hybrid. He used the term Indo (half European) to describe them (Arifin 1983, pp. 113–4). Though directors temporarily invite an actor-choreographer from a traditional genre for a workshop, groups do not have ongoing/common training in such arts.[18] The roots accessed are not generally classical styles with refined characters/repertoires, but popular urban theatres of the early twentieth century that were already secular, hybrid mixes (*lenong/stambul* of *Moths* for example). But content has been changed from popular melodrama to thinking persons' theatre. Traditional clowns, with their mixture of *kasar* (rough) entertainment and strong social commentary, are also tapped. Such characters are ready-made: they always speak to the present and for the underclass. Putu's clown gravediggers take this clown function in *Geez!*, as do Arifin's Waska and companions in *Ozone*. Popular theatre and clowns speak across ethnic divides. Artists are not replicating traditions but "quoting" them to place contemporary ideas into an accessible local frame. Clowns struggling with poverty, injustice and a world in chaos "fit"; noble princes and refined dance do not.

Resistance

Though the scripts discussed here are limited, they represent ongoing concerns. Arifin, Putu and other *teater modern* leaders developed companies that escaped the straightjacket of socialist realism and traumas of mass killings to seek freedom of mind and spirit. Artists saw rising youth cohorts globally, from American hippies and anti-war activists, to French students on the barricades, to 1960s anti-treaty Japanese students. Coming of age after the Second World War, these Indonesians embraced the new and used theatre as a tool to interrogate realities of Suharto-era corruption and brutality. They knew the New Order would not make them free and decided to free themselves. Their theatre reflected the plight of the impover-ished (Abu in *Moths*; Bima in *Geez!*). The humour of the clowns (Waska in *Ozone*; Gravediggers in *Geez!*) was a way to highlight failures in justice. Performances protested containment of the spirit in New Order Jakarta and gave voice to intel-lectuals and students. TIM's acting workshops and performances were carnivalesque sites where what was said sub rosa was played in plain sight: this resulted in packed houses exploding with energy that leaned towards change.

Actor-centred

The works of these artists responded to their political and social moment and it was devised with actors and designers present throughout. Although the director serves as the leader and actors may depend on him for advice, guidance, financial or other support (as in the traditional *guru-murid* system), he is also the leader in a modern communal company aimed at egalitarian development of each performer. All have active roles in the *mis-en-scène* and the crafting of the piece. Although the protagonist depicted in many works is from the underclass, most performers are not, yet they see the impoverished world all around them. The actor develops secular *taksu* not for the self, but to serve the dispossessed.

Self-actualization

The play itself is not the thing. What was important was the space – the nightly rehearsals, the two-hour performance and post-performance conversations – that created space to think outside the New Order box. Young people of Chinese, Javanese, Balinese, Sumatran and other heritages converged. Christian, Muslim and Hindu found common ground. Actors borrowed from Stanislavski, Brecht, absurdism, Grotowski, movement improv, postmodern embodiment, *lenong, kecak*, or clowning. The *gado-gado* (mixed salad) of the workshops and resultant perfor-mances were about becoming modern, urban, intellectual and politico-socially engaged subjects. Actors explored interiorities that helped them identify with the downtrodden, explored pathologies of the bloodletting of 1965–1967, and dreamed of toppling abusive leaders. Acting was stretching souls to reflect both current realities and what the performers wanted for polyglot Jakarta and the nation itself. Acting was becoming post-colonial, a nation comprised of independ-ent persons living in a hybrid transnational world. When this Indonesian work was carried across oceans and shared with American acting students, US actors did not know the political, historical and emotional fires that had fuelled the style. But they felt its fire, which helped them to start thinking globally while still acting in their own locale.

Bio: Kathy Foley is a Professor of Theatre Arts at UCSC and past editor of *Asian Theatre Journal.*

Notes

1 Indonesian authors are best known and alphabetized by first names. I use this convention and in the references give the more complete names that will help readers find the references which are sometimes under the "last" name in Anglophone sources/bibliographies. Arifin C Noer is without a full stop/period after "C".

2 *Tradisi Baru* has normally been traced to W.S. Rendra's *Perjuangan Suku Naga* (Struggle of the Naga Tribe, 1975), which used *gamelan* and had a narrator (*dalang*). Saini K.M. (2001, p. 226) however shows that, as early as 1960, Jim Adhilimas (b. 1936) in *Studiklub Teater Bandung* (STB) used the local comic form *lengser* to parody President Sukarno in *Bung Besar*.

3 In Rafferty (1989), see Zarrilli's "Structure and Subjectivity: Putu Wijaya's Theatre of Surprise" (pp. 31–58), Katherine M. Braun's "*Geez!* The Process" (pp. 129–38), Putu Wijaya's "The Performance of *Geez!* In Madison" (pp. 139–63), and "*Geez!* A Performance Text" (trans. Michael Bodden, pp. 59–128). In other sources Putu and Arifin are seen through the lens of post-colonial studies by Evan Winet (2010), while Michael Bodden (2010) and Barbara Hatley (in Varney et al. 2013) discuss the artists' work as political resistance.

4 Classical arts like modern theatre are continually evolving and have a greater audience than modern theatre. "Classical" is not static, yet generally artists in traditional genres do not routinely emphasize their experience as educated urbanites in national and transnational frames.

5 In the 1970s, Arifin's actor, Ikranagara, had a small grant to enable him to study masking and director Nano Riantiarno toured Indonesia for six months viewing diverse forms. However, when I visited TIM modern theatre people would interview me, a foreigner, about *wayang*. Some groups (i.e. Bengkel Teater [Workshop Theatre]) learnt *penca silat* martial arts, but most had no shared traditional training.

6 I felt at the time that since many of the creators and viewers (journalists, students, intellectuals) shared class, social circles and blood with powerful individuals in government, this perhaps caused authorities to allow a freer space, as a safety valve for the largely youthful audiences, hoping perhaps that what happened at TIM could let off steam.

7 See "Manifesto Kebudayan" as quoted by Ikwanhul Halim, Surat Surat Kepercayaan Gelanggang dan Manifesto Kebudayaan (A Letter of Belief in the Circle and the Cultural Manifesto), *Kompasiana*, 24 October 2015. Available at: http://www.kompasiana.com/ayahkasih/surat-keper cayaan-gelanggang-dan-manifesto-kebudayaan-sebuah-refleksi_562b380263afbd6007eb26f2 [Accessed 22 August 2016].

8 Boleslavsky's *Acting: The First Six Lessons* (1966) and Stanislavski (1936) in the English versions were well known to all the developing troupes. Important examples besides Rendra's first Yogyakarta group include Teguh Karya's *Teater Popular* (Popular Theatre) in Jakarta, and Bandung's *Studiklub Teater* (STB). Rendra was one of the first to start presenting local scripts.

9 Rendra's home in Yogyakarta was the first such live-in studio for actor training. Teguh Karya's studio in Jakarta was an analogous site. As their students broke off from these first studios, TIM was a space to rehearse, eat and even, if needed, sleep.

10 For example, Rendra (Javanese Catholic) and Putu (Balinese Hindu) were both adult converts to Islam; Teguh Karya (founder of *Teater Popular*, 1968) and Nano Riantiarno (leader of *Teater Koma*, 1979) were born Chinese Christians.

11 Debates in the 1970s often focused on the virtues of realism. Teguh Karya's studio highlighted method acting and Western realist scripts. By the 1980s Teguh moved into film. Also Western plays sold; actress Tutu Indra Malaon (personal communication 29 July 1986) noted elite audiences were attracted by Western scripts.

12 Arifin often used death images and mentioned death frequently in 1991. His father and grandfather had died of heart problems by the age of 50. He was anticipating his demise, which came in 1995.

13 Since Arifin's death in 1995 there has been an increase in Muslim sources. But such alternatives are not purely indigenous – Sunni strains from the Middle East can also assert global hegemony over indigenous Islam.

14 In response to Putu's 1985 manifesto on *Tontonan,* Noorca M. Massardi (in Tuti 1986) quoted Arifin's observation that Putu's embrace of offending the audience reminds us of Western work and is not so original. Noorca felt Putu's images (rape, orgasm, etc.) to theorize art-making were gratuitous.

15 Rendra studied at Harvard, NYU and American Academy of Dramatic Art. Although Rendra dismissed American influences and highlights his Javanese roots (Gillitt 2001, p. 131), he absorbed 1960s trends of group theatres under strong heads (Joseph Chaikan and Judith Malina with Julian Beck), and movement improvisation. Exercises were not necessarily from a specific group, since artists from around the world were trading techniques in New York, Amsterdam, Nancy, Iowa, Australia and Tokyo, but Indonesia was part of this international exchange.

16 Exercises described by Katherine Braun in her essay titled "*Geez!* The Process", in Rafferty 1989, p. 132.

17 Benny Yohannes (2013, pp. 87–104) argues transmigration is central for Putu.

18 Some exceptions are Tuti Indra Malaon (Javanese dance) of *Teater Popular;* Ratna Riantiarno (Balinese dance) of *Teater Kecil* and, later, *Teater Koma.* Sardono, primarily known as a choreographer and director, is also trained in Javanese dance.

References

Arifin C. Noer. (1974). *Moths.* Translated by H. Aveling. Kuala Lumpur: Dewan Bahasa dan Pustaka.

Arifin C. Noer. (1983). Teater Indonesia Masa Depan [Indonesian Theatre's Future]. In W. M. Sutardjo, et al., eds., *Bagi Masa Depan Teater Indonesia [On the Future of Indonesian Theatre].* Granesia: Bandung.

Arifin C. Noer. (1991). *Ozone* [English manuscript]. Santa Cruz, CA: University of California, pp. 17–24.

Benny Yohannes [Timmerman]. (2013). *Teater Piktografik: Migrasi Estetik Putu Wijaya dan Membahasa Layar [Visual Theatre: Putu Wijaya's Migration Aesthetic and Screenwork].* Jakarta: Dewan Kesenian Jakarta.

Bodden, M. (2010). *Resistance on the National Stage: Modern Theatre and Politics in Late New Order Indonesia.* Athens: Ohio University Press.

Boleslavsky, R. (1966). *Acting: The First Six Lessons,* 18th ed. New York: Theatre Arts Books.

Gillitt, C. (2001). *Challenging Conventions and Crossing Boundaries: A New Tradition of Indonesian Theatre from 1968–1978.* Thesis (PhD). New York University.

Goenawan Mhd. (1991). *Aspects of Indonesian Culture: Modern Drama.* New York: Festival of Indonesia Foundation.

Knowles, R. (2010). *Theatre and Interculturalism.* London: Palgrave Macmillan.

Lindsay, J. and Liem, M. (eds.). (2012). *Heirs to World Culture: Being Indonesian 1950–1965.* Leiden: KITLV.

Putu Wijaya. (1999). Teater Mandiri. In Tommy F. Awuy, et al., eds., *Teater Indonesian; Konsep, Sejarah, Problema [Indonesian Theatre; Concepts, History, Problems].* Jakarta: Dewan Kesenian Jakarta.

Rafferty, E. (ed.). (1989). *Putu Wijaya in Performance: A Script and Study of Indonesian Theatre.* Madison, WI: University of Wisconsin, Center for Southeast Asian Studies.

Saini, K. M. (2001). Indonesia. In Katherine Brisbane, et al., eds., *World Encyclopedia of Contemporary Theatre.* Vol. V. London: Routledge.

Stanislavski, C. (1936 [1989]). *An Actor Prepares*. Translated by Elizabeth Reynolds Hapgood. New York: Theatre Arts Book Routledge.

Tuti Idra Malaon. (ed.). (1986). Sanggahan [Response of] Norrcia M Massardi Atas Pembic-araan [To Presentation of] Putu Wijaya. In *Mengengok Tradisi [Looking at Tradition]*. Jakarta: Dewan Kesenian Jakarta, pp. 117–122.

Varney, D., Eckersall, P., Hudson, C. and Hatley, B. (2013). *Theatre and Performance in the Asia-Pacific: Regional Modernities in the Global Era*. New York: Palgrave Macmillan.

Winet, E. (2010). *Indonesian Postcolonial Theatre: Spectral Geneologies and Absent Faces*. New York: Palgrave Macmillan.

12

RENDRA 2.0

Cross-cultural theatre, the actor's work and politics in dictatorial Indonesia

Marco Adda

Introduction

Born in Surakarta, W.S. Rendra (7 November 1935–6 August 2009) was an Indonesian theatre director, actor, playwright and poet. A complex personality in a difficult period, Rendra represents one of the most important, and loved, figures in contemporary Indonesian theatre and literature.[1] He remains barely known outside Indonesia. Crucial to consider is Rendra's public criticism of Soekarno and Communism, and later of Suharto's dictatorship.[2] He was arrested several times during the early 1960s. In 1978 he was imprisoned for several months and then banned from performing until 1985.[3] These events reflect both this delicate political period in Indonesia as well as Rendra's involvement in the cultural and political scenes.

From the early 1960s Rendra began adapting Western plays for the Indonesian context. He was experimenting with a mixture of theatrical traditions and intercultural techniques. His Yogyakarta-based drama club *Lingkar Studi Drama Mahasiswa*[4] was a crossroad of experiences, a workshop involving other individuals who also became later prominent figures of the Indonesian culture, as Arifin C Noer and Putu Wijaya.[5] Together with his social commitment, public speaking, and performing, Rendra was already being noticed as rebellious by the authorities. The political tensions in the country and Rendra's arrest on several occasions during the early 1960s influenced his decision to depart for the US in 1964. He joined an international humanities seminar for anti-communist youth at Harvard University, then studied social sciences and humanities at New York University "where he began to think of art related to 'structural analysis' and communal activism" (Winet 2010, p. 152). He attended the American Academy of Dramatic Arts (AADA), which represents the first and only formal training he ever received in theatre and performing.

The American period between 1964 and 1967, and in particular his experience at AADA, were crucial to Rendra's human and artistic development. Little previous research has investigated this dimension of Rendra's development. Moreover, at that time, American theatre was interconnected with European theatre, and the interest in cross-cultural and multi-ethnical ensembles was growing exponentially.[6] Given his interest in the avant-garde in his early career, while in the US Rendra had the opportunity to touch those trends.

Considering the above, this essay explores certain dimensions of Rendra's background to highlight specific facets of his work, compare it to others better known, and thereby contribute to a better international appreciation of his work. I choose here to focus on the actor, training and the human processes that precede the creation of a character. In this attempt to understand certain features of Rendra's work, I collect, consider and interpolate relevant information.

I begin by exploring important aspects regarding the AADA, and highlight key influences Rendra could have received. I do so through pertinent bibliographical sources and via direct email correspondence with the Academy and reputed US acting coach Harry Mastrogeorge. I contextualize some information directly collected through discussions and interviews with key people via email, phone calls, or in person. Particularly important are Rendra's eldest son, Teddy and senior actors of the Bengkel Teater, especially I Gede Tapa Sudana. Interviewed at several stages during the research process, we discussed theatre, meditation and other aspects of Rendra's work. The language used for interviews was English, along with some Indonesian phrases. Quotations most relevant to this investigation are provided with minimal "editing" to preserve each voice.

I suggest correspondences between the American and Indonesian debates around Stanislavsky. I confront some aspects of Rendra's theatre with facets of Stanislavsky. I then discuss the possible presence of, or similarity with, some of Stanislavsky's principles in Rendra's works. I compare Rendra with other prominent personalities of twentieth-century theatre. Historical documents and press are reported where appropriate. Finally, I glimpse at the significance of Rendra's work today in Indonesia.

1. The American period

Already active in theatre and politics in Indonesia since the late 1950s, in 1964 Rendra moved to New York City. America represented an opportunity to study sociology and deepen his thinking about capitalism, communism, colonialism and imperialism.[7] An award from the Rockefeller Foundation allowed Rendra to stay longer than originally planned. He enrolled in the two-year course at the AADA in 1964. In my opinion, this experience was an important influence on Rendra and his future career. To trace those influences, we must venture into the history of the Academy.

The AADA was and is one of the most well-known actor's schools in the US. Founded in 1884, it parallels the creation of pioneering institutions such as the London Academy of Music and Dramatic Art (1861), the Moscow Art Theatre (1898), and the Royal Academy of Dramatic Art in London (1904).

Franklin Sargent directed the Academy from 1885. Charles Jehlinger, graduated in 1886, was an instructor from 1898. Jehlinger's approach determined an important shift in the teaching concept of the Academy, that is, from the Delsarte's mechanical diagrams to subjective naturalism. Jehlinger targeted an inner system of work, and his approach was later noticed as strikingly similar to Stanislavsky's. In 1923, the year of Sargent's death, Jehlinger took over as director of the Academy and head teacher until his death in 1952. The Academy maintained a pivotal position in both creating modern acting and circulating the principles of modern acting within the American acting community.[8] Spencer Tracy, Kirk Douglas, Robert Redford and John Cassavetes, among others, were alumni of the Academy.

1.1 Charles Jehlinger

A closer examination of Charles Jehlinger is crucial for this study.[9] As the acting teacher at AADA, he provided a critical contribution to American actor training during the first half of the twentieth century. The Academy shared with me a document that includes verbatim notes transcribed by Eleanor Cody Gould during rehearsal classes led by Jehlinger at the AADA between 1918 and 1952 (the year of Jehlinger's death).[10] Those notes specifically record some of Jehlinger's phrases used when teaching. Along with other researchers, I particularly note two main resemblances with Stanislavsky, and I report them here in two groups of sentences.[11]

Group 1: Focus on the human being

- You cannot teach acting. You can only teach the laws of human behaviour
- If acting is not founded on nature, it will never reach the realm of art
- All great things are simple and natural
- Human impulse is the only thing that counts, not stage directions
- Unless you develop as men and women, you cannot develop as artists
- There is no limit to the art of acting. You need the understanding of all human nature, the sense of beauty of the artist and poet, the sense of rhythm of the dancer and musician, the mentality of a philosopher and scientist. It is the universal art
- Will you stop acting and directing yourself and be a human being!!
- Life is the only true school of acting
- Give in to instinct in emotional work. Instinct must rule, not intellect

Group 2: Focus on characterization

- Stop and ask yourself. "What would happen here in real life? I would do a thing this way – but how am I different from the character that I am portraying? So – how would the character react to this?"

- Establish the age of your character, his nationality, profession, social standing, temperament; his physical, emotional and mental qualities
- The aim of acting is to create a character, a living human being. In creating, consider the whole past of your character's life
- Watch people in real life; study them; then take this material, condense and simplify it, and use it in your work
- This is not a stage with actors on it acting. It is a four-walled room with human beings in it, living human lives
- The whole basis of acting is listening. [...] Listening is *listening*; it is not acting that you are listening
- Throw your study out the window when you are creating

(AADA 1968)

Eleanor Cody Gould's notes disclose common ground between Stanislavsky and Jehlinger. The importance of Life Study is also glaring.[12] Academy faculty member Aristide D'Angelo confirms the fact that Jehlinger's view of acting and that of the Academy also featured imagination as the key to performance. This contrasts with the role of personal substitutions suggested by Method acting. These facts illustrate how the Academy programme reflects the approach of Modern acting, rather than Method acting principles.[13]

Rendra entered the Academy in 1964 and graduated in 1966. To continue my examination of the tradition of the Academy and the teaching of Jehlinger during these years, I turn to the teaching of Harry Mastrogeorge.

1.2 Harry Mastrogeorge

Among the acting teachers at AADA during the 1960s when Rendra was a student was Harry Mastrogeorge – today still among the most appreciated acting coaches in the US. In a warm-hearted email exchange (July–August 2015), I gave Harry a summary about Rendra's career, and I asked him if he had any memories of Rendra:

> I absolutely do remember Willy, vividly and fondly! I am so deeply pleased that he had such a wonderful career and also that he was so active in his world as a leader! It was evident when he was a student. He was like a sponge, accepting and absorbing everything he was exposed to! A really satisfying pleasure to work with!

In an attempt to understand what might have influenced Rendra, I asked Mastrogeorge about his approach to teaching acting:

> Everything I teach and work on is fundamentally based on the common sense logic of natural law and human behavior. [...] Jehlinger was a tremendous influence on me; therefore I am following through and all these years on the substantial amount of his approach.

While underscoring the limitless power of imagination in his work, Mastrogeorge focuses on five key elements: childlike innocence, imagination, vulnerability, concentration and homework. They are like "muscles".

> If you exercise these muscles, Nature makes them stronger and more proficient. And this is the kind of cornerstone I've been working with. [. . .] Stanislavsky to me is one of the most misinterpreted human beings, certainly in our profession, in history, ok? What he represented makes total sense to me. These are exercises, as the title of his first book says, for human beings to prepare themselves to do the work. I think it has been distorted a lot . . . [. . .] The ideal mentality for an actor is to have a childlike innocent mentality.
>
> *(Moutsatsos 2015, Min. 13.50)*[14]

In Mastrogeorge's approach, acting is a "mentality", a "state of mind", and not a method. He minimizes the technique and targets the behaviour of human being.[15]

1.3 An Indonesian student

What I have explored thus far through figures such as Jehlinger and Mastrogeorge, is the cultural and theatrical environment which Rendra experienced at AADA. Through direct communication with the Academy, I discovered additional information pertinent both to the Academy's approach to acting and Rendra's education.[16]

> As a first year student from Indonesia in 1964, Mr Rendra would have been among the first students in the Academy's new home at 120 Madison Avenue in New York City, designed by the famous American architect, Stanford White. His graduation photo is located on our second-floor lobby outside two of our training theatres. Among his 1966 graduating classmates is the well-known American actor, director, producer Danny DeVito. [. . .] Mr Rendra's Graduation Ceremony was held at the Fashion Institute of Technology. The celebrated American actor, Henry Fonda, introduced by Lillian Gish, gave the commencement address to the 61 seniors from 14 states and four foreign countries.
>
> *(AADA 2015, personal communication, 15 July)*

I also learnt that the curriculum during those years included the study of Classical Acting, Theatre History, American Mime, Radio and Television, Acting, Singing, Fencing, Musical, Make-up and Costume, Speech and Movement. The AADA archive reveals that:

> There were between 25 and 30 formal productions each year with an additional series of Special Projects. Each production was preceded by a dress rehearsal and given two public performances-accompanied by one or more professional critiques analysing the effectiveness of each individual performance.

Rehearsals were scheduled for four hours a day, Monday through Friday between 2 pm. and 6 pm. [. . .] Plays performed during this time period include *The Affairs of Anatole, Othello, Carousel,* and *Hamlet* among many others.

(AADA 2015, personal communication, 15 July)

FIGURE 12.1 Willy Rendra Student at AADA, NYC 1964

Photo courtesy of AADA

In such a thriving environment, Rendra no doubt received critical inputs that influenced both his person and his future career.

1.4 The journey of a debate

After assisting Stanislavsky during the first tour of the Moscow Art Theatre in the US, Boleslavsky was allowed to give a series of six public lessons on Stanislavsky's work. He stressed the importance of emotional memory.[17] In 1933 he wrote *Acting, The First Six Lessons*, which represents the American "version" of Stanislavsky's (early) approach and features psychological realism.[18] The System, as previously learned by Boleslavsky, had already been re-elaborated by Stanislavsky, especially regarding the critical shift in Stanislavsky from emotional memory to actions and physical work. Additionally, Stanislavsky's trilogy of books published in the US was different from the original versions published in the Soviet Union, and emphasized the psychological aspects instead of physical training and actions, as advocated by Stanislavsky later in his career.[19] There was certainly a divergence between the "whole" System of Stanislavsky and the American "lineage". This divergence triggered a huge debate around Stanislavsky's System, especially where it interwove with the Strasberg's Method.[20]

The American acting scenario of the first half of the twentieth century is certainly complex, and the dispute around Stanislavsky reflects the contrast between "Modern acting" and "Method acting". Some of the personalities and groups directly involved in the debate included Stella Adler, Marlon Brando, the Group Theatre, and Lee Strasberg.[21] Some teachers of "Modern acting" distanced themselves from the Method and were reluctant to formulate their approach as "a method". Jehlinger's principles and practices were directly or indirectly consistent with "Modern acting".[22]

The AADA was one of the most significant locations for the development of "Modern acting". That shines through in some features of the AADA approach, such as the importance of the imagination in the preparation of the actor. Another example is script analysis instead of personal memory. The actor's work is based on developing conscious thoughts as essential to an inner process, and not as a psychoanalytical challenge. Work on the body enhances flexibility, coordination, relaxation, observation and concentration. Action–Reaction is directly relevant to the process of characterization, during action on stage, and as the foundation of ensemble-based work. Ultimately, AADA training featured an approach focusing on the actor's creative process. In this review of characteristics of AADA training, I also want to mention how the Academy promoted gender parity. The focus on the human being promoted a democratic approach to acting as well as life – the opposite to the male-based model emerging from the Method.

Both Jehlinger and Mastrogeorge likely distanced themselves from emotional and psychological approaches, namely, Stanislavsky as "negotiated" in the US by Boleslavski and Strasberg.[23] However, in Jehlinger's and Mastrogeorge's work on

"Modern acting" we identify traits that are remarkably similar to Stanislavsky: the relevance of the imagination, the importance given to the rediscovery of human nature, and the prominence of physical work.[24] Strasberg's psychological methodology was based on a Freudian approach, considered by some as a deterioration of Stanislavsky's teaching. From a psychophysical perspective, American psychological realism carried the risk for actors of increasing body-mind dualism. In contrast, Jehlinger and Mastrogeorge, and then Rendra, were pointing towards a process of integration of these aspects of acting – namely, the *bodymind* in its authentic wholeness.[25] This integrated body-mind is an important contribution of Rendra's work as theatre director and leader.

Indonesian theatre director, poet and author Asrul Sani (1926–2004) visited the US several times between 1952 and 1956 (Rosidi 1997), coming in contact with the Boleslavsky's "lineage". In 1955 Sani co-founded the Indonesian National Theatre Academy (ATNI). ATNI's acting courses were influenced by the American version of psychological realism as proposed by Sani, who translated *Acting, The First Six Lessons* of Boleslavsky into Indonesian in 1960.[26] That conveyed Stanislavsky's model directly into the Indonesian acting environment. While Rendra too, in the 1950s, was exposed to the influence of ATNI, he was later a vehicle of a different approach. As Winet explains:

> Although he had already been exposed to Method acting through the work of ATNI and STB in the 1950s, it was here (AADA) that Rendra first became acquainted with improvisational rehearsal techniques.
>
> *(Winet 2010, p. 152)*

Sani's translation of *The First Six Lessons* to some degree replicated in Indonesia the divergence between Boleslavsky and the Strasberg's Method from "Modern acting". Conversely, what Rendra had learned at AADA was likely different, if not the opposite, to what he might have already associated with Stanislavsky in Indonesia. Travelling from the US back to Indonesia in 1967, Rendra was likely carrying "traces" of Stanislavsky as negotiated by the AADA and "Modern acting". Not inclined to the psychological, Rendra focused on a physical approach, on spontaneity and improvisation, on ensemble work, on life study, on the development of the human being and the reconnection with nature as a "must" for the actor. Hence, Rendra was diverging from the emotional and psychological approach. Although familiar with some of Stanislavsky's principles and practices, Rendra absorbed a non-method approach to acting based on physicality, human behaviour, logic and common sense.

It is interesting to note how the US debate around acting, alias Stanislavsky/Boleslavsky-Strasberg, to some degree reverberates in the Indonesian theatre of the 1960s and 1970s through the difference between "Rendra's Modern acting" and "Sani's Method acting".

2. Indonesia

During the extended period between 1967 and 1998, Indonesia was under the dictatorship of its second president, General Suharto. Rendra's activity is parallel to and interconnected with the politics of this era, and his personality needs to be framed within his militancy. Returning to Indonesia in 1967, by the 1970s Rendra was on the front line and directly involved in the political critique of General Suharto's dictatorship. In this regard, Winet[27] offers the following valuable snapshot:

> When Rendra returned to Indonesia in 1967, he began to produce a kind of modern theatre Indonesia had not seen before: ensemble-based, improvisational, abstract and theatrical. His theatre privileged action over text, the visual over the linguistic composition, and the group over the individual actor. Goenawan Mohamad called the style *mini-kata* (minimal word). [. . .] Indonesian artists and political activists had met the first years of Suharto's presidency with optimism following the political turmoil of the preceding decade. [. . .] The *mini-kata* aesthetic suited such times. It was political, but in an exploratory rather than an ideological mode. [. . .] Rendra came to be regarded as an artistic prophet. In this extraordinary transitional moment, people in Yogyakarta claimed him as "our Rendra," academics praised him as a cultural hero, and, in 1969, the Indonesian government presented him with a National Arts Award (Winet 2010, p. 152). [. . .] However, by the early 1970s it became clear to progressive students that Suharto had assumed a familiarly paternalistic and authoritarian stance, and was settling into the role of a latter-day Javanese king. They began to demonstrate against the same sorts of political and economic abuses and "prestige projects" seen under Soekarno. [. . .] In these years, Rendra allied himself with the student movement and its critique of Suharto. [. . .] He was detained briefly in 1970 for taking part in a "night of prayer for the nation," and thus began a new period of police harassment. Rendra would face escalating state opposition during this most productive period of his career. From around 1971 to 1978, he produced his most acclaimed work and faced his most severe persecution. Police authorities banned him from performance in Yogyakarta (1973) and ultimately throughout Indonesia (1978). [. . .] In that first decade of renewed activity with Teater Bengkel after his return from America, Rendra commanded an unprecedented respect as both leading counter-cultural innovator and man of the people.
>
> *(Winet 2010, p. 145)*

Throughout the prosperous period between 1967 and 1978, Rendra developed some remarkable productions, and his theatre was the mirror of post-colonial fractures. His involvement on the front line in political criticism, sociality, and his attention to existentialism and humanity, combined with his interest and choice of a specific international dramaturgy reflect in his work on Shakespeare and Sophocles: 1969 *Oidipus Sang Raja* (Sophocles' *Oedipus Rex*); 1970 *Menunggu Godot* (Beckett's *Waiting For Godot*); 1970 *Machbet* (Shakespeare's *Macbeth*); 1971 *Hamlet* (Shakespeare's *Hamlet*); 1972 *Pangeran Homburg* (Heinrich von Kleist's *Prince of Homburg*); 1974 *Oidipus Berpulang* (Sophocles *Audipus at Colonus*); 1974 *Antigone* (Sophocles'

Antigone); 1975 *Lysistrata* (Aristophanes' *Lysistrata*); 1976 *Lingkaran Kupur Putih* (Bertold Brecht's *The Caucasian Chalk Circle*); 1976 *Perampok* (F. Shiller's *The Robbers*).

The period between 1967–78 is one of the most thriving and yet controversial phases of modern Indonesian theatre. As typically happens with prominent personalities, Rendra was not immune to some pressing critics, especially where the border between the personal and the public was not distinct. Multiple marriages, conversion to Islam, the use of the platform of right-wing politicians for his purposes, working with wealthy impresarios, the high cost of his productions and high fees for his talks and lectures, are among the main criticisms directed at Rendra during his career. And yet, Rendra always remained consistent in his social criticism and with his militancy for the voiceless.[28]

3. Roots

"Teddy" (Theodorus Setya Nugraha 1959) is Rendra's eldest son. He participated in many productions of Bengkel Teater. In our conversations, we have often discussed his father. We met frequently in the period between May and August 2015. Our talks included philosophy and politics, the martial arts, human development, traditions, magic and beliefs, shamanism, healing and nature. For Rendra, theatre and the actors were playgrounds where that knowledge could be cultivated, explored, argued, reconsidered and upgraded. He expected that actors would find and express their deepest human nature. This was conducive to the creation of a character, to the dramatic action, and then to the critical impact on the public that Rendra wanted to generate. Teddy emphasized how everything in that period was intense. On the cultural-political scene, there was no space for decoration or time wasting. Information, emotions and values had to be delivered directly and powerfully.

In one of our conversations (2015, 4 July), Teddy told me a fun story from the late 1960s – a story similar to those in books about Zen or martial arts.

> At that time, I was studying the sword. One day my father (Rendra) asked me to show him about the use of the sword. After having seen some movements, he said: "This is too sharp and too rough, a lot of weakness in this movement!" – "Ok, then let's fight Pa'! – I replied. – 'Come on; you can use my other sword!" But my father took a newspaper. – "No, is ok with this." And he rolled up the newspaper. We got into position and as soon as I moved . . . shhhpà!!!. The newspaper moved and hit me on my front. "Oh, Pa', how you did that? You do not move the way you should move?!" I exclaimed. Then he said "You assume I should move in a certain way. But how about your experience out of what just happened?" – "My experience is that you entered my body without letting me know it" I said. Then he concluded "That's the point. In everything, there is no rule, but you have to be able to respond to the changes of space and time."

After this story, Teddy and I laughed for a while. This anecdote reveals much about Rendra's personality and focus. We agreed to call this "Naturalness in motion" – a move in tune with the reality of a given situation. According to Teddy, this was consistent with what his father asked of actors. On the one hand, this relates to the Action–Reaction approach, an essential dimension of "Modern acting" in the US. On the other hand, we might parallel this to Stanislavsky's *Adaptation*. The sum of information the actor must gather to create a character (*Given Circumstances*) is counterbalanced by *Adaptation* – responding to the reality, to the truth of the present moment that is not predictable in the stage of preparation. *Adaptation* responds to the need of reformulating what is already known. For Rendra, this was a matter of presence, knowledge and freedom.

3.1 Penghayatan

Teddy introduced me to the concept of *Penghayatan* as something essential to his father. I did further research to deepen the understanding of this notion. The root of the word is *Hayat* (noun: Life). The verb *Menghayat* refers to the inner feeling of an experience. The suffix *Pen* refers to the person who lives and appreciates the experience described by the main noun. *Penghayatan* also relates to words such as *Pendalaman* (Deepening), *Peresapan* (Permeation-Absorption) and *Penjiwaan* (Inspiration).

Hence, the literal translation of *Penghayatan* might be "inner experience coming from Life", or, to use a slightly fuller interpretation, "the inner feeling in deep connection to life that brings inspiration". *Penghayatan* also refers to the type of "full comprehension" related to meditation as practised by Rendra and actors of Bengkel Teater. Teddy spoke of *Penghayatan* as an experience that allows actors to achieve a deep connection to the Self in a scene, i.e., going over the known, over the personal

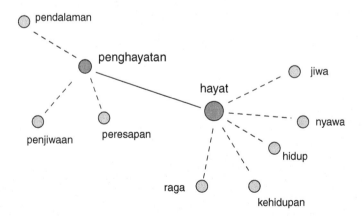

FIGURE 12.2 Visual Penghayatan

understanding, over the structure already created. In fact, Teddy referred to *Penghayatan* as what actors of Bengkel Teater must get . . .

> . . . to live the life of that structure. To live the life of that function. That's what Rendra teaches to actors in order for them to live the role, to bring the life of the role. [. . .] When we study for example Hamlet that's the life of Hamlet . . . [. . .] As a consequence of studying *Penghayatan*, you are aware of that part of you that makes you do things; that attracts certain ideals and behavioural patterns.
>
> *(Theodorus Setya Nugraha 2015, personal*
> *communication, 5 July)*

For actors, embracing the spirit of a character is *Penghayatan*. Rendra and Bengkel Teater's actors were seeking the inspiration, the immediate life of the character and being led by a force overcoming personal habits. There is a dimension of *Penghayatan* relating to the reconnection with something profound, with those roots of the Self that precede the personality and the cultural conditioning. *Penghayatan*, to some extent, also evokes Stanislavsky's *Subconscious*. It relates well to the collective unconscious as coined by Carl Gustav Jung. This aspect too, to some degree, is consistent with "Modern acting" and parallels the contrast with the Freudian personal unconscious relating to the Method.

Expanding on this observation, we might also wish to conjugate Rendra's theatre conceptually by discussing his approach to acting alongside Grotowski's *Theatre of Sources* and the *Art as Vehicle*.

3.2 Laduni

A profound truth within the Self is *Penghayatan*. That relates to characterization and makes me think further about the nature of inner truth advocated by Stanislavsky. The internal world of characters, their emotions and thoughts are the *what*. Stanislavsky proposes a *how* to get there: the *Magic If*. And while thinking about the *Magic If*, Teddy introduced me to another concept important to Rendra:

> If you "*Laduni*" this master, then you incorporate it and move like him. [. . .] Traditionally, and religiously, *Laduni* is considered as a gift, and you suddenly are able to. But through the dramatic process that I've learned from my father, I realised that *Laduni* is not a gift, it is a capacity of the human being, as far as a human is free from cultural conditionings. When you are free, you can do *Laduni*. [. . .] Actors, to a certain extent, have to use *Laduni*. In order to perform Hamlet, they have to experience the world of Hamlet, the love of his parents, the conflict of life, until the creation of Hamlet. How to live that and carry it out in the action? That is already *Laduni*.
>
> *(Theodorus Setya Nugraha 2015, personal*
> *communication, 5 July)*

Laduni can be understood as parallel to the *Magic If*. It enables *Penghayatan* just as the *Magic If* enables inner truth. Moreover, I asked Teddy if *Laduni* reflects in some way the principle of forgetting the structure, the art of the debutant, as it is also advocated for martial arts, or from actors like Richard Cieslak (see Schechner 1973, p. 275).

> Someway yes. It is necessary not to frame yourself into a specific structure. Otherwise, you become a fossil of yourself.[29]

3.3 Gerak Indah

I requested Teddy to tell me something about the practical aspect of *Gerak Indah* in Rendra's work:

> My father used to talk about *Gerak Indah*. All the actors in Bengkel Teater have to study that in order to fit into a certain space or a certain role and come to the right time, and carry the right energy, the right expression. The flexibility of flowing in life, in an unknowing situation, is *Gerak Indah*.
>
> *(Theodorus Setya Nugraha 2015, personal communication, 5 July)*

Gerak (movement) *Indah* (beautiful) refers to something that integrates all parts and moves as a whole. When the movement is coordinated, coherent and organic, then it is *Gerak Indah*. That, in my opinion, can be juxtaposed with the *Through Line of Action* and *Logic* in Stanislavsky. Also, it may be related to *Organicity* in Eisenstein.[30] In *Expressive Movements*,[31] Eisenstein clarifies how movements are organic and efficient when the actor performs with the whole body.[32] Such movements have a double function: they generate in the actor a state of elementary emotional mood, and inspire in the viewer an emotional state similar to that of the performer. If the actor's movement is "organic", then, it resonates in the body of the viewer as a lighter, smaller, but a similar movement. It is a phenomenon of contagious mimicry. Eisenstein called that process kinaesthesia, anticipating by half a century what neuroscientists would have later discovered and named *mirror neurons*.[33] *Gerak Indah*, which must be alive and engage the viewer, reflects Eisenstein's *Organicity* and kinaesthesia.

4. Tapa Sudana

Interested in Balinese traditions, late in the 1960s Rendra observed those with knowledge of Balinese meditation/energetic practices. Already influenced by his collaborating with Putu Wijaya,[34] in 1968 Rendra was introduced to I Gede Tapa Sudana (born in Bali 1945) by Putu Wijaya himself. Tapa Sudana had grown up absorbing the performing traditions of Bali. He was a performer and specialized in meditation and breathing techniques. Due to his cultural background and education, he was also carrying knowledge related to the use of imagination and a strong sense of spirituality.[35] He taught breathing and meditation for the Bengkel Teater actors and then participated as a performer in all the Bengkel Teater's productions from 1968 to 1973. Therefore, regarding intra-cultural knowledge (Balinese in this case), Tapa provided a significant contribution to Bengkel Teater during these years.

In 1974 Tapa Sudana joined a production directed by Sardono Waluyo Kusoumo, left Indonesia and travelled to Europe, where he later stayed to work with Peter Brook from 1979 to 1991.[36] A remarkable actor and pedagogue, I have been studying and then collaborating with Tapa since 1999. We have spoken about Rendra many times. However, in a series of email correspondences (June–August 2015), we deepened certain aspects of my understanding of Rendra's work. I asked Tapa about Rendra's process of training actors:

> (One time) He asked me to find the character, and not come back before that. How? To go walk 30 km. from Yogyakarta to Parangtritis, and work there, directly after rehearsal at 22h00 . . . he gave me Lady Macbeth (Rahayu Effendi) to work with, and an assistant (Azwar). That was once upon a time when I was asked to play as Macbeth while he only directed. It was . . . hmmm 1971? [. . .] Every actor of him, seems he has his own way to work with. His way is many ways, and it is one long chat to make alive, clear and interactively constructive.
>
> *(Tapa Sudana 2015, personal communication, 6 July)*

Tapa seems to be referring to how Rendra wanted actors targeting the main line required by the drama. That is similar to what Stanislavsky proposed to support actors in creating a sense of whole in action: the *Superobjective* which is the mission or the "final goal of every performance" (Moore 1984, pp. 49–50).[37]

I invited Tapa to tell me more about Rendra working with him:

> Referring on how Rendra worked with me: personally. Specifically in theatre, more specific and real on characters I played in his play that he directed and played too. The first play I did with him is Kasidah Barzanji. In this play, I dance based on the work I follow with him through Gerak Indah. I was the second generation on this period of Rendra on Gerak Indah. [. . .] For this creation I don't remember specific indication Rendra gave to me. We were left free to explore. I see now, by distance, Rendra see my Balinese heritage in movement. It seems that my dancing was appreciated by Rendra. I had a solo with the tambourine, leaping jumping . . . in joy. It was a show of celebration. In Oedipus, as Tiresias, he awoke my Balinese elements on mask, movement, and sense of sacred, ritual. No memories of method or technic. In Hamlet, I played Claudius, the father of Hamlet. Rendra was playing Hamlet and directing and also translating the text.
>
> *(Tapa Sudana 2015, personal communication, 13 July)*

BENGKEL TEATER, JOGJA

W.S. RENDRA

DENGAN

HAMLET

KARYA - WILLIAM SHAKESPEARE

PELAKU² : L GDE TAPA SUDANA; RAHAYU EFFENDI;
MOORTRI PURNOMO; AZWAR AN; ROBINSON SIMANDJUNTAK,
SUNARTI RENDRA; ARENG WIDODO dll.

7, 8, 9, APRIL 1971 — DJAM : 20.00

TEATER TERBUKA
TAMAN ISMAIL MARZUKI

KARTJIS DILOKET TJIKINI RAYA 73 — TLP. 42605 DJAKARTA

FIGURE 12.3 Hamlet poster, Jakarta 1971

Photo courtesy of Edi Haryono/Bengkel Teater.

Regarding Rendra's intra-cultural work with actors, Evan Winet notes how

> Rendra's more colloquial translations and locally colored productions in the
> 1970s inspired numerous Shakespeares: a Balinese *Macbeth*, a Batak *Romeo and
> Juliet*, among others.[38]

Tapa Sudana was that very Balinese *Macbeth*. He relates:

> In Macbeth, it was the moment when Rendra (was) looking for a master of
> martial arts and met *Suhu* (*Subur Rahardja*)[39] [. . .] In Macbeth we all dress in
> jeans, *surdjan* (a Javanese traditional shirt/jacket) and using *blankon* (Javanese
> headdress) and a stick. I remember we went to *Sendang Kasihan*, everybody
> with the stick. There was once almost a real fight in rehearsal. [. . .] Ren-
> dra inventing a code in rehearsal: when he uplift both of his arms aside
> open (like Jesus in the cross) that means we are ready to work, everybody in
> guard, like the army in guard, and SILENCE, look at him to be ready to do
> the work. I guess this technic/mode/method/system started at Oedipus, or
> maybe already in *Barzanji*. It was a very efficient way to install discipline and
> efficiency in working together as/in a group.
>
> In "Mastodon dan Burung Kondor", we did a few of "Nyepi" (Balinese
> term). In Javanese we say: meditate in an "angker" (ghostlike) place, "tem-
> pat keramat" (shrine), in the night. Once we went to the cemetery of Kota
> Gede, walking in the night, "lek-lekan" (awake meditate) there, and return
> in silence before the sunrise. Ah ha: I remember there is a journalist com-
> ing with his bike to ask Rendra: "what happen Mas Willy, ada protes apa?"
> (Are you protesting about what?). Rendra and all of us follow Rendra
> indication:"SILENCE", walking till Bengkel. And the journalist follows us.
> Only when we arrived at Bengkel, Ketanggungan Wetan, in his little house,
> he spoke to the journalist to answer his question.
>
> My general impression on his guidance for actors is that he was very tough,
> "keras dan discipline" (hard and discipline) and oriented to open discussions.
> Let's say a democratic way of creating, yet he was the leader that can behave
> like an authoritarian. [. . .] I can add that he seems to honour everybody's
> nature, and try to awaken and use the best of them, in his Javanese "klenik"
> (witchery) way yet with American intelligence [. . .] He is loving and hard
> toward his actor, tegas namun berkasih saying (firm yet compassionate).
>
> *(Tapa Sudana 2015, personal communication, 13 July)*

From these last few lines, a relevant aspect emerges regarding Rendra's attitude.
Tapa notes how Rendra typically had a tough approach towards actors. That is
confirmed by other members of Bengkel Teater I have talked to in recent years (e.g.
Pak Fajar Suharno, and Mas Untung Basuki among others). While he was open to
understanding and taking care of the individual needs of each actor, Rendra was
also resolute and direct, provocative but never arrogant. He wanted to inspire a
transformation in the process of actors. He aimed for those powerful and expressive
qualities essential for both drama and public demonstrations. The actors of Bengkel
Teater remember this aspect well with a mixture of reverence and bitterness. They
agree that was the way of the past – an approach necessary at that time. In this sense,
Rendra is considered to have been a patriarch, an incontestable leader, and yet he is
remembered for his great sense of compassion.

4.1 Theatre and Politics

I asked Tapa about Rendra concerning the political situation in Indonesia at the time. Tapa related:

> He declared (himself) as confronters. He was regarded as an important figure that even the General Minister of Defence of Indonesia came to Yogyakarta to speak with Rendra concerning his play *Mastodon*, that was banned. Rendra was invited to come to the military office in Yogya. Rendra giving them the ultimatum: 'I only speak with the person as human, not as an army general. Only to him. If other staff members in the army speak, I will close myself in the WC'. In result, the *Mastodon Dan Burung Kondor* was allowed to be per-formed in Yogya and Jakarta. [. . .] When the big movement of Jakarta University students want to go down to the road to demonstrate, Rendra stops them on campus, because if students came down the army tank was ready to shoot them. Rendra said: 'hey students, what do you want, let me do it with my friends artist'. (At) That moment Rendra, like Soekarno or Ché Guevara, his charismatic power of orator, declamator, is shaking the atmosphere and the political power. So, when the army tank (was) ready around a round car-refour where the student supposed to manifest, Rendra crossed the road to the round, followed by other artists that looked ordinary. They were 10, they made a circle, and recited '*Allah hu Akbar*, etc.', so Army cannot shoot people praying.[40]
>
> *(Tapa Sudana 2015, personal communication, 13 July)*

4.2 Gerak Indah, Prep, Imagination, Method

Tapa mentioned about *Gerak Indah*, a concept that already emerged in my discus-sions with Teddy. I asked Tapa to elaborate:

> With my bike every night I came to *Bengkel* to see them dancing with American music in the night (first Indonesian wild American nightclub, with music as Misses Robinson [Simon and Garfunkel], Bob Dylan, Joan Baez, Beatles, and all that western Pop Rock. That was forbidden at that time.) We were very happy to dance, to move as a warming-up. We did *Prep* by sitting quietly and feeling each member (of the body), guided by Rendra or Azwar. Then came movement-solo with music, or by 2, improvisation . . . then it became *GERAK INDAH*. After one did a *Gerak Indah*, the others, one by one, making their review, their comment. Rendra said something at the end of each presentation. After my turn, people commented, Rendra too, and I did comment on myself too. Rendra was surprised: '*Ah haaa Tapa nkritik dirnya juga, ha haaa*' ('Ha ha, Tapa also critics himself!'). Rendra laugh. So, what was important in *GERAK INDAH*? The movement was observed in its *Indah*, in its beauty . . . but Rendra eyes awaken his creative poetical

thought. Much later, when we happen to work until 2 or 3 in the morning, then came . . . *GERAK NURANI.*

(Tapa Sudana 2015, personal communication, 13 July)

Gerak (Movement) *Nurani* (Conscience) translates as *Inner Movement* or *Inner Flow,* a flow from the inside, a movement originating in the depth of the heart. In a previous conversation (Skype call, December 2012) Tapa referred to *Gerak Nurani* as an "inner movement that goes into meditation". Those movements were practised at night, 1 am to 3 am.

Prep was a series of exercises put together by Rendra. Tapa suggested that they had American origins. One of them consisted of actors sitting with closed eyes while visualizing/imagining all that they had done during the day from the moment they woke up. The next step was to tell others one by one what they had seen in their imagination. This process allowed the surge of emotions and memories that would have been used later in the process of creation.[41] This exercise has similarities to Stanislavsky's work on imagination, and it may easily link to the importance given to imagination by Charles Jehlinger and Harry Mastrogeorge.

Since I have known him, Tapa has often mentioned Boleslavsky and the *Six Lessons.* I asked where he first encountered Boleslavsky and if Rendra, too, was interested or worked in contrast with Boleslavsky's approach. Was Rendra following or developing any "method"?

> When I study in the afternoon at ASDRAFI at *Keraton Ngasem,* one of the books was *Enam Peladjaran Pertama Bagi Calon Aktor* of Boleslavsky. [. . .] In my memory, Rendra never express it to us. He is not yet writing and sharing his method with us, but maybe all he has done is a method in itself. [. . .] Yes, Mas Willy's method. Very "martial", in the theatrical way of Bengkel Teater Yogyakarta 1968–1973.
>
>
>
> *(Tapa Sudana 2015, personal communication, 13 July)*
>
>

Previously named Cine Drama Institut, ASDRAFI[42] opened in Yogyakarta, Central Java, in 1948. It was the first Indonesian modern drama academy. During the 1960s, Boleslavsky's book translated by A. Sani (1960) was an essential text in the curriculum. Psychological realism was at the core of actors training. That is how Boleslavsky was introduced into the Indonesian acting environment. That confirms how a whole generation of actors and critics may have been influenced by this specific "version" of Stanislavsky. That was the situation when Tapa joined ASDRAFI in 1968. Shortly after, Tapa met Rendra and had to face a rather different path regarding theatre and actor's work.

5. Traditions, training and spirituality

Since his childhood, Rendra was well grounded in traditional roots. While his father represented the rational side of his early education, his mother, herself a dancer, taught him about Javanese traditions. Rendra was introduced to the worlds of mysticism and meditation by his grandfather, while the mystical guru Mas Janadi taught him about awareness and instinct. As a consequence, from early in his career, Rendra vitally drew from intra-cultural sources. Specifically, from a performing perspective, *Wayang Kulit* (Indonesian shadow-puppet theatre) was a significant part of Rendra's background,[43] as well as *Ketoprak*, a popular Javanese theatrical genre based on actors-singers accompanied by the *gamelan*, and other various forms of folk opera. Importantly, Rendra also explored traditions from Bali. In particular, he watched *Arja*, a dance-drama enacting old stories mainly based on the *Panji* Romances (11th–14th century); Balinese *Wayang Kulit*, which may be the older style of *Wayang Kulit* and differs from those of Java in several aspects; and Balinese *gamelan*. As previously mentioned, he also drew on energetic/meditation practices.

Rendra's work incorporated Indonesian traditions, ancient performance-making techniques, mindfulness practices and "Modern acting" – all integrated into a unique approach with a strong personal vision about the human being, spirituality and symbolism. Rendra expected his theatre and actors to be messengers of human values. While some elements of Stanislavsky were possibly "included", through Rendra's work Stanislavsky was being realigned with symbolism and mysticism, the opposite of what happened in Soviet Russia and the US where these aspects of Stanislavsky's work were inhibited. Partaking in rehearsals of *Menunggu Godot* in 1968, Bakdi Soemanto[44] provides an interesting snapshot:

> In contrast to three years ago, that is, before that Rendra went to America and studied at *The American Academy of Dramatic Art*, the exercises held did not revolve uniquely around the script. They include improvisation, beautiful movement, hearing and olfactory sensitivity, spiritual *response* to objects, translating *inner feeling* into expressive, full, shaped in a *form*, and authentic motion. Of course, this requires the spiritual resources of the actors.
>
> At the time Stanislavsky discovered the famous acting technique with inner realism, existing plays were only realistic texts. At the present we see non-realistic texts, no plots, even theaters called anti-theater and others. To confront this, presumably Stanislavski's theory would no longer be sufficient to reveal the mystery contained in these texts. Perhaps Rendra has continued the method that Stanislavsky has discovered. Its name is 'Spiritual Method'.[45]
>
> *(Bakdi Soemanto 1968)*

This fragment reveals several critical dimensions of Rendra's work relating to Stanislavsky. It confirms that the perception of Stanislavski's work in Indonesia was limited to the inner realism. It validates Rendra's spiritual approach. Navigating what Soemanto described, Rendra indeed "continued the method that Stanislavsky has discovered" if we consider what was known about Stanislavsky in the Indonesia of the late 1960s. However, from a broader perspective and consistently with our discussion, Rendra more than continuing was reconnecting Stanislavsky's work to some spiritual and symbolic sources, although in a cultural context so different from Soviet Russia and the US. To some degree, Rendra was restoring Stanislavsky's spiritual dimension. In this sense, Rendra was also shortening the distance between Stanislavsky and Grotowski that reflects both the loss of Stanislavsky's spiritual dimension in the Soviet Union and the absolute absence of that dimension in the US.

In some of Rendra's notes we read the following:

> To meditate by using the BREATH in order to process PRANA envisioned as NING penetrating into all of us, since the first reign of PELENGGAHAN (Tan Tien), and continuing to flow to the whole body through the spine up to the fontanel.[46]
>
> *(Rendra 1987?)*

This fragment of text aligns Rendra with those directors who drew from yoga to support actors in preparing themselves, transcending the physical senses and accessing higher levels of perception, ultimately awakening their consciousness. That was the case for Stanislavsky and Grotowski, among others.[47] Tapa Sudana relates:

> The discovering of the origins is what puts us in touch with the *Brahman*, the Creator. That can be achieved by science and structure, or by the path of spirituality. In this sense, there is a strong similarity between the work of Rendra and that of Grotowski. With Rendra, we have been working in direct contact with nature, going through a very hard training and doing a lot of meditation.
>
> *(Tapa Sudana 2015, personal communication, 18 July)*

6. Martial arts

In 1970–1971 the Bengkel Teater was working on the production of *Hamlet* and Rendra was looking for a master of martial arts. He met Suhu Subur Rahardja, who had established his *Persatuan Gerak Badan Bangau Putih Silat* organization in Bogor, West Java in 1952. The knowledge and charisma of Suhu – an inspiring human being and remarkable master respected in Indonesia and elsewhere – had a significant impact on Rendra. Encountering Suhu allowed Rendra to connect several dots. Rendra had received some martial art training in his younger years through traditional education. Later he tried to use some elements of martial arts in training actors. Rendra's training at AADA included fencing. Rendra most likely observed how martial principles could be conjugated with the actor's work. Besides, Rendra was keen to utilize practices involving meditation combined with movement, and he was likely aware of how martial arts encompassed both. The meeting with Suhu, however, allowed Rendra to give continuity to his previous experiences, to deepen his understanding of movement principles and mindfulness practices, to push forward the physical quality of the actors. Indeed, Bangau Putih Silat provided the actors of Bengkel Teater with a strong body-movement foundation used for both their training and their stage action through the development of dexterity, strength, presence, concentration, focus and the efficacy of the movements in action. Therefore, meeting Suhu represents a crucial shift for Rendra's individual development and all the actors of the Bengkel Teater. Interestingly, that resulted in the fusion, to a certain extent, of the two groups Bengkel Teater and Bangau Putih Silat,[48] which developed a process of exchange and mutual learning.[49]

For some productions, the martial arts were employed for the physical and mental training of the actors. In other cases, elements of the Silat were utilized on-stage. While elements were present in several plays, since 1970s Hamlet, the martial arts were prominent in *Antigone*, staged at Teater Terbuka, TIM, 27–28 July 1974. The martial dimension of Rendra's *Antigone* was widely reported in press coverage.[50] Putu Wijaya observed:

> Look at what we have done for this prominent theater figure. Despite these circumstances, the occasional tongs will actually cause the poet who has studied this *silat* diligently to jump with a bigger step again.[51]
>
> *(Putu Wijaya 1974)*

Conclusions

Before Rendra, modern Indonesian theatre was considered to be suffering from emulation of Western theatre,[52] particularly regarding dramaturgy. Boleslavsky, as conveyed by Sani, did not adequately meet the needs of Indonesian actors. The Bengkel Teater, especially between 1967–1978, was remarkable, and Rendra brought modern Indonesian theatre to its maturity. He combined Western theatre and traditional Indonesian theatre; he conjugated different acting techniques with traditional knowledge and with political and social urgency. All these elements made Rendra a charismatic figure. He gained immense popularity. His theatre became an icon in the overlapping worlds of drama, literature, poetry and politics. His work was crucial through the socio-cultural transformation and the reform of theatre in Indonesia, namely, *teater modern* and *Tradisi Baru* (New Tradition).[53]

Hence, we could look at Rendra as the converging centre of some relevant components, including among others:

(i) The cross-cultural: the actor's work and its revolution that was triggered in the Soviet Union by Stanislavsky, arrived in America, and then travelled (in some elemental form) to Indonesia via Rendra (and Sani). In addition, there were elements of the staging, translation and reconsideration of international playwrights at work
(ii) The intra-cultural: the integration of various forms of traditional Indonesian theatre, folk opera, music and storytelling, among others
(iii) The social: the criticism, the deployment in the Indonesian cultural and political scenario, in the particularly delicate period of Suharto's dictatorship

(iv)   The exoteric: the symbolism, the spiritual quest and the interpolation of knowledge such as yoga, meditation and other practices and principles related to mindfulness

(v)   The transversal: the significant influence of Bangau Putih Silat in Rendra's personal development and theatre

The "connection" of Rendra to Stanislavsky may be observed on two different layers. One is perceptible: elements of Stanislavsky prone to a physical, improvisational and non-methodical approach which Rendra carried in some respects from the US. The second is invisible, yet it can be framed as one of these phenomena that Eugenio Barba has defined as *Recurring Principles* (Barba 1995). I refer to the underlying principles of Rendra's work on the actor, which are similar to some of the principles framed by Stanislavski without necessarily having been derived from Stanislavsky.

Western theatres throughout the twentieth century have been engaged in the process of elevating the art of acting to a "scientific" level.[54] In their search for pertinent principles and practices, researchers and practitioners have been looking at Asian theatres and traditions where performers' training and work were highly formalized, as in Beijing Opera, Balinese dances and Indian Kathakali, among others. As a consequence, other significant Asian theatres remained less visible within the Euro-American contexts. Certainly, this is the case with Rendra who did not pursue a high level of formalization in his performers' actions, nor did he create any specific formal method in training actors. Targeting a fusion of experiences, cross-cultural performing and an improvisational approach to training and acting, Rendra relied upon the actors and their presence, their inner work and their process of transformation as human beings. For the importance given to both physical training and spirituality in the actor's work, Rendra can be placed alongside Stanislavsky and Grotowski. More generally, as a director and leader of actors, Rendra aligns with those "Director-Pedagogues" identified by Fabrizio Cruciani (1995) such as Stanislavsky, Copeau, Meyerhold, Grotowski and Brook, among others. Rendra may fairly be framed as their Asian counterpart.

With Rendra, Indonesian theatre revealed its transformative power. It surely became a place of resistance, a playground to reformulate both the human being and the society.[55] Thus, Rendra and Bengkel Teater can be considered an Indonesian parallel to other important theatre movements happening in the US or Europe in the same period, including The Living Theatre, Odin Teatret and the Theatre of Sources of Grotowski.[56] With reference to his dedication to the voiceless, I would also note the resemblance between Rendra and Augusto Boal.[57] Both were devoted to the oppressed. They exactly parallel in time with activities starting in the 1950s and, by a strange irony of fate, both dying a few months apart in 2009. Ultimately, while having a unique impact on Indonesian theatre and literature, Rendra's work should be reconsidered from a global perspective for his contribution to twentieth-century theatre.

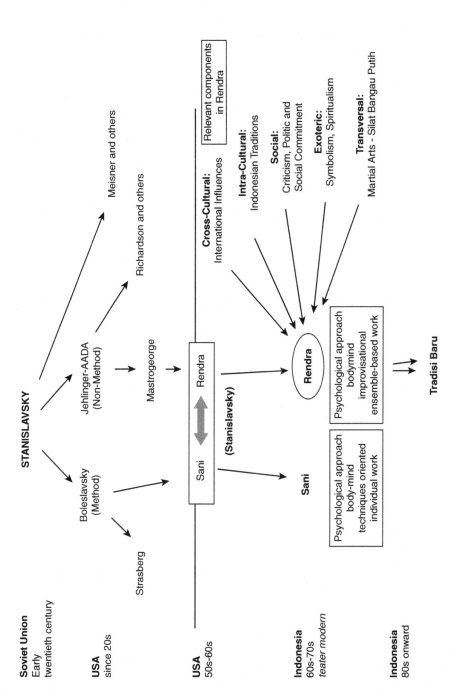

FIGURE 12.4 Stanislavsky and other components in Rendra

Rendra Nowadays

Apart from the universal value of his poetry, some social features make Rendra's work still relevant. From the 1950s until his death, Rendra has been a voice for the voiceless. He has spoken in the name of uneducated children, burdened workers and marginalized people, women, prostitutes and other powerless Indonesians. His poems and plays have represented a heartbeat against the oppression of the government and abuse of power, social injustice, economic inequality and ignorance. Social injustice in Indonesia is still a major issue, so is the destruction of nature perpetuated by events such as the disastrous forest fires in Sumatra and Kalimantan of recent years. Thus, Rendra's body of work continues to reverberate and appear alive and necessary. Consequently, beyond a sense of nostalgia that sometimes characterizes the memory of such personalities, Rendra's work is currently studied and read around Indonesia, especially in universities. As a poet and dramatist, Rendra is respected as an example of social redemption, justice, collective values and spiritual quest. His work continues to inspire various artists active in many fields. His influence is palpable through the work of poets, musicians, painters and architects such as Iwan Fals, Sawung Jabo, Herry Dim, Agus Sarjono and many others. Rendra's work continues to be staged, especially in areas culturally and politically active, socially and ecologically involved, such as Yogyakarta and Bandung. Youth theatre groups often use Rendra's dramaturgy for exploring new forms of theatrical expression.[58]

Notes

1 Prijosusilo, B (2009).
2 The Independence of Indonesia, and the later proclamation of the Republic of Indonesia, occurred in 1945 and 1949, respectively. Sukarno, the first president, led the country until 1967, when Suharto, after a coup d'état, took control. The second President of Indonesia, Suharto, set up a centralized and military-dominated government. His dictatorial era lasted until 1998.
3 A few explosions occurred while Rendra was reading his poetry during a public event at the Taman Ismail Marzuki Arts Centre in Jakarta.
4 Yudiaryani. (2015). W.S. Rendra dan Teater Mini Kata. Yogyakarta: Galang Pustaka.
5 See Foley, K. (2016).
6 In Europe, this trend reaches its climax with Grotowski and Brook, while in the US people such as Schechner, A.C. Scott and P. Zarrilli, among others, were introducing a new stage of a cross-cultural and multidisciplinary theatre, training and performance.
7 Recall that in 1964 President Lyndon B. Johnson had just been elected following the assassination of J.F. Kennedy in 1963.
8 Byron, C. (2016). The American Academy of Dramatic Art. In *Modern Acting*. London: Palgrave Macmillan, pp. 137–54.
9 Charles Jehlinger (1866–1952) was among those advocating a non-method approach to acting. He taught Spencer Tracy, Edward G. Robinson and Anne Bancroft, among others.
10 Mrs Gould was a junior student at the Academy in 1918, and a Senior in 1919, graduating in 1920. Later in 1934, she returned to the Academy by special permission of Jehlinger to take notes. Since 1956 she was a director and instructor at the Academy. Quotations from Gould represent a distillation of Jehlinger's approach.
11 H. Dickens. (1959). The American Academy of Dramatic Arts. *Films in Review*, pp. 597–8, December. John Allen. (1959). Seventy-Five Years of the American Academy. *New York Herald Tribune*, 6 December.

12 Gerard Raymond. (2009). 125 Years and Counting: The American Academy of Dramatic Art. *Backstage*, pp. 6–7, 25 November.

13 A. D'Angelo. (2011). *The Actor Creates* (Clapham Press – Paperback). To some extent, Aristide D'Angelo also represents a link between the Academy and the Group Theatre.

14 www.youtube.com/watch?v=GrWUCkvguUg

15 www.harrymastrogeorge.com. Visit also www.ameliaproductions.com.

16 All the communications with AADA occurred in June–August 2015 via email. My correspondent has been Betty Lawson, Director of External Relations/ALO of the Academy. She has researched the archives of the Academy to facilitate my investigation.

17 Bolesław Ryszard Srzednicki, later known as Richard Boleslavsky (1889–1937). Already an actor at The First Studio at the Moscow Art Theatre, then collaborator of Stanislavsky, in 1923 (with Maria Ouspenskaya) he introduced Stanislavsky's approach in the US.

18 See also Blair, R. (2010).

19 See Stanislavsky, K. (1989).

20 Lee Strasberg (17 November 1901–17 February 1982) was an American director, acting teacher and actor, regarded as the developer of the American Method acting. He co-founded the Group Theatre in 1931 and became director of the Actors Studio in NYC in 1951. He wrote *A Dream of Passion. The Development of the Method* (Strasberg 1987). See also Carnicke 1998.

21 The Group Theatre was established in 1931 by Lee Strasberg, Cheryl Crawford and Harold Clurman. It was a theatre collective based in New York City.

22 See also Richardson, D. (1988).

23 Affective Memory was a component of Stanislavsky's early teachings. The concept was later elaborated by Lee Strasberg (sense memory/emotional memory) and became an essential part of his Method acting. However, sense memory had been considered a distortion of Stanislavsky's ideas and was therefore at the core of the debate Stanislavsky-Strasberg in the US.

24 See also Baron, C. (2016).

25 For a broad and relevant overview about *body-mind* and *bodymind* in performing and actor's work, see *Acting (Re)Considered* (Zarrilli 2002), and *Psychophysical Acting: An Intercultural Approach After Stanislavski* (Zarrilli 2009).

26 See also Winet E. D. (2003).

27 Winet E. D. (2010). See also Yudiaryani (2006).

28 See also Lane, M. (2009).

29 Teddy expanded this problem from the individual to the collective, talking about how sometimes traditions end up being self-referential and not open to integrating new experiences. "They do not update, do not change themselves according to time and situation. When traditions lose that, they lose compassion".

30 Sergei Mikhailovich Eisenstein (Riga 1898–Moscow 1949) was a Soviet film theorist and director, a pioneer in the theory of montage. His theories had a significant influence also on theatre and actor training. Important was the influence of Meyerhold on his career.

31 S. Eisenstein, & S. Tretyakov. (1996). Expressive movement. In A. Law & M. Gordon (Eds.), *Meyerhold, Eisenstein and Biomechanics: Actor Training in Revolutionary Russia*. Jefferson, North Carolina: McFarland and Company, Inc., Publishers.

32 For a review of the theories and practices of organicity in performing arts, also see Ciancarelli and Ruggeri (2009).

33 V. Gallese, L. Fadiga, L. Fogassi and G. Rizzolatti. (1996). Action Recognition in the Premotor Cortex. *Brain*, 119(2), pp. 593–609.

34 Another prominent Indonesian literary figure, I Gusti Ngurah Wijaya (born in Bali 1944), worked with Bengkel Teater from 1967 to 1969, but he gravitated around Rendra during the prolific period of the Bengkel Teater 1969–1978.

35 Tapa's father was an educator and teacher well known in southern Bali.

36 Sardono Waluyo Kusumo (born in Surakarta, 6 March 1945) is an Indonesian choreographer, dancer, actor, theatre director, and film director. In 1973, he founded his own theatre company, Sardono Dance Theatre.

37 The *Superobjective* can be looked at as the skeleton of a body, the principal structure that supports the body to stand versus the gravity. For example, the *Superobjective* of a character might be the conqueror of a kingdom. To achieve that, the character has to go through successive unit objectives, such as setting up an army, gaining the trust of his soldiers, wining a battle, etc.

38 Winet E. D. (2010), p. 151.

39 Suhu Subur Rahardja (4 April 1925–31 December 31 1985), martial art master and founder of Persatuan Gerak Badan – Bangau Putih Silat, on 25 December 1952.

40 Indonesian law in those years prohibited holding a meeting of more than ten people in a public place, considering it as a demonstration.

41 A similar exercise was also proposed on a "higher degree". With closed eyes, actors had to imagine and physically express the creation of life, from the Big Bang and the origin of the Universe until the creation of human beings.

42 Akademi Seni Drama dan Film Indonesia (Indonesian Academy of Drama and Film).

43 The Wayang Kulit also inspired one of the most outstanding productions of Bengkel Teater (1975), Kisah Perjuangan Suku Naga (*The Struggle of the Naga Tribe*), which might be considered Rendra's political manifesto against the New Order and Suharto's dictatorship.

44 Soebakdi Soemanto (1941–2014) was an Indonesian writer, poet, playwright and editor. Later in his career he was a professor at the Faculty of Cultural Sciences (UGM), Yogyakarta. He cooperated with Rendra, especially around *Waiting for Godot,* on several occasions.

45 Bakdi Soemanto, "Menunggu Godot", BASIS, XVII, January 1968. Original selected text: "Berbeda dengan tiga tahun yang lampau sebelum Rendra pergi ke Amerika, dan belajar di *The American Academy of Dramatic Art*, latihan-latihan yang diselenggarakan tidak hanya berkisar pada naskahnya sendiri. Tetapi meliputi improvisasi, gerak indah, kepekaan pendengaran, penciuman, rohani untuk *respons* kepada obyek, menterjemahkan *inner feeling* ke dalam gerak yang ekpresif, penuh, membentuk suatu *form*, dan otentik. Tentu saja, untuk ini diperlukan kekayaan daripada rohani para aktor-aktor itu. Pada waktu Stanilavski menemukan teknik akting yang terkenal dengan *inner realism*, naskah-naskah yang ada pada waktu itu hanyalah naskah-naskah realistis. Pada waktu sekarang kita melihat naskah-naskah yang non-realistis, tanpa plot, bahkan ada teater yang disebut anti teater dan lain-lain. Untuk menghadapi ini, kiranya teori Stanislavski tidak akan memadai lagi, untuk mengungkapkan misteri yang terkandung dalam naskah itu. Kiranya Rendra telah melanjutkan metode yang telah diketemukan oleh Stanislavsky itu. 'Metode Rohani' namanya".

46 Rendra (1987?), unpublished. p. 4. Translated by the original Indonesian: "Meditasi dengan mempergunakan NAPAS untuk mengolah PRANA yang dibayangkan sebagai NING yang merasuk kedalam seluruh diri kita, setelah lebih dulu bertahta di PELENG-GAHAN (Tan Tien) dan terus ter salur ke sekujur tubuh melalui tulang punggung ke ubun-ubun" [sic]. See also Rendra, W. S. (1983).

47 See Carnicke (1998, p. 140), White (2006); and see Grotowski (2002).

48 See also Redana 2010.

49 After Suhu's death in 1986, and following a period of transition, the PGB Bangau Putih Silat has been led by Suhu's son, Guru Besar Gunawan Rahardja, who is also a healthcare practitioner. Nowadays, the PGB organization maintains its role in the community as a Martial Arts School, a health centre, an educational association, and is involved in numerous social projects around Indonesia and abroad.

50 E. Haryono. (2013). Antigone. In *Menonton Bengkel Teater Rendra*. Jakarta: Burungmerak Press, pp. 415–28.

51 Putu Wijaya. (1974). Catatan Pementasan Antigone di TIM. *HORISON/X/165,* Jakarta, 3 August. (Original text: "Lihatlah apa yang telah kita perbuat untuk tokoh teater yang terkemuka ini. Meskipun keadaan ini, yang kadang jepitannya justru akan menyebabkan penyair yang sudah belajar silat ini getol dan meloncat dengan langkah yang lebih besar lagi".)

52 See Winet E. D. (2004).

53 On *Tradisi Baru*, see Asmara, C. (1995) and Cobina Gillitt, A. (1995). For a comprehensive overview of articles and other materials about Rendra and Bengkel Teater productions (up to 2005), see the remarkable collection-book *Menonton Bengkel Teater Rendra*, Edi Haryono (2013).

54 The *super-puppet* of Gordon Craig, the work of *physical actions* of Stanislavsky and later Grotowski, and the *Biomechanics* of Meyerhold are main examples of this notion.

55 See Murray 2015. Keyword 12: Resistance.

56 Grotowski, J. (1997).

57 A. Boal (Rio De Janeiro 1931–2009) was a Brazilian theatre director, writer and politician. He founded the Theatre of the Oppressed.

58 Acknowledgements: I want to express my gratitude to The American Academy of Dramatic Arts (AADA), and specifically Betty Lawson. The Academy provided me with relevant information, pictures and the Transcript Document of Jehlinger/Gould. They also put me in contact with Don Amendolia, a fellow student of Rendra, whom I thank for his effort to recall some memories. My warmest thanks to Harry Mastrogeorge, who was ready to help and share his knowledge, and who was passionate about my research. Thank you to Theodorus Setya Nugraha (Teddy) for his generosity in sharing many aspects about his father's personal and public life. Our discussions facilitated a deeper comprehension of Rendra's work. My heartfelt thanks to Tapa Sudana, whose approach, experience and behaviour have had an enormous impact on me. For this essay, he provided much pertinent information. Thank you to the PGB Bangau Putih Silat association, in particular, Guru Gunawan Rahardja, Pak Irwan Rahardja and all the trainers. Meeting senior Silat practitioners and Bengkel Teater's actors of the period 1967–1978, has supported my understanding about Rendra's work. Thus, thanks to Pak Fajar Suharno, Pak Untung Basuki and Pak Edi Haryono, among others. To Phillip Zarrilli, my gratitude for trusting and supporting the progress of this essay since its early stages. Finally, thanks to Cathirose Petrone and Jonathan Pitches for some editorial suggestions.

References

AADA. (1968). Jehlinger in Rehearsal. Verbatim Notes Transcribed by Eleanor Cody Gould in Rehearsal Classes Conducted by Charles Jehlinger at the American Academy of Dramatic Arts from 1918 to His Death in 1952. *Copyright Eleanor Cody Gould, 1958. Copyright American Academy of Dramatic Arts, 1968.*

Asmara, C. (1995). Tradisi Baru: A 'New Tradition' of Indonesian Theatre. *Asian Theatre Journal*, 12(1).

Barba, E. (1995). *The Paper Canoe: A Guide to Theatre Anthropology*. London and New York: Routledge.

Baron, C. (2016). *Modern Acting. The Lost Chapter of American Film and Theatre*. London: Palgrave Macmillan.

Blair, R. (2010). *Acting: The First Six Lessons: Documents from the American Laboratory Theatre*. New York: Routledge.

Boleslavsky, R. (1960). *Enam Peladjaran Pertama Bagi Tjalon Aktor. 'Tjatatan dari Penterdjemah'*. Jakarta: A. Sani. PT Jaya Sakti.

Carnicke, S. M. (1998). *Stanislavsky in Focus* (Russian Theatre Archive, Volume 17). Amsterdam: Harwood Academic Publishers.

Ciancarelli, R. and Ruggeri, S. (2009). *Il teatro e le leggi dell'organicità*. Roma: Dino Audino.

Cobina Gillitt, A. (1995). Tradisi Baru: A 'New Tradition' of Indonesian Theatre. *Asian Theatre Journal*, 12(1), 164–174, Spring. University of Hawai'i Press.

Cruciani, F. (1995). *Teatro nel novecento. Registi pedagoghi e comunita' teatrali nel XX secolo.* Rev. ed. Rome: Editori Associati.

Foley, K. (2016). Arifin and Putu: *Teater Modern* Acting in New Order Indonesia. *Theatre, Dance and Performance Training*, 7(3), 472–484.

Gallese, V., Fadiga, L., Fogassi, L. and Rizzolatti, G. (1996). Action Recognition in the Premotor Cortex. *Brain*, 119(2), 593–609.

Grotowski, J. (1997). Theatre of Sources. In Richard Schechner and Lisa Wolford, eds., *Grotowski Sourcebook*. London and New York: Routledge, pp. 252–270.

Grotowski, J. (2002). *Towards a Poor Theatre*. London: Routledge.

Haryono, E. (2013). *Menonton Bengkel Teater Rendra*. Jakarta: Burungmerak Press.

Lane, M. (2009). W.S. Rendra (1935–2009): Dissident in the Wind. *Direct Action: For Socialism in the 21st Century*, 15, September.

Moore, S. (1984). *The Stanislavski System*. New York: Penguin.

Moutsatsos, K. (2015). *Harry Mastrogeorge, Hollywood's Most Precious Acting Coach.* Underground Network Interview Streamed live, 28 April. Available at: www.youtube.com/watch?v=2GVf2iViPS8.

Murray, S. (2015). Keywords in Performer Training. *Theatre, Dance and Performance Training*, 6(1), 46–58.

Prijosusilo, B. (2009). Obituary: Farewell WS Rendra, Poet, Playwright and Father of Indonesian Theater. *Jakarta Globe*, 7 August.

Redana, B. (2010). Rendra and Martial Arts. *Inside Indonesia*, 101, July–September.

Rendra, W. S. (1983). From the Mysteries of Nature to Structural Analysis. *Prisma*, 29, 44–49.

Rendra, W. S. (1987?). *Hand Notes*. Unpublished.

Richardson, D. (1988). *Acting Without Agony: An Alternative to the Method*. Boston, MA: Allyn and Bacon.

Rosidi, A. (1997). *Asrul Sani 70 tahun: penghargaan dan penghormatan.* Jakarta: Pustaka Jaya.

Schechner, R. (1973). *Environmental Theater*. New York: Hawthorn.

Stanislavsky, K. (1989). *An Actor Prepares*. London: Routledge (First Published in 1936).

Strasberg, L. (1987). *A Dream of Passion: The Development of the Method*. Boston: Little, Brown and Company.

White, R. A. (2006). Stanislavsky and Ramacharaka: The Influence of Yoga and Turn-of-the-Century Occultism on the System. *Cambridge Journal Online, Theatre Survey, the American Society for Theatre Research*, 1, 73–92.

Winet, E. D. (2003). Interpolating American Method Acting in 1950s Indonesia. *Journal of Dramatic Theory and Criticism*, 89–106, Fall, University of Kansas, US.

Winet, E. D. (2004). Shadow and Method: Indonesian Theatre. In S. E. Wilmer, ed., *Writing and Rewriting National Theatre Histories*. Iowa City, IA: University of Iowa Press.

Winet, E. D. (2010). *Indonesian Postcolonial Theatre: Spectral Genealogies and Absent Faces*. London and New York: Palgrave Macmillan.

Yudiaryani. (2006). Rendra and Teater Mini Kata as a Counter Culture in Yogyakarta on the 1960s: Considering a Tradition for Creating a Modern Theatre. *Culture Resources Management*, 4. URP, Yogyakarta.

Yudiaryani. (2015). *W.S. Rendra dan Teater Mini Kata.* Yogyakarta: Galang Pustaka.

Zarrilli, P. (2002). *Acting (Re)Considered: A Theoretical and Practical Guide.* 2nd ed. London and New York: Routledge.

Zarrilli, P. (2009). *Psychophysical Acting: An Intercultural Approach After Stanislavski*. London: Routledge.

Some Videos about Rendra

www.youtube.com/watch?v=DdwQFoB7Tcc
www.youtube.com/watch?v=Vm8uawLRgpk
www.youtube.com/watch?v=TjlpqlOprcc
www.youtube.com/watch?v=TObTybYkA6A
www.youtube.com/watch?v=IAVngRyTn84

Other links

AADA: www.aada.edu
Harry Mastrogeorge: www.harrymastrogeorge.com
Tapa Sudana: http://tapasudana.blogspot.co.id/

13

BALI IN BRAZIL

Perceptions of "otherness" by the "other"

Carmencita Palermo[1]

Introduction: otherness as discourse

Balinese dance-theatre and music are taught in various parts of the world, often included in the curricula of performing arts and music departments of educational institutions and as part of actors' training at independent theatre groups. This interest in Balinese performance can be seen to originate from an attraction to the exotic "other" mixed with a specific local political-economic narrative. This attraction can be traced back to the description of Bali during the period of colonization by the Dutch, which created a romanticized image of the island where everyone was an artist. Hobart (2007) skilfully deconstructs the romanticization of Balinese dance, encouraging a critical approach to its representation in accounts from pre-colonial times to the present by non-Indonesians and Indonesians alike. Inspired by Hobart's work and drawing on my own personal touring experience, I seek to highlight the roots of the "romanticized" appeal of Balinese dance-drama for some theatre training traditions in Europe and South America and reveal how the weight of this discourse affects me as an "other", an Italian nomad, skilled in Balinese masked dance-drama.

Keeping in mind the discourse on "otherness" established by continental philosophy, I will attempt to demonstrate that the political construction of the "other", by a colonial power, is the source of this attraction to Balinese dance-drama in actor training contexts. At the same time, I will consider the vital role played by the perception of self in otherness in the defining of the other, in particular the sense of belonging which appears in colonial and -postcolonial discourse (Habermas 1975) in which there are two choices: one is either "in" or "out" of the circle – one belongs or does not; the "other" is simply the "other". Zygmunt Bauman asserts that social order is based on a strong concept of otherness, and that a dichotomized approach to building identity is seen clearly at work in the practice of power. "The second member is but the other of the first, the opposite (degraded, suppressed, exiled) side of the first and its creation" (Bauman 1991, p. 11). Part of the identity building of the colonized "other" is a process of essentialization, which in the case of Bali has made the island into, "museum of Hindu civilization", "the last paradise", "the island where everyone is an artist" as well illustrated by Vickers (2012 [1989]). Those images, which originated from the essentialized identity initially promoted to the external world by the Dutch colonizers, have continued to circulate for more than a century, creating all sorts of interpretations and responses, both within and outside Bali.

The politically constructed image of the colonized other produced long-lasting influence seen in unforeseeable domains, as evidenced in Antonin Artaud's essay "On the Balinese Theatre", which he wrote after seeing a Balinese dance troupe in the Dutch East Indies Pavilion at the Colonial Exhibition in Paris in 1931.[2] Artaud portrays the performers' movements in relation to the music, the shape of their bodies, their costumes, the sense of sacredness that he perceives, and prizes the minor role of the word as an example to imitate in order to overcome the limitations of realism/naturalism in Western theatre. Artaud conveys poetically his experience of seeing the performers rather than describing the performance. His article has received abundant critical reactions, leading Nicola Savarese in his work on Artaud's essay (Savarese 2001), to highlight the need to contextualize the event and Artaud's poetic writing style, noting it was not so different from that of others who reviewed the same performance. Savarese demonstrates that some of Artaud's impressions were the result of misinformation within the programme and the adaptation of the performance for a non-Balinese audience. Moreover, it is likely that Artaud saw in Balinese theatre what he needed to see to revitalize Western theatre: a new theatrical language, a language of gesture and the figure of the director. The possibility that Artaud saw the projection of his own vision – of his own self – can perhaps be explained by the works of Zygmunt Bauman and other phenomenologists.

Bauman (1991), in his analysis of the political construction of the "other", saw blurry boundaries between the self and the other in both a psychological and sociological sense. Such a blurring incorporates Lacan's "the other within" (2006[1966]) and the ways this intrinsic other has extrinsic and sociological implications for identity construction, as discussed by both Martin Buber (2000[1923]) and Emmanuel Levinas (1987). This was a stepping stone for the deconstructed, relative concept of otherness developed by Jacques Derrida (1984), who shifts between the phenomenological approach that sees the self in the other and Levinas' approach which considers that it is impossible to know the other (in Reynolds 2001). In terms of the above theories – constructed colonial identity, concurrence of other with self, the impossibility of knowing the other – Artaud could have had no real knowledge of Balinese performance since what he had seen in the Paris Balinese performance was in fact a projection of his own self. If so, how did Artaud's exotic and decontextualized approach to the "other" have such an important impact on Western theatre in the twentieth century? Furthermore, why do we perpetuate this image of the exotic other after Edward Said's exposure in Orientalism (1978) of the concept of otherness as a colonizing vision in which every other is both a perception of otherness in the other but also the self? This was the apparent paradox which became increasingly clear and needed to be faced throughout a visit I made to Brazil to lecture about and demonstrate Balinese dance.

The activities I conducted – performances, demonstrations and workshops – became tools to reflect on my own personal conflict in considering Artaud an "exotic disaster" while being aware of the revolution he created in theatre. In the following discussion I will lead the reader through my reflections; this is going to be my narrative, my "voice" (as in Herbst 1998), relating the perception (by "others") of my otherness in those other lands. Inspired by Herbst, who leads the reader through his journey of learning Balinese music and drama, I will provide an account of my thoughts as they evolved, stimulated by the interaction with my audiences. It is mostly an account of my negotiations with the perception of my own "otherness", while questioning my fascination with Balinese dance-drama. I first contextualize my visit to Brazil; then I review separately my response to the different types of interactions during demonstrations, performances and workshops. My narrative is at times conflicted, reflecting a struggle in my thoughts between rejection of exoticism and re-experiencing through my Brazilian audiences my own initial attraction to Balinese dance and gaining enriched understandings of self and otherness. Eventually, from being a strenuous defender of contextualization I became open to seeing the value of exoticism. In spite of its uncomfortable chaos, the journey allowed me experientially to perceive that same dichotomy that I vigorously seek to hold at bay, yet which also paradoxically creates a liminal space for my own cross-cultural existence.

From writing to touring – my contextualized Bali

My journey to Brazil started when I was invited by Professor Maria Brigida Miranda (Brazilian lecturer with a PhD on Capoeira and actor training from Australia) to contribute an article on Balinese topeng (mask dance-drama) in a book on masks published by the State University of Santa Catarina (Palermo 2012).[3] The publication of the article led to further conversation with Professor Miranda on the idea of spreading my views on actor training in Brazil. The focus of my article in the edited collection was on my training in topeng and the way in which Balinese mask masters explained the process of characterization of the masks. In the article, I record the voices of several performers on characterization, and discuss how their use of cosmological concepts linked to the use of breath is influenced by contemporary cultural policy and the democratization of knowledge. This is strongly connected to the post-colonial context and identity-building process of the Indonesian nation and is also manifest in the discourse of Balinese identity or Balineseness, which is based on religious identity in the wider national Indonesian discourse.

The concept of Balineseness (*kebalian*), is a clear example of the essentialization of identity of the colonized "other" (Vickers 2012 [1989]; Palermo 2007). In the case of Bali, its image was strongly exoticized and sanitized to showcase it for the international community after the atrocities involved in the bloody conquest of the island (Vickers 2012[1989]). As already mentioned, Bali was commonly portrayed as a living museum of Indian Hinduism, the last paradise, the island where all are artists – all aspects included in the concept of Balineseness, which were picked up by the Balinese intelligentsia from the 1920s onwards.Vickers (2012[1989]) clearly shows how the image of Bali as "Paradise" was created in the writings of Dutch colonizers, anthropologists and artists along with various Balinese writers. Picard (1999) points out that Balinese identity "is the outcome of a process of semantic borrowing and conceptual recasting that the Balinese had to make in response to the colonization, the Indonesianization and the touristification of their island" (in Allen and Palermo 2005, p. 239).

The imperialistic practice of essentialization of the identity of the colonized reached European theatre practitioners in the early twentieth century, as they were pursuing otherness in search of themselves, or as part of a renewed self. At the same time, this essentialized identity was adopted by the Balinese themselves to create a space for Balinese under Dutch colonization, in the post-colonial Indonesian nation. In both cases it was "otherness" adopted for the self. Balineseness has always been related to preservation, as a concern of the first visitors to the island was about the preservation of Hindu elements of Balinese culture. For the Balinese intelligentsia, it was initially about surviving colonization, then about not being subsumed by Islam in the process of nation building after independence. More recently, after the Bali bombings in 2002 and 2005, Balineseness has been about the Balinese defending themselves from the influx of too many immigrants from elsewhere in Indonesia, and on enticing back international tourists (Suryawan 2004; Allen and Palermo 2005). Now the concern is about defending their land from excessive tourism while still being "authentically Balinese" in order to attract tourists. In this context, topeng has often been used to represent Balineseness and its practice has been widely promoted through competitions such as those included in the programme of the Pesta Kesenian Bali, Bali Art Festival (Palermo 2007).

My familiarity with the cultural/religious discourse of topeng practice has allowed me to connect such discourse with an analysis of the body of the performer in its context. It was this focus that resonated with Professor Miranda and led to the invitation to teach and perform in Brazil in October–November 2013. I had a vague memory of Brazilians training with my own teachers in the early 1990s and also around 2000–2010. Some of them were involved with commedia dell'arte, and most of them encountered topeng through Eugenio Barba's Odin Teatret and International School of Theatre Anthropology (ISTA) or Ariane Mnouchkine's Théatre du Soleil with I Made Djimat and the late Italian expatriate, Cristina Wistari Formaggia, as artists in residence. I do not recall meeting in the 1990s any Brazilian colleagues involved in "Balinese Studies", or any "Bali experts" who talked or wrote about Brazil in relation to Balinese arts and culture. Although nowadays things are different, Brazilians are still relatively few in number compared to those coming from the US, Japan, France or even Italy to study Balinese dance-theatre in Bali. The international interest in Balinese performance varies according to the country of origin. However, as these are other stories and it is my personal experience and perceptions that are fundamental to this article, I return to the account of my journey to Brazil with flashbacks to Italy where I had my first experience of Bali.

Questioning my own attraction for the exotic other (Bali) via Brazil: reflections from demonstrations

My first stop in Brazil was in Florianopolis, which felt encouragingly familiar. Many places were like a mix of Indonesian and Sicilian villages and towns with the same chaos, dirt and traffic for which my host, Professor Miranda, kept apologizing since she knew me as an "Australian". Over time I noticed similarities with attitudes I had experienced in Australia – in particular, a certain disregard of indigenous traditions and cultures in the domain of the performing arts in favour of a distinct Eurocentric attitude. This attitude was also criticized: I often heard people say, in discussions about theatre, that "Brazilians like foreigners – European foreigners" or that "there is a lot of funding to invite foreign artists and next to nothing for local ones". Throughout my stay, my interlocutors were the participants in workshops and the audience members at work-demonstrations and performances. Some of my interactions with audiences were video recorded, while other feedback was obtained from the students in Florianopolis. I also sent a questionnaire to workshop participants and others. The languages used during my tour and interactions were a combination of Italian, English and Portuguese. In some contexts I would speak in Italian or English, which was translated into Portuguese, but then I listened directly to my interlocutor's reply in Portuguese. During the tour I presented a lecture-demonstration and a workshop in all the cities I visited. I performed three times in Florianopolis and Joinville.

The lecture-demonstrations in Brazil were all organized at universities and dance-theatre schools. During the lecture-demonstrations I would talk about the context of a temple ceremony in Bali and demonstrate the traditional introductory full-mask characters of Balinese topeng to highlight how each part of the body needs to change shape to become the masked character: Patih (the Prime Minister), Boes (the funny and strong character), Tua (the Old Man) and Dalem (the King). Then I would mention the role of the half-masks: servants as storytellers of the dynastic chronicles connecting the past of the Majapahit courts to present-day life and the comic characters. With each of the solo characters I demonstrate their basic walks followed by a cosmological interpretation of the dance technique and its contextualization of daily life. At this point, I would usually allow the audience to ask questions about the presentation. I also took the opportunity to ask them about their reasons for attending a talk on Balinese masks. Especially in Florianopolis, my question to the audience became an opportunity to discuss in a rather critical way the source of their interest in Balinese performance: reading of Artaud's "On the Balinese Theatre" and their encounter with Eugenio Barba's Odin Teatret and ISTA. That was my beginning too. Like me, most of my audience's fascination with

Balinese performance started from ISTA's concept of transcultural pre-expressivity, which has informed the principle of the presence of the performer by focusing on their body-mind (Barba and Savarese 1991; Barba 1995; De Marinis 2000). But as De Marinis (2000) underlines, the focus of the body of the performer outside its cultural context has some limits. In fact, those who learn topeng receive their technical knowledge via kinaesthetic imitation and body manipulation up to a certain level, then the learning process becomes dialogical; talking about the stories used in topeng and their underlying philosophy is as important as (sometimes more important than) a performer's technical ability since it is one of the ways to characterize the mask. A pupil learns by joining the master in performing; the feedback and discussion regarding that experience is fundamental to the process of the transmission of the knowledge, since this knowledge is fully embodied and involves several domains of the human: "personal, social, ritual, aesthetic, political, cosmological" (Zarrilli 2001, p. 35). These are all aspects that will influence both pre-expressive and expressive levels. Without this experience, the risk is to consider the "other" as a decontextualized object or an experimental guinea pig attracting our scientific curiosity. Today, with the relative ease of travelling to the lands of others, we can attempt to avoid such decontextualization.

It was, however, more difficult for someone like Artaud who experienced the distant "other" in the exotic context of the Paris Exhibition. Hence Artaud's decontextualized exoticism requires contextualization. Whereas Rustom Bharucha (1984, p. 3) is critical of Artaud's a-historical view of Balinese theatre, citing him as an example, among others, of cultural appropriation, we have seen how Savarese (2001) has sought to contextualize Artaud's experience in Paris in 1931, analysing the historical context of the Paris Colonial Exhibition and the nature of the performance made for non-Balinese audiences as "constructed otherness", aiming to glorify Dutch colonial power. Rather than attacking Artaud's vision, as Bharucha does, I would use Artaud's work to understand his context, as do Savarese and more recently Tsu-Chung Su. Su draws on Savarese's work and further considers Artaud's experience in Foucauldian terms as a "singular event of interpretation, exposing the dual nature of Orientalism and the double-bind characteristic of the act of interpretation which contaminates and disseminates its target all at the same time" (Su 2009, p. 5). Su (2009, p. 9) suggests that Artaud's "misreadings and misunderstandings" of Balinese theatre are a tool to grasp the power relation between Balinese and European cultures, to understand colonial imperialism in general.

Su explains how Artaud's misinterpretations have given birth to avant-garde movements, studies of interculturalism and theatre anthropology. Risks of appropriation in cross-cultural theatre experiments are always present, as much as the counter-effort of changing the dichotomy of East/West (see Barba 1995). Su's and Savarese's analyses provide contextualization of the imagined Balinese dance and drama in the domain of performing arts theory that I believe can be enriched by a combination of their work with that of Vickers and Picard, which focuses on imagined Balinese culture, and, more specifically, Hobart's research (2000, 2007) that explores imagined Balinese performance. Savarese is well known in the domain of

European performing arts scholars influenced by ISTA, whilst Vickers, Picard and Hobart are prominent specialists in Balinese culture. In rare cases the respective spheres of influence cross. In my case, for instance, I have been exposed to a wide range of ideas and influences through studying and teaching in Italy, the UK, Malta, the Netherlands, Indonesia and Australia. In Tasmania, where I taught a unit on the Performing Arts in Asia, it was often a revelation for students to realize the depth of influence Asian performing arts have had on theatre practitioners in the twentieth century. For many Australian students, Bali is seen as a holiday destination and not a place they would think of as the inspiration for major new directions in contemporary theatre in Europe. For my Italian students, Bali is a faraway "aspiration". These experiences highlight how the perspective of the "other" changes according to where we are and the kind of cultural circles in which we move. But in some cases even if we move around the same circles we can have different perspectives regarding the "other". I did not explicitly discuss these thoughts while in Brazil; they have arisen in recalling my effort to distance myself from the role of "Balinese performer", an effort which was unsuccessful in the context of my performance *Women's Breath*.

My "non-Balinese performance": a window on the audience's reactions

My performance piece *Women's Breath* is a portrait of female archetypes across cultures through dance and movement. While the archetypes I represent are inspired by Balinese topeng in giving an implicit portrait of the cycle of life, I do not use Balinese technique; rather I use the principles of mask embodiment learned from my Balinese teachers. The work with my teachers was based on male characters only. In my work I explore the femininity within the stereotyped court characters and the comic characters of topeng and their different breaths or energies. The performance is the result of the study of the breath necessary to give life to the characters. The breath which transforms the body is represented by dictating the rhythm supported by the sound which becomes the body itself. In order to reach this unity of mask–body–sound, I employ live music that interacts with the performer in a dialogic, somewhat jazz-like manner inspired by the way in which the topeng performer interacts with the *gamelan* orchestra. I endeavoured to avoid having the performance labelled "Balinese", even though audience interaction is a strong feature of Balinese topeng and a point of creative departure for me. Nevertheless, in spite of my clear position, *Women's Breath* was promoted as a performance with Balinese masks and I was told that it was the only way to attract an audience; I had to accept that faraway exotic Bali was a promotional tool beyond my control.

There were three evening performances of the piece – two in Florianopolis and one in Joinville. At the end of the second performance in Florianopolis we decided to allow the audience to ask questions. One question concerned the use of Balinese masks outside of Bali. The audience member had read that masks are entered by a spirit and the spirit enters into the actor, and thus she wondered how it was possible to use Balinese masks outside their "spiritual" place. That was a difficult question to answer. Whilst some of my fellow non-Balinese topeng practitioners explicitly and often "theatrically" call upon Balinese ancestors with offerings and incense, I do not. I explained that all performers in Bali have different ways of treating the masks and it depended on the occasion of the performance, on the performer's personality as well as on the type of mask and whether or not ceremonies of purification and initiation had been performed to allow the spirit of the ancestors to enter the mask. Since I had to talk about my own experience, I explained that what I put into the mask is my own spirit in using the mask over and over, recharging it with life. This question confirmed the "danger" of promoting the performance as "Balinese", because the imagined "other" overshadows the actual form of my work, which has very few explicitly Balinese elements.

During another conversation about the relationship between masks and music, a member of the audience noted that there was some similarity with the Brazilian martial art Capoeira. The connection was explicit and I felt the same way. In fact, in both cities I happily welcomed two different Capoeira practitioners beside classically trained musicians. The observer was picking up on the fact that the music is made up of cycles and performers know exactly when within a cycle they can signal for softer or louder volume, faster or slower rhythm or a longer accent phrase. The performer communicates to the drummer, who then rhythmically signals to the rest of the ensemble. In interacting with the local musicians, I try to reproduce this principle in such a way that I am not bound to a fixed melody, but can continuously adjust the structure of my performance according to the space and the audience. Although this sort of improvisation is common in Indonesia, allowing a performer to interact with unfamiliar musicians almost straight away, it is more difficult to do this with musicians trained in the Western classical tradition. The "dialogue" is between the sound of the musicians and the "sound" of the performing body – a dialogue not unlike what happens in jazz music. Once the language is established, the conversation happens and involves the audience. It is within this conversation between the musicians, the audience, the space and myself that I find the principles of Balinese performance manifest in context, and experience the pleasure of being part of it. I found it interesting that neither the audience nor the musicians in Brazil considered this kind of interaction with the music as something completely foreign or "other"; Capoeira was the familiar, linking element of the performance.

My own roots of exoticism – topeng workshops via commedia dell'arte and beyond

The mask workshops varied in length according to the place: the shortest was a one-day workshop in Joinville, most lasted two to three days, as was the case in Campinas, São Paolo, Belo Horizonte and Brasilia, while the extended stay in Florianopolis allowed for five days. In the workshops I introduced the basic topeng technique through which it was possible to understand the principles such as how the body changes shape according to the characters, and how to distribute energy to animate the masks, to create rhythm and contrasts and to change direction and focus. These principles were applied in learning the basic walks that underpin a character's movement. I always make clear that, although it takes years of training to fully master these principles, a grasp of the basic technique is useful to understand the half-masks used for the bondres/comic characters. These are more open to personal interpretation, and in my workshops I use the basic commedia dell'arte techniques that I learnt from Italian commedia dell'arte actors Enrico Bonavera and Claudia Contin in order to teach comic characters.

My reflection on the use of commedia dell'arte techniques in my current teaching methodology of mask embodiment takes me back to my first experiences of Balinese topeng in Italy in 1990, in Bologna, as part of an ISTA event. The topeng troupe I watched was led by well-known scholar and performer I Made Bandem and an Italian mask performer Pino Confessa, who, in full Balinese costume, was the translator of the faraway culture. During the performance the imprinting happened, as my perception of the "other" was shaped by the possibility of understanding this new form – topeng – as an exciting and improved version of the familiar commedia dell'arte. As a performing arts student I knew that commedia dell'arte, which was considered dead for a few centuries, had been reinvented at the beginning of the twentieth century. By contrast, the topeng performance seemed to me very much part of a living and necessary tradition. It did not matter that the performance was outside its context, as my perception of the "other" was shaped by finding a masked performance form with a more explicit focus on the body. Although the experience elicited my own Artaud-like delirium, it did not last for too long.

Unconsciously influenced by the Italian discourse on an actor's training, it always made more sense to me to combine the two techniques to discover how to build a character in a cross-cultural way or "beyond tradition" in a very personal manner. Later I realized some topeng performers themselves see the similarities between, and the potential for combining, topeng and commedia dell'arte. For example, well-known Balinese performer I Made Djimat calls commedia dell'arte "bondres Italia" and he often mentions the days when he used to perform with Pino Confessa during temple ceremonies in Bali. I have seen I Nyoman Durpa, a well-known topeng performer from north Bali, performing with a Pulcinella-like costume and mask. Teaching Balinese comic characters, inspired by the teachings of Italian masters, was not so out of this world. Enrico Bonavera, in the foundation sessions of his training, teaches that by changing the shape of single sections of the body and combining those, "transformation occurs" as the whole body acquires a new shape. In my workshops in Brazil I adopted this technique and I encouraged the transformed bodies to look for a rhythm, a breath and a sound suitable for any of the masks/characters that I made available. Once these attributes were found, improvisation was used to explore ways to interact within other characters. Another aspect I explored was the interaction between performer and rhythm. I taught groups of participants a basic interlocking pattern typical of Balinese music and then allowed the mask-wearer to learn how to lead the improvised orchestra/chorus through use of their own body. The chorus-like effect of this mechanism is very strong when the body of the mask-wearer and the rhythm of the group become one. This interlocking of rhythms for me has always been the closest thing to my exotic image of choral music used in Ancient Greek theatre, which brings another layer of otherness into play, but one left as a background sensation. In the Brazilian cities I visited, the workshop participants responded particularly well to this part of the work. Although the sound created by the group had no relation with the actual *gamelan* music, the use of the masks did give a taste of how the topeng performers have to lead the *gamelan* ensemble through their bodies. In Campinas and São Paolo, some participants drew comparisons between our work and performance form called Cavalo Marinho in which stories are told through masked characters and rhythms reminiscent of samba; they thus felt more familiar with the sound–music relationship.[4] The intensity and focus of the workshops changed according to the expectations and experiences of the participants, as some of them had some experience of learning topeng in Bali, while others were students or professional actors.

After-tour conversations

Emails, chatting and interactions with a specific questioner kept me in touch with students and audience members and introduced me to Brazilians interested in Balinese topeng. From my conversations I realized that only Maria Bonome and Rafael Protzn from Belo Orizonte, Helo Cardoso from Campinas and Ana Pessoa from São Paolo had ever worked with a Balinese teacher, and they had all studied with I Made Djimat in Bali. Djimat's family have set up the Tri Pusaka Sakti Arts Foundation in Batuan, which makes it easy for foreigners to access regular training and accommodation. Djimat is not surprised he has students from Brazil since he has toured there quite a few times since the 1980s.[5] More adventurous students explore other options, as in the case of Luana L.R. Although I did not meet her in Brazil, I have had email conversations after being introduced by one of my workshop participants. She travelled to Bali in 2012 and 2014, basing herself in Ubud and studying with Ida Bagus Anom from Mas during her first visit and then with I Wayan Yuda in Batuan during her second stay. Luana explained that although she began with no expectations, she is grateful that after some 10 months of training over two years, she is now skilled enough to share the three characters she learntd. When I asked if Balinese theatre is relevant to theatre in Brazil, she answered that her Balinese training is an inspiration, and taught her dedication and patience:

> This is a great learning experience for a Western actor, who often seeks quick results, or also depends more on talent, leaving aside the dedication to a technique. Balinese art also teaches us about humility and respect for tradition and the passing on of skills from a master. It shows the amazing ability of accuracy, refinement, and attention to detail. It shows a theatre tradition that has maintained its origins in ritual, with a latent corporeality, and one that uses masks.[6]

There are two aspects of her assessment that are relevant to my discussion. Firstly, Luana considers herself within the category of "Western actor", a somewhat denigrating label for someone who has lost the sense of actor training, but has had the great opportunity to learn patience and appreciate details through Balinese dance technique. Secondly, her mention of connection with an "original theatre", the connection with "its origins in ritual" that is possible to find in Bali, echoes the description of Balinese dance by Artaud in "On the Balinese Theatre".

The understanding of "Western actor" in the context of Brazil is, according to Juliana Cohelo, somewhat complex as it involves issues of Brazilian identity. Cohelo (2014) describes how she learnt topeng in Bali as a travelling artist and compares her experience with that of fellow Brazilians Ana Teixeira and Felisberto Sabino, and with Roberta Carreri from Odin Teatret. Cohelo analyses the created images of Bali and the impact on everyday reality, reflects on the similarities between her home in northern Brazil and Bali, and thus does not see Bali as exotic. Cohelo, by comparing the Brazilian and Balinese sense of identity in a post-colonial prospective, underlines that Brazil cannot be considered "Oriental" or Western. In particular, she calls for a "collective problematization" of the fact that Brazilians consider themselves as "Western" and the urgent need for "perspective adjustment" as "essential" for further reflection on Brazilians' affiliations and "multiple identities" (Cohelo 2014). In Cohelo's case, she has had the advantage of living in Paris and travelling to Bali for research, allowing her both spatial and existential distance to question her sense of identity as a Brazilian. In other words, her ability to do so in part depends on her own status of otherness, which changes depending on where she lives and works. Change of place and being in the "place of others" allows one to step outside the cultural self and negotiate between the perception of self and the perception of other.

A further step accurs when the experience of "the place of others" allows one to come back to the self and nurture the perception of self: Prof Miranda my host, for example, with her PhD from Melbourne University, looks at the Capoeira as a source for contemporary actor's training and was the one initiating my collaboration with Capoeira performers. In Campinas my host whom I first met in Italy to study commedia dell'arte mask-making, enthusiastically informed me that Candomblé was studied at the department of Performing Arts at the University of Campinas. My host in São Paulo, who has often visited Italy, had me invited to a ritual derived from Candomblé religion where I experienced the sacredness that I considered the root of theatre.

In keeping with the "otherness" that is idealized and decontextualized in Artaud's vision as non-modern tradition rooted in ritual and able to save Western theatre, I could see that strong sense of sacredness in rituals in Brazil and I was attracted to them because I experienced them as otherness. Yet the alterity of the other (Bali), the other constructed via colonial power and national cultural policy introduced to Brazil by a European/Western theatre group, seems to be regarded as a more valid medium than local traditional training and rituals to nurture Brazilian theatre. I became aware that I was invited to Brazil by those who felt that Brazil's own otherness needed to be re-evaluated in actor training. Was I like a latter-day little Pelé who had to remind the nation that playing soccer in Brazilian style, ginga style derived from Capoeira, was the only way to win the World Cup in 1958?

Final thoughts

A dichotomized tension of opposites and multiple opposing layers have character-ized my personal journey. The reader has been led through a non-linear personal account which is permeated by a sense of guilt for being an "Orientalist" in Said's terms.

In order to understand the reasons for my invitation to Brazil, I have sought to interrogate my position as an "other" while also seeking to work against the essen-tialized "Balinese other". I talked about the performances, audiences and partici-pants, which prompted me to reflect upon issues of identity and people's desire to engage with otherness, in particular "far otherness". Despite my repeated attempts to assert that I was not a "Balinese performer", I was still perceived as a conduit through which to access that "exotic otherness", in part due to the trust bestowed on me as the exotic, yet familiar (Italian-born/European) "other" who had also been on a similar journey of discovering Balinese art. In a way, their othering of me as a "Balinese performer" represented a failure of my attempts to avoid the stereotype of the colonized other (Bali), in the land of colonized others (Brazil). Yet it was also a success in that my use of site-specific elements (i.e. relating the performer's body to music) in a cross-cultural manner provided a means to highlight for my audience/participants the closeness of the exotic "otherness" of Bali to common performance and ritual elements in Brazil, and thereby facilitate their rediscovery of the other-ness within. In the section regarding the workshop, I introduced into the otherness of Balinese technique additional "othernesses" such as commedia dell'arte and the chorus-like aspects of Balinese rhymes and the imaginings of how it could have been in the ancient Greek tragedies and comedies. This is a practical way to link all the main "othernesses" that have been sources of inspiration for the theatre of the twentieth century: the "Far Orient", Greek Theatre, commedia dell'arte, faraway in space or faraway in time. The completed questionnaires from some students, audience members and other Brazilian performers revealed a quest for a theatrical tradition that maintained its link to ritual – a quest for details, precision, respect for teachers and dedication to training, all things that Western-trained performers, such as those in Brazil, feel they can still learn from Bali, the last paradise. The colonial and post-colonial discourse on the "other" (Balinese) inevitably resonates within a post-colonial "other" (Brazilian). The cycle of my narrative returns to the begin-ning; it returns to the representation of the colonized other (Bali) as created by the Dutch and perceived and revealed by Artaud.

While I was in Brazil, trying to justify my being the other expert about other-ness and attempting to contextualize the same otherness (Bali), I was rejecting and at the same time thanking Artaud and Eugenio Barba who had inspired me and brought me to Brazil. I now realized that the tension between my "self" and the

other was absolutely fundamental to my narrative, as it created the actual space for
a cross-cultural performance. I believe this space has something in common with
the space created by Artaud. Based on Reynold's interpretation of Merleau-Ponty,
I dare to say that in the case of Artaud, although he inevitably saw himself in the
Balinese performance at the Paris Exhibition, he was also present in the Merleau-
Pontian sense of "the corporeality of consciousness" (Merleau-Ponty 2005 [1945]
in Reynolds 2010, 2001), such that he could have perceived the actual unity of
body-mind achieved by Balinese performers through their practical cosmological-
based training. There is a possibility that Artaud was able to perceive that space
of sacredness in spite of, or thanks to, his own altered state of mind; he was truly
connected with himself, so that what he perceived in Balinese theatre was already
in himself. Beyond speculation, Artaud clearly did perceive in Balinese theatre the
unity of body-mind to achieve presence on-stage, which has become fundamental
in actor training in both Western and non-Western theatre. For my own part, the
experience has allowed me to reconcile the intellectual separation between self and
the other, between the exotic perception of otherness and my need for contextualization at any cost; somehow, I learnt to accept the unavoidable perpetuation
of a decontexualized other as seen by Levinas. According to Levinas, facing the
other or avoiding the other will always result in the impossibility of "assimilating
aspects of the world into prior understanding" (Levinas 1993, p. 108 in Cohen
2010, p. 3). Rather, Levinas calls for respect for the alterity of the other and the
necessity of the other, and sees in the domain of the performance the possibility of
encountering the other where creativity is another liminal space where encounter
of otherness may happen without giving much importance to the aesthetic results
(Cohen 2010, p. 3). I came to value domains of complex othernesses, such as those
in Brazil, where I could enjoy and share the pleasure of the flourishing practice
of cross-cultural performance, an aesthetically pleasant practice I hope, because in
the encounters all the parties involved became a bit closer to each other's alteri-
ties. Above all, the conclusion of my journey is the understanding that exoticism
contributes to that liminal space of cross-cultural creative encounter, exoticism is,
or can be, a window to the other.

Notes

1 Acknowledgements: Thank you to all those in Brazil who invited and hosted me, thanks
  too to all the students and performers, many more than have been mentioned in this paper.
  Thank you to Barbara Hatley, Brett Hough, Margaret Coldiron and Kerensa Johnston
  who read the draft of this paper, provided feedback and helped me to make it sound a bit
  "less Italian".
2 "On the Balinese Theatre" (Sur le théâtre balinais) was initially published in 1931 in Nouvelle Revue Française, as a review of the event (in Savarese 2001, p. 51) and then included
  in The Theatre and Its Double (Le théâtre et son double) (Artaud, 1964 [1938]).
3 The English translation of the title is "Breathing into the Mask. The Body Takes Form in
  Balinese Dance-drama Topeng: A Learning Experience".
4 For an example of this form see https://www.youtube.com/watch?v=WvtOFNShFqc
  viewed 10 August 2015.
5 Personal communication with I Made Djimat, May 2015, Naples.

6 Original text: Isso é um grande aprendizado para o ator ocidental, que muitas vezes busca resultados rápidos, ou aposta também mais no próprio talento, deixando de lado a dedicação à uma técnica. A arte balinesa nos ensina também sobre humildade e também respeito pela tradição e transmissão do mestre. Ela mostra a incrível capacidade de precisão, refinamento, cuidado com o detalhe. Mostra o teatro mantido tal como foi em suas origens, originário do ritual, com a corporeidade latente, e com o uso da máscara.

References

Allen, P. and Palermo, C. (2005). Ajeg Bali: Multiple Meanings, Diverse Agendas. *Indonesia and the Malay World*, 33(97), 239–255.

Artaud, A. (1964 [1938]). *Le théâtre et son double [The Theatre and Its Double]*. Paris: Gallimard.

Barba, E. (1995). *The Paper Canoe: A Guide to Theatre Anthropology*. Translated by R. Fowler. New York: Routledge.

Barba, E. and Savarese, N. (1991). *The Secret Art of the Performer: A Dictionary of Theatre Anthropology*. Translated by R. Fowler. London and New York: Routledge.

Bauman, Z. (1991). *Modernity and Ambivalence*. Ithaca, NY: Cornell University Press.

Bharucha, R. (1984). A Collision of Cultures: Some Western Interpretations of the Indian Theatre. *Asian Theatre Journal*, 1(1), 1–20.

Buber, M. (2000 [1923]). *I and Thou*. Translated by R. G. Smith. Ithaca, NY: Scribner Classics.

Cohelo, J. (2014). Le voyage en tant que dessinateur d'une nouvelle cartographie de la chercheuse (The Journey as a Designer of a New Map of the Researcher). *The Post-colonialist*, 2(1). [online]. Available at: http://postcolonialist.com/culture/le-voyage-en-tant-que-dessinateur-dune-nouvelle-cartographie-de-la-chercheuse/ [Accessed 14–19 August 2015].

Cohen, M. I. (2010). *Performing Otherness: Java and Bali on International Stages, 1905–1952*. London: Palgrave Macmillan.

De Marinis, M. (2000). *In cerca dell'attore. Un bilancio del Novecento teatrale [In Search of an Actor. A Theatre Survey of 20th Century]*. Roma: Bulzoni Editore.

Derrida, J. (1984). Deconstruction and the Other: Dialogue with Derrida. In R. Kearney, ed., *Dialogue with Contemporary Continental Thinkers: The Phenomenological Heritage*. Manchester: Manchester University Press, pp. 145–162.

Habermas, J. (1975). *Legitimation Crisis*. Translated and Introduction by T. McCarthy. Boston: Beacon.

Herbst, E. (1998). *Voices in Bali: Energies and Perceptions in Vocal Music and Dance Theatre*. Hanover, NH: Wesleyan University Press and University Press of New England.

Hobart, M. (2000). *After Culture: Anthropology as Radical Metaphysical Critique*. Yogyakarta: Duta Wacana University Press.

Hobart, M. (2007). Rethinking Balinese Dance. *Indonesia and the Malay World*, 35(101), 107–128.

Lacan, J. (2006 [1966]). *Écrits: The First Complete Edition in English*. Translated by B. Fink. New York: W.W. Norton & Co.

Levinas, E. (1987). *Time and the Other*. Translated by R. A. Cohen. Pittsburgh: Duquesne University Press.

Levinas, E. (1993). *Outside the Subject*. Translated by M. B. Smith. Stanford, CA: Stanford University Press.

Palermo, C. (2007). *Towards the Embodiment of the Mask. Balinese Topeng in Contemporary Practice*. Thesis (PhD). Hobart, Launceston: University of Tasmania.

Palermo, C. (2012). Respirando para dentro da máscara – o corpo toma forma no teatro-dança balinês *topeng*: uma experiência de aprendizado. In V. Beltrame and M. de Andrade, eds., *Teatro de Máscaras (Theatre of Masks)*. Brasil: Universitadade Do Estato De Santa Catarina – UDESC, pp. 153–166.

Picard, M. (1999). The Discourse of *kebalian*: Transcultural Constructions of Balinese Identity. In R. Rubinstein and L. H. Connor, eds., *Staying Local in the Global Village: Bali in the Twentieth Century*. Honolulu: University of Hawai'I Press, pp. 15–49.

Reynolds, J. (2001). The Other of Derridean Deconstruction: Levinas, Phenomenology and the Question of Responsibility. *Minerva*. Available at: www.minerva.mic.ul.ie//vol5/der rida.html [Accessed 14 September 2015].

Reynolds, J. (2010). Problems of Other Minds: Solutions and Dissolutions in Analytic and Continental Philosophy. *Philosophy Compass*, 5(4), 326–335. Available at: http://dro. deakin.edu.au/eserv/DU:30061045/reynolds-problemsof-post-2010.pdf [Accessed 14 September 2015].

Said, E. W. (1978). *Orientalism*. New York: Pantheon Books..

Savarese, N. (2001). Antonin Artaud sees Balinese Theatre at the Paris Colonial Exposition. *Drama Review*, 45(3), 51–77.

Su, T-C. (2009). The Occidental Theatre and Its Other: The Use and Abuse of the Oriental Theatre in Antonin Artaud. *NTU Studies in Language and Literature*, 1(22), 1–30, December.

Suryawan, I. N. (2004). Ajeg Bali dan lahirnya jago-jago kebudayaan [Stand-Up Bali and the Birth of the Champions of Culture]. *Kompas*, 7 January.

Vickers, A. (2012 [1989]). *Bali: A Paradise Created*. Singapore: Tuttle Publishing.

Zarrilli, P. B. (2001). Negotiating Performance Epistemologies: Knowledges 'About', 'In' and 'For'. *Studies in Theatre and Performance*, 21(1), 31–46.

14

"TRADITIONAL" OPERA IN A "MODERN" SOCIETY

Institutional change in Taiwanese *xiqu* education

Josh Stenberg and Tsai Hsin-hsin

Introduction

Discourses of modernization in the twentieth-century Sinophone world engaged Western, Soviet and Japanese influences and models. Both education and theatre were important foci of social reform projects. Traditional Chinese theatre (*xiqu*) was no exception. *Xiqu* theorists and performers borrowed liberally from Western and Soviet models from the beginning of the twentieth century (Tian 2008, pp. 141–74), and by 1930 attempts were being made to adopt "the system of Western music drama schools" for *xiqu* training (Gao 2014, p. 144),[1] including the introduction of classes featuring academic content and higher expectations of cultural literacy. Nonetheless, most performers in the Republic were still trained according to older apprenticeship-based systems (Wu 1999, p. 81). In the years following the end of the Civil War in 1949, governments on both sides of the Taiwan Strait reformed *xiqu* training, deeming older systems incompatible with ideology and/or socio-political conditions and subordinating them to general political programmes. This article argues that since *xiqu* education is a substantial national project in Taiwan, tracing the principal training institution's history shows the socio-political determinants of the contemporary *xiqu* stage. This is particularly important given the identification of *xiqu* as "traditional", an ideological designation which partially obscures its constant reshaping by political forces. Approaching the question through its public institutions provides a concrete history of *xiqu* as a political project, and one answer to the still relevant question of how to make *xiqu* training – once marked by corporal punishment and predicated on fealty to a teacher and a troupe – compatible with a polity concerned to represent itself as modern and, especially in recent years, democratic.

Ideological rationale for institutionalization of *xiqu* education

Chinese *xiqu* education was historically conducted through private instruction, family transmission, or through studies at *keban* (private theatre schools), a system "structured according to paternalistic teacher – disciple bonds" (Goldstein 2007, p. 34).[2] Migration from Fujian to Taiwan in the Ming and Qing dynasties brought *xiqu* and associated training practices to the island. By the Japanese colonial period (1895–1945), there was a rich fabric of *xiqu* performance practice among "native"[3] Hokkien/Hakka Taiwanese as well as frequent touring companies from the Mainland (principally *Jingju* – "Peking/ Beijing Opera" – troupes).[4] Describing training in *gezaixi*, a native Taiwanese theatre form, one scholar notes that "training took place in the theatre company" with a novice performer receiving a "three-year-and-four-month contract that required physical and vocal training in residence" while taking on small parts to acquire stage experience (Hsieh 2008, p. 126).[5] *Xiqu* education was highly formal in its regulation of teacher-student relationships, but state involvement was not heavy. The Japanese colonial state in Taiwan was not much concerned with regulating, let alone instituting, *xiqu* education.

After the (retro)cession of Taiwan to the Republic of China in 1945 and the 1949 flight of Chiang Kai-shek's Nationalist government to Taiwan after defeat by the Communists on the Mainland, *Jingju* became for decades the pre-eminent institutional theatre form there, a function of "the Nationalists' dominant ideology (which valued Mainland Chinese culture over local Taiwanese culture)", granting it "the highest cultural capital of virtually all traditional performing arts" (Guy 2005, p. 4). The elevation of this genre, at the expense of "native" (and more popular, in both senses of the word) Taiwanese genres, formed the basic dynamic of state support for *xiqu* in Taiwan between the late 1940s and the 1980s (Guy 1999, pp. 508–9; Hsu Y.H. 2014, pp. 103–4). Although, unlike the People's Republic in Mainland China, the Republic of China (ROC) on Taiwan never attempted to organize, instrumentalize or politicize the totality of theatre activities, state involvement in *Jingju* was nevertheless high, and the genre "had an important role to play in the governing of Taiwan by the ruling Nationalist [KMT] party" (Guy 1999, p. 509).

Until late in the martial law years (1949–1987) of KMT Taiwan, the financial support and later the nationalization of a system of theatre education was deemed necessary to ensure the continuity of *Jingju* performance, particularly since market forces proved insufficient to sustain training and produce new high-quality performers. *Jingju* was adopted as an important ideological tool in its capacity as the "National Drama", in which role it features (in an attenuated form, to this day) in ROC claims to being the legitimate representative of, and protector of, Chinese culture.[6] Although *xiqu* performance and training in Mainland China was deeply altered by the sometimes radically reformist programme of the Chinese Communist Party,[7] until the 1970s Taiwanese *Jingju* "maintained more of the traditional repertoire and the related acting conventions", even if "professionals and audiences on Taiwan were ... deprived of the opportunity to see the best-trained actors" (Li 2010, p. 221; see also Hsu Y.H. 2014, pp. 108–9).

Beginning with the 1957 establishment of a private vocational school, institutional *xiqu* education in Taiwan has adopted various models, moving from an accredited private to public training school system before the establishment of public junior colleges with affiliated secondary schools. At present, there is a single formal national post-secondary *xiqu* institution, the 12-year (elementary, secondary and post-secondary) National Taiwan College of Performing Arts (NTCPA).[8] Incorporation of non-*Jingju* forms into public training structures has occurred only since 1994, constituting the expansion of institutionalized training to "native" forms, and reflecting a new period of contention between the resource allocation and symbolic importance of Mainland-derived vs. native Taiwan forms and identities.[9] Depending on one's political stance, this might be conceptualized as a national/local, as a native/ imported, or even as an organic/imposed kind of distinction.

From private to public to modern: *xiqu* education as a government project

Having sketched out the ideological background of institutional *xiqu* education in Taiwan, it is necessary to consider the context of nationalization and the manner in which *xiqu* institutions were integrated into a general public education system. In the process, the transformation broadened the education base (and future options) of performers while loosening teacherstudent relations and instituting a constantly evolving compromise between the necessity of training regimens and the legal requirements of a general education.

Up to 2 million Mainland Chinese arrived in Taiwan during the turbulent later-1940s. In that period, it was common for Mainland *Jingju* performers to visit Taiwan, some of whom – given the strife prevailing in the Mainland during the last stages of the KMT–CCP Civil War – chose to remain (Guy 2005, pp. 22–5). One such Mainland group was the "China National Drama Troupe", which arrived in Taiwan in 1949. Adverse conditions caused their disbanding after only a month, but the troupe leader, Wang Chen-tsu (*pinyin*: Wang Zhenzu; 1913–1980), continued to be active for several years as a performer in Taiwan. A student of Mei Lanfang, Wang had earned the moniker "Mei Lanfang of Shandong Province". C.K. Yen,[10] at the time the governor of Taiwan Province, granted Wang the physical space to set up a *Jingju* school, which Wang opened in 1957. This was the "Private Fu-hsing Theatre School". Its ideological purpose was signalled in the name: *fu-hsing* (*pinyin*: *fuxing*) means revival, and alludes, in Republican Chinese discourse, to the rejuvenation or revival of Chinese culture.[11] Beginning in 1955, other schools were set up as "small classes" (*xiaoban*) or "training classes" (*xunlianban*) which fed into the *Jingju* troupes funded by the Ministry of Defence (Su 2002, pp. 59–60).

Wang set up his school largely according to the *keban* system of single-minded, training-intensive *Jingju* teaching popular in China since the late nineteenth century. This entailed close student-teacher interaction, without use of textbooks or a standardized curriculum (Tsai 1999, p. 36). Since the economic base of the school was performance receipts, "academic" (i.e. non-performance) courses were often cancelled in order to ensure a high level of performance technique. The first group of 120 students (80 boys and 40 girls) boarded at the school, and received food and lodging; in return, their performances paid for the school's operations. Students in the "small classes" at military *Jingju* schools as well as at Fu-hsing were accepted at the age of 10, having been recruited mostly from Mainland (rather than "native" Taiwanese) families, many of them lower-ranking military and often "desperate to be relieved of the financial burden of supporting at least one of their children" (Guy 2005, p. 37), thus perpetuating a pre-existing stigma that consigning a child to a career as an actor was a sign of dire poverty. The curriculum consisted of eight years of training and one year of internship with a troupe. Each successive class of students was given a name incorporating a character determined by order of their generation in a slogan beginning "Revive China's Traditional Culture, Disseminate National Ethics and Morality".

As a private institution, the school lasted a little over a decade. However, as it became clear that the market would not sustain the institution, the KMT must have decided that it could not be allowed to fail, particularly given the KMT's

FIGURE 14.1 Students of the Ta-peng Theatre School, the air force Jingju school, late-1950s

Courtesy of Chen Yu-hsia

self-representation as the "true heir and guardian of traditional 'Chinese Culture'" (Su 2002, p. 256) as the People's Republic of China was overwhelmed by the anti-traditional radicalism of the Cultural Revolution (p. 60). As early as January 1967, the official KMT party organ *Central Daily News* announced that:

> because of the difficulties in the Fu-hsing Drama School's development, endangering even its continuation, and in order to protect our nation's artistic culture, the Ministry of Education has decided that, from the beginning of the next academic year, the private Fu-hsing Drama School will become a public higher vocational school, recruiting students separately for high school, middle school, and the third year of elementary school.
>
> *(Zhongyangbao, 13 January 1967)*

The failure of the school as a private endeavour must be understood in the context of more general shifts in the island's education system which began to threaten the supply of students. It had become increasingly difficult to convince parents that they should entrust their children to theatre school rather than placing them in the general education system. Primary education had become all but universal by 1958, and the nine years of compulsory schooling (primary and junior secondary) promulgated by law in 1968 generated a further jump in schooling numbers (Zhang 2003, p. 91). In the 1970s and 1980s, senior vocational and junior colleges grew, as did corresponding expenditure on education and culture (Guo 2005, p. 125; Hsiao and Hsiao 2015, p. 55).[12] In this context, *Jingju* training could no longer subsist as an alternative form of education outside of the mainstream system, as a stigmatized alternative to a basic general education. Moreover, many thought that *Jingju* was fated to decline in Taiwan, in which case "why waste seven years on this hopeless thing? [*meichuxi de wanyi'r?*]", especially if one expected to "be unemployed as soon as one graduated" (Li 1969, p. 214). In order to survive, it had to be nationalized and integrated into the mainstream system as a specialized but compatible strain of junior secondary, secondary and post-secondary education.

Consequently, in February 1968, the Ministry of Education formally announced the restructuring of the institution as a public school, retaining Wang as the principal, a post he held until his death in 1980. In July, the school was renamed the National Fu-hsing Experimental Theatre School and turned over to the Ministry of Education, becoming the first *xiqu* training institution within the formal education system. Its mandate was "not only to foster new talents in the National Drama, but also to be responsible for the reorganization [*zhengli*] and improvement [*gailiang*] of National Drama" (*Lianhebao* [United Daily News] 1968). The law nationalizing the school defined its mission as the fostering of new talent and the progress of "National Drama" as an art form, and legislators who supported the motion usually situated the move in terms of the responsibility to maintain the greatness of Chinese culture in the fight against the Communists on the Mainland.[13] A later history of the Fu-hsing school sums up the justification for nationalization: "A nation's strength or weakness, rise or fall, depends entirely on the high or low level of its

FIGURE 14.2   Children training in the early years of the Fu-hsing Drama School.
Photo courtesy of the NTCPA

culture. The level of culture and the theatre arts, moreover, are inextricably related",
going on to argue that, therefore, "children who really love the national drama [i.e.
Jingju] cannot really turn out bad" (Cao 1993, p. 99). The new curriculum included
both general education and specialized *xiqu* classes, with students (barring grievous
offences) moving directly through the levels of the institution without reapplica-
tion. The campus was moved to the outer Taipei district of Neihu, and students'
costs were now defrayed from the public purse (Tsai 1999, p. 37).

The "experimental" in the school's name was meant to indicate not so much
artistic innovation as constant progress and indefatigable self-improvement. The
principal mission of the newly public institution was therefore to establish an educational system, design a curriculum and develop textbooks. The move to Neihu
substantially improved resources, accommodation, equipment and teacher quality
(Jiang 1988, p. 99). The Fu-hsing school also underwent a complete administrative
overhaul, establishing accounting, personnel and guidance offices, not to mention a
new *Jingju* troupe attached to the school. Dedicated permanent staff were hired for
academic courses, and the general dramatic education was expanded in scope, and
conducted alongside the *Jingju* training classes.

Critics in the Legislative Yuan (the Republic of China's parliamentary body),
however, were ready to point out that even so, "the school's curriculum was not in
accord with standardized educational requirements" (Guy 2005, p. 71). If previously

Wang had been free to establish his school along the traditional lines of *Jingju* training, its nationalization in 1968 meant that it had become subject to general rules for public educational bodies. Since nationalization over 50 years ago, the school has featured periodically in the public and parliamentary debate surrounding the place of traditional theatre in Taiwan's shifting cultural politics. In 1970, Wang's tradition-derived *xiqu* education system came into direct conflict with legislators, when highly regarded academic and Legislative Yuan member Hung Yen-chiu[14] decried the school's operations as unconstitutional on the grounds that it infringed articles guaranteeing a right to basic education for children (*Lifayuan gongbao* 1970, pp. 8–9). Quoting from a description of the school's curriculum, Hung remarked that three-quarters of education time was spent on theatre courses, with only one-quarter on "knowledge courses" (i.e. academic subjects), accusing it of making a mockery of the national principle of "civic education" for all (*Lifayuan gongbao* 1970, p. 9). Anticipating the argument that early training was needed to attain proficiency in the acrobatic scenes, Hung remarked that "one cannot for *this single reason* deprive school-age children of their constitutionally guaranteed rights and opportunities" and suggested that the age to begin vocational education be raised to 15 (*Lifayuan gongbao* 1970, p. 9).[15] Hong proposed that the school would be financially and bureaucratically more sensibly managed if placed once more in private hands (*Lifayuan gongbao* 1970, p. 10). In the ensuing debate, other legislators brought forth a litany of deficiencies of the schools: *inter alia* the absence of a library, a curriculum, or a pleasant campus. While the debate concluded without any formal attempt being made to privatize the school, pressures to make the institution comply with general educational regulations led to the recurrent necessity to defend and redefine itself.[16]

In response to political pressure, initiatives developed at the school over the following decades in order to standardize and regularize a training system, such as the "Small Consultative Group for the Progress of National Drama Education" (1976), dedicated to the establishment of a fixed curriculum. Under new school leadership in the 1980s and 1990s, more definite shifts in training can be identified. In 1985, for instance, the institution's press issued a "National Drama Vocation School Course List" providing a detailed programme for *xiqu* training, showing notable broadening of the curriculum. According to "Theatre Art Schools Curriculum Standards", issued by the Department of Education in 1989, courses on close script reading, *xiqu* spectatorship and appreciation, overview of performance psychology and a general introduction to the arts were mandated, with much of the material being drawn from Western-inspired performance types, especially from spoken theatre. By the 1990s, six to ten hours per week of non-performance classes were included in the training programme for actors, including theoretical overview, *xiqu* stories, *xiqu* origins, performance overview, overview of playwriting and direction, stage management and viewing discussion. In addition, high school students followed the national curriculum in sciences, maths, civics, social sciences and English – in some cases, students who excelled in these subjects could apply for post-secondary education in these disciplines, and the rigidity of the school-to-theatre pathway receded as, simultaneously, professional outlets for actors began to contract with the post–Martial Law consolidation of *Jingju* troupes.

To support this new curriculum, throughout the 1990s the school published a number of textbooks for a broad *xiqu* education[17] (Tsai 1999, p. 40). At the same time, the Ministry of Defence's *xiqu* school, Kuo-kuang, also included an overview of contemporary theatre in its curriculum, in order to allow students "to recognize and adopt contemporary theatre performance and dance techniques" (Tsai 1999, p. 39). Teaching staff, however, voiced (and continue to voice) concern about the viability of generating high levels of performance technique in students where so much time is devoted to non-performance coursework.

Institutional consolidation and diversification

As *Jingju* education was being adapted, the political capital of *Jingju* was shrinking. Training institutions were reducing in number, a process that continued throughout the 1980s and 1990s. In 1985, the three Ministry of Defence *Jingju* schools (Ta-peng, Hai-kuang and Lu-kuang) were consolidated into one (Kuo-kuang), which in turn fused with Fu-hsing in 1999 to become the National Taiwan Junior College of Performing Arts (NTJCPA) (Jiang 1988, p. 100, Niu 1998, p. 55). This consolidation occurred in the context of a general Taiwanese education reform, which proclaimed that, "among the public higher education institutes, a portion are too small, which results in overlapping educational resources" leading to the conclusion that they "should be considered for consolidation or expansion to an appropriate size for the effective use of resources and the improvement of their quality" (Xingzhengyuan 1996, p. 61). As some smaller programmes were fused, others were simply abolished: 1994 saw the removal of *Jingju* from the programme of the National Taiwan College of Arts in the process of its promotion to National Taiwan University of the Arts (Tsai 1999, p. 2). This struck *Jingju* enthusiasts as especially ominous, since *Jingju* had been a part of the institution's core material since its establishment nearly 40 years earlier.[18]

At the same time, the number of government-supported *Jingju* troupes was shrinking. The Ministry of Defence's role as *Jingju*'s "primary patron came under increasingly serious scrutiny throughout the early 1990s" (Guy 2005, p. 39), culminating in the disestablishment of these troupes in 1995, leaving the NTJCPA school troupe and the newly founded Kuo-kuang troupe (under the auspices of the Ministry of Education) as the major state-funded *Jingju* troupes (Chang 2007, p. 64). Thus, from six or seven state-funded troupes in the 1950s, *Jingju* was reduced to two by 1995, of which one was attached to what had now become the sole training institute, NTJCPA (Guy 2005, p. 39). It was clear that *Jingju* was losing its position as a genre central to national political projects.

As the curriculum changes rendered the training institution more similar to a Western-style arts high school or university-based training programme, the contentious addition of non-*Jingju* departments brought more genres and students into this "modernizing" *xiqu* training system. In 1982, upon orders of the Ministry of

Education, the Fu-hsing School was required to add a "general arts" (i.e. acrobatics) course. Starting from the early 1990s, in the more critical atmosphere of post-martial law Taiwan, journalists and legislators challenged the divergence in resources between *Jingju* and the more "native" *gezaixi* at the same time that they queried whether the former could legitimately claim to be the "National Drama" (Guy 1995, pp. 93–5; Hsieh 2008, p. 211). Thus, since 1994 and 2001 respectively, *gezaixi* and *kejiaxi* (Hakka theatre) have been formally incorporated into the NTCPA's programme, partly under the political pressure of politicians from these communities in an era of growing "Taiwan consciousness".

In contrast to *Jingju*, earlier efforts to establish *gezaixi* training schools were not state-supported, and the one school founded in the 1960s by entrepreneur Chen Chengsan had received no state recognition, making the degrees it granted of limited usefulness.[19] The incorporation of *gezaixi* and *kejiaxi* into the national *xiqu* institution thus had important symbolic meaning, and signalled the arrival of "native" Taiwanese arts at the heart of the national bureaucracy; indeed, the move to consolidate the military troupes and to bring *gezaixi* into the national training mould were related and simultaneous (Hsieh 2008, p. 11). It was acknowledged by a Ministry of Education official that the inclusion of "native" genres reflected a consideration of *shengji* (i.e. provincial origin, specifically Mainlander/Taiwanese; Chang 2007, pp. 63–4). It is also significant that in 1999, as the Fu-hsing and Kuo-kuang schools merged, two names ("revival" and "national glory") associated with the ideological projects of the KMT were given up in favour of one name: National Taiwan College of Performing Arts, which highlights a shift in symbolic emphasis from *xiqu* as Chinese Republican political project to an element of Taiwanese heritage.

Not unreasonably, the inclusion of native genres has been interpreted as a diminution of *Jingju* support, and this expansion has thus met with some resistance from the *Jingju* establishment. In 2010, several prominent *Jingju* performers, including international stars Wei Hai-min and Wu Hsing-kuo, protested that *Jingju* standards were not being upheld at the school, claiming that:

> noted Peking opera teachers have been shifted to the teaching of Hakka opera, and that the practice established during the National Fu Hsing Dramatic Arts Academy era of inviting mainland Chinese teaching masters to train local students has rarely been seen at the college over the past few years.
> *(United Daily News [Lianhebao] 2010)*

Informally, teachers are concerned that there is not enough training time, or close enough student-teacher bonds, to ensure high-quality transmission of *Jingju* technique.

The institutionalization of *gezaixi* has also proven contentious. A journalist writing for the KMT-affiliated National Policy Foundation opined that there was a "historical rationale" for state *Jingju* support, while NTCPA *gezaixi* students had difficulty finding employment upon graduation. The report, entitled "Please

Abolish Public *Gezaixi* Troupes" – i.e. principally the NTCPA's *gezaixi* troupe – argued also that the singing and speaking technique of the students was too heavily influenced by Mandarin, even if their movement technique (learned from *Jingju*) was commendable. The author of the report opined that students would be unable to adapt to temple performance, meaning that the government initiative in integrating *gezaixi* troupes had been "wasted", making the programme "a source of regret for grassroots *gezaixi* troupes" (Ji 2007). This analysis, though hardly unbiased, is partly corroborated by fieldwork friendlier to *gezaixi* as a whole, which also suggests that NTCPA's *gezaixi* graduates face employment difficulties (Hsu 2010, pp. 11, 47).

Neither the existence nor the mission of a special national college of *xiqu* training is ever quite assured or secure, especially since (in an increasingly metric age) its achievements as a post-secondary institution may be difficult to measure against other, purely academic schools. In a motion passed by the Legislative Yuan in 2005 in support of the elevation of the school from junior college to college, a private member commented that:

> Due to the nativeness, special and traditional qualities of the National Taiwan Junior College of Performing Arts, one cannot use the standards of ordinary schools to evaluate and examine it, even less can it be merged with other arts universities, by which it would lose its meaningful traditional significance and subjectivity . . . Thus, it is suggested that, as regards the Ministry of Education's assessment and development of the National Taiwan Junior College of Per-forming Arts, it ought to consider it a special case, a specialised school, so as to ensure that Taiwan has one traditional *xiqu* vocational school.
>
> *(Fan 2006)*

In 2006, the Ministry of Education upgraded the school to full college status. Its mission was redefined as "grounding tradition and incorporating innovation; embracing the local, and facing the international" (NTCPA n.d.). The primary school students are mainly concerned with basic skills while the high school students are separated into *xiqu* specializations, and the college students are expected to fuse traditional technique with a modern innovative education. This pluralistic curriculum is intended to combine practice and theory, allowing "traditional *xiqu* to bring Taiwan out [in the world] and become a new international highlight" (NTCPA 2012, p. 18). The upgrading of the school to college (and the repudiation of nascent projects to merge it with the National Taiwan University of the Arts) was also vigorously advocated by some members of the Legislative Yuan as necessary for the promotion of local Taiwanese culture, proclaiming that "in order to maintain and develop the flame of *kejiaxi* and *gezaixi*, we want a Taiwan College of Performing Arts" (Fan 2006). For the time being, public *xiqu* education still enjoys the necessary political backing.

FIGURE 14.3 Students of the NTCPA in 2012

Courtesy of the NTCPA and Tsai Hsin-hsin

Conclusions

Even though NTCPA exists specifically in order to preserve a standard of *xiqu* performance, here as elsewhere the institutionalization of performance genres "often heightens rather than prevents the transformation of cultural forms as they become embedded in institutional mechanisms for cultural preservation and promotion, mechanisms shaped by the logics and conventions of broader political and economic systems" (H.W. Hsu 2014, pp. vii–viii). Writing about a Mainland *xiqu* genre, musicologist Hui Yu remarks that "there is always an educational imbalance between *xiqu* artists' high level of performing skills and their low levels of formal education, which is, in fact, a big theoretical and practical dilemma for the Chinese *xiqu* education system" (Yu 2001, p. 164). The NTCPA (like its predecessor institutions) exists as an attempt to resolve this dilemma, providing an officially recognized diploma and offering a general education for pupils, while seeking to maintain a high standard of theatre skills.[20] These two goals, however, have consistently been in tension, sometimes publicly.

Under the influence of Western ideas, *xiqu* education moved into the formal sphere of education, helping to nearly eradicate the older stigma surrounding the acting profession, and to mitigate the assumption in KMT Taiwan (and other Chinese societies) that having a child educated in *xiqu* was a sign of dire poverty. The institutionalization of *gezaixi* in the curriculum, though largely unsuccessful in securing employment for its graduates in the temple circuit, is also seen as having reduced the stigma of the *gezaixi* performer (P. Hsu 2010, pp. 11, 74–5). On the other hand, the long period of education "equivalent to that of a junior high school graduate" undermined performer "confidence in their own ability to create" and generated shame and embarrassment (Guy 2005, pp. 116–7).

Xiqu training in Taiwan is best understood as a constant negotiation between a traditional model of apprenticeship training and the demands of a modernizing society to make all forms of secondary and post-secondary education adhere to "modern", often Western-inspired, models. Performer training, like any other social practice, is responsive to broader shifts in educational policy and agendas of social reform as these are felt in the institutions through which training is conducted and the environment in which artists and troupes must perform. This is particularly true when a theatre form has historically relied on a system of training which depends for its effectiveness on both the single-mindedness and youth of its trainees. Patrice Pavis (1996, p. 17) has written: "[t]raining does not do away with the choice of a form; it presupposes it". The institutionalization of the training system within the broader education system thus affects the development of the genre.

The now-fading ideological importance of *Jingju* in Taiwan first assured the economic basis of *xiqu* training through state support. Subsequently, the subordination of older training practices to the demands for a modern education model for the arts altered and perhaps threatened the technical basis for the art. Later, the political necessity to include other "native" Taiwanese forms in *xiqu* (*gezaixi* and *kejiaxi*) in the NTCPA curriculum meant that resources have been spread more evenly between the three genres, possibly at the expense of *Jingju* technical virtuosity, and perhaps without signal benefits for *gezaixi* graduates.

This is rather in contrast to Mainland China, where most performers receive a theatre education often only nominally supplemented by other courses, and who are in consequence more committed (or restricted) to the stage than their Taiwanese counterparts (whose diplomas give them the basic qualifications for other professions or for other studies). Moreover, the heavy (if precarious) state support for *xiqu* companies in China, coupled with the inflexible (but reforming) *danwei* work-unit system,[21] provided all willing *xiqu* school graduates with employment within the theatre, even if not all trainees will become actors. This is not the case for graduates of NTCPA, most of whom must find employment in the competitive and often low-paid *xiqu* market. Recent shifts in the structure of labour in Mainland Chinese *xiqu* are, however, also tending in that direction.

Before closing, there is room here only to make some cursory suggestions about the effects of this institutionalization of training on stage practices. On the one hand, the diminution of training time contributes to the widely acknowledged deterioration in *Jingju* technique in Taiwan, especially compared to Mainland China's relatively single-minded training system. The total absence of other Taiwanese-language genres, such as *beiguanxi* or *nanguanxi*, from training institutions has contributed to their highly precarious status on the Taiwanese stage. The inclusion of courses on drama during *xiqu* education is one factor in the openness of *Jingju*-trained performers such as Wu Hsing-kuo (who founded the innovative Contemporary Legend troupe) and troupes such as Kuo-kuang to experimentation, or to collaboration with foreign artists.[22] On balance, the development of *Jingju* in Taiwan in recent decades has seen a shift towards genre-bending and experimentalism, and the broadening of the *xiqu* curriculum has played a key role in this development. The presence of *Jingju* instructors in *gezaixi* and *kejiaxi* classrooms has meant a strong influence of martial movement and of Mandarin declamation on NTCPA graduates in these genres. The fact that NTCPA's two troupes are publicly funded also creates a tendency to adapt the grand narratives of ROC and Taiwan history – including recent biographies of Sun Yat-sen and George Leslie Mackay (Stenberg 2017).

The NTCPA and its predecessors constitute a major state investment in *xiqu* valorization, a fact which first justified the nationalization of its predecessor institution, and has more recently driven the push to include native Taiwanese arts. Its reforms and expansions have responded to shifts in education (driven by Western-inspired views on universal education and an education market responding to both American models and Western economic demand) and to changes in the Taiwanese political landscape. It has never, however, occupied an unproblematic position, as successive leaderships have tried to reconcile a heritage of rigorous training practices for children with the demands of the formal public education system.

Xiqu education is defended as a form of heritage protection, but heritage protection is not itself a neutral act. Designating "a practice or a site as heritage is not so much a description as an intervention", since "heritage reorders relations between persons and things, and among persons them-selves, objectifying and recontextualizing them with reference to other sites and practices designated as heritage" (Hafstein 2014, p. 36). The ideology of heritage preservation, ultimately an endeavour designed to project a specific, usually national, image, is imposed from above on existing cultural practices. The NTCPA operates today as an establishment intended to protect what is regarded as a constituent of either possible nation (*Jingju* to China or *gezaixi/kejiaxi* for Taiwan), and the distribution of the resources allocated to various forms of *xiqu* reflects shifts in the forces that define the nation and control public funds. And like any public institution in Taiwan, its definitions and goals remain under negotiation.

Funding

This work was supported in part by Social Sciences and Humanities Research Council of Canada.

Notes

1 Gao's essay details the programme for modernizing *Jingju* at the Zhonghua xiqu zhuanke xuexiao (Zhonghua Chinese Opera Music College), which operated from 1930 to 1940 in Beiping (the Republican-era name of Beijing). Other similarly innovative projects included the Shanghai xiju xuexiao (Shanghai Theatre School) and Xi'an's Xiasheng xiju xuexiao (Xiasheng Theatre School).

2 Goldstein (2007, pp. 32–9) also gives an extensive account of the *keban* system in late nineteenth-century *Jingju*. When *keban* was used in 1950s Taiwan *Jingju* training, practices were only somewhat milder.

3 Taiwan's political history has generated myriad terms for ethnicities and sub-ethnicities. Since this article is in no way concerned with aboriginal performance, "native" will be used to indicate the descendants of Hokkien and Hakka settlers who arrived in the seventeenth to early twentieth centuries and form the bulk of Taiwan's ethnic Chinese population. This group, often known as *bensheng* (within-province) has usually been contrasted with *waisheng* (outside-province) – i.e. those who arrived in Taiwan in the late 1940s, during the closing stages of the Chinese Civil War. In terms of *xiqu*, which has always been almost exclusively a Han family of performance arts, the distinction has been between *bensheng* Taiwanese genres such as *gezaixi* and *waisheng* Mainland-originating genres, principally *Jingju*.

4 All *xiqu* forms were under pressure from Japanese authorities starting in 1937 as part of the *kominka/ huangminhua* movement. While *gezaixi* did not disappear, it seems that there were probably no *Jingju* performances during 1937–1945 (Guy 1995, p. 88, 2005, pp. 15–22; Chang 2007, pp. 54–9; Hsu Y.H. 2014, p. 103). Despite the complex terminological history, *Jingju* is now the consensus term for the genre, and for this reason will be used to refer to "Peking opera" consistently in this essay, even if such usage is somewhat anachronistic.

5 This does not seem very different from the case in the English-speaking world until the emergence of drama schools in the mid-nineteenth century. The *Continuum Companion to Twentieth Century Theatre* notes that in the early nineteenth century, actors in the UK generally were "touring the provinces and learning the craft as an apprentice, through practical experience, particularly by observing the work of the leading artists in the company" (Jenkins 2006).

6 Not incidentally, *Jingju* was known for decades in Taiwan as "Guoju" (National Drama), a "sign of Peking opera's position of superiority over other traditional opera forms" (Guy 1999, p. 518) before conforming to the Mainland name *Jingju* in the 1990s (Guy 1995, p. 85).

7 For instance, *Jingju* repertoire on the Mainland "underwent significant revisions in order to accommodate the presumed tastes of international audiences by highlighting movement and dance while sacrificing dialogue and singing, to emanate an upbeat face for the new China or to convey specific messages mandated by officials through significant revisions" (Liu 2013, p. 2).

8 The authors' views on the subject are inevitably informed by their past affiliations with the institution. Tsai Hsin-hsin was vice president of NTCPA in 2011–2015. Josh Stenberg was a Fulbright Taiwan fellow at NTCPA in 2014–2015.

9 Other *xiqu* forms, such as puppetry or *nanguanxi*, are less directly institutionalized, although their support through arts-funding mechanisms also means the indirect influence of the West on training in the form of models of arts support.

10 Yen Chia-kan (*pinyin* Yan Jiagan; 1905–1993) was a Mainland-born KMT politician who also served as minister of finance and became premier, vice president, and finally, upon the death of Chiang Kai-shek, president of the Republic of China (1975–1978). The office of governor of Taiwan Province was, until streamlining in 1998, an important political post, even if the "province" and the actually controlled territory of the entire Republic were in Yen's time nearly coterminous.

11 It was meant at that time also to contrast with the PRC, where according to the ROC, Chinese culture was being destroyed. As part of the PRC's efforts to re-establish a continuity with pre-1949 Chinese historical narratives, the term *fuxing* has recently been revived there also, since it "implies that China is not 'newly rising' but just 'recovering' a status it had before the West humiliated it in the nineteenth century" (Müller 2013, p. 128).

12 This expansion was funded by the Republic of China's principal ally: the US, and the system of education that developed featured "education principles based on Western economic capitalism" (Chou and Chuing 2012, p. 40; see also Altbach 1998, p. 186, Li and Li 1998, pp. 172–3).

13 In 1966, the Cultural Revolution had begun on the Mainland. As Nancy Guy (2005, p. 57) notes, "[t]he violence against traditional culture in China provided an opportunity for the Nationalist regime" to represent itself nationally and internationally as "the guardian of Chinese culture".

14 Hung Yen-chiu, *pinyin* Hong Yanqiu, 1899–1980. Taiwanese-born, Hung studied in Beijing, co-founded the *Mandarin Daily News* and became a professor at National Taiwan University (NTU). He became a legislator in 1969, at the age of 71. NTU provides a biography at http://homepage.ntu. edu.tw/~chinlit/ch/html/ MA3d005.htm.

15 Hung's basis of criticism draws explicitly on the 1947 ROC constitution, which in turn seems to have derived its demand for universal education from the constitution of the Weimar Republic (Chang 2014, pp. 1–2).

16 This partially accounts for the four name changes it has undergone in one half-century.

17 Such works include *National Drama Division Textbooks for Theatre Schools* (Juxiao guoju ke jiaokeshu), *Stories from Chinese Traditional Theatre* (Xiqu gushi), *Voice and Recitation in National Drama* (Guoju de fasheng yu changnian), *Overview of Performance Psychology* (Biaoyan xinlixue gainian) and *Theatre History of China* (Zhongguo xiju shi).

18 Although it had been part of the initial programme when founded in 1955, it had been discontinued after four years since there were insufficient students, then reinstated in 1982 as further education for the graduates from the theatre training attached to the military. Other *Jingju* education in this period of note include the major at Chinese Culture University (from 1963, becoming a "Chinese Theatre Division" in 1972 and a Chinese Theatre Studies department since 1999) and at the private secondary Hwa Kang Arts School (established in 1975 with Peking University part of the inaugural programme, transforming into a Theatre department in 1986 of which the *Jingju* element was discontinued in 1988) (Su 2002, p. 60).

19 The school lasted only three years, leading one scholar to remark that the "*gezaixi* school received lukewarm, even oppressive, treatment from the state" especially given the "wholehearted support" available for *Jingju* (Hsieh 2008, p. 198).

20 The underlying presumption is that education must begin at a young age for technical proficiency to be achieved. Indeed, there has never been a performer of any note who began training after puberty. This means the best Western analogy may be ballet. Indeed, the Royal Ballet School (RBS) "expanded to include academic studies" in the 1940s and 1950s, facing the same challenge of providing academic studies and professional training (Craine and Mackrell 2010), although while the RBS must provide only secondary education, the NTCPA must provide primary, secondary and post-secondary programmes.

21 Under the *danwei* system, the place of work has been a basic and decisive factor for many aspects of an employee's life. The *danwei* has been drastically weakened in the private sector, but remains important for those who work in the public sector, like most *xiqu* workers, especially in cities. The *danwei* system has meant that, relative to Taiwan or the West, there is still much less free agency of creative workers, including theatre actors and directors, most of whom will remain with one theatre company for their entire careers.
22 Kuo-kuang's most famous Western-inspired work is probably *Orlando*, a 2009 collaboration with Robert Wilson, but such projects are not uncommon.

References

Altbach, P. (1998). *Comparative Higher Education: Knowledge, the University, and Development.* Greenwich: Ablex.

Cao, J. L. (1993). Guoli fuxing juyi shiyan xuexiao fazhan shilüe (1). *Fuxing juyi xuekan*, (3), [A Brief History of National Fu-Hsing Experimental Theatre School's Development], 99–108.

Chang, B. Y. (2007). Disclaiming and Renegotiating National Memory: Taiwanese *Xiqu* and Identity. In C. Storm and M. Harrison, eds., *The Margins of Becoming: Identity and Culture in Taiwan.* Wiesbaden: Harassowitz, pp. 51–68.

Chang, W. C. (2014). *Comparative Discourse in Constitution-Making. Conference, World Congress of Constitutional Law. International Association of Constitutional Law IXth World Congress 'Constitutional Challenges: Global and Local'*, University of Oslo. Available at: www.jus.uio.no/english/research/news-and-events/events/con-ferences/2014/wccl-cmdc/wccl/papers/ws5/w5-chang.pdf [Accessed 1 October 2016].

Chou, P. C. and Chuing, G. (2012). *Taiwan Education at the Crossroad: When Globalization Meets Localization.* New York: Palgrave Macmillan.

Craine, D. and Mackrell, J. (eds.). (2010). *The Royal Ballet School. The Oxford Dictionary of Dance.* 2nd ed. Oxford: Oxford University Press.

Fan, T. S. (2006). Yiyou nian juyue jiayue liwei guangu wenjiao yiti [Concerns of Legislators on the Topic of Cultural Education in the Ninth and Eleventh Months of the Yiyou Year (2005)], *National Policy Foundation Research Report.* Available at: http://old.npf.org.tw/PUBLICATION/IA/095/IA-R-095-004.htm [Accessed 1 October 2016].

Gao, Y. (2014). Zhonghua xiqu yinyue zhuanke xuexiao de xiqu jiaoyu yanjiu [Research on *xiqu* Education at the China *Xiqu* Music College]. *Jiaoyu pinglun*, 1, 144–146.

Goldstein, J. (2007). *Drama Kings: Players and Publics in the Re-Creation of Peking Opera.* Berkeley: University of California Press.

Guo, Y. (2005). *Asia's Educational Edge: Current Achievements in Japan, Korea, Taiwan, China, and India.* Lanham: Lexington Books.

Guy, N. (1995). Peking Opera as 'National Drama' in Taiwan: What's in a Name? *Asian Theatre Journal*, 12(1), 85–103.

Guy, N. (1999). Governing the Arts, Governing the State: Peking Opera and Political Authority in Taiwan. *Ethnomusicology*, 43(3), 508–526.

Guy, N. (2005). *Peking Opera and Politics in Taiwan.* Urbana: University of Illinois Press.

Hafstein, V. (2014). Protection as Dispossession: Government in the Vernacular. In D. Kapchan, ed., *Cultural Heritage in Transition: Intangible Rights as Human Rights.* Philadelphia: University of Pennsylvania Press, pp. 25–57.

Hsiao, F. S. T. and Hsiao, M. C. W. (2015). *Economic Development of Taiwan: Early Experiences and the Pacific Trade Triangle.* Singapore: World Scientific.

Hsieh, H. M. (2008). *Across the Strait: History, Performance, and Gezaixi in China and Taiwan.* Doctoral Thesis. Northwestern University, Evanston.

Hsu, H. W. (2014). *Institutionalizing Cultural Forms: A Comparative Analysis of the Social Organization of Finnish Pelimanni and Taiwanese Hakka Music*. Doctoral Thesis. Indiana University, Bloomington.

Hsu, P. (2010). *Living Taiwanese Opera: Improvisation, Performance of Gender, and Selection of Tradition*. Doctoral Thesis. University of Berkeley, Berkeley, CA.

Hsu, Y. H. (2014). Shidai xianying: zhanhou Taiwan Jingju shenfen de duozhong zhuanhuan (1945–1995) [Exposing Eras: The Many Shifts in Post-War Taiwan *Jingju* Identity (1945–1995)]. *Wenyi yanjiu*, 1, 103–113.

Jenkins, J. E. (2006). Drama Schools. In C. Chambers, ed., *The Continuum Companion to Twentieth Century Theatre*. London: Continuum.

Ji, H. L. (2007). Qing ting guojia gezaixi tuan [Please Abolish Public Gezaixi Troupes]. *National Public Foundation Backgrounder*. Available at: http://old.npf.org.tw/PUBLICA TION/EC/096/EC-B-096-003.htm [Accessed 1 October 2016].

Jiang, H. (1988). Taiwan xixiao gaikuang [Overview of Taiwan Drama Schools]. *Xiqu yishu*, 1, 99–100.

Li, F. S. (1969). *Zhonghua Guoju shi [Chinese National Drama History]*. Taipei: Zhengzhong shuju.

Li, R. (2010). *The Soul of Beijing Opera: Theatrical Creativity and Continuity in the Changing World*. Hong Kong: Hong Kong University Press.

Li, X. and Li, H. (1998). *China and the United States: A New Cold War History*. Lanham: University Press of America.

Lianhebao [United Daily News]. (1968). Fuxing juxiao gaiwei guoli [The Fu-hsing Drama School Is Nationalised]. *Lianhebao*, 6 February.

Lifayuan gongbao [Legislative Yuan Gazetteer]. (1970). *Lifayuan gongbao*, 59(pt. 61), 8–26.

Liu, S. (2013). The Case of *Princess Baihua*: State Diplomatic Functions and Theatrical Creative Process in China in the 1950s and 1960s. *Asian Theatre Journal*, 30(1), 1–29.

Müller, G. (2013). *Documentary, World History and National Power in the PRC: Global Rise in Chinese Eyes*. New York: Routledge.

Niu, P. (1998). Jingju zai Taiwan (shang) [*Jingju* in Taiwan, Part One], *Zhongguo xiju*, 9, 52–55.

NTCPA (National Taiwan College of Performing Arts). (2012). *Guoli Taiwan Xiqu Xueyuan gaishan jiaoxue shebei jihua shu [National Taiwan College of Performing Arts Report on Improved Teaching Equipment]*. Available at: http://b001.tcpa.edu.tw/ezfiles/1/1001/img/285/101-02.pdf [Accessed 19 September 2016].

NTCPA (National Taiwan College of Performing Arts). (n.d.). *Xiaowu jiben ziliao' [Basic Materials on School Affairs]*. Available at: www.tcpa.edu.tw/files/11-1000-931.php [Accessed 19 September 2016].

Pavis, P. (1996). *The Intercultural Performance Reader*. New York: Routledge.

Stenberg, J. (2017). Staging the International Embrace: George Leslie Mackay Narratives on Taiwanese Stages. *Theatre Research in Canada*, 38(1), 52–73.

Su, K. K. C. (2002). *Guojiazhuyi xia de yiwen zhengce: Taiwan jieyan qianhou Jingju, gezaixi fazhan zhi yanjiu [Arts Policy Under Statism: A Study of the Development of Government Policy on Traditional Opera Before and After the Lifting of Martial Law in Taiwan]*. Doctoral Thesis. Leiden University, Leiden.

Tian, M. (2008). *The Poetics of Difference and Displacement: Twentieth-Century Chinese-Western Intercultural Theatre*. Hong Kong: Hong Kong University Press.

Tsai, H. H. (1999). Taiwan jingju jiaoyu fazhan gaikuang [Overview of the Development of Taiwan *jingju* Education]. *Xiqu yishu*, 2, 36–44.

United Daily News [Lianhebao]. (2010). Peking Opera Stars Want College Head Replaced. hosted by *Taiwan Today*, 2 June. Available at: http://taiwantoday.tw/ct.asp?xItem=105470&CtNode=445 [Accessed 1 October 2016].

Wu, Q. (1999). Xin Zhongguo xiqu jiaoyu shishu (lianzai yi) [A Historical Record of xiqu Education in New China (First Instalment)]. *Xiqu yishu*, 4, 81–85.

Xingzhengyuan jiaoyu gaige shenyi weiyuanhui (Education Reform Consultative Committee, Executive Yuan). (1996). *Jiaoyu gaige zong ziyi baogaoshu [General Discussion Report on the Reform of Education]*. Taipei: Xingzhengyuan yanjiu fazhan kaohe weiyuanhui.

Yu, H. (2001). *Political Economy of Music in China: The Impact of Danwei System on Luju*. Doctoral Thesis. Wesleyan University, Middletown.

Zhang, W. B. (2003). *Taiwan's Modernization: Americanization and Modernizing Confucian Manifestations*. Singapore: World Scientific.

INDEX

Note: Page numbers in *italic* indicate a figure on the corresponding page.